Macintosh™
Revealed

Volume One: Unlocking the Toolbox

Stephen Chernicoff

HAYDEN BOOK COMPANY
a division of Hayden Publishing Company, Inc.
Hasbrouck Heights, New Jersey and Berkeley, California

Apple believes that good books are important to successful computing. The Apple Press imprint is your assurance that this book has been published with the support and encouragement of Apple Computer Inc., and is the type of book we would be proud to publish ourselves.

For

Ann,

who likes the one with the mouse.

Acquisitions Editor: MICHAEL MCGRATH
Consulting Editor: SCOT KAMINS
Production Editors: MARY PICKLUM, ANDREW RONEY, RONNIE GROFF
Editorial Production Service: GANIS & HARRIS, INC.: CLAIRE MCKEAN
Cover design: JIM BERNARD
Cover photo: LOU ODOR
Composition: MCFARLAND GRAPHICS & DESIGN, INC.: JULIE QUICKEL
Printed and bound by: COMMAND WEB OFFSET, INC.

Library of Congress Cataloging in Publication Data

Chernicoff, Stephen.
  Macintosh revealed.

  Includes bibliographical references and index.
  Contents: v. 1. Unlocking the toolbox—
  1. Macintosh (Computer)   I. Title.
QA76.8.M3C48   1985   001.64   85-8611
ISBN 0-8104-6551-5

Macintosh is a trademark of Macintosh Laboratory, Inc., licensed to Apple Computer Inc., neither of which is affiliated with Hayden Book Company. QuickDraw, Finder, and Apple Press are trademarks of Apple Computer Inc.

Printed in the United States of America

	2	3	4	5	6	7	8	9	Printing
	86	87	88	89	90	91	92	93	Year

Preface

If you're reading this book, you probably don't need to be told that Apple Computer's Macintosh is an extraordinary personal computer. It does things you may never have seen a computer do before, in ways you may never have imagined. If you've wondered what goes on behind the scenes to make the magic happen, this book is for you. By the time you've finished reading it, you will be able to see the inner workings of the Macintosh revealed. You'll also be able to use the User Interface Toolbox, which is built into the Macintosh, to perform the same magic in your own programs.

Bear in mind before you begin programming that the Toolbox is for experienced computer users, not for beginners. So to get the most out of this book and the Toolbox, you should have experience (the more the better) in at least one high-level programming language. The programming examples given here are written in Pascal, but their general principles are applicable in other languages as well. If Pascal isn't your native programming tongue, you should still be able to pick up enough of it to follow the logic of the programming examples so that you can apply them in the language you prefer. The book will offer a few hints to help you over the rough spots, but in general it's assumed that you're acquainted with the syntax and semantics of standard Pascal. (For hard-core bit bangers, we've also included information on how to use the Toolbox in assembly language.)

The only other assumption we've made in writing this book is that you, the reader, want to know how the Macintosh user interface works from the inside. Whether you're a professional software developer, a college student, a midnight hacker, or simply a person who likes to take watches apart and see what makes them tick, read on and behold the Macintosh revealed.

STEPHEN CHERNICOFF
Belmont, California

Acknowledgments

No book is ever the product of one person working alone—particularly when a book is of the size and complexity of this one. These are some of the people who have helped me bring the book to completion, and to whom I owe a special debt of gratitude and appreciation:

First and forever, to my wife, **Helen,** whose love and understanding through the ordeal of living with an author have brought new meaning to the word "patience"; and to my parents, **Murray and Annette Chernicoff,** for their unwavering encouragement and support.

To **Chris Espinosa,** manager of Macintosh User Education, and **Mike Murray,** manager of Macintosh Marketing, who graciously gave me the freedom to pursue this project as an independent agent.

To **Mike McGrath, Mary Picklum,** and **Nancy Ragle** of Hayden Book Company, professionals all in the noblest sense of the word, whose contributions were manifold and invaluable.

To **David Casseres** of Apple Computer, for his indispensable assistance with the programming examples and his wise and thoughtful counsel throughout.

To the redoubtable **Scot Kamins** of Technology Translated, Inc., whose candid judgment and incisive suggestions have helped make this a better book in countless ways.

To **Steve Smith** of Technology Translated, who executed the illustrations with brilliance and panache.

And finally, to the men and women of Apple Computer's Macintosh Division, who are as talented and creative a group of people as I have ever been privileged to work with; and to **Steven Jobs,** Apple's chairman of the board and general manager of its Macintosh Division, who provided the vision and inspiration for these remarkable people to bring Macintosh to reality.

Contents

Chapter 3	**Thanks for the Memory**	**49**

Chapter 4   **Any Port in a Storm**   **97**

Chapter 5   **Quick on the Draw**   **171**

Chapter 7   **Getting Loaded**   **301**

Chapter 8   **Upstanding Characters**   349

CHAPTER

All the Tools You Need

What sets the Macintosh apart from other personal computers is its revolutionary *user interface*. In plain English, the word *interface* means a junction or boundary where two things meet. In computerese, it refers to the set of rules and conventions by which one part of an organized system (like the Macintosh) communicates with another. Wherever two components of the system come together, they exchange information through an interface.

The Macintosh system consists of hardware (physical components such as chips, circuits, and other electronic and mechanical devices) and of software (programs). The most important component of all is the human being peering at the screen and fiddling with the mouse and keyboard. This system's flesh-and-blood component is known, in technical parlance, as the *user*. So the user interface is the set of conventions that allows the human user to communicate with the rest of the system.

Before the Macintosh, user interfaces were typically based on a screen full of text characters (usually displayed in garish green) and a keyboard for typing those characters. To tell the computer what to do, you had to memorize a complex command language, so you could press exactly the right keys in exactly the right order. If your actions didn't conform to what the computer expected of you, it would tell you so in terms ranging from curt to unintelligible. On the whole, it was sometimes hard to tell that the human was the boss and the computer, the servant.

The Macintosh changes all that. In place of the time-honored character screen and keyboard, it uses a high-resolution, "bit-mapped" display and a hand-held pointing device, called a mouse. This results in a whole new way of communicating between people and computers. The bit-mapped screen can present information in vivid visual form, using

1

pictorial "icons," elaborate graphical effects, and varied patterns and textures. Text can be depicted exactly as it will appear on the printed page—in black characters on a white background, with a variety of typefaces, sizes, and styles. The mouse provides a direct, natural way of giving commands. This is done by using the mouse to point and manipulate images directly on the screen instead of typing arcane command sequences using the keyboard.

The programmers at Apple have put a great deal of thought and effort into taking advantage of these features to produce a user interface that feels natural and comfortable to people who aren't computer experts as well as those who are. To achieve this they produced the User Interface Toolbox, 64 kilobytes of tightly engineered, hand-crafted machine-language code that's built into every Macintosh in *read only memory* (*ROM*). With it, you can write programs that use overlapping windows, pull-down menus, scroll bars, dialog boxes, and all the other wonders you see on the Macintosh screen. This book will teach you how.

Strictly speaking, the Macintosh ROM is divided into three parts: the Macintosh Operating System, which handles low-level tasks such as memory management, disk input/output, and serial communications; the QuickDraw graphics routines, which are responsible for everything displayed on the screen; and the User Interface Toolbox, which implements the higher-level constructs of the user interface, such as windows and menus. As a rule, we'll be using the term "Toolbox" to refer loosely to the entire body of built-in code that's available to a running program; only occasionally will we use it in the narrower sense of the user-interface code alone, to distinguish it from the Operating System and QuickDraw.

How This Book Is Organized

The book is divided into two volumes. Volume One, *Unlocking the Toolbox* (which you now have before you), presents the foundations of the Toolbox:

- Chapter 2, "Putting the Tools to Work," introduces the basic conventions for calling the Toolbox from an application program and discusses several general-purpose Toolbox facilities useful in your programs.
- Chapter 3, "Thanks for the Memory," tells how the Macintosh's memory is laid out and how to allocate memory space for your program's needs.

- Chapter 4, "Any Port in a Storm," presents the fundamental concepts behind the QuickDraw graphics routines.
- Chapter 5, "Quick on the Draw," shows how to use QuickDraw to draw.
- Chapter 6, "Summoning Your Resources," introduces the resources, one of the cornerstones of the Macintosh software design.
- Chapter 7, "Getting Loaded," covers the way programs are started and how code is loaded into memory for execution.
- Chapter 8, "Upstanding Characters," tells how character text is represented inside the computer and displayed on the screen.

Once you've mastered these fundamentals, you'll be ready for Volume Two, *Programming with the Toolbox*. There you'll learn about the parts of the Macintosh user interface and how they work: events (the mechanism for monitoring the user's actions with the mouse and keyboard), windows, menus, cut-and-paste text editing, controls (including scroll bars), alert and dialog boxes, and disk input/output.

Because the Toolbox includes such a broad range of facilities and features, it's impossible to cover them all in this book. Unavoidably, some topics were left out because of time and space limitations. But we've included those features most programmers need for most applications. The ultimate, comprehensive source of information on the Toolbox is Apple's own forthcoming *Inside Macintosh* manual.

A central feature of Volume Two is a fully worked example program, a simple interactive text editor named **MiniEdit**, which serves two purposes. First, it illustrates concretely how to use the Toolbox. Second, it gives you a framework for developing your own application programs. The example program includes all the Toolbox calls needed to implement the standard features of the user interface—for instance, to display pull-down menus when the user presses the mouse in the menu bar, or to move windows around on the screen when the user drags them by their title bars—so it can save you from having to "reinvent the wheel" every time you write a program of your own. By returning the mail-order card provided in Volume Two, you can order a software disk containing the source code of the example program. Then instead of writing your own programs from scratch, you can just modify the existing program for whatever application you choose.

How to Use This Book

With the exception of Chapter 1, each chapter in this book consists of two complementary parts, the basic text of the chapter, referred to as the *Guidebook*, and the subsequent reference section, referred to as the *Handbook*. They are designed to be used together. For an overview of the Toolbox and how to use it, you should read the Guidebook from beginning to end. Cross-references enclosed in square brackets, such as [2.1.1], indicate the Handbook's relevant sections, where you'll find detailed descriptions of individual Toolbox procedures, functions, constants, variables, and data types. When you encounter one of these for the first time, follow the cross-reference to the Handbook for the details. Together, the Guidebook and Handbook will teach you step by step how to use the Toolbox in your own programs.

After you know the basic concepts, you'll find the Handbook useful on its own for refreshing your memory or looking up information. The Handbook is organized for quick reference rather than sequential reading. Although the Handbook's structure generally parallels that of the Guidebook, it doesn't always treat topics in the same order or build logically on what's gone before as does the Guidebook. Thus you may find some of the Handbook's material hard to understand at first, because it refers to topics you haven't yet learned. Try not to let this bother you—just skip the parts that don't make sense and come back to them later when you're better prepared to understand them. You'll also find some subjects covered in the Handbook that aren't discussed in the Guidebook at all; once you've acquired a working knowledge of the Toolbox, you can pick up these extra topics by browsing the Handbook on your own.

What's in the Reference Sections

Each section of the Reference Handbook is headed by a set of Pascal declarations defining the Toolbox entities such as procedures, functions, constants, variables, and data types that are discussed in that section. The declarations give the names of the entities being defined, plus other practical information, such as the number, order, and types of a procedure's parameters, the type of value a function returns, or the names and types of a record's fields. Following the declarations are a series of notes explaining the meaning and use of the Toolbox entities being discussed. Finally, most reference sections end with a data box containing further information, valuable only to assembly-language programmers.

```
type
  PenState = record
              pnLoc  : Point;     {Current location of graphics pen in local coordinates}
              pnSize : Point;     {Width and height of pen in pixels}
              pnMode : INTEGER;   {Transfer mode for line drawing and area fill}
              pnPat  : Pattern    {Pen pattern for line drawing}
            end;
```

Program 1-1 A type declaration

For readers unfamiliar with Pascal, let's look at examples of the reference declarations and discuss how to read them. Program 1-1 shows a Pascal declaration typical of those you'll find in the Handbook. (This particular one is taken from section [5.2.1].) The declaration says that **PenState** is the name of a record type with four components, or *fields*. The first field is named **pnLoc** and holds a value of type **Point**; the second, **pnSize**, also holds a **Point**; the third is named **pnMode** and is the type **INTEGER**; and the fourth, **pnPat**, is of the type **Pattern**. To the right of each field definition is a comment (enclosed in the Pascal comment brackets { and }) describing the meaning of that field: for instance, field **pnLoc** represents the graphics pen's current location in local coordinates. (We'll be learning about the graphics pen in Chapter 5 and the meaning of "local coordinates" in Chapter 4.) If **thePenState** is the name of a record in your program of type **PenState**, the expression

```
thePenState.pnLoc
```

denotes a value of type **Point** giving the pen location in local coordinates.

```
procedure MoveTo
              (horiz : INTEGER;   {Horizontal coordinate to move to, in pixels}
               vert  : INTEGER);  {Vertical coordinate to move to, in pixels}
```

Program 1-2 A procedure declaration

Program 1-2 shows an example of a procedure declaration, taken from section [5.2.4] of the Handbook. This declaration defines the procedure **MoveTo**, used to reposition the graphics pen to a new set of coordinates. The procedure accepts two parameters named **horiz** and **vert**, both of type **INTEGER**; as the explanatory comments state, these represent the pen's new horizontal and vertical coordinates, respectively. To move the pen to coordinates **h** and **v**, you would use the statement

```
MoveTo (h, v)
```

```
function EqualPt
            (point1 : Point;              {First point to be compared}
             point2 : Point);             {Second point to be compared}
             : BOOLEAN;                   {Are they equal?}
```

Program 1-3 A function declaration

Program 1-3 shows the declaration for the Toolbox function **EqualPt**, taken from section [4.4.1] of the Handbook. This function compares two points and tells whether or not they are equal. Similar to the procedure declaration we just looked at, a function declaration defines the names and types of the parameters the function expects you to supply. In addition, it also specifies the type of value the function returns as a result, following the colon (:) on the declaration's last line. In this case the function accepts two parameters named **point1** and **point2**, both of type **Point**, and returns a result of type **BOOLEAN**. You might call this function with a statement such as

```
equalFlag := EqualPt (firstPoint, secondPoint)
```

where **equalFlag** is a variable of type **BOOLEAN** declared in your program, and **firstPoint** and **secondPoint** are of type **Point**.

If you compare the procedure and function declarations shown in our Reference Handbook with those given in Apple's *Inside Macintosh* manual, you'll find that the names of the parameters are often different. Since you don't actually use the parameter names when you call a routine in your program, the names given in the declaration don't affect the way the routine is used. Because of that we've taken the liberty of changing many of the names to suggest more clearly the meaning or purpose of the parameters.

Names that you *do* use directly in your own program, such as those of constants and variables or of the fields in a record, are, of course, listed the same way in our Handbook as in the Apple documentation. Even here, however, you may notice slight variations in capitalization style; these make no difference, since Apple's Pascal compiler doesn't distinguish between corresponding upper- and lowercase letters. Similarly, the compiler uses only the first eight characters of any name, so variations occurring after the eighth character have no significance.

Some Terms and Conventions

Before we start, we'll explain some terms and conventions used. The Macintosh's microprocessor (the Motorola MC68000, usually referred to simply as the "68000") works with data items of three different sizes: *bytes* of 8 bits each, *words* of 16 bits (2 bytes), and *long words* of 32 bits (2 words, or 4 bytes). All memory addresses are long words, 32 bits in length, of which only the last 24 bits are actually significant. Each address designates a single 8-bit byte in memory. As a rule, word-length and long-word data items in memory must begin at an even-numbered byte address, known as a *word boundary*.

Throughout the book, we signal **computer-voice** expressions which appear in text lines by using a **bold** or ***italic bold*** typeface; such a convention serves as a kind of implicit quotation mark to distinguish actual program code from ordinary body text. In all other cases, we will use an alternate

    computer-voice typeface

to distinguish program code from ordinary body text. The computer voice is also used occasionally for characters typed on the Macintosh keyboard or displayed on the screen.

In keeping with the convention used in many programming languages, including Apple's versions of Pascal and assembly language for the Macintosh, we use a dollar sign (**$**) to denote hexadecimal (base-16) constants. For instance, the constant **$43** represents the same numerical value as decimal **67** (4 sixteens plus 3). As usual, the letters **A** to **F** stand for hexadecimal digits with numerical values from **10** to **15**—so the hexadecimal constant **$BD** stands for 11 sixteens plus 13, or decimal **189**.

We've already mentioned that section numbers enclosed in square brackets, such as [2.1.1], denote cross references to the designated section of the Reference Handbook. References to Volume Two are prefixed with a Roman numeral II and a colon: for instance, [II:2.1.1] refers to Volume Two, section 2.1.1.

> Throughout the Guidebook, you'll see shaded boxes like this one. These "by-the-way" boxes enclose side comments, helpful hints, exceptional cases, and other material subordinate to the main discussion.

Several chapters of the Guidebook end with a section titled "Nuts and Bolts." This section is for miscellaneous topics that don't fit anywhere else in the chapter—the little unclassified odds and ends rattling around in the bottom of the Toolbox. In general these are minor points of only limited interest, or things that are useful only in unusual or highly specialized circumstances.

That does it for the preliminaries, so now it's time to get to the business at hand. If you're ready to see the Macintosh revealed, turn the page and let's get started.

C H A P T E R

Putting the Tools to Work

Like a genie in a bottle, the Toolbox waits patiently inside every Macintosh, ready to perform its wonders for any program that cares to summon it. But before it will serve you, you need to know how to call it forth and command it to do your bidding. In this chapter, we'll start learning the spells needed to make the Toolbox work its magic. We'll learn about the underlying trap mechanism that's used at the machine-language level to call the Toolbox routines in the Macintosh ROM, as well as the higher-level calling conventions used in Pascal and assembly language. Then we'll talk about some nonstandard features of Apple's version of Pascal that are particularly useful for programming with the Toolbox. Finally we'll discuss some of the general-purpose utility routines that are included in the Toolbox for things like working with character strings, low-level bit manipulation, arithmetic operations, and reading or setting the date and time on the Macintosh's built-in clock chip.

The Language Problem

Exactly how you go about using the Toolbox depends on the language you're programming in. The Toolbox doesn't care what language you use, as long as you follow the proper rules and conventions to communicate with it. At the underlying machine level, these rules are always the same; but in a higher-level language, like Pascal or BASIC or C, you normally don't have to deal with them directly. Instead, each language has its own way of representing Toolbox calls and its own set of conventions that you, as a programmer, have to follow.

When Apple first began developing the software for the Macintosh, there wasn't any Macintosh to develop it on. Fortunately, Mac's big sister Lisa (now known as the Macintosh XL) was around to lend a hand. The Lisa already had a complete software development system based on the same microprocessor used in the Macintosh, the Motorola MC68000. This Lisa programming environment, with its Pascal compiler and 68000 assembler, became the *de facto* standard for programming the Macintosh. All of Apple's own Mac software—including the Toolbox itself—was written in Lisa Pascal or assembly language, compiled or assembled on a Lisa, and "ported" to the Macintosh to run. Then all the application software was produced by independent developers under special pre-release licenses from Apple. In those early days, if you wanted to program the Macintosh, you had to have a Lisa.

Since Macintosh was released, that situation has been changing rapidly. A growing number of languages now are available for programming directly on the Macintosh. Those include Pascal, BASIC, FORTRAN, COBOL, C, LISP, Logo, and FORTH. Most of these systems include a facility for calling the Toolbox routines in the Macintosh ROM from within a running application program. Apple soon will be introducing a software development system that will include a Pascal compiler and a 68000 assembler, along with an interactive program editor, linker, symbolic debugger, and full Toolbox support.

If you do have access to a Lisa, of course, you can write your Macintosh programs in the Lisa Workshop software development system mentioned earlier. A set of special software tools specifically for Macintosh programming on the Lisa is available from Apple under the name Macintosh Software Supplement. As this book goes to press, the Software Supplement is not a retail product and can be obtained only by direct mail order from Apple. Eventually it will be replaced by the Macintosh-based development system described in the preceding paragraph, which will run either on a Macintosh or on a Lisa under the "MacWorks" emulator.

Because the Toolbox has its historical roots in the Lisa development system, its internal data formats and calling conventions are based on those of Lisa Pascal. In a sense, Pascal is the Toolbox's "native language." We'll be using it for all our programming examples in this book, and our descriptions of Toolbox routines and data structures will be given in Pascal form (along with additional information on how to use them in assembly language). If you're writing in another language, you'll have to consult your documentation to find out how to convert the information given here into the form you need.

When I was writing this book, Apple's Macintosh software development system wasn't yet available. The example program **MiniEdit** that forms the core of Volume Two was actually compiled on a Lisa and ported to the Macintosh for execution. In theory, the Pascal compiler in the development system is supposed to be completely compatible with Lisa Pascal at the language level, but in practice there may be slight differences. Please forgive any confusion that arises because of such minor language incompatibilities. (As any programmer knows, there's no difference between theory and practice in theory, but often a great deal of difference between theory and practice in practice!)

The Trap Mechanism

At the machine level, all calls to Toolbox routines have to be translated into subroutine jumps to the appropriate addresses in the Macintosh ROM. The way this is done is rather ingenious. It's based on a feature of the 68000 processor called the "emulator trap," which adds new operations to the processor's instruction set. These new operations look like ordinary machine instructions, but the processor doesn't actually execute them directly: their effects are emulated in software instead of hardware. The Macintosh uses such emulated instructions to represent all the Toolbox operations built into the ROM.

A *trap* (also called an *exception*) occurs when the processor detects an error or abnormal condition in the course of executing a program. This causes it to suspend normal execution and save the address of the next instruction to be executed, along with some additional information about the processor's internal state. It then executes a *trap handler* routine to deal with the abnormal condition. On completion, the handler routine restores the internal state of the processor, using the state information and return address saved earlier, and resumes normal execution from the point of suspension.

Traps can occur for a variety of reasons, such as an attempt to divide by zero, a reference to an illegal address, or an interrupt signal from an input/output device. Each type of trap has its own trap handler. The addresses of the various trap handlers are called *trap vectors*, and are kept in a *vector table* in the first kilobyte of memory. When a trap occurs, the processor fetches the vector for that type of trap from the vector table and uses it to locate the proper handler routine to execute.

In particular, an *emulator trap* occurs when the processor, in the course of program execution, encounters an instruction word that it doesn't recognize as a valid machine-language instruction. On the Macintosh, the trap vector for such unimplemented instructions is set up to point to a handler routine called the Trap Dispatcher. The Trap Dispatcher locates the offending instruction, examines its bit pattern to determine what Toolbox operation it represents, and jumps to the corresponding Toolbox routine in ROM. On completion, the Toolbox routine will return control to the program instruction following the trap.

The unimplemented instruction used to represent a Toolbox operation is called a *trap word* (see Figure 2-1). As the name implies, a trap word is always one word (16 bits) long. Its first 4 bits are always **1010** (hexadecimal **$A**), the pattern that the 68000 processor recognizes as an unimplemented instruction. The particular Toolbox operation the trap word stands for is identified by a *trap number* in the last 8 or 9 bits of the word, depending on the operation. The remaining bits are flags giving additional information to the Trap Dispatcher about how to carry out the operation; the details needn't concern us here.

a. Toolbox Trap Word Format

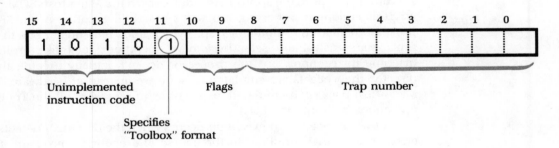

b. Operating System Trap Word Format

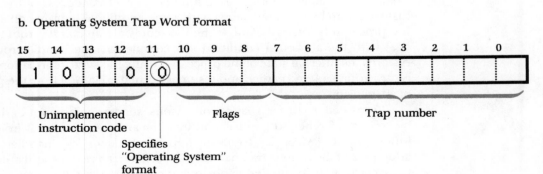

Figure 2-1 Format of a trap word

The Trap Dispatcher locates the ROM routine for a given Toolbox operation by looking it up in a table in memory called the *dispatch table*. The 8- or 9-bit trap number taken from the trap word is actually an index to an entry in the dispatch table, which in turn gives the address of the corresponding routine in ROM. The ROM itself contains a compressed version of its own dispatch table, which is used to reconstruct the actual table in RAM whenever the system starts. This makes it easy to upgrade the machine as newer versions of the ROM appear: what's needed is to substitute the new ROM chips for the older ones, and everything will work just as before, even though all the Toolbox routines may be at different locations in the new ROM.

In reality, the dispatch table entry is more complicated than the raw address of a routine in ROM. Some of the Toolbox routines may actually reside in RAM instead—for instance, to fix bugs discovered after the Toolbox code was already "frozen" into ROM. In that case the corrected version of the routine is loaded into RAM from the disk when the system is started up, and the relevant entry in the dispatch table is "patched" to lead to the proper RAM address. Again, the details aren't important here; what matters is that each entry in the dispatch table leads to the correct address of the corresponding routine in memory.

The Stack

Routines written in Pascal receive their parameters and return their results on a *pushdown stack* in memory. To understand how the stack works, picture a stack of trays in a self-service cafeteria. Trays are always added or removed at the top of the stack, never at the bottom; the base of the stack remains fixed on the counter top. The next tray removed is always the last one added, so the stack grows and shrinks in "LIFO" order (LIFO stands for last in, first out).

A program's subroutines (procedures and functions) also behave in LIFO fashion: the last routine called is always the first to return to its caller. This means that their parameters and private storage can be kept in a contiguous area of memory that grows and shrinks at one end, just like the stack of trays on the lunch counter (see Figure 2-2). One end of this area (the *base* of the stack) remains fixed in memory, while items are added or removed at the other end (the *top*). One of the processor's registers, address register **A7**, is reserved for use as the *stack pointer*: this register always holds the address of the top of the stack.

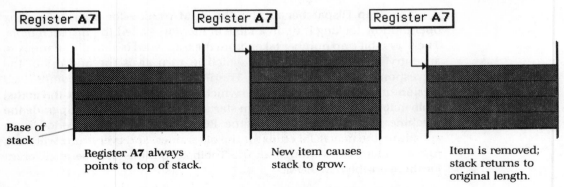

Register **A7** always points to top of stack.

New item causes stack to grow.

Item is removed; stack returns to original length.

Figure 2-2 The stack

When you call a routine in Pascal (or any other language that follows the same calling conventions), the compiler generates machine instructions to "push" the parameter values you supply onto the top of the stack, along with the routine's *return link* (the instruction address where execution will continue when the routine is finished). If the routine is a function, space is also reserved on the stack for the result value that it will return. The routine can then allocate additional stack space for its own local variables, if any.

If this routine in turn calls any others, the space for *their* parameters and local variables will be added to the top of the stack above those of the calling routine. Before returning control to the point of call, each routine "pops" its parameters, local variables, and return link from the stack, leaving it in the same state it was in before the routine was called. (In the case of a function, it leaves its result on the top of the stack for the calling routine to do with as it pleases.)

The Pascal Interface

All of the Toolbox routines and data structures that we'll be discussing in this book are defined in a set of Pascal *interface units*. A *unit* is a collection of precompiled constant, type, procedure, and function declarations that can be incorporated wholesale into any Pascal program. The units that make up the Toolbox interface are provided as part of the Lisa-based software development system (the Macintosh Software Supplement), and will also be included along with the Pascal compiler and other tools in Apple's forthcoming Macintosh-based development system. The interface consists of the following units:

- **MemTypes** defines a set of basic, general-purpose data types that are used by all the other units.
- **OSIntf** contains the interface to the Macintosh Operating System.

- **QuickDraw** contains the interface to the QuickDraw graphics routines.
- **ToolIntf** contains the interface to the User Interface Toolbox proper.
- **PackIntf** contains the interface to the disk-based subroutine packages that supplement the Toolbox; these are discussed further in Chapter 7.

There are also a few other units for specialized uses not covered in this book, such as printing, floating-point arithmetic, and transcendental functions; see *Inside Macintosh* for information.

Each unit consists of two files: a text *interface file* containing the declarations that make up the unit in Pascal source form, and an *object module* containing the corresponding compiled code. To use the Toolbox in Pascal, you name the interface units in a *uses* declaration:

uses MemTypes, OSIntf, QuickDraw, ToolIntf, PackIntf;

This makes all the constant, variable, type, and routine names declared in the units available to your program at compilation time, just as if they were Pascal standard identifiers such as **INTEGER** or **SQRT**. (Of course, you only need to include those units that you actually use in your program: if you don't use any of the routines in the disk-based packages, for instance, you can omit the **PackIntf** unit from your *uses* declaration.) After compiling your program, you link it with the corresponding object modules to incorporate the compiled code of the units; see the documentation provided with the software development system for further information on this process.

Stack-Based and Register-Based Routines

Most of the Toolbox routines are *stack-based:* they accept their parameters and return their results on the stack, as described in the preceding section. This allows the Pascal compiler to generate the same machine instructions to set up the parameters for these routines that it would use for an ordinary Pascal routine defined in your program. Remember, though, that routines in ROM have to be called through the trap mechanism we discussed earlier, rather than by going directly to a memory address in the normal way. The Toolbox interface units use a special "*inline* declaration" for all stack-based ROM routines, telling the compiler to place an appropriate trap word in-line—that is, directly into the compiled object code—instead of the usual **JSR** (Jump to Subroutine) instruction.

Not all the ROM routines are stack-based, however; some of them are *register-based* instead. In general these are Operating System routines that perform relatively low-level operations such as memory management and file input/output, and were originally intended to be called only from assembly language rather than Pascal. So instead of using the stack like a

Pascal routine, they pass their parameters and results directly in the processor's registers.

Later it was decided that some of these register-based routines would be useful in Pascal as well as assembly language, so they were added to the Pascal interface. Because of the difference in calling conventions, however, an extra level of indirection had to be introduced. When you call a register-based routine in Pascal, what you're actually calling is a special *interface routine* that mediates between the stack- and register-based calling conventions. The interface routine moves the parameters from the stack, where the Pascal calling program leaves them, to the registers where the ROM routine expects to find them; then it traps to the ROM routine. On return from the trap, it moves the results, if any, back from the registers to the stack for the Pascal program's benefit. The interface routine serves as a kind of "glue" between your Pascal program and the register-based routine in ROM, and is sometimes referred to as a "glue routine."

> When you use the Pascal interface units, you don't have to worry about the distinction between stack- and register-based routines. You simply use the normal Pascal syntax for all your routine calls, and the interface units see to it that everything gets fixed up to work the way you expect it to. The difference between stack- and register-based routines is really important only if you're using the Toolbox in assembly language, as discussed in the next section.

The Assembly-Language Interface

To call a Toolbox routine in assembly language, you use a *trap macro* that expands into the proper trap word for that routine. For example, to call the routine **HidePen** [5.2.3], which hides the "graphics pen" that the Toolbox uses to draw lines on the screen, you would use the instruction

```
_HidePen
```

When assembled, this macro produces the trap word **$A896**, which causes a trap to the **HidePen** routine in ROM.

The trap macros are defined in a set of assembly-language files that you incorporate into your program with an **.INCLUDE** directive:

- **SysTraps**, containing the macros for calling Operating System routines
- **QuickTraps** for the QuickDraw graphics routines
- **ToolTraps** for the User Interface Toolbox
- **PackMacs** for the disk-based packages

There is also a set of *definition files* that uses **.EQU** directives to define assembly-language constants and addresses of global variables for use with the Toolbox:

- **SysEqu** for constants and variables relating to the Operating System
- **QuickEqu** for those relating to QuickDraw
- **ToolEqu** for those relating to the Toolbox proper
- **SysErr** for Operating System error codes

Like the Pascal interface units, the assembly-language macro and definition files are provided as part of the Lisa-based Macintosh Software Supplement and will also be included in the Macintosh-based development system.

You'll find the names of all the trap macros (along with the corresponding trap words) listed in summary boxes at the end of each section in our Reference Handbook. Trap macro names always begin with an underscore character (_), followed by the routine's name. The routine's name is generally spelled the same way as in Pascal, but there are occasional exceptions; these are noted where appropriate in the Reference Handbook. The Handbook also lists useful Toolbox constants, addresses of global variables, field offsets within Toolbox data structures, and so forth, taken from the definition files.

> Be warned that the values of constants, and especially the addresses of global variables, may be subject to change in future versions of the Toolbox. To stay on the safe side, always refer to them by name, rather than relying on the values and addresses shown in the Handbook.

Before calling a Toolbox routine with a trap macro, you have to set up its parameters the way it expects to find them. For stack-based routines, this means pushing the parameters onto the stack in the order they're listed in the routine's Pascal definition. All parameter values must be in the same data formats used by the Pascal compiler:

- Integers are 2 bytes long, long integers 4 bytes, both in the two's-complement form.
- All pointers (including handles, discussed in Chapter 3) are 4 bytes long.
- Booleans occupy 2 bytes on the stack, with the actual value in bit 8, the low-order bit of the first byte: **1** for **TRUE**, **0** for **FALSE**. The other 15 bits are ignored.
- Single characters (type **CHAR**) occupy 2 bytes, with the ASCII character code in the second byte. The first byte is ignored.

- Character strings are represented on the stack by a 4-byte pointer to the actual string in memory. The format of the string itself is described later in this chapter and in section [2.1.1] of the Reference Handbook.
- Data structures such as records and arrays are usually represented by a 4-byte pointer to the structure in memory. However, if the contents of the structure are no more than 4 bytes long, they're stored directly on the stack instead of a pointer.
- All variable parameters, regardless of type, are represented by a 4-byte pointer giving the address of the variable in memory.

The routine will remove its parameters from the stack before returning, so there's no need for you to do this yourself. If the routine is a function, you must reserve stack space for its result by decrementing the stack pointer the appropriate number of bytes *before* pushing the parameters; on return from the trap, you'll find the result on top of the stack.

For register-based routines, of course, you have to set up the parameters in the appropriate registers rather than on the stack. Register usage conventions for all such routines are given in the Reference Handbook; if no register information appears, you can assume the routine is stack-based.

A few of the routines listed in the Handbook don't reside in ROM, but belong to the Pascal interface itself. These routines are inaccessible via the trap mechanism and so are unavailable in assembly language. In general, they exist only to provide a way of doing something in Pascal that can be done more directly and easily at the assembly-language level, such as by reading or setting a global variable. Routines in this category are identified wherever applicable in the Reference Handbook.

Extended Features of Pascal

The version of the Pascal language supported by Apple's compiler has a few nonstandard features that we'll be using in our programming examples. One of these is the data type **LONGINT** ("long integer"), representing integers of twice the normal length: 32 bits including sign, instead of only 16. This provides a range of ±**2147483647**, compared with ±**32767** for ordinary integers. You can apply all the standard arithmetic operators to long-integer operands as well as to ordinary integers. An ordinary integer will automatically be converted to the equivalent long integer if you combine it with a long integer in an arithmetic expression, or assign it to a long-integer variable, or pass it to a routine that expects a long integer as a parameter.

Many of the Toolbox routines accept long-integer parameters or return long-integer results. Since memory addresses in the 68000 processor are 32 bits long, this type is particularly useful for working with addresses and related quantities, such as the lengths of memory blocks. For the same reason, all pointers on the Macintosh (including handles, which we'll learn about in the next chapter) are 32 bits long.

The built-in function **ORD** is a standard Pascal function for converting any scalar value to a corresponding integer: for instance, a character to its equivalent integer character code. On the Macintosh, **ORD** will also accept a pointer and return the equivalent long-integer address. For converting in the other direction, there's a built-in function named **POINTER** that accepts a long integer representing a memory address and converts it into a pointer to that address. The result is a "blind pointer" similar to the standard Pascal constant **NIL**: it can be assigned to a variable of any pointer type, regardless of the underlying base type the variable is declared to point to.

The **ORD** and **POINTER** functions can be used in combination to convert from one pointer type to another. For instance, if you've declared

```
var
   this : ThisPtr;
   that : ThatPtr;
```

where **ThisPtr** and **ThatPtr** are two different pointer types, you can convert one into the other by writing

```
this := POINTER(ORD(that))
```

or

```
that := POINTER(ORD(this))
```

ORD converts the original pointer to a long-integer address, then **POINTER** takes it back into a blind pointer that you can assign to a variable of the other type.

However, Apple's Pascal compiler provides a more direct way to convert data values (including pointers) from one type to another. Just use the name of the target type as a function, giving it as a parameter the value to be converted to that type. In the example above, for instance, you could convert the pointers directly with the statements

```
this := ThisPtr(that)
```

or

```
that := ThatPtr(this)
```

This technique is known as "typecasting." It doesn't change the underlying data representation (in this case, the memory address that the pointers point to) but changes only the high-level data type that it's considered to represent. We'll see many examples of this technique later on, particularly when we begin to develop our example program **MiniEdit** in Volume Two.

Another useful feature is the @ operator, which produces a pointer to whatever variable or routine you give it as an operand. Once again, the result is a blind "pointer to anything." For instance, if you declare

```
var
    aThing     : Thing;
    aThingPtr  : ^Thing;
```

then the statement

```
aThingPtr := @aThing
```

sets **aThingPtr** to point to the address of variable **aThing**. After you've executed this assignment, the expression

```
aThingPtr^
```

(which denotes whatever **aThingPtr** points to) is equivalent to the variable **aThing** itself. You can use this expression on either the left or right side of an assignment statement, or anywhere else that variable **aThing** could be used: for instance, if **something** is another variable of type **Thing**, the statement

```
something := aThingPtr^
```

is equivalent to

```
something := aThing
```

and

```
aThingPtr^ := something
```

is equivalent to

```
aThing := something
```

The @ operator can be applied to routines (that is, procedures or functions) as well as to variables. Some of the Toolbox routines and data structures have parameters or fields of type **ProcPtr** [2.1.1], representing a pointer to a program routine. You can use the @ operator to create such routine pointers: for example, if **Twiddle** is the name of a routine in your program, then the expression

```
@Twiddle
```

denotes a pointer to it. You can assign this routine pointer to a variable of type **ProcPtr**, embed it in a data structure, or pass it to any Toolbox routine that expects a **ProcPtr** as a parameter.

> Technically, though, a **ProcPtr** is just defined as a pointer to a byte in memory—presumably the address of the first instruction in the routine. This means that there's no way in Pascal to "open up" the **ProcPtr** and execute the underlying routine it points to. That can only be done at the machine- or assembly-language level, either by the Toolbox or by an assembly-language routine of your own, using a **JSR** (Jump to Subroutine) instruction.

One last built-in function worth mentioning is **SIZEOF**, which accepts a variable of any type as a parameter and returns the number of bytes that variable occupies in memory. If the parameter is the name of a type, **SIZEOF** gives the number of bytes occupied by a value of that type. For instance, if **x** is an integer variable, then the expressions **SIZEOF(x)** and **SIZEOF(INTEGER)** both have the value **2** (since an integer is 2 bytes long).

General-Purpose Utilities

In the rest of this chapter, we'll be talking about some of the general-purpose utility routines that are included in the Toolbox. Generally, these are simple, straightforward operations dealing with such things as character strings, bit-level manipulation, and arithmetic. Knowing these topics well isn't essential to your overall understanding of the Toolbox but if you're in a hurry, you might want to skim this section for a general idea of the utilities available. Later refer to them when you need more detailed information.

Strings

For working with strings of character text, the Toolbox uses the same data format found in Apple's Pascal compiler. A string is stored internally as a variable-length data structure consisting of 1 byte giving the length of the string in characters, followed by the characters themselves (Figure 2-3). Since the character count is 1 byte long, it can accommodate strings of up to 255 characters. The actual character codes used to stand for the various characters will be given in Chapter 8.

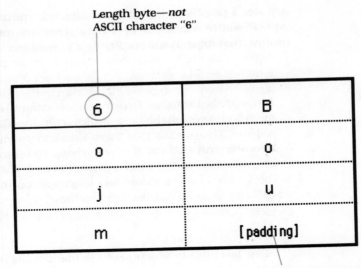

Length byte—*not* ASCII character "6"

String format must be a whole number of words so an extra byte of "padding" is needed here

Figure 2-3 Internal string format

Strings of this form are normally represented in the Toolbox interface by the data type **Str255** [2.1.1], used for things like the titles of windows and the names of menu items. Values of this type take up only as many bytes of memory as are needed to hold the actual characters of the string (along with the length byte, of course). For instance, the string '**Snark**' would be 6 bytes long: 1 byte for the character count and 5 more for the characters of the string. However, the string must always occupy a whole number of words—that is, an even number of bytes. If the number of bytes actually needed is odd, an extra, unused byte is added at the end for "padding." So the string '**Boojum**' would take up 8 bytes altogether: one for the character count, 6 for the characters, and 1 more to keep the overall length even. The empty string takes up 2 bytes of memory: a character count of **0** and a byte of padding.

The Toolbox function **EqualString** [2.1.2] compares two strings and returns a Boolean result telling whether they are equivalent. You can specify whether you want corresponding upper- and lowercase letters to be considered the same or different. The **UprString** routine [2.1.2] converts all letters in a string to uppercase while leaving all other characters unchanged.

The Macintosh character set includes a variety of accented letters and diacritical marks for use in foreign languages. The **EqualString** and **UprString** routines both accept Boolean parameters telling them whether to take such foreign characters into account or whether to ignore them or remove them from the string. There's also an International Utilities Package for adapting a program to the needs of foreign languages and countries. This package includes a more sophisticated string comparison routine named **IUEqualString** (IU for "International Utilities") that can be customized to the spelling conventions used in a particular language. (For instance, in German it can be set up to treat the umlauted vowels **ä**, **ö**, and **ü** as equivalent to the combinations **ae**, **oe**, and **ue**.) See the *Inside Macintosh* manual for information on the International Utilities Package.

Bit-Level Operations

For testing or changing single bits in memory, the Toolbox includes routines named **BitSet** to set a bit to **1**, **BitClr** to clear it to **0**, and **BitTst** to test its current value [2.2.1]. These routines all accept two parameters: a pointer to a base address and a bit number relative to that address. Bits are numbered consecutively throughout memory, beginning with **0** for the leftmost (high-order) bit at the designated base address (Figure 2-4). Thus bit numbers **0** to **7** refer to the byte at the base address itself, **8** to **15** refer to the following byte, and so on through consecutive bytes of memory. You can designate a bit at any distance forward from the given base address by making the bit number as big as you like, but negative bit numbers are not allowed.

Notice that this bit-numbering convention is the reverse of the one generally used on the 68000 processor, where bits are numbered from right to left within a byte or word.

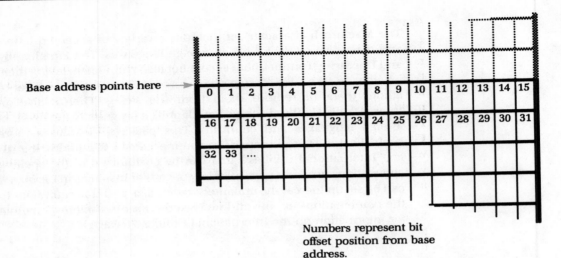

Numbers represent bit
offset position from base
address.

Figure 2-4 Bit numbering for single-bit operations

The utility routines **BitAnd**, **BitOr**, **BitXOr**, and **BitNot** [2.2.2] perform the standard bitwise logical operations on 32-bit operands. **BitShift** [2.2.2] shifts its operand a specified number of bit positions in either direction. The shift is a logical one, in which bits shifted out at one end of the operand are lost and **0**s are shifted in at the other end. **HiWord** and **LoWord** [2.2.3] extract the high-order and low-order 16 bits, respectively, of a 32-bit operand.

The **StuffHex** procedure [2.2.4] "stuffs" consecutive bytes of memory, beginning at an assigned destination address, with the contents defined by a string of hexadecimal digits. The string should contain no characters other than **0** to **9** and **A** to **F**; in particular, it should *not* begin with the leading dollar sign (**$**) usually used to denote hexadecimal constants.

StuffHex is a dangerous operation that can easily get you in trouble if you use it carelessly. It does no range or validity checking, but blindly stores into the specified locations in memory. If you give it the wrong destination pointer, the consequences can be catastrophic. Be careful what you stuff and where you stuff it!

Arithmetic Operations

The Toolbox includes facilities for working with 32-bit "fixed point" numbers. Type **Fixed** [2.3.1] is defined as equivalent to the built-in Pascal type **LONGINT**, but is interpreted in a different way. Instead of a full 32-bit integer, a fixed-point number is considered to have a binary point in the middle, splitting it into a 16-bit integer part and a 16-bit fraction. The **FixRatio** routine [2.3.2] divides two 16-bit integers and produces a 32-bit **Fixed** result. You can add and subtract fixed-point numbers in the usual way, with the standard arithmetic operators + and—, but for multiplication you must use the special Toolbox function **FixMul** [2.3.2]. There is no built-in routine for dividing fixed-point numbers.

The **FixRound** function [2.3.1] converts a positive fixed-point number to the nearest 16-bit integer. (**FixRound** doesn't work on negative numbers; to round a negative fixed-point number, you have to multiply it by −**1** to make it positive, round it with **FixRound**, then multiply the result back by −**1**, to make it negative again.) There's also a routine named **LongMul** [2.3.3] that multiplies two 32-bit long integers and produces a 64-bit integer result. A pair of conversion routines, **NumToString** and **StringToNum** [2.3.4], convert between long integers and their equivalent representations as strings of decimal digits.

```
function Randomize (range : INTEGER)          {Desired range of random numbers}
                 : INTEGER;                    {Random number between 0 and (range - 1)}


   { Generate random numbers over a specified range.  }


   var
      rawResult : LONGINT;                     {"Raw" random number received from Toolbox}


   begin {Randomize}

      rawResult := ABS(Random);               {Get random number between 0 and 32767 [2.3.5]}
      Randomize := (rawResult * range) div 32768   {Scale to specified range}

   end;  {Randomize}
```

Program 2–1 Generate random numbers

Finally, there's a **Random** function [2.3.5] that returns a different integer result each time you call it. The results are distributed uniformly over the entire range of integer values, from **−32768** to **32767**. Program 2-1 shows how to scale the result to the range you need: to generate an integer between **0** and (**range −1**), convert the "raw" result you receive from the **Random** function to a positive value, multiply by **range**, and divide by the original range of **32768**. Notice the use of a **LONGINT** variable for the intermediate result.

The method used to generate random numbers is based on a "seed" value kept in a global variable named **RandSeed** [2.3.5], which is changed each time you call the **Random** function. The sequence of numbers is really only "pseudo-random," since you can reproduce the same sequence again by starting out with the same seed value. The seed is ordinarily initialized to a standard value of **1** at the beginning of your program; if you want to produce a different sequence of random numbers each time the program is run, you must change this setting to start with a different seed each time. The easiest way to do this is to initialize the seed to the current setting of the clock chip (see next section) at the time the program is started.

Date and Time

The Macintosh has a built-in clock chip that continuously keeps track of the current date and time. The clock chip is powered independently by a battery, and continues to keep time even when the machine's main power is off. The date and time are expressed internally as a total number of seconds since the beginning of time, which according to Apple's painstaking research occurred at midnight, January 1, 1984. You can read the clock in this "raw" form with the Toolbox routine **GetDateTime** or set it with **SetDateTime** [2.4.1].

Often, however, it's more convenient to work with a *date and time record* [2.4.2], which has separate fields for the year, month, day of the month, day of the week, hour, minute, and second. To read or set the clock in this form, use **GetTime** or **SetTime** [2.4.2] instead of **GetDateTime** or **SetDateTime**. There's also a pair of utility routines named **Secs2Date** and **Date2Secs** [2.4.3] for converting between raw seconds on the one hand and date and time records on the other.

To convert the date and time into a readable character string for human consumption, use **IUDateString** and **IUTimeString** [2.4.4]. These routines accept the clock reading in raw seconds and return a string representing the date or time of day, respectively. You can ask for the date in any of three formats: short

12/18/84

long

Tuesday, December 18, 1984

or abbreviated

Tue, Dec 18, 1984

and the time with seconds included

1:47:22 PM

or without

1:47 PM

REFERENCE

2.1 Elementary Data Structures

2.1.1 Strings and Procedures

Definitions

```
type
    Str255  = STRING[255];    {Any text string, maximum 255 characters}

    ProcPtr = Ptr;            {Pointer to a procedure or function [3.1.1]}
```

Notes

1. **Str255** stands for a string of text with a maximum length of 255 characters.

2. Just enough bytes are actually included as are needed to hold a given string. The first byte (element **0**) gives the length of the string in characters; the remaining 1 to 255 bytes contain the characters themselves.

3. The string must always physically occupy a whole number of 16-bit memory words. If necessary, an unused byte of "padding" is added at the end to fill out the physical length to an even number of bytes.

4. **ProcPtr** is a pointer to a procedure or function.

5. To denote a **ProcPtr** to a given routine, prefix the name of the routine with the pointer operator @.

2.1.2 String Operations

Definitions

```
function  EqualString
          (string1     : Str255;      {First string to be compared}
          string2      : Str255;      {Second string to be compared}
          caseCounts   : BOOLEAN;     {Distinguish upper- and lowercase?}
          marksCount   : BOOLEAN)     {Ignore diacritical marks?}
           : BOOLEAN;                 {Are the two strings equivalent?}

procedure UprString
          (var theString : Str255;    {String to be converted}
          stripMarks     : BOOLEAN);  {Eliminate diacritical marks?}
```

Notes

1. **EqualString** compares two strings for equality and returns a Boolean result.

2. If **caseCounts** is **FALSE**, corresponding upper- and lowercase letters are considered identical for purposes of comparison; if **TRUE**, they're considered different.

3. If **marksCount** is **TRUE**, foreign-language accents and diacritical marks are taken into account in the comparison; if **FALSE**, they're disregarded.

4. A more sophisticated form of string comparison, allowing for specialized spelling conventions used in foreign languages, is available through the **IUEqualString** routine of the International Utilities Package. See *Inside Macintosh* for details.

5. **UprString** converts a string to full capitals, replacing any lowercase letters with their uppercase equivalents.

6. Characters other than letters of the alphabet are left unchanged.

7. If **stripMarks** is **TRUE**, foreign-language accents and diacritical marks are removed from the converted string.

8. The trap macro for **EqualString** is **_CmpString** ("compare string").

9. When called from assembly language, these routines are register-based: see register usage information below.

10. In assembly language, the Boolean parameters are represented by flag bits in the trap word: **1** for **TRUE, 0** for **FALSE. caseCounts** and **marksCount** correspond to bits **10** and **9**, respectively, of the **_CmpString** trap, and **stripMarks** to bit **9** of the **_UprString** trap. The trap macros accept optional parameters named **CASE** and **MARKS** for setting these flag bits to **1**: for example,

```
_UprString      ,MARKS
_CmpString      ,CASE
_CmpString      ,MARKS,CASE
```

Assembly Language Information

Trap macros:

(Pascal) Routine name	(Assembly) Trap macro	Trap word
EqualString	**_CmpString**	**$A03C**
UprString	**_UprString**	**$A854**

Register usage:

Routine	Register	Contents
EqualString	**A0.L** (in)	pointer to **string1**
	A1.L (in)	pointer to **string2**
	D0.L (in)	high word: length of **string1**
		low word: length of **string2**
	D0.B (out)	= **0** if strings equal ≠ **0** if unequal
UprString	**A0.L** (in)	pointer to **theString**
	D0.B (in)	length of **theString**
	A0.L (out)	pointer to **theString**

2.2 Bit-Level Operations

2.2.1 Single Bit Access

Definitions

```
procedure BitSet
          (bitsPtr    : Ptr;            {Pointer to bits [3.1.1]}
           bitNumber : LONGINT);        {Number of bit to be set to 1}

procedure BitClr
          (bitsPtr    : Ptr;            {Pointer to bits [3.1.1]}
           bitNumber : LONGINT);        {Number of bit to be cleared to 0}

function   BitTst
          (BitsPtr    : Ptr;            {Pointer to bits [3.1.1]}
           bitNumber : LONGINT);        {Number of bit to be tested}
            : BOOLEAN;                  {Is bit set to 1?}
```

Notes

1. These routines operate on single bits in memory.

2. **BitSet** sets a bit to **1**; **BitClr** clears it to **0** ; **BitTst** tests it and returns a Boolean result representing its value.

3. **bitsPtr** is a pointer to a base address in memory (the elementary data type **Ptr** is defined in [3.1.1]). **bitNumber** identifies a single-bit relative to the base address.

4. Bits are numbered from left to right within each byte; notice that this is the reverse of the usual 68000 convention.

5. **bitNumber** can have any nonnegative value, and can designate a bit at any distance in memory from the base address. Bit numbers **0** to **7** refer to the byte designated by the base address, **8** to **15** refer to the byte following it, and so on through consecutive bytes of memory.

6. Negative bit numbers are not allowed.

7. **BitTst** returns **TRUE** for a **1** bit, **FALSE** for a **0** bit.

Assembly Language Information

Trap macros:

(Pascal) Routine name	(Assembly) Trap macro	Trap word
BitSet	**_BitSet**	**$A85E**
BitClr	**_BitClr**	**$A85F**
BitTst	**_BitTst**	**$A85D**

2.2.2 Logical Operations

Definitions

```
function BitAnd
        (bits1 : LONGINT;          {First operand}
         bits2 : LONGINT)          {Second operand}
         : LONGINT;                {Bitwise "and"}

function BitOr
        (bits1 : LONGINT;          {First operand}
         bits2 : LONGINT)          {Second operand}
         : LONGINT;                {Bitwise "or"}

function BitXOr
        (bits1 : LONGINT;          {First operand}
         bits2 : LONGINT)          {Second operand}
         : LONGINT;                {Bitwise "exclusive or"}

function BitNot
        (bits : LONGINT)           {Bits to be complemented}
         : LONGINT;                {Bitwise complement}

function BitShift
        (bits      : LONGINT;      {Bits to be shifted}
         shiftCount : INTEGER)     {Number of places to shift}
         : LONGINT;                {Result of shift}
```

Notes

1. These routines perform bitwise logical operations on 32-bit (long word) operands.

2. For **BitAnd**, **BitOr**, and **BitXOr**, each bit of the result is obtained by applying the given logical operation to the bits found at the corresponding position in the two operands.

3. For **BitNot**, each bit of the result is the logical complement of the corresponding bit in the operand. That is, each **1** bit in the operand is transformed into a **0** bit in the result, and vice versa.

4. The result returned by **BitShift** is obtained by shifting the operand **bits** by the number of bit positions specified by **shiftCount**.

5. **shiftCount** is interpreted modulo **32**.

6. Positive shift counts shift to the left, negative to the right.

7. **BitShift** performs a *logical* shift. Bits shifted out at one end of the operand are lost; positions vacated at the other end are filled with **0**s.

Assembly Language Information

Trap macros:

(Pascal) Routine name	(Assembly) Trap macro	Trap word
BitAnd	**_BitAnd**	**$A858**
BitOr	**_BitOr**	**$A85B**
BitXOr	**_BitXOr**	**$A859**
BitNot	**_BitNot**	**$A85A**
BitShift	**_BitShift**	**$A85C**

2.2.3 Word Access

Definitions

```
function HiWord
        (longWord : LONGINT)        {32-bit operand}
            : INTEGER;              {High-order 16 bits}

function LoWord
        (longWord : LONGINT)        {32-bit operand}
            : INTEGER;              {Low-order 16 bits}
```

Notes

1. These routines extract and return the high- and low-order, 16-bit words of a 32-bit long word.

2. **HiWord** and **LoWord** can be used to extract the integer and fractional parts, respectively, of a fixed-point number [2.3.1].

Assembly Language Information

Trap macros:

(Pascal) Routine name	(Assembly) Trap macro	Trap word
HiWord	**_HiWord**	**$A86A**
LoWord	**_LoWord**	**$A86B**

2.2.4 Direct Storage

Definitions

procedure StuffHex
(destPtr : Ptr;   {Pointer to data structure to be stuffed}
hexString : Str255);   {String representing data in hexadecimal}

Notes

1. **StuffHex** stores "raw" bits into any designated data structure in memory.

2. **destPtr** is a pointer to the beginning of the destination data structure. The specified data will be "stuffed" into consecutive locations beginning at this address.

3. **hexString** is a string representing the data to be stuffed, in hexadecimal form.

4. **hexString** should contain no characters other than the hexadecimal digits **0-9** and **A-F**. It should *not* begin with a dollar sign (**$**).

5. Nominally, the maximum length of **hexString** is 255 hexadecimal digits. However, since data structures generally must consist of a whole number of 16-bit words, the effective maximum is actually 252 digits, or 63 words.

6. *BEWARE:* No range checking of any kind is performed.

Assembly Language Information

Trap macro:

(Pascal) Routine name	(Assembly) Trap macro	Trap word
StuffHex	**_StuffHex**	**$A866**

2.3 Arithmetic Operations

2.3.1 Fixed-Point Numbers

Definitions

```
type
  Fixed = LONGINT;              {Fixed-point number}


function FixRound
        (theNumber : Fixed)     {Fixed-point number to be rounded}
          : INTEGER;            {Number rounded to an integer}
```

Notes

1. Type **Fixed** represents a 32-bit, fixed-point number, with 16 bits before the binary point and 16 bits after it.
2. The value of a fixed-point number is equivalent to that of the corresponding long integer divided by **65536** (2 to the 16th power).
3. Use **HiWord** and **LoWord** [2.2.3] to extract the integer and fractional parts of a fixed-point number, respectively.
4. **FixRound** rounds a positive fixed-point number to the nearest integer.
5. To round a negative fixed-point number, multiply it by −1, round with **FixRound**, then multiply the result back by −1.

Assembly Language Information

Trap macro:

(Pascal) Routine name	(Assembly) Trap macro	Trap word
FixRound	**_FixRound**	**$A86C**

2.3.2 Fixed-Point Arithmetic

Definitions

```
function FixMul
        (number1 : Fixed;           {First fixed-point operand}
         number2: Fixed)            {Second fixed-point operand}
         : Fixed;                   {Fixed-point product}
function FixRatio
        (numerator    : INTEGER;    {Integer numerator}
         denominator  : INTEGER)    {Integer denominator}
         : Fixed;                   {Fixed-point quotient}
```

Notes

1. **FixMul** multiplies two fixed-point numbers and produces a fixed-point result.

2. **FixRatio** divides two integers and produces a fixed-point result.

3. To add and subtract fixed-point numbers, just use the standard operators + and −.

Assembly Language Information

Trap macros:

(Pascal) Routine name	(Assembly) Trap macro	Trap word
FixMul	**_FixMul**	**$A868**
FixRatio	**_FixRatio**	**$A869**

2.3.3 Long Multiplication

Definitions

```
type
  Int64Bit = record
                hiLong : LONGINT;          {High-order 32 bits}
                loLong: LONGINT            {Low-order 32 bits}
             end:

procedure LongMul
             (number1    : LONGINT;        {First 32-bit operand}
              number2    : LONGINT;        {Second 32-bit operand}
              var product : Int64Bit);     {Returns 64-bit product}
```

Notes

1. **LongMul** multiplies two 32-bit long integers and produces a 64-bit result.

Assembly Language Information

Trap macro:

(Pascal) Routine name	(Assembly) Trap macro	Trap word
LongMul	**_LongMul**	**$A867**

2.3.4 Binary/Decimal Conversion

Definitions

```
procedure NumToSring
            (theNumber    : LONGINT;    {Number to be converted}
        var theString    : Str255);    {Returns equivalent string}
procedure StringToNum
            (theString    : Str255;     {String to be converted}
        var theNumber : LONGINT);    {Returns equivalent number}
```

Notes

1. These routines convert a number between its internal binary representation and its external representation as a decimal character string.

2. The string consists entirely of decimal digits (**0-9**), except possibly for a leading sign (+ or −).

3. **NumToString** doesn't produce a + sign for positive numbers, but **StringToNum** will accept one.

4. **NumToString** suppresses leading zeros except in the case of the numerical value **0**, which produces the one-character string '**0**'.

5. The magnitude of the string provided to **StringToNum** should not exceed 2 to the 31st power minus 1 (**2147483647**).

6. The binary/decimal conversion routines are not actually part of the Toolbox proper; they're contained in a package, the Binary/Decimal Conversion Package, that resides in the system resource file and is automatically loaded into memory when needed. Package routines are defined in the interface file **PackIntf**. See Chapter 7 for further information on the package mechanism.

7. The trap macros for these routines expand to call **_Pack7** [7.2.1] with the routine selectors given below.

Assembly Language Information

Trap macros and routine selectors:

(Pascal) Routine name	(Assembly) Trap macro	Trap word	Routine selector
NumToString	**_NumToString**	**$A9EE**	**0**
StringToNum	**_StringToNum**	**$A9EE**	**1**

2.3.5 Random Numbers

Definitions

```
function Random
          : INTEGER;        {Random Number}

var
  RandSeed : LONGINT;       {"Seed" for random number generation}
```

Notes

1. **Random** returns a different integer each time it's called, distributed uniformly over the interval from **−32768** to **32767**.

2. The sequence of numbers generated is "pseudo-random": the same sequence can be duplicated by starting with the same "seed" value in the global variable **RandSeed**.

3. **RandSeed** is initialized to **1** by the QuickDraw initialization procedure **InitGraf** [4.3.1].

4. **RandSeed** is actually a QuickDraw global variable [4.3.1]. To access it in assembly language, find the pointer to QuickDraw's globals at the address contained in register **A5**, then locate the variable relative to that pointer using the offset constant **RandSeed** (below). See Chapters 3 and 4 for further discussion.

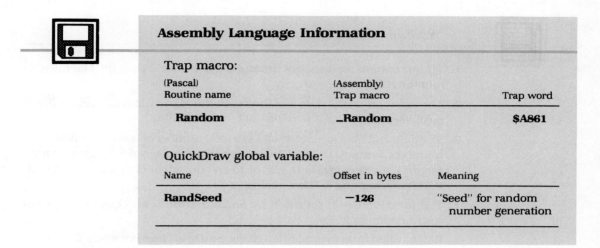

Assembly Language Information

Trap macro:

(Pascal) Routine name	(Assembly) Trap macro	Trap word
Random	**_Random**	**$A861**

QuickDraw global variable:

Name	Offset in bytes	Meaning
RandSeed	**−126**	"Seed" for random number generation

2.4 Date and Time

2.4.1 Date and Time in Seconds

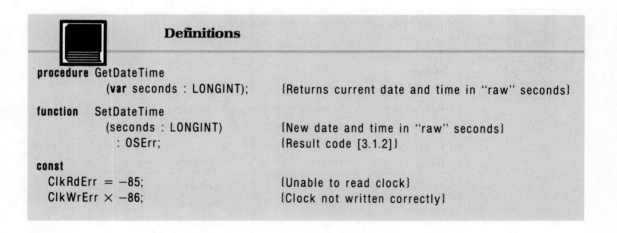

Definitions

```
procedure GetDateTime
           (var seconds : LONGINT);      {Returns current date and time in "raw" seconds}
function   SetDateTime
           (seconds : LONGINT)           {New date and time in "raw" seconds}
           : OSErr;                       {Result code [3.1.2]}
const
  ClkRdErr = −85;                         {Unable to read clock}
  ClkWrErr × −86;                         {Clock not written correctly}
```

Notes

1. These routines read and set the current date and time in the Macintosh's built-in clock chip.

2. The user can set the date and time with the Alarm Clock or Control Panel desk accessory.

3. The date and time are expressed as a total number of "raw" seconds since midnight, January 1, 1904. This value can be converted to a date and time record with **Secs2Date** [2.4.3], or to an equivalent character string with **IUDateString** and **IUTimeString** [2.4.4].

4. The function result returned by **SetDateTime** is an Operating System result code [3.1.2].

5. When called from assembly language, **SetDateTime** is register-based; see register usage information below.

6. **GetDateTime** is not available in assembly language via the trap mechanism. Instead, the current reading of the clock chip is directly accessible in the global variable **Time**.

Assembly Language Information

Trap macro:

(Pascal) Routine name	(Assembly) Trap macro	Trap word
SetDatetime	**_SetDateTime**	**$A03A**

Register usage:

Routine	Register	Contents
SetDateTime	**D0.L** (in)	**seconds**
	D0.W (out)	result code

Assembly-language global variable:

Name	Address	Meaning
Time	**$20C**	Current date and time in "raw" seconds

2.4.2 Date and Time Records

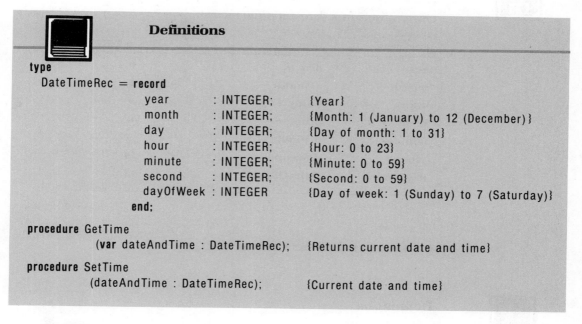

Definitions

```
type
  DateTimeRec = record
          year       : INTEGER;      {Year}
          month      : INTEGER;      {Month: 1 (January) to 12 (December)}
          day        : INTEGER;      {Day of month: 1 to 31}
          hour       : INTEGER;      {Hour: 0 to 23}
          minute     : INTEGER;      {Minute: 0 to 59}
          second     : INTEGER;      {Second: 0 to 59}
          dayOfWeek  : INTEGER       {Day of week: 1 (Sunday) to 7 (Saturday)}
        end;

procedure GetTime
        (var dateAndTime : DateTimeRec);    {Returns current date and time}

procedure SetTime
        (dateAndTime : DateTimeRec);        {Current date and time}
```

Notes

1. **GetTime** and **SetTime** read and set the current date and time in the Macintosh's built-in clock chip.

2. The user can set the date and time with the Alarm Clock or Control Panel desk accessory.

3. The date and time are represented in the form of a record of type **DateTimeRec**.

4. These routines are not available in assembly language via the trap mechanism. Instead, you can read the clock chip directly via the global variable **Time** or set it with **SetDateTime** [2.4.1] and convert between "raw" seconds and date and time records with **Secs2Date** and **Date2Secs** [2.4.3].

Assembly Language Information

Field offsets in a date and time record:

(Pascal) Field name	(Assembly) Offset name	Offset in bytes
year	dtYear	0
month	dtMonth	2
day	dtDay	4
hour	dtHour	6
minute	dtMinute	8
second	dtSecond	10
dayOfWeek	dtDayOfWeek	12

2.4.3 Date and Time Conversion

Definitions

```
procedure Secs2Date
          (seconds          : LONGINT;        {Date and time in "raw" seconds}
       var dateAndTime : DateTimeRec);        {Returns equivalent date and time record}

procedure Date2Secs
          (dateAndTime : DateTimeRec;         {Date and time record}
       var seconds   : LONGINT);              {Returns equivalent in "raw" seconds}
```

Notes

1. These routines convert the date and time between "raw" seconds, as reported directly by the built-in clock chip [2.4.1] and the more convenient form of date and time records [2.4.2].

Assembly Language Information

Trap macros:

(Pascal) Routine name	(Assembly) Trap macro	Trap word
Secs2Date	**_Secs2Date**	**$A9C6**
Date2Secs	**_Date2Secs**	**$A9C7**

2.4.4 Date and Time Strings

Definitions

```
type
    DateForm = (ShortDate, LongDate, AbbrevDate);

procedure IUDateString
            (seconds    : LONGINT;       {Date and time in "raw" seconds}
             format     : DateForm;      {Format desired for date}
         var theString  : Str255);       {Returns equivalent character string}

procedure IUTimeString
            (seconds    : LONGINT;       {Date and time in "raw" seconds}
             withSeconds : BOOLEAN;      {Include seconds in string?}
         var theString  : Str255);       {Returns equivalent character string}
```

Notes

1. These routines convert a date and time in "raw" seconds, as reported by **ReadDateTime** [2.4.1], to a character string representing the corresponding calendar date or time of day.

2. These routines are not actually part of the Toolbox proper; they're contained in a package, the International Utilities Package, that resides in the system resource file and is automatically loaded into memory when needed. Package routines are defined in the interface file **PackIntf**. See Chapter 7 for further information on the package mechanism, and *Inside Macintosh* for more on the International Utilities Package.

3. The exact formats used for dates and times may vary from one country to another, under the control of the International Utilities Package. The formats shown below are the standard ones for American use.

4. The **format** parameter to **IUDateString** identifies the format desired for the date, as in the following examples:

   Short: **6/ 8/84**
                       10/15/84

   Long: **Friday, June 8, 1984**
                       Monday, October 15, 1984

   Abbreviated: **Fri, Jun 8, 1984**
                       Mon, Oct 15, 1984

5. Dates in the short format carry leading blanks or zeros if necessary, so that they're always the same length (8 characters in the standard American format).

6. The **withSeconds** parameter to **IUTimeString** specifies whether or not to include a seconds field in the time, as in the following examples:

   With seconds: **10:47:13 AM**
                       3:23:08 PM

   Without seconds: **10:47 AM**
                       3:23 PM

7. Times, whether with or without seconds, carry leading blanks or zeros if necessary, so that they're always the same length (8 or 11 characters in the standard American format).

8. The trap macros for these routines expand to call **_Pack6** [7.2.1] with the routine selectors given below.

Assembly Language Information

Trap macros and routine selectors:

(Pascal) Routine name	(Assembly) Trap macro	Trap word	Routine selector
IUDateString	**_IUDateString**	**$A9ED**	**0**
IUTimeString	**_IUTimeString**	**$A9ED**	**2**

C H A P T E R

3

Thanks for the Memory

This chapter is about memory, how it's organized and how to manage it. We'll learn what's where in the Macintosh's memory, how to allocate blocks of memory for a program's use, how to refer to those blocks from within the program, how to copy and combine them, and how to release them when they're no longer needed. These are basic techniques that you'll use in every program you write for the Macintosh.

Memory Organization

Every Macintosh has 64 kilobytes—that is, 64 times 1024, or 65,536 bytes—of *read only memory* (ROM). ROM occupies hexadecimal addresses **$400000–$40FFFF** and contains the built-in machine code of the Toolbox. Since its contents are permanent and unchangeable, this portion of memory is not available for general use by a running program.

When we talk about memory allocation, we're referring only to the remaining *read/write memory* (commonly known by the misleading term "random access memory," or RAM). The original version of the Macintosh has 128K of RAM, occupying addresses **$0–$1FFFF**. The more spacious "Fat Mac" has 512K, or four times as much, running from **$0–$7FFFF**. The Macintosh XL (formerly Lisa) comes in 512K and 1-megabyte models. The Toolbox is designed to adapt automatically to different memory configurations, so that programs written for one version of the machine will run without change on other versions and will automatically use the available RAM.

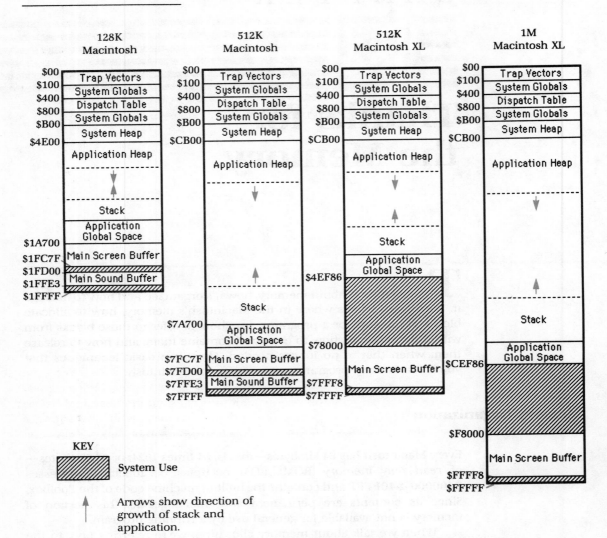

Figure 3-1 Memory organization

Figure 3-1 shows how RAM is laid out. On all models of Macintosh, the first $800 bytes are reserved for use by the system itself. Addresses **$0–$FF** hold the 68000 processor's trap vectors, which we discussed in the last chapter; the dispatch table, containing the ROM addresses of the various Toolbox routines, is at addresses **$400–$7FF**. The Toolbox keeps its *system globals* (memory locations reserved for its own private use) at addresses **$100–$3FF** and **$800–$AFF**.

Table 3-1 Buffer addresses

Model	Memory size	Main screen buffer	Main sound buffer	Alternate screen buffer	Alternate sound buffer
Macintosh	128K	$1A700–$1FC7F	$1FD00–$FFE3	$12700–$17C7F	$1A100–$1A3E3
Fat Mac	512K	$7A700–$7FC7F	$7FD00–$7FFE3	$72700–$77C7F	$7A100–$7A3E3
Macintosh XL (Lisa)	512K	$78000–$7FFF7	. . .	. . .	. . .
Macintosh XL (Lisa)	1M	$F8000–$FFFF7	. . .	. . .	. . .

All of the addresses given in this chapter may differ in future models of the Macintosh.

At the end of memory are the *screen buffer*, which contains the bits that define the image to be displayed on the Macintosh screen, and the *sound buffer*, which controls the sounds emitted by the built-in speaker. Table 3-1 shows the addresses of the screen and sound buffers in the various models. (Notice that the Macintosh XL has no sound buffer, since it lacks the built-in speaker of the 128K and Fat Mac models.) Just before these buffers in memory is the *application global space*, which contains the application program's global variables and other information about the program as a whole. The space between the end of the system globals and the beginning of the application globals is available for dynamic memory allocation.

Although most programs will use the main screen and sound buffers at the addresses just given, there are also alternate buffers available for unusual needs, at the locations shown in Table 3-1. (Again, notice that there are no alternate buffers in a Macintosh XL.) Since the application global space is always located right before the lowest-addressed screen or sound buffer in use, using either or both of the alternate buffers lowers the position of the global space in memory and reduces the space available for dynamic allocation accordingly. For the alternate sound buffer, the reduction is $600 bytes, or 1.5K; for the alternate screen buffer, it's a whopping $8000 bytes, or 32K.

The Application Global Space

The application global space holds three kinds of information pertaining to a program. They are *global variables, application parameters*, and the *jump table* (see Figure 3-2). The space needed for these varies among programs and is allocated when the particular program is started. (We'll discuss how this is done and describe the contents and purpose of the jump table in Chapter 7.)

At the machine-language level, the processor's address register **A5** always holds a pointer to the beginning of the application parameters. If you're programming in a higher-level language such as Pascal, of course, you never have to think about processor registers; your language software will see to it that **A5** is properly maintained. Even so, you should understand how this register is used at the machine level. The Toolbox initializes **A5** when a program is started, and uses it as a base address from which to locate everything in the application global space: global variables at negative offsets from **A5**, application parameters and the jump table at positive offsets. (The global variables are allocated in the reverse of the order they're declared. That is, the first variable declared is last in memory, at the smallest negative offset from the base address in **A5**.)

If you're using assembly language, you must remember that register **A5** is special and be careful not to disturb its contents. If you absolutely must "borrow" this register temporarily, be sure to restore it from the system global **CurrentA5** before calling any Toolbox routine.

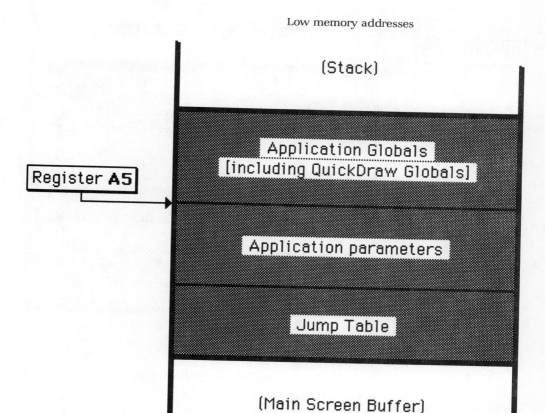

Figure 3-2 Application global space

This "**A5** world" is a vestige of the Lisa Pascal environment from which much of the Macintosh software grew. On the Lisa, the application parameters hold important descriptive information about the program that's used by various parts of the system. Most of these parameters are unused on the Macintosh, but a few still are needed by parts of the Toolbox that preserve traces of their Lisa origins. To keep these archaic parts of the Toolbox happy, space (normally 32 bytes) still is reserved for the application parameters when a program is started, and a pointer to them is placed in **A5.**

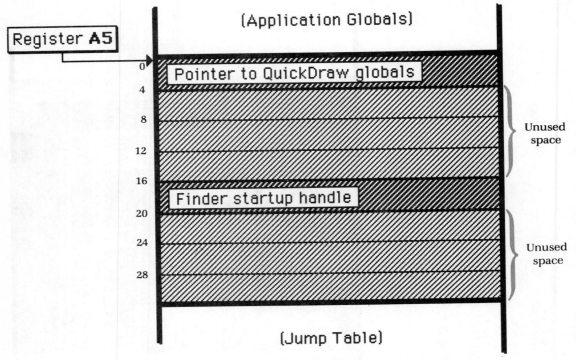

Figure 3-3 Application parameters

Only two of the application parameters are used on the Macintosh (Figure 3-3). At address **0(A5)** (that is, at an offset of **0** bytes from the base address in register **A5**) is a pointer that the QuickDraw graphics routines use to find global variables; we'll return to this subject in Chapter 4. At **16(A5)** is the *startup handle*, used by the Finder to tell the program what files to open on starting up. (We'll be learning what a handle is later in this chapter; the Finder startup handle is discussed in Chapter 7.) The rest of the 32-byte application parameter area is reserved for possible future use.

The Stack and the Heap

As noted earlier, the space available for dynamic memory allocation runs from the end of the system globals to the beginning of the application globals. This area is shared between two different forms of allocation, the *stack* and the *heap*, which grow toward each other from opposite ends of the space (see Figure 3-4). The stack is used mainly for holding parameters,

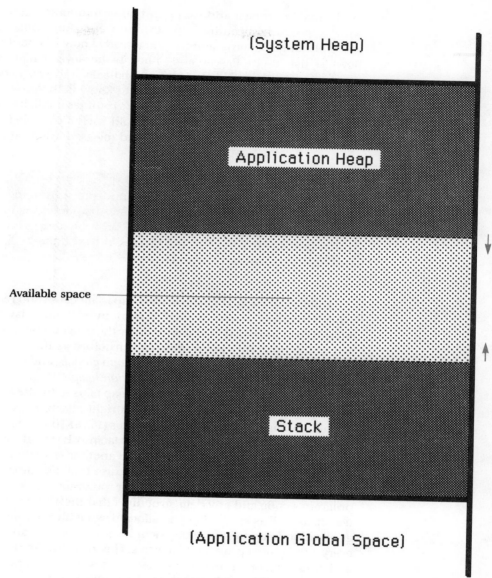

Figure 3-4 Stack and heap

local variables, return addresses, and other temporary storage associated with a program's routines (procedures and functions). If you're an assembly-language programmer, you already know all about the stack and how to use it. In Pascal and other higher-level languages, all stack management is handled for you automatically and you needn't concern yourself with it; what you really need to know is that every variable you declare by name in one of your program's routines implicitly resides on the stack. The memory space needed to hold such a variable is allocated on entry to the routine that declares it, and released again on exit.

> The stack actually grows backward in memory, from higher- toward lower-numbered addresses. If you're an experienced programmer, you should be used to this (you also probably draw your trees with their roots at the top and their leaves at the bottom!)

Unlike stack space, space in the heap is allocated and released only by explicit request, never implicitly, even in high-level languages. These requests can be issued in whatever order the program requires, and are not tied to the program's subroutine call structure as the stack is. The heap extends forward from the end of the system globals, and is divided into two parts, the *system heap* and the *application heap*.

As you might expect, the system heap is used by the system software for its private memory needs. It begins right after the end of the system globals, and has a fixed size of $4300 bytes (16.75K) on a 128K Macintosh, or $C000 bytes (48K) on a Fat Mac or Macintosh XL. Its contents aren't destroyed when one program ends and another is started; this allows the system to maintain its private data structures from one program to the next.

The application heap is for your program's use; it contains the program's code and any data structures that the Toolbox creates on your behalf, as well as space that you allocate explicitly for your own data. The application heap follows the system heap in memory, and is reinitialized every time a new program is started. This destroys its previous contents and gives each program a brand-new, empty heap to work with. The initial size of the application heap is $1800 bytes (6K), but, if more space is needed, it can grow bigger as the program runs.

Technically, what we're calling the system heap and application heap are actually *heap zones*. The Toolbox can maintain any number of heap zones: if you want, you can subdivide your original application heap into two or more separate zones and allocate space from each of them independently. This is an unusual thing to do, though, and we won't go into it any further here; see Apple's *Inside Macintosh* manual if you want the details. Unless you explicitly specify otherwise, all the memory allocation operations described in this chapter will automatically apply to the single application heap zone.

Handles and Master Pointers

You can allocate space from the heap in *blocks* of any size; when you no longer need a block, you should release it so that the space can be reused for another purpose. As blocks are allocated and released, the available free space tends to become fragmented into lots of little blocks scattered randomly throughout the heap. Such fragmentation can sometimes make it impossible to allocate a block of a given size even though the needed amount of free space is available, because no single free block is big enough. When this happens, the Toolbox tries to create a block of the needed size by moving all the allocated blocks together and coalescing the free space into one big block. This is known as *compacting* the heap (see Figure 3-5).

For heap compaction to work, there must be a way to keep track of the allocated blocks as they're moved from one location to another. Suppose you ask the Toolbox to allocate a block; it gives you back a pointer to the new block, which you save in a variable or embed in a data structure. Later, the heap is compacted and the block is moved to a different location (see Figure 3-6). This leaves your pointer indicating where the block used to be instead of where it is; what's actually there now is anybody's guess.

Before

After

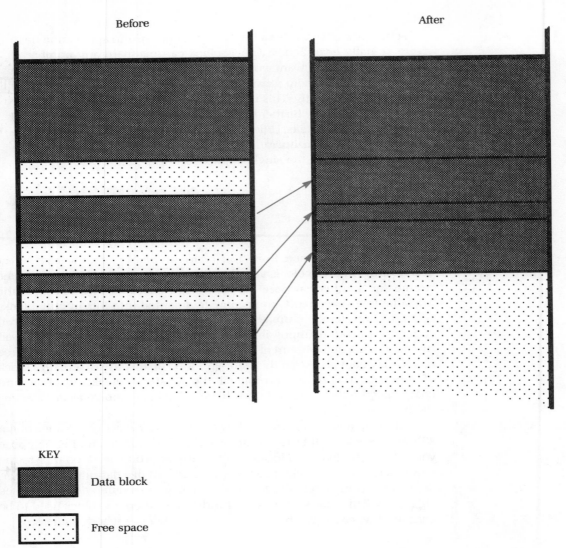

KEY

Data block

Free space

Figure 3-5 Heap compaction

The solution is simple and elegant. Instead of giving you a pointer when it allocates a block, the Toolbox keeps its own *master pointer* to the block and gives you a pointer to the master pointer, known as a *handle* to the block (Figure 3-7). Like the block itself, the master pointer resides in the heap; but unlike the block, the master pointer is never moved, even when the heap is compacted. Since it remains at a known, fixed location, the Toolbox can easily update it whenever the block is moved, so that it always

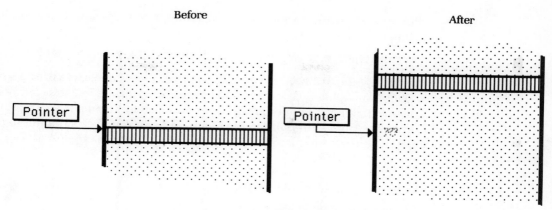

Figure 3-6 Dangling pointer

points correctly to the block's current location. When you refer to the block, you do it by double indirection: the handle leads you to the master pointer, which in turn leads you to the block. Since the master pointer never moves, you'll never lose track of the block, no matter where or how often it's moved within the heap.

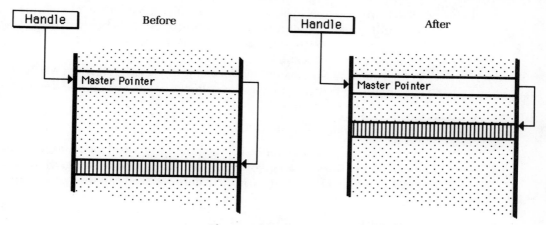

Figure 3-7 Handle and master pointer

Relocatable and Nonrelocatable Blocks

Blocks that are referred to by handles are called *relocatable* blocks, since they can safely be moved around within the heap. You create a relocatable block by calling the Toolbox routine **NewHandle** [3.2.1], specifying the size of the block in bytes. For instance, suppose your program defines a data type named **Thing**. To allocate a new **Thing** from the heap, you would use a statement like

```
thatThing := NewHandle(SIZEOF(Thing))
```

(Recall that the **SIZEOF** function, applied to a type name, gives the number of bytes occupied by a value of that type.) **NewHandle** will allocate heap space for a block of the requested size and also for its master pointer, set the master pointer to point to the block, and give you back a pointer to the master pointer—that is, a handle to the block. Thus the expression

```
thatThing^
```

denotes the master pointer, and

```
thatThing^^
```

refers to the underlying **Thing** itself. If a **Thing** is a record with a field named **widget**, you can access the field with the expression

```
thatThing^^.widget
```

Once you allocate a block, its size isn't frozen forever. You can make it bigger or smaller at any time with the Toolbox routine **SetHandleSize** [3.2.3]. (When you make a block bigger, things may have to be moved around in the heap to make room; but of course the master pointers will be fixed up properly, so all your handles will remain correct.) To find out the current size of a block, use **GetHandleSize** [3.2.3]. When you're all through with a block, release it by calling **DisposHandle** [3.2.2] to make its space available for reallocation.

You can also create *nonrelocatable* blocks, which will never be moved even during heap compaction. To allocate such a block, use **NewPtr** [3.2.1] instead of **NewHandle:**

```
otherThing := NewPtr(SIZEOF(Thing))
```

Since the block will never be moved, there's no need for a master pointer—so **NewPtr** doesn't create one. Instead of a handle, it just gives you back a pointer directly to the block itself (Figure 3-8). You can then use this pointer to refer to your **Thing** by single rather than double indirection

```
otherThing^
```

and access its fields with expressions like

```
otherThing^.widget
```

Like a relocatable block, a nonrelocatable one can be lengthened or shortened at any time. You can change its size with **SetPtrSize** [3.2.3], find out its current size with **GetPtrSize** [3.2.3], and release it when the time comes with **DisposPtr** [3.2.2].

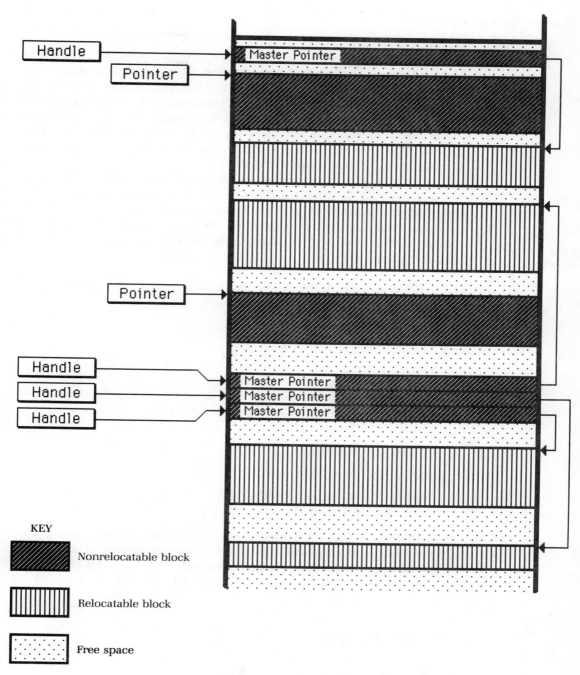

Figure 3-8 Relocatable and nonrelocatable blocks

Elementary Data Types

The Toolbox interface defines general-purpose data types [3.1.1] for talking about pointers and handles. Type **Ptr** stands for a pointer to an arbitrary byte in memory, and **Handle** for a pointer to a **Ptr**. Both are based on the underlying type **SignedByte**, which represents a single-memory byte as an integer between -128 and $+127$. (There's also an alternate type named **Byte**, which represents a byte as an unsigned integer between **0** and **255**.) For specifying the size of a block on the heap, there's the type **Size**, equivalent to a long integer (**LONGINT**).

The heap allocation routines **NewPtr** and **NewHandle** return results of type **Ptr** and **Handle**, respectively—that is, a pointer or a handle to a **SignedByte**. In order to access a block's contents, you have to convert these to some other type that more specifically describes the block's internal structure. For instance, suppose your program defines the following types:

```
type
   LinkHandle = ^LinkPtr;
   LinkPtr    = ^Link;
   Link       = record
                   data : INTEGER;
                   next : LinkHandle
                end;
```

To allocate a new **Link** record from the heap and store into its data field, you can't simply declare a variable

```
var
   theLink : LinkHandle;
```

and write something like

```
theLink := NewHandle(SIZEOF(Link));
theLink^ .data := 0
```

The first of these statements is not a valid assignment, because the types don't match: **NewHandle** returns a general **Handle** (a handle to a **SignedByte**), whereas the variable **theLink** expects a **LinkHandle** (a handle to a **Link** record). Nor can you correct the problem by changing the declared type of **theLink**:

```
var
   theLink : Handle;
```

Now the second statement

```
theLink^^.data := 0
```

is invalid, because **theLink^^** is now a **SignedByte** instead of a **Link**, and so it doesn't have a field named **data**.

The solution is to use the "typecasting" technique described in Chapter 2 to convert the general **Handle** you get from the Toolbox into a **LinkHandle** that you can work with:

```
var
   theHandle : Handle;
   theLink   : LinkHandle;

. . . ;

   theHandle := NewHandle(SIZEOF(Link));
   theLink   := LinkHandle(theHandle);

   theLink^^.data := 0
```

Of course, you could do it in one step by dispensing with the intermediate variable **theHandle** and writing

```
theLink := LinkHandle(NewHandle(SIZEOF(Link)))
```

We did it in two steps in the example to make sure it's clear exactly what's going on.

Error Reporting

Strictly speaking, the memory management routines are part of the Macintosh Operating System, rather than the Toolbox proper. Along with other Operating System routines, most of them post a *result code* of type **OSErr** [3.1.2] to report errors or signal successful completion. At the machine level, the result code is returned in a register—the lower half of **D0**, to be precise. To allow you to access it from Pascal, the interface unit **OSIntf** includes a special function named **MemError** [3.1.2] that returns the result code posted by the last memory management operation.

Notice, however, that **MemError** is part of the *interface* to the memory management routines, not one of the routines actually built into ROM. Other languages may have different mechanisms for accessing Operating System result codes, or none at all. You'll have to consult your own language documentation for details.

Result codes are always less than or equal to **0**. A value of **0** (**NoErr**) means the routine was able to complete its job successfully; a negative result code means that it was prevented from doing so because of an error. The most important error reported by the memory management routines is **MemFullErr**, which means that an allocation operation failed for lack of heap space.

If you're programming in assembly language, you can just look in register **D0** for the result code returned by a memory management (or other Operating System) routine. However, not all such routines do in fact post a result code in this register; the register usage information in the Reference Handbook will tell you which ones do and which don't.

Before returning from any Operating System trap, the Trap Dispatcher sets the processor's condition codes to reflect the result code (if there is one) by executing the instruction

```
TST.W D0
```

You can then just branch on the condition codes without performing a test of your own: for example,

```
MOVEQ D0,#blockSize      ; Indicate size of block
_NewHandle               ; Allocate block
BMI    Error             ; Branch on error
```

Locking Blocks

Whenever you allocate a block from the heap, you can choose whether to make it relocatable (with **NewHandle**) or nonrelocatable (with **NewPtr**). In general you should use relocatable blocks whenever possible, since this allows the Toolbox to make the most efficient use of the available heap space. However, relocatable blocks also have their costs, in both space and time: they take up an extra 4 bytes for the master pointer and require an extra memory fetch to access, because of the second level of indirection. Usually this is a negligible price to pay, but sometimes that extra memory reference can be costly, if it occurs inside a tight inner loop or some other part of your program where speed is critical.

In such cases, you can save time by converting the block's handle to a copy of the master pointer

```
masterPtr := theHandle^
```

and then referring to the block by single indirection

```
masterPtr^
```

within the loop. This is known as *dereferencing* the handle (a general term meaning to convert any pointer into the thing it points to). However, keep in mind that all you have is a *copy* of the master pointer, not the master pointer itself. If the heap is compacted and the block is moved, the Toolbox will only update the actual master pointer; the copy will be left pointing, indiscriminately.

To keep your pointers from dangling, you can "lock" the block before dereferencing its handle. This temporarily prevents the block from being moved, even if the heap is compacted. You can then safely dereference the handle and refer to the block by single indirection. When you're finished with your critical program section, you can discard your copy of the master pointer and "unlock" the block, so that it can again be moved around to make room in the heap for other blocks. The Toolbox routines for locking and unlocking a block are **HLock** and **HUnlock** [3.2.4]; Program 3-1 shows how to use them in dereferencing a handle. (Notice that only a relocatable block can be locked; this makes it "temporarily" unmovable, while a nonrelocatable block is "permanently" unmovable.)

```
{ Skeleton code to illustrate use of a dereferenced handle.  }

type
   LinkHandle = ^LinkPtr;
   LinkPtr    = ^Link;

   Link       = record
                   data : INTEGER;
                   next : LinkHandle
                end;

var
   theHandle : Handle;                              {Untyped handle for creating the block}
   theLink   : LinkHandle;                          {Typed handle for referring to the block}
   masterPtr : LinkPtr;                             {Typed pointer for dereferencing the handle}

begin

   theHandle := NewHandle(SIZEOF(Link));            {Allocate a relocatable block [3.2.1]}
   theLink   := POINTER(ORD(theHandle));            {Convert to typed handle}

   . . . ;

   HLock (theLink);                                 {Lock the block [3.2.4]}

      masterPtr := theLink^;                        {Dereference the handle}

      while . . . do
         begin
            . . . ;
            ...masterPtr^...;                        {Use single indirection inside loop}
            . . .
         end;

   HUnlock (theLink);                               {Unlock the block [3.2.4]}

   . . .

end
```

Program 3-1 Dereferencing a handle

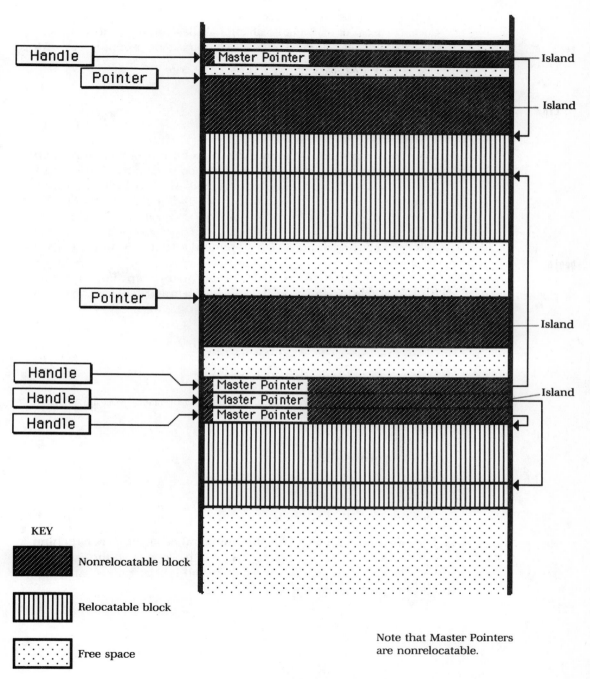

Figure 3-9 Islands in the heap

Certain Pascal constructs involving handles can also cause Apple's compiler to generate dangling pointers. For example, a *with* statement based on a relocatable record

```
with aHandle^^ do
   begin
      . . .
   end
```

will cause problems if the underlying record is moved or purged because of memory allocation performed within the statement's body. To avoid problems, you always should lock the block with

```
HLock (aHandle)
```

before executing such a *with* statement and then unlock it again afterward.

Similarly, any call to a routine that can do heap allocation may cause trouble if you pass it a field of a relocatable record as a variable

```
ARoutine (aHandle^ .field)
```

or assign its result to such a field

```
aHandle^^.field := ARoutine ( . . . )
```

Instead of locking the block in these cases, you can use a temporary variable:

```
temp := aHandle^^ .field;
ARoutine (temp)
```

or

```
temp := ARoutine ( . . . );
aHandle^^ .field := temp
```

Keep in mind that many Toolbox routines allocate heap space behind the scenes, without your being aware of it. To stay on the safe side, you should assume that any Toolbox call is "dangerous" and take suitable precautions.

In general, try not to keep a block locked any longer than needed, and remember to unlock it again as soon as it's safe to do so. An unmovable block, whether it's temporarily locked or permanently nonrelocatable, forms an "island" in the heap that can interfere with compaction and prevent the available free space from being gathered (Figure 3-9). You can avoid this problem, however, by arranging to keep all the unmovable blocks together at the beginning of the heap, away from the movable ones. For nonrelocatable blocks, the Toolbox does this automatically: it allocates them as near as possible to the start of the heap, moving other blocks out of the way if necessary to make room. To do the same for a relocatable block (if you know it will be locked for long periods of time), you can use the Toolbox routine **ResrvMem** [3.2.1]. This routine creates space near the beginning of the heap for a block of a specified size, but doesn't actually allocate the block. You have to follow it with a call to **NewHandle** to do the actual allocation:

```
ResrvMem (blockSize);
theHandle := NewHandle (blockSize)
```

Copying and Combining Blocks

The Toolbox includes a number of utility routines for copying and combining blocks in the heap. **HandToHand** [3.2.5] creates a new relocatable block that's a copy of another. You give it a variable containing a handle to the block you want to copy; it returns a handle to the copy in this same variable (see Figure 3-10). For example, if **thisHandle** is a handle to the block to be copied, the statements

```
thatHandle := thisHandle;
resultCode := HandToHand(thatHandle)
```

make **thatHandle** a handle to the fresh copy.

Notice that **HandToHand,** as well as the other routines discussed in
this section, returns its result code as a function result rather than
through the **MemError** function.

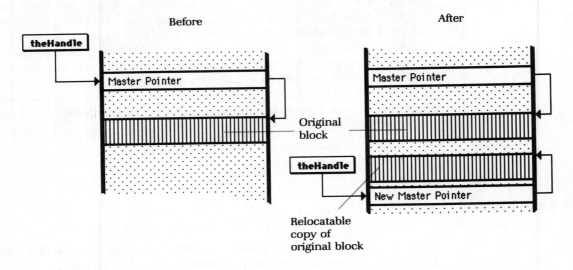

result := **HandToHand (theHandle)**

Figure 3-10 HandToHand

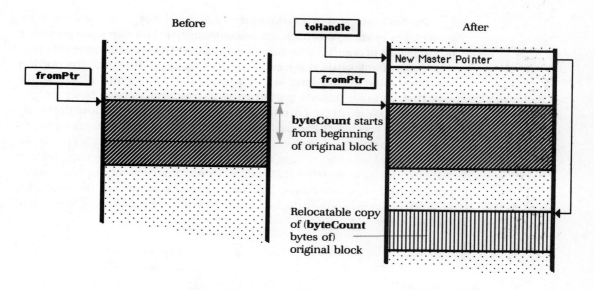

result := PtrToHand (from Ptr, toHandle, byteCount)

Figure 3-11 PtrToHand

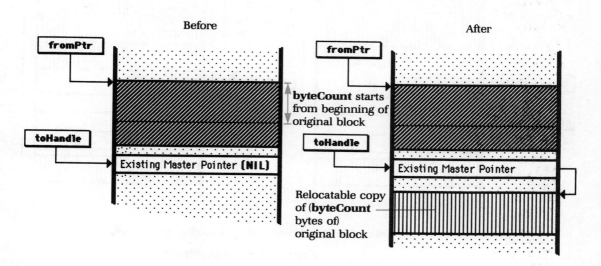

result := PtrToXHand (fromPtr, toHandle, byteCount)

Figure 3-12 PtrToXHand

PtrToHand and **PtrToXHand** [3.2.5] both copy an existing non-relocatable block to a brand-new relocatable one. You can copy an entire block or part of one; both routines accept a **byteCount** parameter that tells them how many bytes of the original block to copy. (However, the portion you copy must always start at the beginning of the original block. Notice also that you can make a partial copy of a nonrelocatable block only; a relocatable block must be copied in its entirety, using **HandToHand**.) **PtrToHand** creates a new master pointer to the copy and returns a pointer to it (a handle) through a variable parameter (Figure 3-11), while **PtrToXHand** sets an existing master pointer to point to the copy (Figure 3-12). In the case of **PtrToXHand,** the previous contents of the master pointer are lost; normally you'll want to give it an empty handle (a pointer to a **NIL** master pointer) to be "stuffed" with the address of the newly created copy.

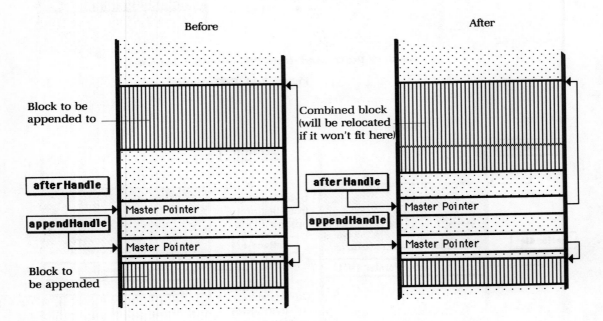

result := HandAndHand (appendHandle, afterHandle)

Figure 3-13 HandAndHand

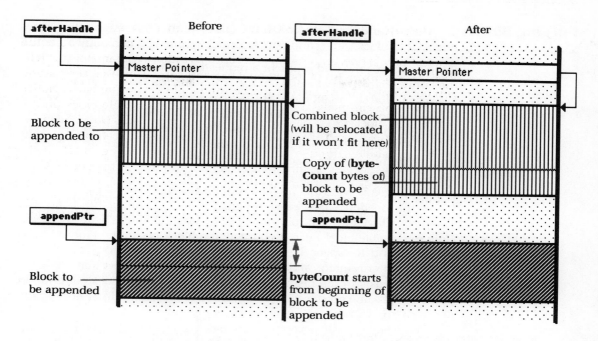

$$result := PtrAndHand\ (appendHandle,\ afterHandle,\ byteCount)$$

Figure 3-14 PtrAndHand

HandAndHand and **PtrAndHand** [3.2.6] are used to combine existing blocks by appending a copy of one block onto the end of another. The block you're appending to is always relocatable, and is lengthened to include the appended information. You can append a copy of either a relocatable block (**HandAndHand,** Figure 3-13) or all or part of a nonrelocatable block (**PtrAndHand,** Figure 3-14); in either case, the original block being copied remains intact.

The most general copying utility of all is **BlockMove** [3.2.5] which just copies "raw" bytes between memory locations. Watch your step because this is a dangerous operation! It doesn't check for errors, but simply copies the bytes. The source and destination pointers you give it aren't restricted to the heap, but can lie anywhere in memory. Give it the wrong parameters and it will cheerfully reduce your program to a pile of rubble.

Purging Blocks

If the Toolbox can't find room for a requested block even after compacting the entire heap, its next step is to try expanding the size of the heap itself. From its initial size of 6K bytes, the heap can grow in increments of 1K at a time, but only up to a certain limit. Recall that the heap and the stack grow toward each other from opposite ends of the same area in memory (Figure 3-4). The Toolbox imposes a limit on the heap's expansion to prevent it from colliding with the stack. This *application heap limit* is set at first to allow a maximum stack depth of 8K bytes, but you can adjust it to your program's needs with the Toolbox routine **SetApplLimit** [3.3.4].

If the needed space can't be created by expanding the heap, the Toolbox will try to make room by *purging* existing blocks from the heap. Only relocatable blocks can be purged; the block is simply removed from the heap and its space is made available for reallocation. The block's master pointer remains allocated, but is set to **NIL** to show that the block no longer exists in the heap. All former handles to the block continue to point to this same master pointer, but since the master pointer now points nowhere, the handles are considered *empty*.

The Toolbox will never purge a block from the heap without your permission. A block is always *unpurgeable* when it's first created; you can make it *purgeable* with the Toolbox routine **HPurge,** and unpurgeable again with **HNoPurge** [3.2.4]. Before attempting to access a purgeable block, you have to test its handle to check whether or not it's been purged. If the handle is empty (that is, if it points to a **NIL** master pointer), you have to *reallocate* the block with the Toolbox routine **ReallocHandle** [3.3.3] before you can access it. This allocates fresh space for the block and updates the master pointer to point to it (see Figure 3-15). However, it does nothing to restore the information the block contained before it was purged; you have to do that for yourself after reallocating the block.

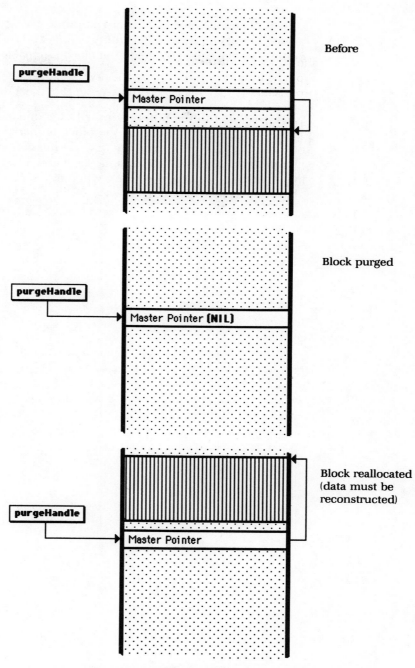

Figure 3-15 Purging and reallocating a block

Since all relocatable blocks are unpurgeable at first, you needn't worry about checking for an empty handle and reallocating the block unless you've explicitly made the block purgeable.

The Toolbox routine **EmptyHandle** [3.3.3] unconditionally purges a block from the heap, even if the block is marked unpurgeable. By calling this routine, you tacitly "give permission" for the block to be purged; the Toolbox will assume you know what you're doing and will obediently purge the block, whether it's purgeable or not. (The block must be "unlocked," however.)

REFERENCE

3.1 Elementary Data Types

3.1.1 Pointers and Handles

Definitions

```
type
    Byte       =     0..255;        {Any byte in memory}
    SignedByte = −128..127;         {Any byte in memory}

    Ptr        = ^SignedByte;       {General pointer}
    Handle     = ^Ptr;              {General handle}

    Size       = LONGINT;           {Size of a heap block in bytes}
```

Notes

1. Both **Byte** and **SignedByte** designate an arbitrary byte in memory, as either an unsigned or a signed 8-bit integer.

2. **Ptr** represents a general, untyped pointer to any byte in memory; **Handle** represents an untyped handle, a pointer to a master pointer.

3. **Size** is a long integer representing the size of a heap block in bytes.

3.1.2 Error Reporting

Definitions

```
type
  OSErr       = INTEGER;        {Operating System result (error) code}

const
  NoErr        =    0;          {No error; all is well}
  MemFullErr   = −108;          {No room; heap is full}
  NilHandleErr = −109;          {Illegal operation on empty handle}
  MemWZErr     = −111;          {Illegal operation on free block}
  MemPurErr    = −112;          {Illegal operation on locked block}

function MemError
              : OSErr;          {Result code of last memory operation}
```

Notes

1. **OSErr** represents an integer result code returned by an Operating System routine (such as those dealing with memory allocation).

2. The **MemError** function returns the result code posted by the last call to a memory allocation routine.

3. A result code of **NoErr** means that all is well; no error has occurred.

4. **MemFullErr** means that not enough heap space is available to satisfy an allocation request.

5. **NilHandleErr** means that a requested operation can't be performed because the specified handle is empty (points to a **NIL** master pointer).

6. **MemWZErr** means that a memory allocation routine that operates on already-allocated blocks was given a free block instead. (The **WZ** in **MemWZErr** stands for **WhichZone**, a low-level routine that tells which heap zone a given block is in. Although **WhichZone** itself is not covered in this book, it's called by many of the routines that are.)

7. **MemPurErr** means that an attempt was made to purge a locked block.

8. The **MemError** function isn't available in assembly language. On return from a memory allocation routine, the result code is in the lower 16 bits of register **D0** and the processor's condition codes are set accordingly.

Assembly Language Information

Assembly-language constants:

Name	Value	Meaning
NoErr	**0**	No error; all is well
MemFullErr	**−108**	No room; heap is full
NilHandleErr	**−109**	Illegal operation on empty handle
MemWZErr	**−111**	Illegal operation on free block
MemPurErr	**−112**	Illegal operation on locked block

3.2 Heap Allocation

3.2.1 Allocating Blocks

Definitions

```
function   NewHandle
              (blockSize : Size)    {Size of needed block in bytes}
                : Handle;           {Handle to new relocatable block}

function   NewPtr
              (blockSize : Size)    {Size of needed block in bytes}
                : Ptr;              {Pointer to new nonrelocatable block}

procedure  ResrvMem
              (blockSize : Size);   {Size of needed block in bytes}

function   RecoverHandle
              (masterPtr : Ptr)     {Master pointer to relocatable block}
                : Handle;           {Handle to block}
```

Notes

1. **NewHandle** allocates a new relocatable block and returns a handle to it; **NewPtr** allocates a new nonrelocatable block and returns a pointer to it.

2. **blockSize** gives the size of the needed block in bytes.

3. The block allocated by **NewHandle** is initially unlocked and unpurgeable.

4. If necessary, both **NewHandle** and **NewPtr** may compact the heap, expand it, or purge blocks from it.

5. **ResrvMem** reserves a requested number of bytes as near as possible to the beginning of the heap, by moving existing blocks upward, expanding the heap, or purging blocks if necessary.

6. **ResrvMem** doesn't actually allocate a block, just creates space for it near the beginning of the heap.

7. Call **ResrvMem** before allocating any relocatable block that will be locked for long periods of time, to minimize interference with heap compaction. This isn't necessary for nonrelocatable blocks, since they're automatically allocated near the beginning of the heap.

8. **NewHandle, NewPtr,** and **ResrvMem** will post the error code **MemFullErr** [3.1.2] if a block of the requested size can't be allocated or reserved.

9. In case of an error, **NewHandle** and **NewPtr** return a **NIL** handle or pointer.

10. **RecoverHandle** reconstructs a relocatable block's handle from a copy of its master pointer.

Assembly Language Information

Trap macros:

(Pascal) Routine name	(Assembly) Trap macro	Trap word
NewHandle	**_NewHandle**	**$A122**
NewPtr	**_NewPtr**	**$A11E**
ResrvMem	**_ResrvMem**	**$A040**
RecoverHandle	**_RecoverHandle**	**$A128**

Register usage:

Routine	Register	Contents
NewHandle	**D0.L** (in)	**blockSize**
	A0.L (out)	function result
	D0.W (out)	result code
NewPtr	**D0.L** (in)	**blockSize**
	A0.L (out)	function result
	D0.W (out)	result code
ResrvMem	**D0.L** (in)	**blockSize**
	D0.W (out)	result code
RecoverHandle	**A0.L** (in)	**masterPtr**
	A0.L (out)	function result
	D0 (out)	unchanged

3.2.2 Releasing Blocks

Definitions

```
procedure DisposHandle
        (theHandle : Handle);        {Handle to relocatable block to be deallocated}
procedure DisposPtr
        (thePtr : Ptr);              {Pointer to nonrelocatable block to be deallocated}
```

Notes

1. **DisposHandle** and **DisposPtr** deallocate a relocatable or non-relocatable block, respectively. The space occupied by the block becomes available for reuse.

2. All handles or pointers to the deallocated block become invalid. Don't use them after deallocating the block.

3. If the specified block is already free, both routines will post the error code **MemWZErr** [3.1.2].

Assembly Language Information

Trap macros:

(Pascal) Routine name	(Assembly) Trap macro	Trap word
DisposHandle	**_DisposHandle**	**$A023**
DisposPtr	**_DisposPtr**	**$A01F**

Register usage:

Routine	Register	Contents
DisposHandle	A0.L (in)	**theHandle**
	A0.L (out)	**0**
	D0.W (out)	result code
DisposPtr	A0.L (in)	**thePtr**
	A0.L (out)	**0**
	D0.W (out)	result code

3.2.3 Size of Blocks

Definitions

```
function    GetHandleSize
               (theHandle : Handle)      {Handle to a relocatable block}
               : Size;                   {Size of block in bytes}

function    GetPtrSize
               (thePtr : Ptr)            {Pointer to a nonrelocatable block}
               : Size;                   {Size of block in bytes}

procedure   SetHandleSize
               (theHandle : Handle;      {Handle to a relocatable block}
                newSize : Size);         {New size of block in bytes}

procedure   SetPtrSize
               (thePtr : Ptr;            {Pointer to a nonrelocatable block}
                newSize : Size);         {New size of block in bytes}
```

Notes

1. **GetHandleSize** and **GetPtrSize** return the size of a block in bytes.

2. **SetHandleSize** and **SetPtrSize** change the size of a block to **newSize** bytes. The block may be either lengthened or shortened.

3. If necessary to lengthen a block, **SetHandleSize** and **SetPtrSize** may compact the heap, expand it, or purge blocks from it.

4. If the room needed to lengthen a block can't be found, **SetHandleSize** and **SetPtrSize** post the error code **MemFullErr** [3.1.2].

5. **GetHandleSize** and **SetHandleSize** post the error code **NilHandleErr** [3.1.2] if the given handle is empty (points to a **NIL** master pointer).

6. All four routines post the error code **MemWZErr** [3.1.2] if the specified block is free (not allocated).

7. In case of an error, **GetHandleSize** and **GetPtrSize** return **0** as the block size.

8. In assembly language, the condition codes on return from the **_GetHandleSize** and **_GetPtrSize** traps are not valid, since they reflect only the lower 16 bits of register **D0** and these routines return a result in the full 32-bit register (see table below). To test the status of **D0** after the trap, use your own **TST.L** instruction.

Assembly Language Information

Trap macros:

(Pascal) Routine name	(Assembly) Trap macro	Trap word
GetHandleSize	**_GetHandleSize**	**$A025**
GetPtrSize	**_GetPtrSize**	**$A021**
SetHandleSize	**_SetHandleSize**	**$A024**
SetPtrSize	**_SetPtrSize**	**$A020**

Register usage:

Routine	Register	Contents
GetHandleSize	**A0.L** (in)	**theHandle**
	D0.L (out)	if $\geq$ **0**, function result if $<$ **0**, result code
GetPtrSize	**A0.L** (in)	**thePtr**
	D0.L (out)	if $\geq$ **0**, function result if $<$ **0**, result code
SetHandleSize	**A0.L** (in)	**theHandle**
	D0.L (in)	**newSize**
	D0.W (out)	result code
SetPtrSize	**A0.L** (in)	**thePtr**
	D0.L (in)	**newSize**
	D0.W (out)	result code

3.2.4 Properties of Blocks

Definitions

```
procedure HLock
        (theHandle : Handle);      {Handle to a relocatable block}
procedure HUnlock
        (theHandle : Handle);      {Handle to a relocatable block}
procedure HPurge
        (theHandle : Handle);      {Handle to a relocatable block}
procedure HNoPurge
        (theHandle : Handle);      {Handle to a relocatable block}
```

Notes

1. **HLock** locks a relocatable block; **HUnlock** unlocks it. A locked block can neither be moved nor purged from the heap.

2. **HPurge** makes a relocatable block purgeable; **HNoPurge** makes it unpurgeable. An unpurgeable block can't be purged, but can be moved within the heap.

3. On creation, a relocatable block is unlocked and unpurgeable.

4. All four routines will post the error code **NilHandleErr** [3.1.2] if the given handle is empty (points to a **NIL** master pointer), or **MemWZErr** if the specified block is free (not allocated).

Assembly Language Information

Trap macros:

(Pascal) Routine name	(Assembly) Trap macro	Trap word
HLock	**_HLock**	**$A029**
HUnlock	**_HUnlock**	**$A02A**
HPurge	**_HPurge**	**$A049**
HNoPurge	**_HNoPurge**	**$A04A**

Register usage:

Routine	Register	Contents
HLock	**A0.L** (in) **D0.W** (out)	**theHandle** result code
HUnlock	**A0.L** (in) **D0.W** (out)	**theHandle** result code
HPurge	**A0.L** (in) **D0.W** (out)	**theHandle** result code
HNoPurge	**A0.L** (in) **D0.W** (out)	**theHandle** result code

3.2.5 Copying Blocks

Definitions

function	HandToHand		
	(**var** theHandle : Handle)		{Handle to relocatable block to be copied}
	: OSErr;		{Result code}
function	PtrToHand		
	(fromPtr	: Ptr;	{Pointer to nonrelocatable block to be copied}
	var toHandle	: Handle;	{Returns handle to relocatable copy}
	byteCount	: LONGINT)	{Number of bytes to be copied}
	: OSErr;		{Result code}
function	PtrToXHand		
	(fromPtr	: Ptr;	{Pointer to nonrelocatable block to be copied}
	toHandle	: Handle;	{Handle to be set to relocatable copy}
	byteCount	: LONGINT)	{Number of bytes to be copied}
	: OSErr;		{Result code}
procedure	BlockMove		
	(fromPtr	: Ptr;	{Pointer to data to be copied}
	toPtr	: Ptr;	{Pointer to destination location}
	byteCount	: Size);	{Number of bytes to be copied}

Notes

1. **HandToHand**, **PtrToHand**, and **PtrToXHand** all copy an existing block. The result in each case is a relocatable block, newly allocated from the heap.

2. **HandToHand** copies a relocatable block. On entry, **theHandle** designates the block to be copied; on exit, it returns a handle to the copy.

3. **PtrToHand** and **PtrToXHand** both copy all or part of a nonrelocatable block, designated by the parameter **fromPtr**.

4. The **byteCount** parameter tells how many bytes of the block to copy, and must not exceed the overall size of the block. The portion to be copied always starts at the beginning of the block.

5. For **PtrToHand**, **toHandle** is a variable parameter that returns a handle to the copy. For **PtrToXHand**, it's an existing handle (a pointer to an existing master pointer), which will be set to point to the copy.

6. All three routines may compact the heap, expand it, or purge blocks from it in order to make room for the copy.

7. All three routines return the error code **MemFullErr** [3.1.2] if there isn't enough room in the heap for the copy.

8. The result code is returned as the function result; it is *not* posted in the usual way and is not available through **MemError** [3.1.2].

9. **BlockMove** copies **byteCount** bytes of "raw" data between two arbitrary locations in memory, designated by the pointers **fromPtr** and **toPtr**.

10. *BEWARE:* **BlockMove** does no error checking of any kind.

Assembly Language Information

Trap macros:

(Pascal) Routine name	(Assembly) Trap macro	Trap word
HandToHand	**_HandToHand**	**$A9E1**
PtrToHand	**_PtrToHand**	**$A9E3**
PtrToXHand	**_PtrToXHand**	**$A9E2**
BlockMove	**_BlockMove**	**$A02E**

Register usage:

Routine	Register	Contents
HandToHand	**A0.L** (in) **A0.L** (out) **D0.W** (out)	**theHandle** **theHandle** result code
PtrToHand	**A0.L** (in) **D0.L** (in) **A0.L** (out) **D0.W** (out)	**fromPtr** **byteCount** **toHandle** result code
PtrToXHand	**A0.L** (in) **A1.L** (in) **D0.L** (in) **A1.L** (out) **D0.W** (out)	**fromPtr** **toHandle** **byteCount** **toHandle** result code
BlockMove	**A0.L** (in) **A1.L** (in) **D0.L** (in) **D0.W** (out)	**fromPtr** **toPtr** **byteCount** result code

3.2.6 Combining Blocks

Definitions

```
function HandAndHand
      (appendHandle : Handle;      {Handle to relocatable block to be appended}
       afterHandle   : Handle)     {Handle to relocatable block to append to}
       : OSErr;                    {Result code}

function PtrAndHand
      (appendPtr   : Ptr;          {Pointer to nonrelocatable block to be appended}
       afterHandle : Handle;       {Handle to relocatable block to append to}
       byteCount   : LONGINT)      {Number of bytes to append}
       : OSErr;                    {Result code}
```

Notes

1. Both of these routines append a copy of one block to the end of another.

2. The block appended to is always an existing relocatable block.

3. For **HandAndHand**, the block to be appended is an existing relocatable block. For **PtrAndHand**, it's all or part of an existing nonrelocatable block; the **byteCount** parameter tells how many bytes to append, and must not exceed the overall size of the block. The portion to be copied always starts at the beginning of the block.

4. Both routines may compact the heap, expand it, or purge blocks from it in order to allocate more space for the destination block.

5. Both routines return the error code **MemFullErr** [3.1.2] if there isn't enough room in the heap to lengthen the destination block.

6. The result code is returned as the function result; it is *not* posted in the usual way and is not available through **MemError** [3.1.2].

Assembly Language Information

Trap macros:

(Pascal) Routine name	(Assembly) Trap macro	Trap word
HandAndHand	**_HandAndHand**	**$A9E4**
PtrAndHand	**_PtrAndHand**	**$A9EF**

Register usage:

Routine	Register	Contents
HandAndHand	**A0.L** (in)	**appendHandle**
	A1.L (in)	**afterHandle**
	A1.L (out)	**afterHandle**
	D0.W (out)	result code
PtrAndHand	**A0.L** (in)	**appendPtr**
	A1.L (in)	**afterHandle**
	D0.L (in)	**byteCount**
	A1.L (out)	**afterHandle**
	D0.W (out)	result code

3.3 Reclaiming Heap Space

3.3.1 Free Space

Definitions

```
function FreeMem
              : LONGINT;              {Total free bytes in the heap}

function MaxMem
         (var growBytes : Size)       {Returns maximum bytes by which heap can grow}
              : Size;                 {Size of largest free block in heap}

function TopMem
              : Ptr;                  {Pointer to end of memory}
```

Notes

1. **FreeMem** returns the total number of free bytes in the heap.

2. Because of heap fragmentation, it may not actually be possible to allocate a block this big.

3. **MaxMem** reclaims all available heap space by purging all purgeable blocks and compacting the heap.

4. The function result is the size in bytes of the largest available free block after purging and compaction.

5. The **growBytes** parameter returns the number of bytes by which the heap can grow. The heap is not actually expanded.

6. **TopMem** returns a pointer to the first address beyond the end of physical memory (*not* the last address actually existing in memory). For example, in a 512K Fat Mac, whose last byte of physical memory is at address **$7FFFF**, **TopMem** returns a pointer to address **$80000**.

7. **TopMem** can be called only through the Pascal interface units, not through the assembly-language trap interface. In assembly language, the global variable **MemTop** holds a pointer to the end of physical memory.

Assembly Language Information

Trap macros:

(Pascal) Routine name	(Assembly) Trap macro	Trap word
FreeMem	**_FreeMem**	**$A01C**
MaxMem	**_MaxMem**	**$A11D**

Register usage:

Routine	Register	Contents
FreeMem	**D0.L** (out)	function result
MaxMem	**A0.L** (out)	**growBytes**
	D0.L (out)	function result

Assembly-language global variable:

Name	Address	Meaning
MemTop	**$108**	Pointer to end of physical memory

3.3.2 Heap Compaction

Definitions

function CompactMem
        (sizeNeeded : Size)   {Size of needed block in bytes}
        : Size;   {Size of largest free block after compaction}

Notes

1. **CompactMem** does a complete or partial compaction of the heap.
2. Compaction ends when a free block of at least **sizeNeeded** bytes is found or created or when the entire heap has been compacted.
3. The function result is the size of the largest free block found or created during compaction. The block is not actually allocated.

Assembly Language Information

Trap macro:

(Pascal) Routine name	(Assembly) Trap macro	Trap word
CompactMem	**_CompactMem**	**$A04C**

Register usage:

Routine	Register	Contents
CompactMem	**D0.L** (in) **D0.L** (out)	**sizeNeeded** function result

3.3.3 Purging Blocks

Definitions

procedure EmptyHandle
      (theHandle : Handle);   {Handle to relocatable block to be purged}
procedure ReallocHandle
      (theHandle : Handle;   {Empty handle to be reallocated}
      sizeNeeded : Size);   {Size of block to be allocated in bytes}
procedure PurgeMem
      (sizeNeeded : Size);   {Size of needed block in bytes}

Notes

1. **EmptyHandle** purges a relocatable block from the heap.

2. The purged block's master pointer remains allocated, but is set to **NIL**. All existing handles to the block become empty.

3. The designated block is purged even if it's marked as unpurgeable; however, a locked block will not be purged.

4. **ReallocHandle** reallocates space for a purged block; the **sizeNeeded** parameter tells how many bytes to allocate.

5. The master pointer pointed to by **theHandle** is updated to point to the reallocated block. All existing handles to the block become valid again.

6. If **theHandle** already points to an existing block, that block is de-allocated before updating the handle.

7. **ReallocHandle** may compact the heap, expand it, or purge blocks from it in order to make room for the reallocated block. If the needed space can't be found, it will post the error code **MemFullErr** [3.1.2].

8. Both **EmptyHandle** and **ReallocHandle** will post the error code **MemPurErr** or **MemWZErr** [3.1.2] if they're given the handle of a locked block or one that's free (unallocated).

9. **PurgeMem** purges all blocks from the heap that are relocatable, unlocked, and purgeable.

10. Purging ends when a free block of at least **sizeNeeded** bytes is found or created or when the entire heap has been purged. The block is not actually allocated.

11. If a free block of the specified size can't be found, **PurgeMem** will post the error code **MemFullErr** [3.1.2].

Assembly Language Information

Trap macros:

(Pascal) Routine name	(Assembly) Trap macro	Trap word
EmptyHandle	**_EmptyHandle**	**$A02B**
ReallocHandle	**_ReallocHandle**	**$A027**
PurgeMem	**_PurgeMem**	**$A04D**

Register usage:

Routine	Register	Contents
EmptyHandle	**A0.L** (in)	**theHandle**
	D0.W (out)	result code
ReallocHandle	**A0.L** (in)	**theHandle**
	D0.L (in)	**sizeNeeded**
	A0.L (out)	**theHandle,** or **0** if block not reallocated
	D0.W (out)	result code
PurgeMem	**D0.L** (in)	**sizeNeeded**
	D0.W (out)	result code

3.3.4 Heap Expansion

Definitions

procedure SetApplLimit
        (newLimit : Ptr);   {Pointer to new application heap limit}

procedure MaxApplZone;

Notes

1. **SetApplLimit** sets the *application heap limit,* which controls how far the application heap can be expanded.

2. **newLimit** is a *limit pointer* to an address one byte beyond the maximum to which the heap can be expanded. All allocatable space beyond this address is reserved for the stack.

3. Notice that **newLimit** is a pointer to an address in memory; it is *not* a number of bytes representing the maximum size of the heap.

4. The application heap limit is initially set to allow 8K bytes for the stack.

5. **MaxApplZone** expands the application heap to its maximum permissible size, as defined by the current application heap limit.

6. **MaxApplZone** is part of the Pascal Toolbox interface, not part of the Toolbox itself. It doesn't reside in ROM and can't be called from assembly language via the trap mechanism.

Assembly Language Information

Trap macro:

(Pascal) Routine name	(Assembly) Trap macro	Trap word
SetApplLimit	**_SetApplLimit**	**$A02D**

Register usage:

Routine	Register	Contents
SetApplLimit	**A0.L** (in)	**newLimit**
	D0.W (out)	result code

C H A P T E R

4

Any Port in a Storm

At the heart of the Macintosh user interface lies a remarkably fast and versatile set of graphics routines called QuickDraw. Everything you see on the Macintosh screen—text, pictures, windows, menus—is put there by QuickDraw. When you call a Toolbox routine to, say, draw a window at a certain location on the screen, the Toolbox in turn calls QuickDraw to do the actual drawing. When the Toolbox text-handling routines need to display text in a window, QuickDraw is used to draw the characters. The basic principles of QuickDraw are fundamental to the way the rest of the Toolbox works.

Your program can also call QuickDraw directly. For instance, after the Toolbox has drawn a window's frame for you, you use QuickDraw to fill in the window. Although QuickDraw is mainly for drawing on the screen, you also can use it for printing on a dot-matrix printer or preparing animation frames off-screen and then transferring them to the screen all at once. In this chapter we'll discuss the underlying principles and concepts behind QuickDraw. In Chapter 5 we'll learn how to actually draw with QuickDraw.

Initializing QuickDraw

Before attempting any QuickDraw operation, you first have to call **InitGraf** [4.3.1] to initialize QuickDraw's global variables and internal data structures. As we mentioned in the last chapter, QuickDraw locates its globals by means of a pointer at address **0(A5)** in the application parameters area of the program's "**A5** world." When you initialize QuickDraw you supply this pointer as a parameter; **InitGraf** stores it at address **0(A5)**, where the rest of the QuickDraw routines expect to find it.

97

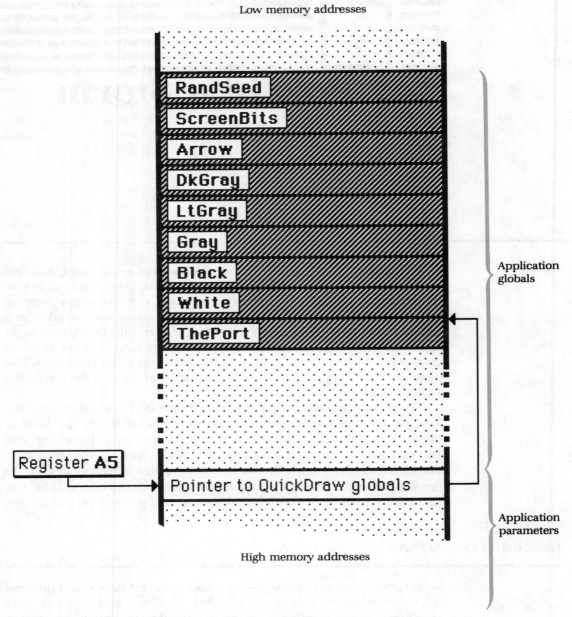

Figure 4-1 QuickDraw globals

Figure 4-1 shows how QuickDraw's global variables are arranged in memory. The pointer at **0(A5)** points to the first of the QuickDraw globals, **ThePort** [4.3.1]. Recall, though, that global variables are always allocated in the reverse of the order they're declared. So this "first" global is physically positioned *last* in memory, with all the other globals located at *negative* offsets from the pointer. In Pascal, the space for the QuickDraw globals is automatically reserved in your program's own application globals area, and all your own references to the variables are directed to the corresponding addresses in this area. To make sure everything works right, you should always pass a pointer to **ThePort** as the parameter to **InitGraf:**

```
InitGraf (@ThePort)
```

In assembly language you can technically place the QuickDraw globals anywhere in memory, provided that you reserve enough space for them. (The number of bytes you need is defined in the assembly-language interface as a constant named **GrafSize** [4.3.1].) The normal practice is to handle the QuickDraw globals the same way they're treated in Pascal: that is, to include them as part of the program's own global variables and place them in the application global space, as in Figure 4-1.

In any case, since the globals are referenced with a simple pointer instead of a handle, you had better make sure they're nonrelocatable. The pointer you pass to **InitGraf** must be the address of the *last* 4 bytes in this space, which will hold the variable **ThePort**. Then make sure you direct your own references to the QuickDraw globals to the proper offsets relative to this same pointer.

Bits, Pixels, and Images

QuickDraw manipulates graphical images made up of white and black dots called *pixels* (short for "picture elements"). The pixels are arranged in a two-dimensional array of rows and columns to form the image, as shown in Figure 4-2. When displayed on the Macintosh screen, each pixel appears as a square, white or black dot approximately 1/72 of an inch on each side.

16 bits = 2 bytes = 1 word

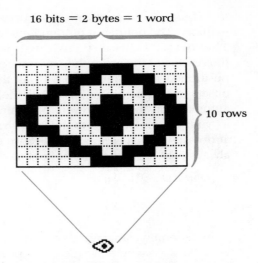

10 rows

Figure 4-2 A graphical image

Internally, a graphical image is stored in the computer's memory as a collection of bits called a *bit image*. Each bit represents one pixel of the image: **0** for a white pixel, **1** for a black one. Notice that bits and pixels aren't the same thing. A pixel is an element of a graphical image; a bit is its internal representation in the computer's memory. In casual reference the distinction is often blurred, however, and we speak loosely of drawing bits on the screen or setting pixels in memory.

To work with a bit image in Pascal, you group the bits into 16-bit memory words. You can then treat each word as an integer and define the bit image as an array of integers. For example, the bit image in Figure 4-2, which consists of 10 rows of 16 bits each, might be declared as

```
var
   anImage : array [1..10] of INTEGER;
```

with each element of the array representing one row of the image.

This image conveniently happens to be exactly 16 pixels wide, but, of course, this won't always be the case. When represented in bits, however, each row of an image must consist of some whole number of 16-bit words. If the image's width is not a multiple of 16 pixels, there will be some unused bits at the end of each row. These extra bits are just "padding" added to fill out the row to a whole number of words. For example, the image shown in Figure 4-3 is 18 pixels wide by 12 high. To represent it in bits, you have to allow two full words (32 bits) for each row

```
var
   otherImage : array [1..12, 1..2] of INTEGER;
```

leaving 14 bits unused at the end of the row.

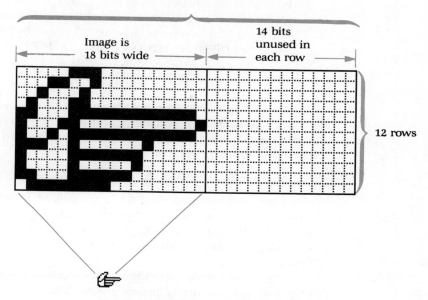

Figure 4-3 Bit image with unused bits

The number of *bytes* (not words or bits) in each row is called the image's *row width*. Since each row must be a whole number of words and a word is 2 bytes, the row width is always an even number. For the image in Figure 4-2, the row width is 2 bytes; in Figure 4-3, it's 4 bytes.

The most important bit image is the *screen image*, which defines what the user sees displayed on the Macintosh screen. The screen is 512 pixels wide by 342 high, a total of 175,104 pixels. Its internal representation, the screen image, is equivalent to an array of type

array [1..342, 1..32] **of** INTEGER

—that is, it consists of 342 rows of 32 words (512 bits) each.

The screen image occupies 175,104 bits (21,888 bytes, or 10,944 words) at a certain fixed block of locations in the computer's memory. This special area of memory is the *screen buffer*, which was mentioned in our discussion of memory organization in Chapter 3. The Macintosh's video display circuitry automatically "paints" the contents of the screen buffer onto the screen 60 times each second. When you ask QuickDraw to draw something on the screen, it does so by storing the appropriate bits into the screen buffer in memory.

The screen dimensions given above, and used throughout this book, are for the standard 128K Macintosh or the 512K Fat Mac. The Macintosh XL has a larger screen: 720 pixels by 364, totaling 262,080 bits (32,760 bytes, or 16,380 words).

In principle, you can store bits directly into a bit image by writing them as hexadecimal constants and assigning them to elements of the array. For instance, to set row 6 of **anImage** (declared earlier) to alternating black and white pixels, you could write

```
anImage[6] := $AAAA
```

(since the hexadecimal digit **$A** is equivalent to binary **1010**). However, storing directly into individual words is not recommended for drawing in a bit image. It's generally safer and more convenient to use QuickDraw's specialized drawing routines. After all, drawing into bit images is what QuickDraw is for!

If you must store a specific sequence of bits into a bit image, the easiest way is to use the utility procedure **StuffHex** [2.2.4]. For example, to set **anImage** to the image shown in Figure 4-2, you could write

```
StuffHex (@anImage, CONCAT('01E0',
                           '0738',
                           '1C0C',
                           '70C6',
                           'C1E3',
                           'C1E3',
                           '70C6',
                           '1C0C',
                           '0738',
                           '01E0'))
```

(Here, since a string constant isn't allowed to run across a line break, we've split the string into pieces and joined them together with the built-in Pascal function **CONCAT**.)

Coordinates, Points, and Rectangles

Since a bit image may have to contain some unused bits at the end of each row to fill out a whole number of 16-bit words, you have to tell QuickDraw how many bits of each row are valuable and how many are just padding. You do this by specifying a *boundary rectangle* for the bit image, as shown in Figure 4-4. The width and height of the boundary rectangle define the dimensions of the actual image, in pixels. Bits in the bit image that lie beyond the right edge of the boundary rectangle are ignored, and it doesn't matter what they contain; the same goes for any extra rows below the rectangle's bottom edge.

The boundary rectangle also imposes a system of coordinates on the bit image. QuickDraw measures coordinates on a grid of horizontal and vertical lines drawn *between* the pixels (not through them), as in the figure. The top-left corner of the boundary rectangle is always assumed to be positioned just outside the first pixel in the image. This top-left corner is called the *origin* of the boundary rectangle, and you can give it any integer coordinates you like; in the figure its coordinates are **125** horizontally and **−75** vertically. The coordinates of any other point on the grid are then determined relative to that point.

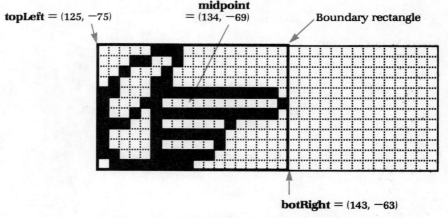

Figure 4-4 Bit image with boundary rectangle

Here are some important facts to remember about coordinates in QuickDraw:

- All coordinates are expressed as 16-bit integers, running from a minimum of **−32768** to a maximum of **+32767**.

- Horizontal coordinates increase from left to right, vertical coordinates from top to bottom. This matches the way English is written (whether on the Macintosh screen or on a printed page), but runs counter to the usual mathematical convention that vertical coordinates increase from bottom to top.

- The coordinates on the grid *enclose* the pixels in the image, rather than coincide with them. In Figure 4-4, for example, the top left pixel in the bit image doesn't lie at coordinates **125** and **−75**, but rather *between* **125** and **126** horizontally and between **−75** and **−74** vertically. If you think of the coordinate grid as a sheet of graph paper, the pixels fall in the squares between the lines, not at the intersections.

For designating positions on the coordinate grid, QuickDraw provides a fundamental data type named **Point** [4.1.1]. It's defined as a Pascal variant record structure, so that you can treat the point's horizontal and vertical coordinates either as two separate fields of the record or as a single two-element array indexed by the scalar type **VHSelect** [4.1.1]. For example, if **midpoint** is a variable of type **Point**, you can refer to its horizontal coordinate as either

    midpoint.h

or

    midpoint.vh[H]

and its vertical coordinate as either

    midpoint.v

or

    midpoint.vh[V]

at your convenience. So to set **midpoint** to the coordinates shown for it in Figure 4-4, you can write either

```
with midpoint do
   begin
      h := 134;
      v := −69
   end
```

or

```
with midpoint do
   begin
      vh[H] := 134;
      vh[V] := −69
   end
```

or you can use the QuickDraw procedure **SetPt** [4.1.1]:

```
SetPt (midpoint, 134, −69)
```

Notice in the figure that **midpoint** denotes a point on the coordinate grid, *not* a pixel in the image.

Notice carefully that **Point** records reverse the customary mathematical convention and place the vertical coordinate before the horizontal. In Pascal this makes no difference, since you always refer to the coordinates by name (**h** or **v**). But if you're programming in assembly language, you must be careful to keep the vertical coordinate first. To further confound the perplexed, notice that the arguments to **SetPt** (as opposed to the fields of a **Point**) *are* given in the conventional order, horizontal before vertical. Aren't computers fun?

A rectangle on the coordinate grid can be defined in either of two ways: as a pair of points specifying the top-left and bottom-right corners of the rectangle, or as four integers giving the top, left, bottom, and right coordinates separately. Again, QuickDraw uses a variant record structure, **Rect** [4.1.2], so you can define your rectangles in whichever way is convenient. If **r** is a variable of type **Rect**, all the expressions shown on each line below are equivalent:

```
r.top        r.topLeft.v      r.topLeft.vh[V]
r.left       r.topLeft.h      r.topLeft.vh[H]
r.bottom     r.botRight.v     r.botRight.vh[V]
r.right      r.botRight.h     r.botRight.vh[H]
```

To set **r** to the boundary rectangle shown in Figure 4-4, you can write

```
with r do
  begin
    top      := −75;
    left     := 125;
    bottom   := −63;
    right    := 143
  end
```

or use the QuickDraw procedure **SetRect** [4.1.2]:

```
SetRect (r, 125, −75, 143, −63)
```

Or, if **origin** and **corner** are points with coordinates (**125**, **−75**) and (**143**, **−63**), respectively, you can use the assignments

```
with r do
  begin
    topLeft  := origin;
    botRight := corner
  end
```

or the QuickDraw procedure **Pt2Rect** [4.1.2]:

```
Pt2Rect (origin, corner, r)
```

The points you give to **Pt2Rect** can be any pair of diagonally opposite corners of the rectangle, not just the top-left and bottom-right.

Calculations with Points and Rectangles

QuickDraw includes a wealth of utility routines for performing various calculations on graphical entities. In this section we'll see how to compare points or rectangles for equality, add or subtract their coordinates, and transform or combine them in a variety of ways. In the next section we'll talk about similar operations on two classes of more complex figures, polygons and regions.

You can compare two points or two rectangles to find out whether they're equal with **EqualPt** [4.4.1] or **EqualRect** [4.4.5]. Each of these functions takes a pair of arguments (points for **EqualPt**, rectangles for **EqualRect**), compares them coordinate by coordinate, and returns a Boolean result: **TRUE** if the arguments are equal, **FALSE** if they're unequal. Another useful comparison function is **PtInRect** [4.4.3], which tests whether a given point lies within a given rectangle.

The procedures **AddPt** and **SubPt** [4.4.1] perform simple arithmetic on points. These procedures add or subtract the two points you give them, coordinate by coordinate, and set the coordinates of the second point to the result. The first point is unaffected.

EmptyRect [4.4.4] tests whether a given rectangle is "empty." Remember that the boundaries of a rectangle run *between* the pixels of an image, not through them. If the specified bottom-right corner doesn't lie strictly below and to the right of the rectangle's origin in the cases of either

r.top ≥ r.bottom

or

r.left ≥ r.right

then the rectangle encloses no pixels and is considered empty. In this case, **EmptyRect** returns a value of **TRUE;** otherwise it returns **FALSE.**

OffsetRect [4.4.4] adjusts a rectangle's coordinates by a given horizontal and vertical offset, as shown in Figure 4-5. This is equivalent to moving the rectangle within its coordinate system while keeping its width and height fixed. If the horizontal offset is positive, the rectangle is moved to the right; if it's negative, the rectangle is moved to the left. Similarly, a positive vertical offset moves the rectangle down and a negative offset moves it up.

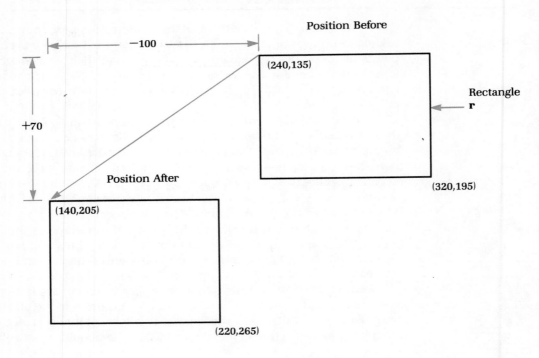

OffsetRect, in this example, moves rectangle **r**
100 pixels to the left and 70 pixels down.

Figure 4-5 Offsetting a rectangle

InsetRect [4.4.4] adjusts a rectangle's size by a horizontal and vertical inset, as shown in Figure 4-6. The left and right edges of the rectangle are both moved inward (toward the center) by the specified horizontal inset, and the top and bottom by the vertical inset. A negative value for either inset adjusts the edges of the rectangle outward instead of inward in that dimension.

InsetRect (r, 15, 10)

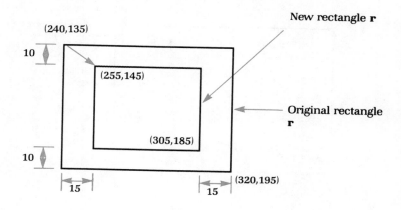

InsetRect, in this example, moves rectangle **r**'s sides in
by 15 pixels left and right, 10 pixels at the top and bottom.

Figure 4-6 Insetting a rectangle

OffsetRect and **InsetRect** operate on a rectangle as a purely
mathematical entity. What they do is adjust the values of the
rectangle's coordinates; they have nothing to do with moving or
changing pixels in a bit image.

    UnionRect and **SectRect** [4.4.5] form the union and intersection of a
pair of rectangles and return the result as the value of their third parameter
(**resultRect**). The union of two rectangles is the smallest rectangle that
encloses them both (see Figure 4-7); the intersection is the largest rectangle
that lies entirely within both (Figure 4-8). **SectRect** also returns a Boolean
result that's **TRUE** if the two rectangles intersect at all (that is, if their
intersection is not empty), **FALSE** if they don't.

UnionRect (r1, r2, union)

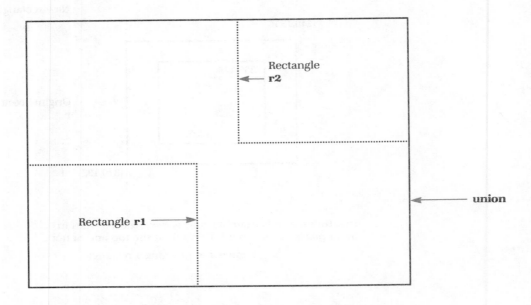

UnionRect returns the smallest rectangle, **union**, that
contains both rectangles **r1** and **r2.**

Figure 4-7 Union of two rectangles

Calculations involving two or more points or rectangles are
meaningful only if the arguments are expressed in the same system of
coordinates. If they aren't, you have to transform them into a
common coordinate system before performing the calculation. The
procedures **LocalToGlobal** and **GlobalToLocal** [4.4.2] are useful for
this purpose; they're discussed below under "Local and Global
Coordinates."

result := SectRect (r1, r2, intersection)

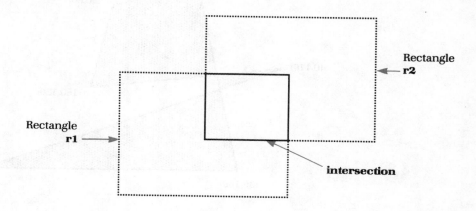

SectRect returns the largest rectangle, **intersection,** contained within both rectangle **r1** and rectangle **r2.**

Figure 4-8 Intersection of two rectangles

Polygons and Regions

QuickDraw provides two special types of structure, polygons and regions, that you can use to define and manipulate graphical figures of any shape. A polygon can be any shape that you can describe with a closed series of connected straight lines, such as the one in Figure 4-9. ("Connected" means that each line begins where the previous one ended; "closed" means that the last line ends where the first one began, so that the figure's outline connects back to where it started.) A region is even more general, and can be any form that can be built up out of simpler shapes such as rectangles, ovals, polygons, and even other regions. It can have curved as well as straight edges, and can even have holes in it or consist of two or more separate pieces (see Figure 4-10).

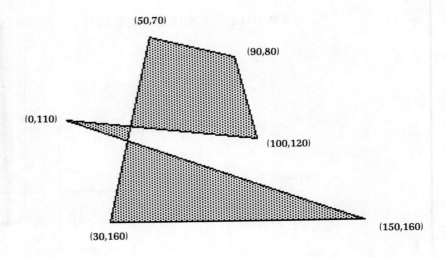

(50,70)

(90,80)

(0,110)

(100,120)

(30,160)

(150,160)

KEY

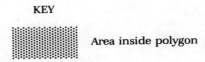

Area inside polygon

Figure 4-9 A polygon

Both polygons and regions are represented internally by variable-length data structures whose size depends on the figure's complexity. Both structures, **Polygon** [4.1.3] and **Region** [4.1.5], begin with a couple of fixed fields, followed by variable-length data to define the figure's shape. The first field (**polySize** or **rgnSize**) is an integer giving the data structures overall length in bytes. The second (**polyBBox** or **rgnBBox**) is the figure's *bounding box*, the smallest rectangle that encloses it on the coordinate grid. QuickDraw maintains these fields for you automatically; you can access their contents, but normally you shouldn't store into them yourself.

The rest of the data structure consists of the variable-length data defining the figure's shape. This part of the structure can't be properly described in a Pascal type definition, so there's no way to access it directly from a Pascal program. You can only manipulate it indirectly, by calling the appropriate QuickDraw routines to do the job for you. You define the shape of a polygon or region by drawing it using QuickDraw's various drawing routines. Since drawing is the subject of the next chapter we'll postpone our discussion of polygon and region definitions until then.

Entire shaded area can be
defined as one region.

Figure 4-10 A region

There are QuickDraw routines for performing a full range of
calculations on regions:

- **EmptyRgn** [4.4.7] tests whether a region is empty.
- **EqualRgn** [4.4.8] tests whether two regions are identical.
- **PtInRgn** [4.4.3] tests whether a point lies within a given region.
- **RectInRgn** [4.4.3] tests whether a given rectangle and region intersect.
- **OffsetRgn** and **InsetRgn** [4.4.7] are analogous to the rectangle operations **OffsetRect** and **InsetRect**, discussed earlier. (There's also an **OffsetPoly** routine [4.4.6] for polygons.)
- **UnionRgn** [4.4.8] unites the two regions, the set of all pixels that lie within either of them (Figure 4-11).
- **SectRgn** [4.4.8] forms the intersection of two regions, the set of all pixels that lie within both of them (Figure 4-12).
- **DiffRgn** [4.4.8] forms the difference of two regions, the set of all pixels that lie within the first but not the second (Figure 4-13).
- **XOrRgn** [4.4.8] forms the "exclusive or" of two regions, the set of all pixels that lie within either one of them but not the other (Figure 4-14).

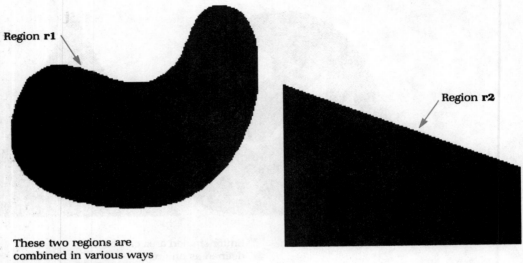

Region **r1**

Region **r2**

These two regions are
combined in various ways
in the next five figures.

UnionRgn (rgn1, rgn2, union)

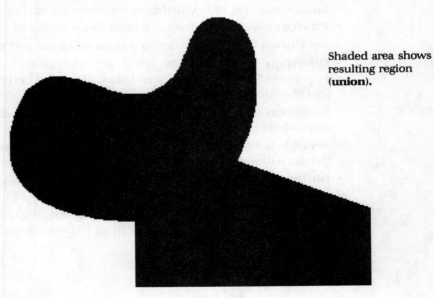

Shaded area shows
resulting region
(**union**).

Figure 4-11 Union of two regions

SectRgn (rgn1, rgn2, intersection)

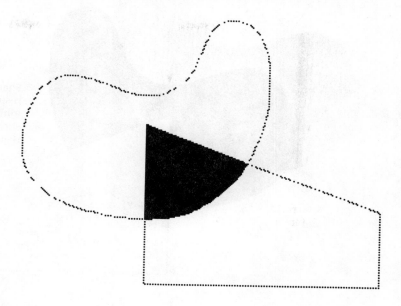

Shaded area shows resulting region (**intersection**); dotted lines
show boundaries of original regions.

Figure 4-12 Intersection of two regions

DiffRgn (rgn1, rgn2, difference)

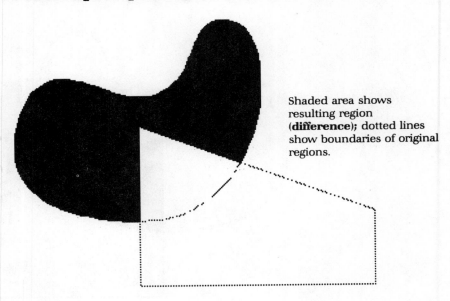

Shaded area shows resulting region (**difference**); dotted lines show boundaries of original regions.

DiffRgn (rgn2, rgn1, difference)

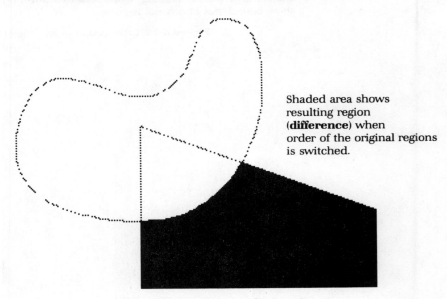

Shaded area shows resulting region (**difference**) when order of the original regions is switched.

Figure 4-13 Difference of two regions

XOrRgn (rgn1, rgn2, exclusiveOr)

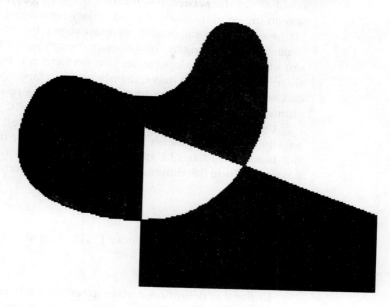

Shaded area shows the
resulting region,
exclusiveOr. (ExclusiveOr
= union − intersection.)

Figure 4-14 "Exclusive or" of two regions

Bit Maps

We said earlier that a bit image needs a boundary rectangle to tell QuickDraw how many bits of each row are valuable and how many are padding. This combination of a bit image and a boundary rectangle is called a *bit map*. Bit maps are the basic medium in which QuickDraw does all of its drawing. The bit image provides the bit map's content; the boundary rectangle defines its extent and gives it a system of coordinates.

Different bit maps can share the same bit image: for example, every window on the screen has its own bit map, but they all share the same screen image in memory. The boundary rectangle limits the portion of the bit image that a particular bit map refers to. The rest of the image is regarded as padding by this bit map (though possibly not by others), and is not affected by any operation you perform on the bit map. Notice that, since a given bit map may use only part of a larger, shared bit image, there can be any amount of padding at the end of a row in the image, not just enough to fill out the row to a multiple of 16 bits.

Conceptually, a bit map could be represented by a record containing two fields: one for the bit image and another for the boundary rectangle. But because of Pascal's strong typing rules, the record definition would have to include the dimensions of the array containing the bit image, such as

```
type
   BitMap = record
               image  : array [1..12, 1..2] of INTEGER;
               bounds : Rect
            end;
```

Under this definition, a bit map record could refer only to bit images of one particular size—12 rows of two words each. To work with images of different sizes, there would have to be a different type of bit map for each size. So instead of including the bit image itself as part of the bit-map record, QuickDraw just uses a pointer to the first byte of the image (its *base address*). That way, since pointers have no dimensions, a single type of bit map can refer to bit images of any size.

But now some important information has been lost. The height and width of the boundary rectangle tell how many rows there are and how many bits of each row count as part of the bit map. But QuickDraw also needs to know how many bits of padding to skip at the end of each row, in order to find the beginning of the next row in memory. So the bit map record has to include another field giving the row width of the bit image— the total width of each row in bytes, including padding. Putting all this together, the actual type definition for bit maps is as follows [4.2.1]:

```
type
   BitMap = record
               baseAddr : Ptr;
               rowBytes : INTEGER;
               bounds   : Rect
            end;
```

To create a bit map in your program corresponding to the one shown earlier in Figure 4-4, you might declare

```
var
    theImage : array [1..12, 1..2] of INTEGER;
    theMap   : BitMap;
```

and then write something like

```
StuffHex (@theImage, CONCAT('07000000',
                            '19000000',
                            '22000000',
                            '46000000',
                            'C7FF8000',
                            '8C004000',
                            '97FF8000',
                            'E4080000',
                            '87F00000',
                            '84100000',
                            'C7E00000',
                            '7F800000'));

with theMap do
  begin
    baseAddr := @theImage;
    rowBytes := 4;
    SetRect (bounds, 125, −75, 143, −63)
  end
```

Remember that **rowBytes** is expressed in *bytes,* not words, so it has to be set to *twice* the number of integers in each row of the bit image.

Like a child with a coloring book, QuickDraw will carefully keep all of its drawing in a bit map "inside the lines" defined by the boundary rectangle. But it has to trust your judgment as to where the lines are. Make sure the bit map's base address pointer really points to a bit image in memory, and that the image array is as big as the bit map's row width and boundary rectangle say it is! If it isn't, QuickDraw will "color outside the lines" and ruin your pretty picture. Specifically, the number of bytes allocated for the bit image must not be less than the row width times the height of the boundary rectangle:

```
SIZEOF(theImage) ≥ theMap.rowBytes *
  (theMap.bounds.bottom - theMap.bounds.top)
```

Similarly, the width of the boundary rectangle must be no greater than the actual number of bits in each row:

```
(theMap.bounds.right - theMap.bounds.left)
  ≤ theMap.rowBytes * 8
```

As the screen image is the most important bit image of all, the most important bit map is the *screen map*, which QuickDraw keeps in a global variable named **ScreenBits** [4.2.1]. The screen map's base address field points to the beginning of the screen buffer in memory, with a row width of 64 bytes (512 bits). Its boundary rectangle is the same size as the Macintosh screen, 512 pixels wide by 342 high; the origin of the rectangle has coordinates (**0, 0**), placing its bottom-right corner at (**512, 342**).

On the Macintosh XL, with its larger screen, **ScreenBits** has a row width of 90 bytes (720 bits) and a boundary rectangle 720 pixels wide by 364 high.

Graphics Ports

There's much more to QuickDraw's drawing environment than just a bit map to draw into. Among the features are foreground and background patterns for filling in areas of an image; a pen size and location for line drawing; a typeface, size, and style for displaying text. Often a program needs to use more than one drawing environment: for example, the program may have several windows on the screen, each with several things including its own pen location, fill patterns, and text characteristics.

Graphics ports enable you to switch quickly and easily from one drawing environment to another. A graphics port is a complete drawing environment containing all the information needed for QuickDraw drawing operations. Each port has its own bit map, fill patterns, pen properties, and everything else QuickDraw needs to do its job. A program can have as many separate graphics ports as it needs; in particular, every window on the screen has its own port.

All the information associated with a graphics port is kept in a record of type **GrafPort** [4.2.2], which normally resides in the heap. For obscure reasons shrouded in the mists of antiquity, graphics ports are nonrelocatable objects and are referred to by single indirection, with simple pointers of type **GrafPtr** [4.2.2] rather than handles. To create a new graphics port, you first allocate a **GrafPort** record with **NewPtr** [3.2.1], then open the port for use with **OpenPort** [4.3.2]:

```
rawPointer := NewPtr(SIZEOF(GrafPort));
newPort  := GrafPtr(rawPointer);
OpenPort (newPort)
```

(where **rawPointer** is of type **Ptr** and **newPort** is of type **GrafPtr**). **OpenPort** initializes the port's fields and allocates its internal data structures; always be sure to call this routine after creating a port and before attempting to use it in any way. (Another routine, **InitPort** [4.3.2], reinitializes the fields of an existing port but doesn't reallocate its internal structures.) When you're finished with a port, remember to release the internal structures with **ClosePort** [4.3.2] before destroying the port itself:

```
ClosePort (oldPort);
rawPointer := Ptr(oldPort);
DisposPtr (rawPointer)
```

At any given time, only one graphics port, called the current port, is in use. Many QuickDraw routines operate implicitly on the current port, so you must make sure the port you want is current before calling the routine. You can always find out what port is current with the QuickDraw procedure **GetPort** or change the current port with **SetPort** [4.3.3]. (A pointer to the current port is also kept in the global variable **ThePort** [4.3.3].) If you're working with more than one graphics port, it's a good idea to use **GetPort** and **SetPort** in any procedure (or function) that changes the current port, in order to save the previous port at the beginning of the procedure and restore it again at the end. Program 4-1 illustrates the technique. Any routine written in this way is "transparent" to the setting of the current port: it leaves the same port current on return from the routine as when it was called.

Every graphics port has its own bit map to draw into, kept in the **portBits** field of the **GrafPort** record. **portBits** is the port's "canvas": QuickDraw operations directed to the port will draw into the bit image belonging to this bit map, and the bit map's boundary rectangle establishes the port's coordinate system. When you open or initialize a port, its **portBits** field is set to a copy of the screen map **ScreenBits**, with the screen image as its bit image, a row width of 64 bytes (90 on a Macintosh XL), and a boundary rectangle the same size as the screen (512 pixels wide by 342 high, or 720 by 364 on an XL) with its origin at coordinates (**0, 0**). If necessary, you can then use the QuickDraw routine **SetPortBits** [4.3.4] to change the bit map (for example, to one based on a bit image other than on the screen), or change the port's coordinate system by adjusting the bit map's boundary rectangle. Since the port's bit map is only a copy of the screen map, any changes you make to its fields won't affect the screen map itself.

```
procedure DrawInPort (whichPort: GrafPtr);

  { Skeleton procedure showing use of GetPort and SetPort to preserve current port setting.  }

  var
    oldPort : GrafPtr;                              {Pointer to previous current port}
    . . . ;

  begin {DrawInPort}

    GetPort (oldPort);                              {Save old port on entry [4.3.3]}

    SetPort (whichPort);                            {Switch to specified port [4.3.3]}

      . . . ;                                       {Draw in port}

    SetPort (oldPort)                               {Restore old port on exit [4.3.3]}

  end;  {DrawInPort}
```

Program 4-1 Saving and restoring the current port

The **portRect, visRgn**, and **clipRgn** fields of a graphics port all define *clipping boundaries* for drawing into the port. QuickDraw will automatically confine its drawing activities within the intersection of all these boundaries, as well as the port's boundary rectangle (see Figure 4-15). Any drawing you attempt that lies outside any one of the clipping boundaries will be suppressed (*clipped*) and will have no effect on the bit image.

The *port rectangle* (**portRect**) defines the portion of the bit map that the port can draw into. For a newly opened or initialized port, the port rectangle is a copy of the screen map's boundary rectangle: top-left corner at coordinates (**0, 0**), bottom-right at (**512, 342**) or (**720, 364**). You can then change the port rectangle to whatever coordinates are appropriate. For a port belonging to a window on the screen, the port rectangle corresponds to the interior of the window, inside the window's frame. For the window shown in Figure 4-15, the port rectangle extends from coordinates (**160, 80**) at the top-left to (**340, 300**) at the bottom-right.

a.

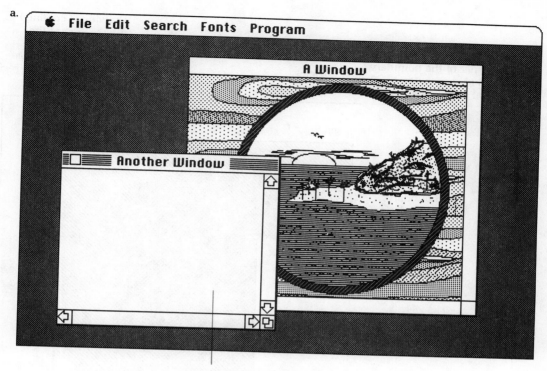

This window obscures part
of the window behind it.

Figure 4-15 Clipping boundaries

The *clipping region* (**clipRgn**) is a general-purpose clipping boundary that you can use any way you like. Notice that it's a *region*, not a rectangle, which means you can make it any shape you need. For example, in an adventure game you might use a circular clipping region, as in the figure, to simulate the view through a telescope or a ship's porthole. Opening or initializing a port sets its clipping region to an arbitrarily large rectangular region extending from coordinates (**−32768, −32768**) to (**32767, 32767**), sometimes called the "wide-open" region. You can then install a different clipping region with **SetClip** or **ClipRect**, or access the port's current clipping region with **GetClip** [4.3.6]. In Chapter 5, we'll look at an example of the use of a clipping region.

The *visible region* (**visRgn**) also can be any shape, but it's there for use by the Toolbox, not by your program. As windows are moved around on the screen, the Toolbox uses this field to keep track of the portion of each window's port rectangle that's exposed to view. Any part of the window that's hidden behind another window is excluded from the visible region,

b.

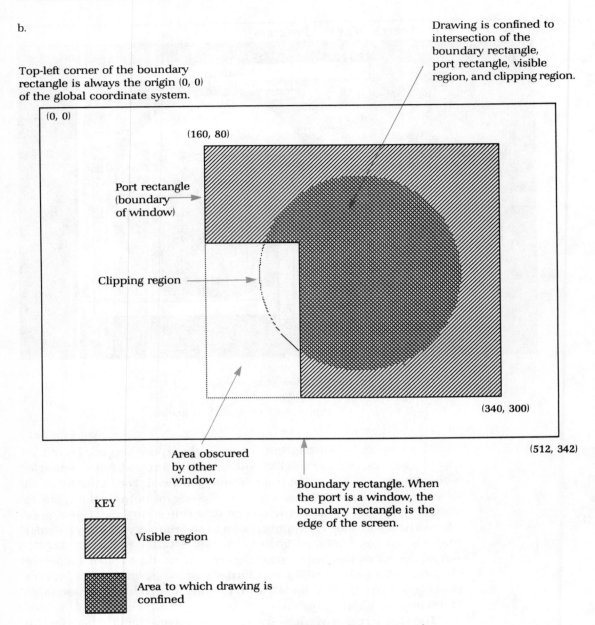

Top-left corner of the boundary rectangle is always the origin (0, 0) of the global coordinate system.

Drawing is confined to intersection of the boundary rectangle, port rectangle, visible region, and clipping region.

Port rectangle (boundary of window)

Clipping region

Area obscured by other window

Boundary rectangle. When the port is a window, the boundary rectangle is the edge of the screen.

KEY

Visible region

Area to which drawing is confined

Figure 4-15 (*continued*)

so drawing in that part of the window is suppressed and won't appear on the screen. Figure 4-15 illustrates how a window's visible region is determined by its position on the screen in relation to other, overlapping windows.

Most of the remaining fields of the **GrafPort** record are discussed in Chapter 5 (**bkPat, fillPat, pnLoc, pnSize, pnMode, pnPat, pnVis**) and Chapter 8 (**device, txFont, txFace, txMode, txSize, spExtra**). The **fgColor, bkColor**, and **colrBit** fields are reserved for future use with color displays or printers; **patStretch, picSave, rgnSave**, and **polySave** are for QuickDraw's private use. **grafProcs** is used for "customizing" QuickDraw operations to your own needs; this is an unusual operation, but if you're interested, see Apple's *Inside Macintosh* manual for further information.

Local and Global Coordinates

A port's bit map belongs only to that port. Even ports that draw into the same bit image have separate bit maps based on that same image. For instance, all ports that draw on the screen share the one screen image in the Macintosh's memory, but refer to it through different bit maps. Each has its own boundary rectangle, whose coordinates can be set independently of all the others.

Since the bit map's boundary rectangle determines the coordinate system of the graphics port, it follows that each port has its own coordinate system, called the *local* coordinate system of that port. The origin (top-left corner) of the boundary rectangle always lies just outside the first pixel in the bit image; everything else in the port is measured relative to the coordinates of that point.

Remember, though, that the area of the bit image that a port can draw into is defined by the port rectangle, not by the boundary rectangle of the port's bit map. Often it's more natural to measure your coordinates relative to the port rectangle instead of the boundary rectangle. The QuickDraw procedure **SetOrigin** [4.3.4] allows you to set a port's local coordinate system in terms of the port rectangle. Like most QuickDraw routines, **SetOrigin** applies implicitly to the current graphics port. It adjusts (the 10-dollar word is "translates") the port's coordinate system to give the top-left corner of the port rectangle the designated coordinates, **hOrigin** and **vOrigin**. In so doing, it recalculates the coordinates of the boundary rectangle, port rectangle, and visible region to keep them all in the same spatial relationships in the new coordinate system. You might call it "simultaneous translation."

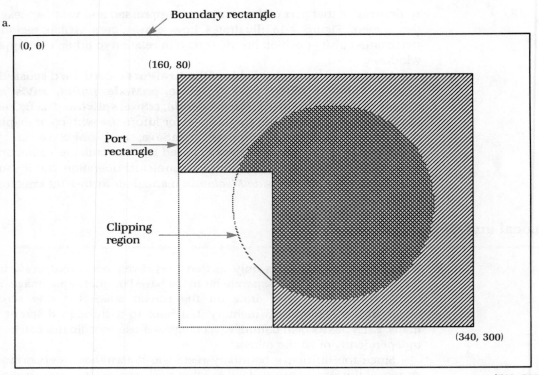

a.

Boundary rectangle

(0, 0)

(160, 80)

Port
rectangle

Clipping
region

(340, 300)

(512, 342)

KEY

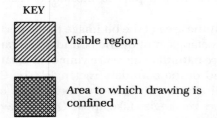

Visible region

Area to which drawing is
confined

Figure 4-16 Adjusting coordinates with **SetOrigin**

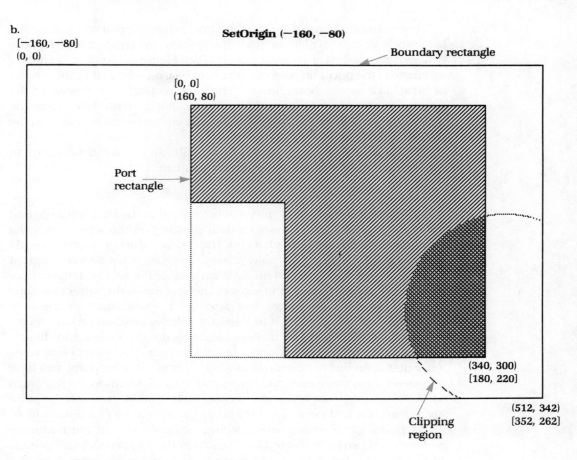

b.

[−160, −80]
(0, 0)

SetOrigin (−160, −80)

Boundary rectangle

[0, 0]
(160, 80)

Port
rectangle

(340, 300)
[180, 220]

Clipping
region

(512, 342)
[352, 262]

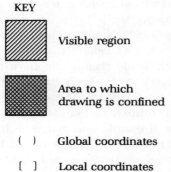

KEY

Visible region

Area to which
drawing is confined

( )   Global coordinates

[ ]   Local coordinates

Figure 4-16 (*continued*)

For example, Figure 4-16a shows a port belonging to a window on the Macintosh screen, which is partially hidden by another, overlapping window; this is just a repeat of our earlier Figure 4-15b. The boundary rectangle of the port's bit map extends from coordinates (**0, 0**) at the top-left to (**512, 342**) at the bottom-right. The port rectangle, representing the interior of the window, extends from (**160, 80**) to (**340, 300**). Since the window is partially hidden on the screen, its visible region is limited to the shaded area shown in the figure.

If you would prefer to express coordinates in this window relative to the window itself instead of the screen, you can write

```
SetOrigin (0, 0)
```

The result is shown in Figure 4-16b. Notice that the port rectangle and the visible region haven't changed their position on the screen; only the coordinate system has been changed. The origin of the boundary rectangle now has coordinates (**−160, −80**), placing the origin of the port rectangle at (**0, 0**), as requested. The bottom-right corners of the two rectangles have been recalculated, to keep the sizes of the rectangles the same as before. The window's visible region has also been transformed to the new coordinate system, keeping it in the same relative position on the screen.

Because each port has its own local coordinate system, coordinates expressed in different ports aren't directly comparable. Before performing any calculation involving coordinates taken from different ports, you have to convert them into a common coordinate system. A convenient system to use for such purposes is the *global* coordinate system, in which the point just outside the first pixel of a port's bit image always has coordinates (**0, 0**).

A port's global coordinate system is independent of the boundary rectangle, and so isn't affected by changes in the local coordinate system. In Figure 4-16a, for instance, the port's local coordinate system coincides with the global system, since the origin of the boundary rectangle has coordinates (**0, 0**). In Figure 4-16b, the local system has been transformed, but the global system remains the same as before. Expressed in global coordinates, the port rectangle and visible region still have the same coordinates shown for them in Figure 4-16a, even though their local coordinates have been changed to those in Figure 4-16b. Global coordinates provide a handy basis of comparison between different ports, provided that the ports are based on the same underlying bit image. For instance, for all ports corresponding to windows on the screen, the global coordinate system measures coordinates with respect to the screen instead of the window.

Suppose you want to find the intersection of two windows on the screen. Since each window's port rectangle is expressed in that window's own local coordinates, you can't just apply **SectRect** directly to the two rectangles. First you have to convert the rectangles into a common coordinate system. Since the two windows' graphics ports are based on the same bit image (the screen), you can use global coordinates as a common basis of comparison.

QuickDraw provides a pair of utility procedures, **LocalToGlobal** and **GlobalToLocal** [4.4.2], for converting between coordinate systems. The local coordinate system involved is always implicitly that of the current port, so you have to make sure the right port is current for each conversion. Program 4-2 shows one way to do the job:

1. Convert both windows' port rectangles into global coordinates.

2. Find the intersection of the two port rectangles in global coordinates.

3. Convert the result back into the local coordinates of one of the two windows.

A slightly more efficient way of doing the same thing is shown in Program 4-3:

1. Convert one window's port rectangle into global coordinates.

2. Convert this same rectangle from global coordinates into the local coordinates of the other window.

3. Find the intersection directly in the second window's local coordinates.

This method requires only two coordinate conversions instead of three.

```
{ Program fragment to find the intersection of two windows' port
  rectangles by converting both to global coordinates.  }

var
    portA, portB        : GrafPtr;
    rectA, rectB, inter : Rect;
    nonEmpty            : BOOLEAN;
    . . . ;
```

Program 4-2 Converting to global coordinates

```
begin

   . . . ;

   portA := . . . ;                          {Port A is first window's port}
   portB := . . . ;                          {Port B is second window's port}
   rectA := portA^.portRect;                 {First window's port rectangle [4.2.2]}
   rectB := portB^.portRect;                 {Second window's port rectangle [4.2.2]}

   SetPort (portA);                          {Get into port A [4.3.3]}
   with rectA do
      begin
         LocalToGlobal (topLeft);            {Convert port rectangle to     }
         LocalToGlobal (botRight)            {   global coordinates [4.4.2]}
      end;

   SetPort (portB);                          {Switch to port B [4.3.3]}
   with rectB do
      begin
         LocalToGlobal (topLeft);            {Convert port rectangle to     }
         LocalToGlobal (botRight)            {   global coordinates [4.4.2]}
      end;

   nonEmpty :=  SectRect (rectA, rectB, inter);   {Find intersection [4.4.5]}
   if nonEmpty
      then                                   {Intersection is nonempty:            }
         begin
            with intersection do
               begin
                  GlobalToLocal (topLeft);   {   convert intersection to           }
                  GlobalToLocal (botRight)   {   port B's local coordinates [4.4.2]}
               end;
            . . .                            {   and proceed with normal processing}
         end
      else                                   {Intersection is empty:     }
         . . . ;                             {   handle exceptional case}
   . . .

end
```

Program 4-2 (*continued*)

```
{ Program fragment to find the intersection of two windows' port
  rectangles by converting one to local coordinates of the other }

var
   portA, portB        : GrafPtr;
   rectA, rectB, inter : Rect;
   nonEmpty            : BOOLEAN;
   . . . ;

begin

   . . . ;

   portA := . . . ;                                {Port A is first window's port}
   portB := . . . ;                                {Port B is second window's port}
   . . . ;
   rectA := portA^.portRect;                       {First window's port rectangle [4.2.2]}
   rectB := portB^.portRect;                       {Second window's port rectangle [4.2.2]}

   SetPort (portA);                                {Get into port A [4.3.3]}
   with rectA do
      begin
         LocalToGlobal (topLeft);                  {Convert port rectangle to   }
         LocalToGlobal (botRight)                  {   global coordinates [4.4.2]}
      end;

   SetPort (portB);                                {Switch to port B [4.3.3]}
   with rectA do
      begin
         GlobalToLocal (topLeft);                  {Convert to port B's          }
         GlobalToLocal (botRight)                  {   local coordinates [4.4.2]}
      end;

   nonEmpty := SectRect (rectA, rectB, inter);     {Find intersection [4.4.5]}
   if nonEmpty
      then                                         {Intersection is nonempty: }
         . . .                                     {   handle normal case      }
      else                                         {Intersection is empty:     }
         . . . ;                                   {   handle exceptional case}

   . . .

end
```

Program 4-3 Converting between coordinate systems

REFERENCE

4.1 Mathematical Foundations

4.1.1 Points

Definitions

```
type
  VHSelect = (V, H);                              {Selector for coordinates of a point}

  Point     = record
                case INTEGER of

                  0: (v  : INTEGER;               {Vertical coordinate}
                      h  : INTEGER);              {Horizontal coordinate}

                  1: (vh : array [VHSelect] of INTEGER)   {Coordinates as a two-element array}

              end;

procedure SetPt
            (var thePoint : Point;               {Point to be set}
             hCoord       : INTEGER;             {Horizontal coordinate}
             vCoord       : INTEGER);            {Vertical coordinate}
```

Notes

1. A **Point** is a data structure representing a point on the QuickDraw coordinate grid.

2. The variant record structure allows the point's coordinates to be accessed as two separate integers

   thePoint.v
   thePoint.h

   or as a two-element array

   thePoint.vh[V]
   thePoint.vh[H]

3. The vertical coordinate comes first, contrary to the usual mathematical convention.

4. **SetPt** sets **thePoint** to a point with coordinates **hCoord** and **vCoord**.

5. Notice that the order of the coordinates in a call to **SetPt** is not the same as in the **Point** record itself.

Assembly Language Information

Field offsets:

(Pascal) Field Name	(Assembly) Offset name	Size in bytes
v	**v**	**0**
h	**h**	**2**

Trap macro:

(Pascal) Routine name	(Assembly) Trap macro	Trap word
SetPt	**_SetPt**	**$A880**

4.1.2 Rectangles

Definitions

```
type
  Rect = record
            case INTEGER of

              0: (top     : INTEGER;        {Top coordinate}
                  left    : INTEGER;        {Left coordinate}
                  bottom  : INTEGER;        {Bottom coordinate}
                  right   : INTEGER);       {Right coordinate}

              1: (topLeft  : Point;         {Top-left corner}
                  botRight : Point)         {Bottom-right corner}

          end;
procedure SetRect
            (var theRect : Rect;            {Rectangle to be set}
             left       : INTEGER;          {Left coordinate}
             top        : INTEGER;          {Top coordinate}
             right      : INTEGER;          {Right coordinate}
             bottom     : INTEGER);         {Bottom coordinate}

procedure Pt2Rect
            (point1     : Point;            {First corner}
             point2     : Point;            {Diagonally opposite corner}
             var theRect : Rect);           {Rectangle to be set}
```

Notes

1. A **Rect** is a data structure representing a rectangle on the coordinate grid.

2. The variant record structure allows the rectangle's coordinates to be accessed as four separate integers

        theRect.top
        theRect.left
        theRect.bottom
        theRect.right

or as a pair of points

```
theRect.topLeft
theRect.botRight
```

representing the top-left and bottom-right corners.

3. If **right** ≤ **left** or **bottom** ≤ **top**, the rectangle is considered empty.

4. **SetRect** sets **theRect** to a rectangle with coordinates **left, top, right,** and **bottom.**

5. Notice that the order of the coordinates in a call to **SetRect** is not the same as in the **Rect** record itself.

6. **Pt2Rect** sets **theRect** to a rectangle defined by a pair of diagonally opposite points **point1** and **point2.**

7. If **point1** and **point2** have the same horizontal or vertical coordinate, the resulting rectangle will be empty.

Assembly Language Information

Field offsets:

(Pascal) Field name	(Assembly) Offset name	Size in bytes
top	**top**	**0**
left	**left**	**2**
bottom	**bottom**	**4**
right	**right**	**6**
topLeft	**topLeft**	**0**
botRight	**botRight**	**4**

Trap macros:

(Pascal) Routine name	(Assembly) Trap macro	Trap word
SetRect	**_SetRect**	**$A8A7**
Pt2Rect	**_Pt2Rect**	**$A8AC**

4.1.3 Polygons

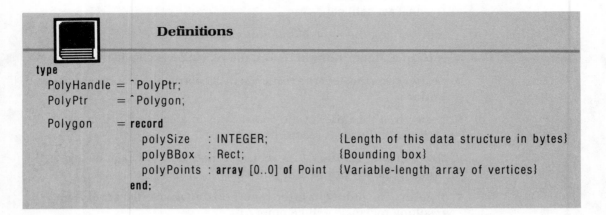

```
type
  PolyHandle = ^PolyPtr;
  PolyPtr    = ^Polygon;

  Polygon    = record
                 polySize   : INTEGER;              {Length of this data structure in bytes}
                 polyBBox   : Rect;                 {Bounding box}
                 polyPoints : array [0..0] of Point {Variable-length array of vertices}
               end;
```

Notes

1. A **Polygon** is a variable-length data structure representing an arbitrary polygon on the QuickDraw coordinate plane.

2. The shape of the polygon is defined by a series of connected sides, specified with the line-drawing operations **Line** and **LineTo** [5.2.4]. Each side begins where the previous side ended; their endpoints are the polygon's vertices.

3. If the first and last vertices don't coincide, an extra side is added automatically to close the polygon.

4. The dummy field **polyPoints** stands for a variable-length array of points (not directly accessible in Pascal) representing the polygon's vertices. The Toolbox maintains the contents of this array for you—you'll never need to access or store into it yourself.

5. **polySize** is the overall length of this **Polygon** data structure in bytes, including the variable-length **polyPoints** array.

6. **polyBBox** is the polygon's *bounding box*, the smallest rectangle that completely encloses it.

Assembly Language Information

Field offsets:

(Pascal) Field name	(Assembly) Offset name	Size in bytes
polySize	**polySize**	**0**
polyBBox	**polyBBox**	**2**
polyPoints	**polyPoints**	**10**

4.1.4 Defining Polygons

Definitions

function	OpenPoly : PolyHandle;	{Handle to new polygon}
procedure	ClosePoly;	
procedure	KillPoly (thePolygon : PolyHandle);	{Handle to polygon to be destroyed}

Notes

1. **OpenPoly** creates a new **Polygon** record [4.1.3], opens it for definition, and returns a handle to it.

2. Subsequent calls to the line-drawing routines **Line** and **LineTo** [5.2.4] will be accumulated into the **Polygon** record to define the shape of the polygon.

3. The graphics pen is hidden [5.2.3] while a polygon is open; the line-drawing operations that define the polygon will not appear on the screen.

4. The polygon's outline is infinitely thin, and is unaffected by pen characteristics such as size, pattern, and mode [5.2.1].

5. Only one polygon may be open at a time; don't attempt to open another without closing the one that's already open.

6. **ClosePoly** closes the polygon currently open for definition, if any.

7. The polygon's bounding box [4.1.3] is recomputed to enclose all of the points in the polygon.

8. The graphics pen is reshown [5.2.3]; subsequent line-drawing operations will appear on the screen instead of being accumulated into the polygon definition.

9. **KillPoly** destroys a **Polygon** record and deallocates the memory space it occupies. The polygon is no longer usable after this operation.

10. The trap macro for **ClosePoly** is spelled **_ClosePgon.**

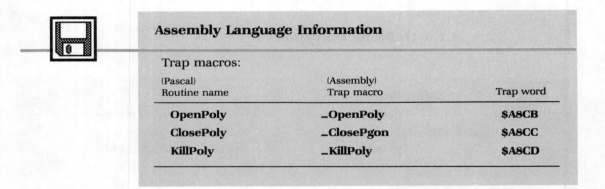

Assembly Language Information

Trap macros:

(Pascal) Routine name	(Assembly) Trap macro	Trap word
OpenPoly	**_OpenPoly**	**$A8CB**
ClosePoly	**_ClosePgon**	**$A8CC**
KillPoly	**_KillPoly**	**$A8CD**

4.1.5 Regions

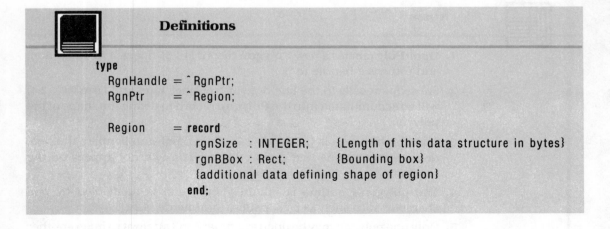

Definitions

```
type
   RgnHandle = ^RgnPtr;
   RgnPtr    = ^Region;

   Region    = record
                  rgnSize  : INTEGER;    {Length of this data structure in bytes}
                  rgnBBox  : Rect;       {Bounding box}
                  {additional data defining shape of region}
               end;
```

Notes

1. A **Region** is a variable-length data structure representing an arbitrary region on the QuickDraw coordinate plane.

2. The shape of the region is defined by a series of lines and shapes specified with the line-drawing operations **Move, MoveTo, Line,** and **LineTo** [5.2.4] and the shape-drawing operations **FrameRect** [5.3.2], **FrameRoundRect** [5.3.3], **FrameOval** [5.3.4], **FramePoly** [5.3.6], and **FrameRgn** [5.3.7]. The region's outline is formed by the specified lines and the boundaries of the specified shapes.

3. At the end of the **Region** record is variable-length data (not directly accessible in Pascal) defining the shape of the region in compact, encoded form. The Toolbox maintains this data for you—you'll never need to access or store into it yourself.

4. **rgnSize** is the overall length of this **Region** data structure in bytes, including the variable-length data defining the shape of the region.

5. **rgnBBox** is the region's *bounding box*, the smallest rectangle that completely encloses it.

6. For a strictly rectangular region, the variable-length data is absent; the bounding box completely defines the shape of the region. In this case **rgnSize = 10** (2 bytes for the size and 8 for the bounding box).

Assembly Language Information

Field offsets:

(Pascal) Field name	(Assembly) Offset name	Size in bytes
rgnSize	**rgnSize**	0
rgnBBox	**rgnBBox**	2
————	**rgnData**	10

4.1.6 Defining Regions

Definitions

function	NewRgn	
	: RgnHandle;	{Handle to new region}
procedure	OpenRgn;	
procedure	CloseRgn	
	(theRegion : RgnHandle);	{Handle to be set to defined region}
procedure	DisposeRgn	
	(theRegion : RgnHandle);	{Handle to region to be destroyed}

Notes

1. **NewRgn** creates a new **Region** record [4.1.5] and returns a handle to it. The new region is initially empty.

2. **OpenRgn** begins a new region definition; subsequent calls to the line-drawing routines **Move, MoveTo, Line**, and **LineTo** [5.2.4] and the shape-drawing routines **FrameRect** [5.3.2], **FrameRoundRect** [5.3.3], **FrameOval** [5.3.4], **FramePoly** [5.3.6], and **FrameRgn** [5.3.7] will be accumulated to define the shape of the region.

3. The graphics pen is hidden [5.2.3] while a region is open; the line- and shape-drawing operations that define the region will not appear on the screen.

4. The region's outline is infinitely thin, and is unaffected by pen characteristics such as size, pattern, and mode [5.2.1].

5. Only one region may be open at a time; don't attempt to open another without closing the one that's already open.

6. **CloseRgn** closes the region definition currently open and sets an existing region to the defined shape.

7. The region must already have been created previously with **NewRgn.**

8. The graphics pen is reshown [5.2.3]; subsequent line- and shape-drawing operations will apear on the screen instead of being accumulated into the region definition.

9. **DisposeRgn** destroys a **Region** record and deallocates the memory space it occupies. The region is no longer usable after this operation.

10. The trap macro for **DisposeRgn** is spelled **_DisposRgn.**

Assembly Language Information

Trap macros:

(Pascal) Routine name	(Assembly) Trap macro	Trap word
NewRgn	**_NewRgn**	**$A8D8**
OpenRgn	**_OpenRgn**	**$A8DA**
CloseRgn	**_CloseRgn**	**$A8DB**
DisposeRgn	**_DisposRgn**	**$A8D9**

4.1.7 Setting Regions

Definitions

```
procedure SetEmptyRgn
        (theRegion  : RgnHandle);      {Handle to region to be set empty}

procedure RectRgn
        (theRegion  : RgnHandle;       {Handle to region to be set}
        theRect    : Rect);           {Rectangle to set it to}

procedure SetRectRgn
        (theRegion  : RgnHandle;       {Handle to region to be set}
        left       : INTEGER;         {Left coordinate of rectangle to set it to}
        top        : INTEGER;         {Top coordinate of rectangle to set it to}
        right      : INTEGER;         {Right coordinate of rectangle to set it to}
        bottom     : INTEGER);        {Bottom coordinate of rectangle to set it to}

procedure CopyRgn
        (fromRegion : RgnHandle;       {Region to be copied}
        toRegion   : RgnHandle);      {Region to copy it to}
```

Notes

1. **SetEmptyRgn** sets an existing region to empty, erasing its previous structure.

2. The region remains in existence, but becomes empty (encloses no pixels). The **Region** record itself [4.1.5] is not destroyed.

3. **RectRgn** and **SetRectRgn** both set an existing region to a specified rectangle. For **RectRgn,** the rectangle is given as a **Rect** record [4.1.2]; for **SetRectRgn,** it's given as four separate coordinates.

4. If **right ≤ left** or **bottom ≤ top,** the region is set to empty.

5. **CopyRgn** sets an existing region to the same shape as another.

6. In each case, the destination region (**theRegion** or **toRegion**) must already have been created previously with **NewRgn** [4.1.6].

7. The trap macro for **SetRectRgn** is spelled **_SetRecRgn.**

Assembly Language Information

Trap macros:

(Pascal) Routine name	(Assembly) Trap macro	Trap word
SetEmptyRgn	**_SetEmptyRgn**	**$A8DD**
RectRgn	**_RectRgn**	**$A8DF**
SetRectRgn	**_SetRecRgn**	**$A8DE**
CopyRgn	**_CopyRgn**	**$A8DC**

4.2 Graphical Foundations

4.2.1 Bit Maps

Definitions

```
BitMap = record
              baseAddr : Ptr;              {Pointer to bit image}
              rowBytes : INTEGER;          {Row width in bytes}
              bounds   : Rect              {Boundary rectangle}
            end;
var
   ScreenBits : BitMap;                    {Bit map for Macintosh screen}
```

Notes

1. **baseAddr** is a pointer to the bit map's *bit image*. The bits of the bit image define the pixels of the bit map.

2. **rowBytes** is the bit map's *row width*, the number of bytes in each row of the bit image.

3. The row width should always be even, representing a whole number of 16-bit words.

4. **bounds** is the bit map's *boundary rectangle*, which defines its extent and coordinate system.

5. The first pixel in the bit image lies just inside the top-left corner of the boundary rectangle.

6. The width of the boundary rectangle must not exceed the row width of the bit image in bits (that is, **8 * rowBytes**). Its height must not exceed the number of rows in the bit image.

7. Any bits of the bit image that lie beyond the right or bottom edge of the boundary rectangle are ignored.

8. The global variable **ScreenBits** holds the *screen map*, a bit map representing the Macintosh screen.

9. The screen map's bit image is the screen buffer in memory; its row width is 64 bytes (512 bits); its boundary rectangle extends from coordinates (**0, 0**) at the top-left to (**512, 342**) at the bottom-right. On a Macintosh XL, its row width is 90 bytes (720 bits) and its boundary rectangle extends from (**0, 0**) to (**720, 364**).

10. To access the screen map in assembly language, find the pointer to QuickDraw's globals at the address contained in register **A5,** then locate the variable relative to that pointer using the offset constant **ScreenBits** (below). See [4.3.1] for further discussion.

Assembly Language Information

Field offsets:

(Pascal) Field name	(Assembly) Offset name	Size in bytes
baseAddr	**baseAddr**	**0**
rowBytes	**rowBytes**	**4**
bounds	**bounds**	**6**

Assembly-language constant:

Name	Value	Meaning
BitMapRec	**14**	Size of bit map record in bytes

QuickDraw global variable:

Name	Offset in bytes
ScreenBits	**−122**

4.2.2 Graphics Ports

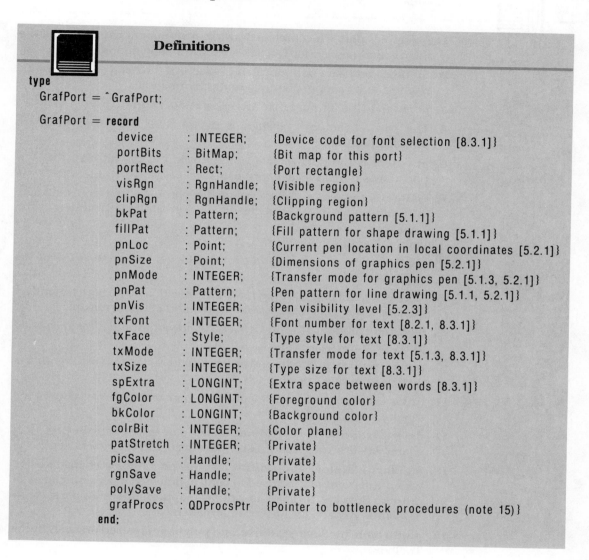

Definitions

```
type
    GrafPort = ^GrafPort;

    GrafPort = record
                device     : INTEGER;    {Device code for font selection [8.3.1]}
                portBits   : BitMap;     {Bit map for this port}
                portRect   : Rect;       {Port rectangle}
                visRgn     : RgnHandle;  {Visible region}
                clipRgn    : RgnHandle;  {Clipping region}
                bkPat      : Pattern;    {Background pattern [5.1.1]}
                fillPat    : Pattern;    {Fill pattern for shape drawing [5.1.1]}
                pnLoc      : Point;      {Current pen location in local coordinates [5.2.1]}
                pnSize     : Point;      {Dimensions of graphics pen [5.2.1]}
                pnMode     : INTEGER;    {Transfer mode for graphics pen [5.1.3, 5.2.1]}
                pnPat      : Pattern;    {Pen pattern for line drawing [5.1.1, 5.2.1]}
                pnVis      : INTEGER;    {Pen visibility level [5.2.3]}
                txFont     : INTEGER;    {Font number for text [8.2.1, 8.3.1]}
                txFace     : Style;      {Type style for text [8.3.1]}
                txMode     : INTEGER;    {Transfer mode for text [5.1.3, 8.3.1]}
                txSize     : INTEGER;    {Type size for text [8.3.1]}
                spExtra    : LONGINT;    {Extra space between words [8.3.1]}
                fgColor    : LONGINT;    {Foreground color}
                bkColor    : LONGINT;    {Background color}
                colrBit    : INTEGER;    {Color plane}
                patStretch : INTEGER;    {Private}
                picSave    : Handle;     {Private}
                rgnSave    : Handle;     {Private}
                polySave   : Handle;     {Private}
                grafProcs  : QDProcsPtr  {Pointer to bottleneck procedures (note 15)}
            end;
```

Notes

1. A graphics port is a complete drawing environment containing all the information needed for QuickDraw drawing operations.

2. Graphics ports are nonrelocatable objects in the heap and are always referred to by simple pointers rather than handles.

3. **portBits** is the bit map that this graphics port draws into.

4. The port's *boundary rectangle* is the same as that of its bit map, **portBits.bounds**.

5. **portRect** is the *port rectangle*, the portion of the bit map that the port draws into, in local coordinates.

6. **visRgn** is the port's *visible region*, the portion of the port rectangle currently exposed to view on the screen. It's maintained privately by the Toolbox to keep track of overlapping windows; never attempt to manipulate this field yourself.

7. **clipRgn** is the *clipping region*, provided for general-purpose use by the application.

8. All drawing in a port is clipped to the intersection of the port's boundary rectangle, port rectangle, visible region, and clipping region.

9. **bkPat** and **fillPat** are the port's *background pattern* and *fill pattern*, used in shape drawing; see [5.1.1].

10. **pnLoc, pnSize, pnMode**, and **pnPat** are characteristics of the graphics pen, used in line drawing; see [5.2.1].

11. **pnVis** is the *pen level*, which controls whether the pen is visible on the screen; see [5.2.3].

12. **device, txFont, txFace, txMode, txSize,** and **spExtra** are the port's text characteristics, which control the drawing of text characters; see [8.3.1].

13. **fgColor, bkColor,** and **colrBit** are the port's color characteristics, which will eventually be used to control drawing on a color display or printer. Drawing in color is not yet supported; see Apple's *Inside Macintosh* manual for further information.

14. **patStretch, picSave, rgnSave,** and **polySave** are used privately by the Toolbox.

15. **grafProcs** is a pointer to the port's low-level drawing procedures (sometimes called "bottleneck procedures"). These procedures are used to "customize" QuickDraw operations; see *Inside Macintosh* for further information.

Assembly Language Information

Field offsets in a graphics port:

(Pascal) Field name	(Assembly) Offset name	Size in bytes
device	**device**	**0**
portBits	**portBits**	**2**
portRect	**portRect**	**16**
visRgn	**visRgn**	**24**
clipRgn	**clipRgn**	**28**
bkPat	**bkPat**	**32**
fillPat	**fillPat**	**40**
pnLoc	**pnLoc**	**48**
pnSize	**pnSize**	**52**
pnMode	**pnMode**	**56**
pnPat	**pnPat**	**58**
pnVis	**pnVis**	**66**
txFont	**txFont**	**68**
txFace	**txFace**	**70**
txMode	**txMode**	**72**
txSize	**txSize**	**74**
spExtra	**spExtra**	**76**
fgColor	**fgColor**	**80**
bkColor	**bkColor**	**84**
colrBit	**colrBit**	**88**
patStretch	**patStretch**	**90**
picSave	**picSave**	**92**
rgnSave	**rgnSave**	**96**
polySave	**polySave**	**100**
grafProcs	**grafProcs**	**104**
portBits.bounds	**portBounds**	**8**

Assembly-language constant:

Name	Value	Meaning
portRec	**108**	Size of graphics port record in bytes

4.2.3 Pixel Access

Definitions

```
function GetPixel
        (hCoord : INTEGER;        {Horizontal coordinate of pixel}
         vCoord : INTEGER)        {Vertical coordinate of pixel}
         : BOOLEAN;               {Is it a black pixel?}
```

Notes

1. **GetPixel** returns the state of a designated pixel in the current graphics port.

2. **hCoord** and **vCoord** are expressed in the local coordinate system of the current port. The pixel returned will be the one immediately below and to the right of these coordinates.

3. The function result is **TRUE** for a black pixel, **FALSE** for a white one.

4. For a graphics port on the screen (such as a window), the result is meaningful only if the given coordinates lie within the port's visible region.

Assembly Language Information

Trap macro:

(Pascal) Routine name	(Assembly) Trap macro	Trap word
GetPixel	_Get Pixel	**$A865**

4.3 Operations on Graphics Ports

4.3.1 Initializing QuickDraw

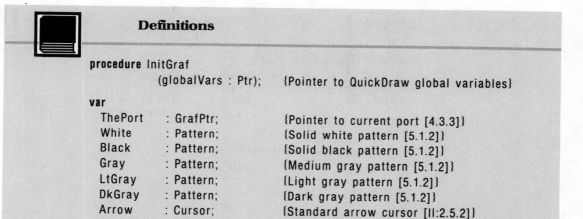

Definitions

```
procedure InitGraf
              (globalVars : Ptr);      {Pointer to QuickDraw global variables}
var
    ThePort    : GrafPtr;      {Pointer to current port [4.3.3]}
    White      : Pattern;      {Solid white pattern [5.1.2]}
    Black      : Pattern;      {Solid black pattern [5.1.2]}
    Gray       : Pattern;      {Medium gray pattern [5.1.2]}
    LtGray     : Pattern;      {Light gray pattern [5.1.2]}
    DkGray     : Pattern;      {Dark gray pattern [5.1.2]}
    Arrow      : Cursor;       {Standard arrow cursor [II:2.5.2]}
    ScreenBits : BitMap;       {Bit map for Macintosh screen [4.2.1]}
    RandSeed   : LONGINT;      {Seed for random number generation [2.3.5]}
```

Notes

1. This routine must be called before any other QuickDraw operation, to initialize QuickDraw's global variables and internal data structures.

2. **globalVars** is a pointer to an area in memory where QuickDraw can store its global variables.

3. In Pascal, **globalVars** should always be set to **@ThePort.**

4. In assembly language, QuickDraw's global variables can be placed anywhere in memory where enough space is available. The parameter passed to **InitGraf** must be the address of the *last* global variable, **ThePort,** in the last 4 bytes of the space reserved for the globals. **InitGraf** will store this pointer at the address contained in register **A5;** all the other globals can then be found at negative offsets relative to this pointer, using the offset constants given in the table below. See Chapter 3 for further discussion.

5. The number of bytes needed for QuickDraw's globals is defined by the assembly-language constant **GrafSize.**

6. Don't call **InitGraf** more than once in the same program.

Assembly Language Information

Trap macro:

(Pascal) Routine name	(Assembly) Trap macro	Trap word
InitGraf	**_InitGraf**	**$A86E**

Assembly-language constant:

Name	Value	Meaning
GrafSize	**206**	Size in bytes of QuickDraw global variables

QuickDraw public global variables:

Name	Offset in bytes
The Port	**0**
White	**−8**
Black	**−16**
Gray	**−24**
LtGray	**−32**
DkGray	**−40**
Arrow	**−108**
ScreenBits	**−122**
RandSeed	**−126**

4.3.2 Creating and Destroying Ports

Definitions

```
procedure OpenPort
          (whichPort : GrafPtr);        {Pointer to port to open}

procedure InitPort
          (whichPort : GrafPtr);        {Pointer to port to initialize}

procedure ClosePort
          (whichPort : GrafPtr);        {Pointer to port to close}
```

Initial values of QuickDraw globals:

Field	Initial value
device	**0** (screen)
portBits	Copy of **ScreenBits** [4.2.1]
portRect	**(0, 0)** to **(512, 342)**
visRgn	Rectangular region **(0, 0)** to **(512, 342)**
clipRgn	Rectangular region **(−32768, −32768)** to **(32767, 32767)**
bkPat	**White** [5.1.2]
fillPat	**Black** [5.1.2]
pnLoc	**(0, 0)**
pnSize	**(1, 1)**
pnMode	**PatCopy** [5.1.3]
pnPat	**Black** [5.1.2]
pnVis	**0** (visible) [5.2.3]
txFont	**0** (system font) [8.2.1]
txFace	Plain [8.3.1]
txMode	**SrcOr** [5.1.3]
txSize	**0** (standard size) [8.3.1]
spExtra	**0**

Notes

1. **OpenPort** initializes a graphics port and opens it for use; **InitPort** reinitializes a port that's already been opened.

2. Both routines set the fields of the **GrafPort** record to their standard initial values, as shown in the table.

3. In both cases, the designated port becomes the current port.

4. On a Macintosh XL, **portRect** and **visRgn** extend to coordinates **(720, 364)** at the bottom-right, instead of **(512, 342)** as in the table.

5. **Open Port** allocates space for the port's internal data structures (the visible region and clipping region); **InitPort** does not.

6. The **GrafPort** record representing the port must already have been allocated previously with **NewPtr** [3.2.1].

7. **ClosePort** destroys a port's internal data structures (visible region and clipping region), but not the **GrafPort** record itself.

8. Call this routine to deallocate the space occupied by the visible and clipping regions before deallocating the port itself with **DisposPtr** [3.2.2].

Assembly Language Information

Trap macros:

(Pascal) Routine Name	(Assembly) Trap macro	Trap word
OpenPort	**_OpenPort**	**$A86F**
InitPort	**_InitPort**	**$A86D**
ClosePort	**_ClosePort**	**$A87D**

4.3.3 Current Port

Definitions

```
procedure SetPort
            (newPort : GrafPtr);     {Pointer to port to be made current}

procedure GetPort
            (var curPort : GrafPtr);  {Returns pointer to current port}

var
  ThePort : GrafPtr;                  {Pointer to current port}
```

Notes

1. **SetPort** makes a designated graphics port the current port; **GetPort** returns the current port.

2. Most QuickDraw operations apply implicitly to the current port.

3. A port must be opened with **OpenPort** [4.3.2] before it can be made current with **SetPort.**

4. The global variable **ThePort** always contains a pointer to the current port.

5. To access variable **ThePort** in assembly language, find the pointer to QuickDraw's globals at the address contained in register **A5;** this pointer leads directly to **ThePort.** See [4.3.1] for further discussion.

Assembly Language Information

Trap macros:

(Pascal) Routine name	(Assembly) Trap macro	Trap word
SetPort	**_SetPort**	**$A873**
GetPort	**_GetPort**	**$A874**

QuickDraw global variable:

Name	Offset in bytes
ThePort	**0**

4.3.4 Bit Map and Coordinate System

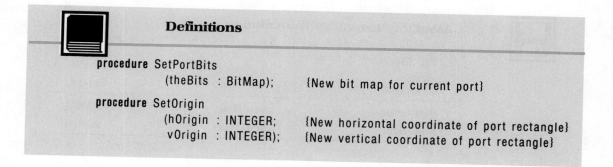

Definitions

```
procedure SetPortBits
        (theBits : BitMap);      {New bit map for current port}
procedure SetOrigin
        (hOrigin : INTEGER;      {New horizontal coordinate of port rectangle}
         vOrigin : INTEGER);     {New vertical coordinate of port rectangle}
```

Notes

1. **SetPortBits** assigns a new bit map to the current port.

2. The bit map **theBits** is stored into the port's **portBits** field [4.2.2].

3. The rectangle **theBits.bounds** becomes the port's boundary rectangle and establishes a new local coordinate system for the port.

4. **SetOrigin** changes the local coordinate system of the current port so as to give the top-left corner of its port rectangle (*not* its boundary rectangle!) the local coordinates **hOrigin** and **vOrigin.**

5. The bottom-right corner of the port rectangle, as well as the boundary rectangle and the visible region, are adjusted to keep the same spatial relationships relative to the port rectangle's new origin.

6. The port's clipping region and pen location are not adjusted. Their coordinates remain unchanged, but are now interpreted relative to the new coordinate system; this changes their spatial positions relative to the port rectangle.

7. **SetOrigin** has no visible effect on the screen.

8. A port's initial bit map (after **OpenPort** or **InitPort** [4.3.2]) is a copy of the screen map **ScreenBits** [4.2.1]. Its initial boundary rectangle, port rectangle, and visible region all extend from coordinates (**0, 0**) at the top-left to (**512, 342**) at the bottom-right, or (**720, 364**) on a Macintosh XL.

9. The trap macro for **SetPortBits** is spelled **_SetPBits.**

Assembly Language Information

Trap Macros:

(Pascal) Routine name	(Assembly) Trap macro	Trap word
SetPortBits	**_SetPBits**	**$A875**
SetOrigin	**_SetOrigin**	**$A878**

4.3.5 Port Rectangle

Definitions

```
procedure MovePortTo
           (leftGlobal  : INTEGER;    {New left edge of port rectangle in global coordinates}
            topGlobal   : INTEGER);   {New top edge of port rectangle in global coordinates}

procedure PortSize
           (portWidth   : INTEGER;    {New width of port rectangle}
            portHeight  : INTEGER);   {New height of port rectangle}
```

Notes

1. **MovePortTo** moves the current port's port rectangle to a new position within its bit map.

2. **leftGlobal** and **topGlobal** are the new *global* coordinates of the port rectangle's top-left corner, and will be converted to the port's *local* coordinate system.

3. The bottom-right corner of the port rectangle is adjusted so that its width and height remain the same.

4. Unlike **SetOrigin** [4.3.4], **MovePortTo** does not affect the port's coordinate system; it simply moves the port rectangle to a new location *within* the existing coordinate system.

5. **PortSize** adjusts the size of the current port's port rectangle.

6. The coordinates of the port rectangle's bottom-right corner are adjusted to give it the new dimensions **portWidth** and **portHeight**. The top-left corner of the rectangle is unchanged.

7. These routines are used by the Toolbox to move and size windows on the screen; application programs normally have no need for them.

8. Neither routine has any immediate visible effect on the screen.

9. A port's initial port rectangle (after **OpenPort** or **InitPort** [4.3.2]) extends from coordinates (**0, 0**) at the top left to (**512, 342**) at the bottom right, or (**720, 364**) on a Macintosh XL.

Assembly Language Information

Trap macros:

(Pascal) Routine name	(Assembly) Trap macro	Trap word
MovePortTo	**_MovePortTo**	**$A877**
PortSize	**_PortSize**	**$A876**

4.3.6 Clipping Region

Definitions

procedure SetClip
        (newClip : RgnHandle);   {Handle to new clipping region}

procedure ClipRect
        (clipRect : Rect);   {Rectangle defining new clipping region}

procedure GetClip
        (curClip : RgnHandle);   {Handle to current clipping region}

Notes

1. **SetClip** sets the current port's clipping region to a specified region, which can be of any shape; **ClipRect** sets it equivalent to a given rectangle.

2. The handle in the port's **clipRgn** field is unchanged, but its master pointer is set to point to the new clipping region.

3. **SetClip** *copies* the region designated by **newClip,** rather than using the region itself.

4. The new clipping region or rectangle is expressed in the port's local coordinate system.

5. **GetClip** returns the current port's clipping region in the handle **curClip.**

6. The handle itself is unchanged, but its master pointer is set to point to a copy of the port's clipping region.

7. A port's initial clipping region (after **OpenPort** or **InitPort** [4.3.2]) extends from coordinates (**−32768, −32768**) at the top-left to (**32767, 32767**) at the bottom-right.

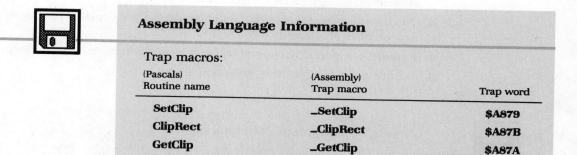

Assembly Language Information

Trap macros:

(Pascals) Routine name	(Assembly) Trap macro	Trap word
SetClip	_SetClip	$A879
ClipRect	_ClipRect	$A87B
GetClip	_GetClip	$A87A

4.4 Calculations on Graphical Entities

4.4.1 Calculations on Points

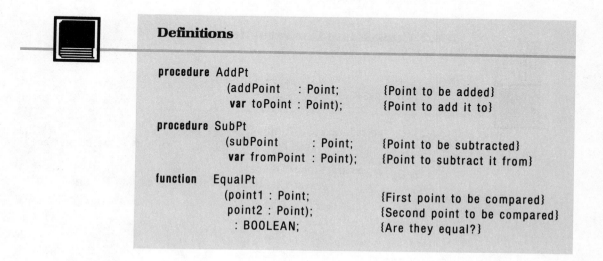

Definitions

```
procedure AddPt
        (addPoint    : Point;        {Point to be added}
         var toPoint : Point);       {Point to add it to}

procedure SubPt
        (subPoint     : Point;       {Point to be subtracted}
         var fromPoint : Point);     {Point to subtract it from}

function   EqualPt
        (point1 : Point;             {First point to be compared}
         point2 : Point);            {Second point to be compared}
         : BOOLEAN;                  {Are they equal?}
```

Notes

1. **AddPt** adds one point to another; **SubPt** subtracts one point from another.
2. The horizontal and vertical coordinates of the two points are added or subtracted independently.
3. The coordinates of the second point are set to the calculated results; the first point is unaffected.
4. **EqualPt** compares two points for equality and returns a Boolean result.
5. Neither point is affected by the comparison.

Assembly Language Information

Trap macros:

(Pascal) Routine name	(Assembly) Trap macro	Trap word
AddPt	_AddPt	$A87E
SubPt	_SubPt	$A87F
EqualPt	_EqualPt	$A881

4.4.2 Coordinate Conversion

Definitions

```
procedure LocalToGlobal
          (var thePoint : Point);     {Point to be converted}
procedure GlobalToLocal
          (var thePoint : Point);     {Point to be converted}
```

Notes

1. These two routines convert a point between local and global coordinates.

2. The local coordinate system involved is always that of the current port.

3. In the local coordinate system, the top-left corner of the port's bit image has the coordinates given by the top-left corner of the boundary rectangle.

4. In the global coordinate system, the top-left corner of the bit image has coordinates (**0, 0**), independent of the boundary rectangle. This provides a convenient basis of comparison between different ports sharing the same bit image, such as the screen.

5. To convert a point from one port's coordinate system to that of another, make the first port current with **SetPort** [4.3.3], convert the point from local to global coordinates, make the second port current, and convert from global to local coordinates.

6. To convert a rectangle, polygon, or region from one coordinate system to another, use **OffsetRect** [4.4.4], **OffsetPoly** [4.4.6], or **OffsetRgn** [4.4.7].

Assembly Language Information

Trap macros:

(Pascal) Routine name	(Assembly) Trap macro	Trap word
LocalToGlobal	**_LocalToGlobal**	**$A870**
GlobalToLocal	**_GlobalToLocal**	**$A871**

4.4.3 Testing for Inclusion

Definitions

```
function PtInRect
          (thePoint   : Point;          {Point to be tested}
           theRect    : Rect)           {Rectangle to test it against}
            : BOOLEAN;                  {Is the point in the rectangle?}

function PtInRgn
          (thePoint   : Point;          {Point to be tested}
           theRegion  : RgnHandle)      {Handle to region to test it against}
            : BOOLEAN;                  {Is the point in the region?}

function RectInRgn
          (theRect    : Rect;           {Rectangle to be tested}
           theRegion  : RgnHandle)      {Handle to region to test it against}
            : BOOLEAN;                  {Does the rectangle intersect the region?}

function PinRect
          (theRect    : Rect;           {Rectangle to pin to}
           thePoint   : Point)          {Point to be pinned}
            : LONGINT;                  {Point pinned to rectangle}
```

Notes

1. **PtInRect** and **PtInRgn** test whether a given point lies inside a given rectangle or region.

2. The test actually applies not to the point itself, but to the *pixel* just below and to the right of it. For example, **PtInRect** will return **TRUE** if the given point lies on the top or left edge of the rectangle, but **FALSE** if it's on the right or bottom edge (since the corresponding pixel is then outside the rectangle).

3. **RectInRgn** tests whether a given rectangle and region intersect. It returns **TRUE** if there is at least one pixel that lies inside both the rectangle and the region, **FALSE** if they have no pixels in common.

4. **PinRect** "pins" a point to a designated rectangle: that is, if the point lies outside the rectangle, **PinRect** converts it to the nearest point along the rectangle's boundary.

5. If the point is already inside the rectangle, it's returned unchanged.
6. The resulting point is returned as a long integer, with its vertical coordinate in the high-order word and its horizontal coordinate in the low-order word. Use **HiWord** and **LoWord** [2.2.3] to extract the coordinates, or typecasting (Chapter 2) to convert the long integer to a **Point.**

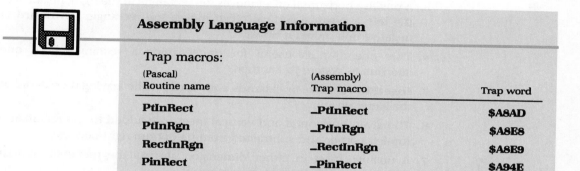

Assembly Language Information

Trap macros:

(Pascal) Routine name	(Assembly) Trap macro	Trap word
PtInRect	**_PtInRect**	**$A8AD**
PtInRgn	**_PtInRgn**	**$A8E8**
RectInRgn	**_RectInRgn**	**$A8E9**
PinRect	**_PinRect**	**$A94E**

4.4.4 Calculations on One Rectangle

Definitions

```
procedure OffsetRect
          (var theRect : Rect;        {Rectangle to be offset}
           hOffset     : INTEGER;     {Horizontal offset in pixels}
           vOffset     : INTEGER);    {Vertical offset in pixels}

procedure InsetRect
          (var theRect : Rect;        {Rectangle to be inset}
           hInset      : INTEGER;     {Horizontal inset in pixels}
           vInset      : INTEGER);    {Vertical inset in pixels}

function  EmptyRect
          (theRect : Rect);           {Rectangle to be tested}
            : BOOLEAN;                {Is the rectangle empty?}
```

Notes

1. **OffsetRect** moves a rectangle to a new position within its coordinate system without affecting its width and height.

2. The given horizontal and vertical offsets are added to both the rectangle's top-left and bottom-right corners.

3. A positive horizontal offset moves the rectangle to the right, negative to the left; a positive vertical offset moves the rectangle downward, a negative one moves it upward.

4. This operation is useful for transforming a rectangle from one coordinate system to another.

5. **InsetRect** shrinks or expands a rectangle while leaving it centered at the same position.

6. The given horizontal and vertical insets are added to the rectangle's top-left corner and subtracted from its bottom-right corner.

7. A positive inset in either dimension shrinks the rectangle in that dimension; a negative inset expands it.

8. If the rectangle becomes empty (**right** $\leq$ **left** or **bottom** $\leq$ **top**), all four of its coordinates are set to **0**.

9. **EmptyRect** tests whether a rectangle is empty.

10. None of these operations has any visible effect on the screen.

Assembly Language Information

Trap macros:

(Pascal) Routine name	(Assembly) Trap macro	Trap word
OffsetRect	**_OffsetRect**	**$A8A8**
InsetRect	**_InsetRect**	**$A8A9**
EmptyRect	**_EmptyRect**	**$A8AE**

4.4.5 Calculations on Two Rectangles

Definitions

```
procedure UnionRect
          (rect1          : Rect;     {First rectangle}
           rect2          : Rect;     {Second rectangle}
           var resultRect : Rect);    {Returns union of two rectangles}

function  SectRect
          (rect1          : Rect;     {First rectangle}
           rect2          : Rect;     {Second rectangle}
           var resultRect : Rect)     {Returns intersection of two rectangles}
             : BOOLEAN;               {Do the rectangles intersect?}

function  EqualRect
          (rect1 : Rect;              {First rectangle}
           rect2 : Rect)              {Second rectangle}
             : BOOLEAN;               {Are the rectangles equal?}
```

Notes

1. **UnionRect** forms the union of two rectangles, the smallest rectangle that completely encloses both of them.

2. **SectRect** forms the intersection of two rectangles, the largest rectangle completely enclosed within both of them.

3. **SectRect** returns a Boolean result telling whether the intersection of the two rectangles is nonempty (encloses at least one pixel).

4. If the intersection is empty, all four coordinates of **resultRect** will be set to **0**.

5. **EqualRect** tests whether two rectangles are equal (agree in all four coordinates).

6. For any of these routines to produce meaningful results, both rectangles must be expressed in the same coordinate system.

7. None of these operations has any visible effect on the screen.

Assembly Language Information

Trap macros:

(Pascal) Routine name	(Assembly) Trap macro	Trap word
UnionRect	**_UnionRect**	**$A8AB**
SectRect	**_SectRect**	**$A8AA**
EqualRect	**_EqualRect**	**$A8A6**

4.4.6 Calculations on Polygons

Definitions

```
procedure OffsetPoly
            (thePolygon : PolyHandle;     {Polygon to be offset}
            hOffset     : INTEGER;        {Horizontal offset in pixels}
            vOffset     : INTEGER);       {Vertical offset in pixels}
```

Notes

1. **OffsetPoly** moves a polygon to a new position within its coordinate system without affecting its shape and size.

2. A positive horizontal offset moves the polygon to the right, negative to the left; a positive vertical offset moves the polygon downward, a negative one moves it upward.

3. This operation is useful for transforming a polygon from one coordinate system to another.

4. The operation has no visible effect on the screen.

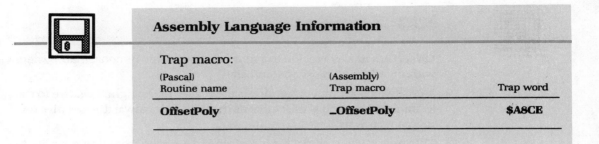

Assembly Language Information

Trap macro:

(Pascal) Routine name	(Assembly) Trap macro	Trap word
OffsetPoly	**_OffsetPoly**	**$A8CE**

4.4.7 Calculations on One Region

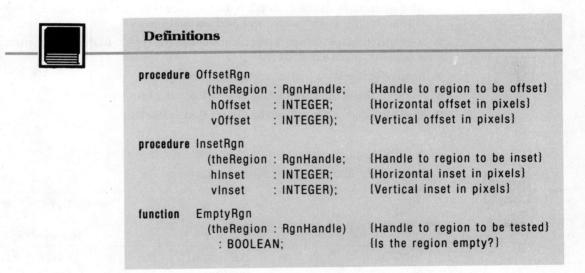

Definitions

```
procedure OffsetRgn
          (theRegion : RgnHandle;      {Handle to region to be offset}
           hOffset   : INTEGER;        {Horizontal offset in pixels}
           vOffset   : INTEGER);       {Vertical offset in pixels}

procedure InsetRgn
          (theRegion : RgnHandle;      {Handle to region to be inset}
           hInset    : INTEGER;        {Horizontal inset in pixels}
           vInset    : INTEGER);       {Vertical inset in pixels}

function  EmptyRgn
          (theRegion : RgnHandle)      {Handle to region to be tested}
           : BOOLEAN;                  {Is the region empty?}
```

Notes

1. **OffsetRgn** moves a region to a new position within its coordinate system without affecting its shape and size.

2. A positive horizontal offset moves the region to the right, negative to the left; a positive vertical offset moves the region downward, a negative one moves it upward.

3. This operation is useful for transforming a region from one coordinate system to another.

4. **InsetRgn** shrinks or expands a region while leaving it centered at the same position.

5. All coordinates in the region's definition are moved inward (toward the center) by the given horizontal and vertical insets.

6. A positive inset in either dimension shrinks the region in that dimension; a negative inset expands it.

7. **EmptyRgn** tests whether a region is empty.

8. None of these operations has any visible effect on the screen.

9. The trap macro for **OffsetRgn** is spelled **_OfsetRgn.**

Assembly Language Information

Trap macros:

(Pascal) Routine name	(Assembly) Trap macro	Trap word
OffsetRgn	**_OfsetRgn**	**$A8E0**
InsetRgn	**_InsetRgn**	**$A8E1**
EmptyRgn	**_EmptyRgn**	**$A8E2**

4.4.8 Calculations on Two Regions

Definitions

procedure UnionRgn
    (region1   : RgnHandle;   {Handle to first region}
    region2   : RgnHandle;   {Handle to second region}
    resultRegion : RgnHandle);   {Handle to be set to union of two regions}

procedure SectRgn
    (region1   : RgnHandle;   {Handle to first region}
    region2   : RgnHandle;   {Handle to second region}
    resultRegion : RgnHandle);   {Handle to be set to intersection of two regions}

procedure DiffRgn
    (region1   : RgnHandle;   {Handle to region to be subtracted from}
    region2   : RgnHandle;   {Handle to region to subtract from it}
    resultRegion : RgnHandle);   {Handle to be set to difference of two regions}

procedure XOrRgn
    (region1   : RgnHandle;   {Handle to first region}
    region2   : RgnHandle;   {Handle to second region}
    resultRegion : RgnHandle);   {Handle to be set to "exclusive or" of two regions}

function EqualRgn
    (region1 : RgnHandle;   {Handle to first region}
    region2 : RgnHandle)   {Handle to second region}
    : BOOLEAN;   {Are the regions equal?}

Notes

1. **UnionRgn** forms the union of two regions, the smallest region that completely encloses both of them.

2. **SectRgn** forms the intersection of two regions, the largest region completely enclosed within both of them.

3. **DiffRgn** forms the difference of two regions, the portion of the first region that doesn't lie within the second.

4. **XOrRgn** forms the "exclusive or" of two regions, the difference between their union and intersection.

5. In each case, the destination region **resultRegion** must already have been previously created with **NewRgn** [4.1.6].

6. In each case, if the result of the calculation is the empty region, **resultRegion** will be set to a rectangular region with all four coordinates equal to 0.

7. **EqualRgn** tests whether two regions are equal (have the same shape, size, and location).

8. Any two empty regions are considered equal.

9. For any of these routines to produce meaningful results, both regions must be expressed in the same coordinate system.

10. None of these operations has any visible effect on the screen.

Assembly Language Information

Trap macros:

(Pascal) Routine name	(Assembly) Trap macro	Trap word
UnionRgn	**_UnionRgn**	**$A8E5**
SectRgn	**_SectRgn**	**$A8E4**
DiffRgn	**_DiffRgn**	**$A8E6**
XOrRgn	**_XOrRgn**	**$A8E7**
EqualRgn	**_EqualRgn**	**$A8E3**

4.4.9 Scaling and Mapping

Definitions

```
procedure ScalePt
        (var thePoint : Point;          {Point to be scaled}
         fromRect     : Rect;           {Rectangle to scale it from}
         toRect       : Rect);          {Rectangle to scale it to}

procedure MapPt
        (var thePoint : Point;          {Point to be mapped}
         fromRect     : Rect;           {Rectangle to map it from}
         toRect       : Rect);          {Rectangle to map it to}

procedure MapRect
        (var theRect  : Rect;           {Rectangle to be mapped}
         fromRect     : Rect;           {Rectangle to map it from}
         toRect       : Rect);          {Rectangle to map it to}

procedure MapPoly
        (thePolygon   : PolyHandle;     {Polygon to be mapped}
         fromRect     : Rect;           {Rectangle to map it from}
         toRect       : Rect);          {Rectangle to map it to}

procedure MapRgn
        (theRegion    : RgnHandle;      {Region to be mapped}
         fromRect     : Rect;           {Rectangle to map it from}
         toRect       : Rect);          {Rectangle to map it to}
```

Notes

1. **ScalePt** scales a point by the ratio of the dimensions of two rectangles.

2. Each coordinate of **thePoint** is scaled by the ratio of **toRect** to **fromRect** in the corresponding dimension. That is, the horizontal coordinate of the point is multiplied by the ratio of the rectangles' widths, and the vertical coordinate by the ratio of their heights.

3. **MapPt** maps a point in one rectangle to the corresponding point in another.

4. The mapping takes into account both the ratio of the rectangles' dimensions and the offset between their top-left corners. The effect is as if rectangle **fromRect** were moved and stretched or shrunk to coincide with **toRect.**

5. **MapRect, MapPoly,** and **MapRgn** map an entire figure from one rectangle to another by mapping each point of the figure as in **MapPt.**

6. In each case, the figure should be entirely contained within the rectangle **fromRect.**

Assembly Language Information

Trap macros:

(Pascal) Routine name	(Assembly) Trap macro	Trap word
ScalePt	_ScalePt	$A8F8
MapPt	_MapPt	$A8F9
MapRect	_MapRect	$A8FA
MapPoly	_MapPoly	$A8FC
MapRgn	_MapRgn	$A8FB

C H A P T E R

5

Quick on the Draw

QuickDraw places at your disposal a wide variety of drawing facilities. You can draw

- *Lines,* using a "pen" of any size and pattern (Figure 5-1a), which produce various graphical effects.
- *Shapes,* including rectangles with square or rounded corners, circles, ovals, arcs, wedges, and polygons of any shape. All can be outlined with any pen or filled with any pattern (Figure 5-1b).
- *Regions* made up of any combination of lines and shapes forming a closed area. A region can have any shape whatever—even one with two or more pieces or with holes in it. For instance, the shaded area in Figure 5-1c could be defined as a single region.
- *Text characters,* in distinct typefaces, sizes, and styles (Figure 5-1d).

In addition, you can take any of these graphical elements and stretch or condense it to desired proportions, horizontally, vertically, or both ways independently. You can "clip" one element to the boundaries of another—for instance, to make one object appear to be hidden behind another. (This is how the Toolbox makes the windows overlap on your screen.) You also can define *pictures* consisting of any combination of these elements and operations, which you can then treat as a unit and redraw in a single operation.

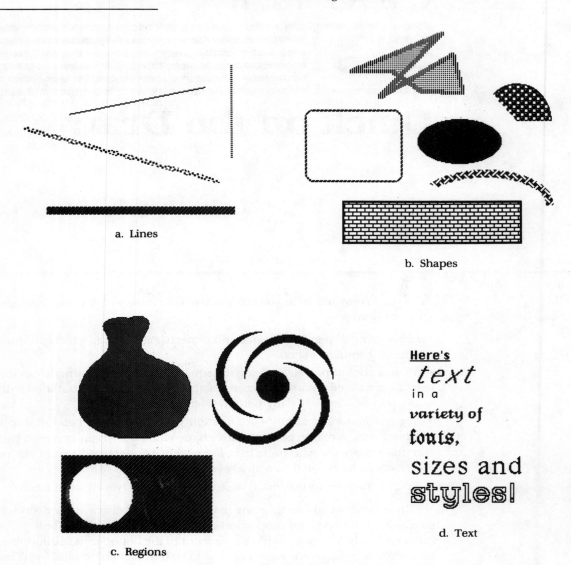

a. Lines

b. Shapes

c. Regions

d. Text

Figure 5-1 QuickDraw graphical elements

Line Drawing

All line drawing in a graphics port is done with the *graphics pen*. Every port has its own pen; you draw lines in the port's bit map by moving the pen from point to point on the coordinate grid. The pen's current location is kept in the **pnLoc** field of the graphics port [4.2.2]; you can read it out at any time with the QuickDraw procedure **GetPen** [5.2.4].

The routines for drawing lines with the pen are **Move, MoveTo, Line,** and **LineTo** [5.2.4]. **MoveTo** simply moves the pen to a designated pair of coordinates, without drawing anything; it's like picking the pen up off the paper (that is, the bit map) before moving it. **LineTo** puts the pen down on the paper and then moves it from its current location to a new set of coordinates, drawing as it goes. The result is a straight line directly from one point to another. The pen is then left at the new location, ready to begin the next line. For example, the statements

```
MoveTo ( 50, 50);

LineTo (150, 50);
LineTo (150, 150);
LineTo ( 50, 150);
LineTo ( 50, 50)
```

draw a square 100 pixels on a side, with its top-left corner at coordinates (**50, 50**).

Everything the pen draws is clipped to the intersection of the port's boundary rectangle, port rectangle, clipping region, and visible region [4.2.2]. The pen will go anywhere you tell it on the coordinate grid, even outside these boundaries, but only those lines (or parts of lines) that fall inside the clipping boundaries will actually be drawn. Anything drawn outside the clipping boundaries is lost: even if you later enlarge the boundaries, the clipped parts of the drawing won't reappear.

The procedures **Move** and **Line** are similar to **MoveTo** and **LineTo,** but interpret the coordinates you give as a motion relative to the current pen location, rather than as an absolute location on the coordinate grid. A positive value for the horizontal coordinate moves the pen to the right, negative to the left; a positive vertical coordinate moves the pen downward, a negative one moves it upward. For example, the statements

```
MoveTo (50,   50);    {Move to starting point}

Line ( 100,    0);    {Draw 100 pixels to the right, }
Line (   0,  100);    {  100 down,                    }
Line (-100,    0);    {  100 to the left,             }
Line (   0, -100)     {  and 100 up                   }
```

draw the same square as in the previous example.

When you shift the origin of the coordinate system with **SetOrigin** [4.3.4], the pen goes along for the ride. The coordinates of the pen remain unchanged, but those coordinates now lie at a new position within the port's bit map. The pen is said to "stick to" the coordinate system. Anything you've already drawn in the port, however, sticks to the image: the existing pixels in the bit image remain the same, but the coordinates of each pixel change because the origin has been changed.

```
procedure StopSign (figureTop  : INTEGER      {Top edge of figure in local coordinates}
                    figureLeft : INTEGER;     {Left edge of figure in local coordinates}
                    scale      : INTEGER);    {Size of scale unit in pixels}


   { Example of simple line drawing.  }


   var
      currentPort : GrafPtr;                  {Pointer to current port [4.2.2]}
      oldOrigin   : Point;                    {Origin of port rectangle on entry [4.1.1]}


   begin {StopSign}

      GetPort (currentPort);                  {Get pointer to current port [4.3.3]}
      oldOrigin := currentPort^.portRect.topLeft;   {Save old origin of port rectangle [4.2.2, 4.1.2]}
      with oldOrigin do
         SetOrigin (h - figureLeft, v - figureTop); {Offset to origin of figure [4.3.4]}

      MoveTo ( 5 * scale, 0        );         {Draw the octagon [5.2.4]}
      Line   ( 8 * scale, 0        );
      Line   ( 5 * scale, 5 * scale);
      Line   ( 0        , 8 * scale);
      Line   (-5 * scale, 5 * scale);
      Line   (-8 * scale, 0        );
      Line   (-5 * scale, -5 * scale);
      Line   ( 0        , -8 * scale);
      Line   ( 5 * scale, -5 * scale);
```

Program 5-1 Line drawing

```
      MoveTo ( 0        ,  5 $ scale);            {Draw the horizontal lines [5.2.4]}
      Line   (18 $ scale, 0       );
      MoveTo ( 0        , 13 $ scale);
      Line   (18 $ scale, 0       );

      MoveTo ( 4 $ scale, 7 $ scale);            {Draw the "S" [5.2.4]}
      Line   (-2 $ scale, 0       );
      Line   ( 0        , 2 $ scale);
      Line   ( 2 $ scale, 0       );
      Line   ( 0        , 2 $ scale);
      Line   (-2 $ scale, 0       );

      MoveTo ( 7 $ scale, 7 $ scale);            {Draw the "T" [5.2.4]}
      Line   ( 0        , 4 $ scale);
      Move   (-1 $ scale, -4 $ scale);
      Line   ( 2 $ scale, 0       );

      MoveTo (10 $ scale, 7 $ scale);            {Draw the "O" [5.2.4]}
      Line   ( 2 $ scale, 0       );
      Line   ( 0        , 4 $ scale);
      Line   (-2 $ scale, 0       );
      Line   ( 0        , -4 $ scale);

      MoveTo (14 $ scale, 7 $ scale);            {Draw the "P" [5.2.4]}
      Line   ( 0        , 4 $ scale);
      Move   ( 0        , -4 $ scale);
      Line   ( 2 $ scale, 0       );
      Line   ( 0        , 2 $ scale);
      Line   (-2 $ scale, 0       );

   with oldOrigin do
      SetOrigin (h, v)                           {Restore old origin [4.3.4]}

end; {StopSign}
```

Program 5-1 (*continued*)

Program 5-1 shows a simple example of line drawing. Procedure **StopSign** draws the stop sign shown in Figure 5-2 into the current graphics port, at any specified location and to any specified scale. The parameters **figureTop** and **figureLeft** locate the figure within the port's local coordinate system; **scale** gives the size of the scale units in which the figure is drawn.

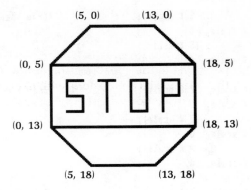

All coordinates are
expressed in scale units.

Figure 5-2 Output of procedure **StopSign**

To simplify our drawing operations, we will temporarily transform the coordinate system to give the origin (that is, the top-left corner) of the figure the coordinates (**0, 0**). First we call **GetPort** [4.3.3] to get a pointer to the current port, which we use to find the origin of the port rectangle,

```
currentPort^.portRect.topLeft
```

Before transforming the coordinates of this point, we first save it in the variable **oldOrigin** so that we can later restore the coordinate system to its original state. Then we use **SetOrigin** [4.3.4] to subtract the coordinates of the figure's origin, **figureLeft** and **figureTop,** from those of the port rectangle's origin. This has the effect of subtracting these same two values from the coordinates of every other point in the port as well: in particular, it transforms the point (**figureLeft, figureTop**), which will be the origin of the figure, to (**0, 0**) as we want.

Now we're ready to draw the figure: first the octagonal outline of the stop sign, then the two horizontal lines, then each of the letters in turn. All our drawing operations are defined in terms of the specified scale unit; overall, the figure is 18 units wide by 18 high. Finally, we restore the port's original coordinate system with **SetOrigin** and exit.

Pen Size

The "pen point" that you draw with is always rectangular in shape, but it can be any size you like. When you open or reinitialize a graphics port, its pen is set to the finest possible point, 1 pixel wide by 1 pixel high. You can then change its dimensions with the QuickDraw procedure **PenSize** [5.2.2]. For example, to make the pen 3 pixels wide by 7 high, you would write

```
PenSize (3, 7)
```

> If you make either dimension of the pen zero or negative, the pen vanishes and then, naturally, won't draw anything.

A port's pen location always refers to the top-left corner of the pen; the rest of the pen "hangs" below and to the right of those coordinates. It's important to keep this in mind when you use pen sizes bigger than (**1, 1**). Lines drawn with **Line** or **LineTo** don't necessarily end at the coordinates you specify: they extend to include the width and height of the pen as well. For example, in Figure 5-3, a line drawn from coordinates (**65, 140**) to (**80, 145**), using a pen 3 pixels wide by 7 high, will extend to coordinates (**83, 152**), the bottom-right corner of the pen.

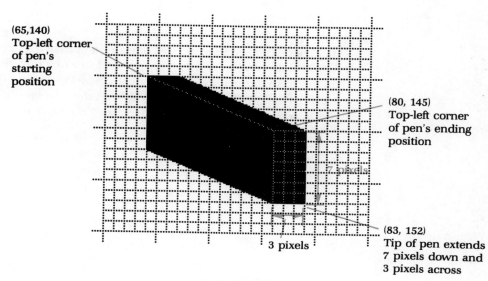

Figure 5-3 Pen size

Hiding the Pen

The pen draws into a port's bit image only when it's *visible*. It also can be *hidden*, in which case none of your drawing operations have an effect on the image. You can hide the pen with **HidePen** and later make it visible again with **ShowPen** [5.2.3]. These routines control the pen's visibility by manipulating the **pnVis** field of the current graphics port.

You might think that **pnVis** would be a simple Boolean field: **TRUE** if the pen is visible, **FALSE** if it's hidden. More correctly, it's an integer called the *pen level;* the pen is hidden if the pen level is negative, visible if it's zero or positive. The pen level is set at **0** when you open a new port, making the pen visible at first. **HidePen** decrements the level by **1,** which hides the pen by making the pen level negative; **ShowPen** increments the level by **1,** undoing the effect of the last **HidePen.** Notice that this doesn't necessarily cause the pen to become visible again: it just restores the pen level to whatever value it had before the pen was last hidden. In effect, the pen level counts how many times the pen has been hidden and not yet reshown. This allows calls to **HidePen** and **ShowPen** to be "nested" to any depth; only when every **HidePen** has been balanced by a corresponding **ShowPen** will the pen become visible again.

This arrangement is useful for writing routines that leave the pen in the same state of visibility as when they found it. If a routine needs to hide the pen, it can restore the previous pen level by calling **ShowPen** before returning. If the pen was visible (**pnVis = 0**) on entry to the routine, this will make it visible again; if it was already hidden (**pnVis < 0**), the routine will leave it hidden at the same depth of nesting as before.

Notice that if the pen level ever becomes greater than **0,** decrementing it with **HidePen** won't make it negative and so won't hide the pen. To keep this from happening, don't ever call **ShowPen** except to balance a previous call to **HidePen.** This will keep the pen level from going above **0,** so the pen will always hide when you tell it to.

Patterns and Transfer Modes

You can achieve interesting graphical effects by varying two more of the pen's characteristics, its *pattern* and *transfer mode*. A pattern [5.1.1] is a special bit image, always 8 pixels wide by 8 high, that can be repeated indefinitely to fill an area in a bit map, like identical floor tiles laid end to end (see Figure 5-4). You can use the graphics pen to paint any pattern by setting the *pen pattern* kept in the port's **pnPat** field [4.2.2]. A port's pen pattern is initially set to solid black, but you can change it to some other pattern with **PenPat** [5.2.2]. The pen will then paint in that pattern, just like the paintbrush tool in MacPaint.

When you paint with a pattern, QuickDraw automatically aligns each "tile" so that its top-left corner falls at an even multiple of 8 pixels from the origin of the port rectangle. This ensures that adjacent areas of the same pattern will blend into one another without creating visible "seams" along the boundaries.

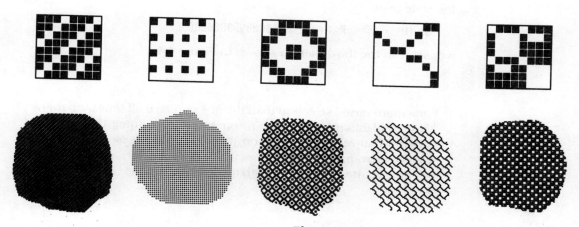

Figure 5-4 Patterns

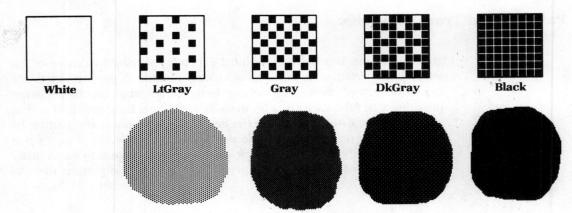

Figure 5-5 Standard fill tones

The Toolbox provides five standard patterns representing a range of tones from solid white to solid black (Figure 5-5). These standard fill tones are available in the global variables **White, LtGray, Gray, DkGray,** and **Black** [5.1.2], which are initialized when you call **InitGraf** [4.3.1]. You can also define your own patterns by storing the desired bits into them with **StuffHex** [2.2.4]. For example, if **myPattern** is a variable of type **Pattern,** the statement

    StuffHex (@myPattern, '3C66C39999C3663C')

will set it to the third pattern shown in Figure 5-4.

> For a more varied selection than the five standard fill tones, a *pattern list* is available in the system resource file containing the same 38 patterns that MacPaint offers on its pattern palette (see Figure 5-6). We'll be learning about resources in the next chapter; you can access individual patterns in the list with the Toolbox routine **GetIndPattern** [5.1.1].

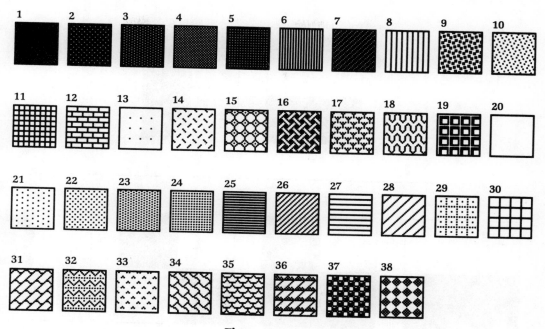

Figure 5-6 Standard pattern list

Besides a pen pattern, every graphics port also has a *background pattern* (**bkPat**) and a *fill pattern* (**fillPat**). The background pattern is used for erasing things. It's normally solid white, but you can set it to some other pattern with **BackPat** [5.1.1]. The fill pattern is used privately by QuickDraw for shape drawings; you'll never need to set it yourself.

A port's *pen mode* [5.1.3] controls the way the pen paints its pattern into the bit map. There are four basic pen modes, and four more that are variants of the basic ones (see Figure 5-7). The most straightforward is **PatCopy,** which simply copies the pixels of the pattern directly to the bit map, replacing whatever was there before. The existing pixels of the bit map are simply "painted over" by those of the pattern, both black and white. This is the mode the pen is set to when you open a brand-new graphics port; to switch to one of the other modes instead, use **PenMode** [5.2.2].

Each of the other three basic pen modes perform a specific operation on the existing pixels of the bit map. They all use the pattern as a "mask" to select which pixels of the bit map the operation will affect. Wherever the pattern has a black pixel (that is, a **1** bit), the corresponding pixel of the bit map will be affected; a white pixel (**0** bit) in the pattern leaves the existing pixel in the bit map unchanged. The pen mode **PatOr** sets the selected bits in the bit map to black, **PatBic** ("bit clear") clears them to white, and **PatXOr** ("exclusive or") inverts them from one color to the other.

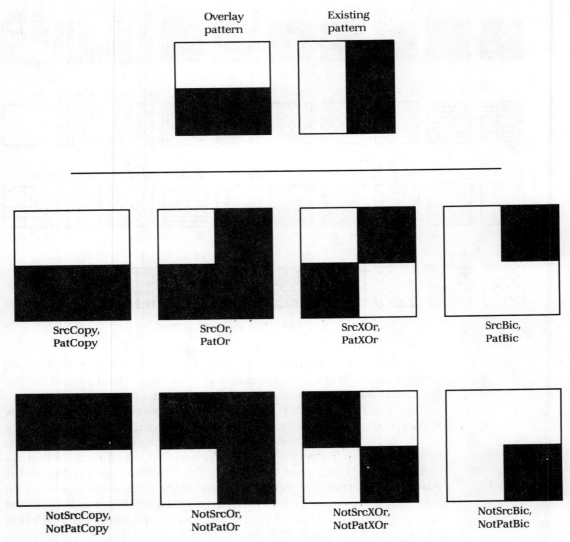

Figure 5-7 Transfer modes

The four variant pen modes work the same as the four basic ones, but reverse the roles of the white and black pixels in the pattern. So **NotPatCopy** paints the inverse of the pattern: white pixels where the pattern has black, and vice versa. **NotPatOr, NotPatXOr,** and **NotPatBic** perform the same operations as their counterparts described, but they affect only those pixels in the bit map corresponding to white in the pattern, leaving those corresponding to black unchanged. (The bits of the pattern itself aren't inverted, they're just interpreted the opposite way.)

Together, the pen's location, size, pattern, and mode make up the port's *pen state*. If you have to change any of the pen's characteristics for any reason, you can save the old state with **GetPenState** and restore it later with **SetPenState** [5.2.1]. The routine **PenNormal** [5.2.2] resets the pen to its initial state: 1 pixel wide by 1 high, with a solid black pattern and a pen mode of **PatCopy.**

Direct Bit Transfer

QuickDraw's fundamental drawing operation, which all the others are based on, is **CopyBits** [5.1.4]. It copies pixels directly from any rectangle in one bit map (the source) to any rectangle in another (the destination), in any of the eight transfer modes and with optional scaling and clipping. You can use **CopyBits** to "stamp" a copy of a small bit image into a designated location in another. For example, to stamp the pointing hand of Figure 4-3, which we defined in the last chapter as a bit map named **theMap,** into a larger bit map named **theCanvas** at coordinates (**85, 60**), you could write

```
SetRect  (atRect, 85, 60, 103, 72);
CopyBits (theMap, theCanvas,
          theMap.bounds, atRect,
          SrcCopy, NIL)
```

(In this example the rectangle you're copying from is **theMap.bounds,** the entire boundary rectangle of the source bit map; you could also specify a smaller source rectangle to transfer just a part of the bit map instead of the whole thing.)

Notice that the transfer mode in the example is specified as **SrcCopy,** not **PatCopy** as in the preceding section. **CopyBits** has its own set of eight *source transfer modes* [5.1.3], analogous to the *pattern transfer modes* used with the graphics pen. It's important to keep the two kinds of transfer modes straight, and to use the right kind in a given situation. The pattern modes are for painting patterns with the pen; the source modes are for transferring bits from one bit map to another. As we'll see when we talk about character text in Chapter 8, the characters in a font are also represented as a bit map, so source transfer modes are used for "painting" text characters as well.

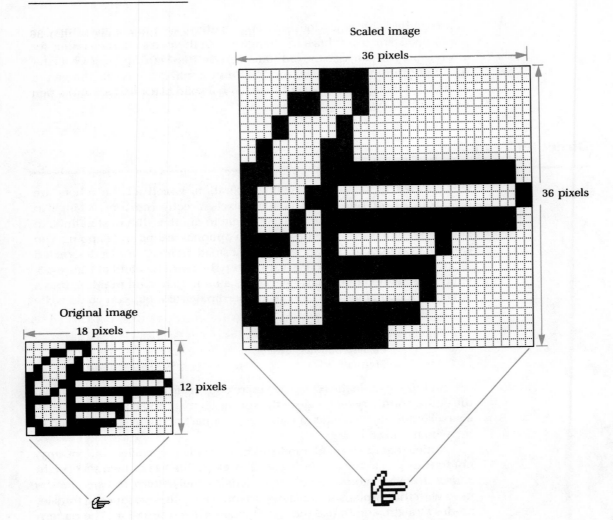

Figure 5-8 Scaling an image

Notice also in the example previous that the destination rectangle **atRect** has the same dimensions as the source rectangle **theMap.bounds**, 18 pixels wide by 12 high. This means the source map will be copied directly, pixel for pixel, to the destination. The two rectangles aren't required to be the same size, however. If they aren't, the source pixels will be stretched or condensed to fit the destination rectangle. For instance, if you used a destination rectangle twice as wide and three times as high, 36 pixels by 36,

```
SetRect (atRect, 85, 60, 121, 96);
```

the source image would be scaled accordingly and would come out looking as in Figure 5-8.

Scaling an image to a different-size rectangle works best if both dimensions of the destination rectangle are exact multiples or divisors of the source dimensions. Otherwise the image tends to come out looking distorted and ugly, like text scaled to an unavailable point size in MacPaint or MacWrite.

QuickDraw has utility routines for mapping standard figures such as points, rectangles, polygons, and regions from one rectangle to another [4.4.9]. These routines transform each point in the original figure, relative to the origin of the source rectangle, to the corresponding coordinates relative to the origin of the destination rectangle, scaled by the ratio of the two rectangles' widths and heights (see Figure 5-9). For polygons and regions, the source rectangle is normally the figure's bounding box (**polyBBOX** [4.1.3] or **rgnBBOX** [4.1.5]). There's also a **ScalePt** routine [4.4.9] that scales a point by the proportion between two rectangles' dimensions, without reference to their origins (Figure 5-10).

The last parameter to **CopyBits** is an arbitrary clipping region, expressed in the coordinate system of the destination bit map. You can use this to confine the bit transfer within any desired boundary of any shape—only those bits that lie inside the given boundary will actually be transferred. If you don't want to specify a clipping region, you can set this parameter to **NIL,** as in our example above. However, **CopyBits** will *always* clip automatically to the boundary rectangle of the destination bit map, and in the common case where the destination is the bit map belonging to the current graphics port (**ThePort.portBits**), it will also clip to the port's port rectangle, visible region, and clipping region.

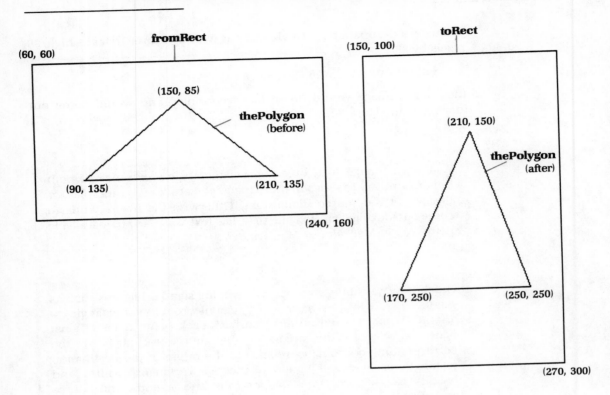

MapPoly (thePolygon, fromRect, toRect)

Figure 5-9 Mapping a figure

A specialized form of bit transfer is **ScrollRect** [5.1.5], which shifts the contents of a rectangle within the current port by a given horizontal and vertical distance. As the name suggests, this operation is useful mainly for scrolling the contents of a window on the screen. The results are clipped to the specified rectangle, as well as to the usual clipping boundaries (boundary rectangle, port rectangle, clipping region, and visible region). Pixels scrolled out of the rectangle at one end are lost forever; the empty space vacated at the other end is "erased" by filling it with the port's background pattern, normally solid white (see Figure 5-11).

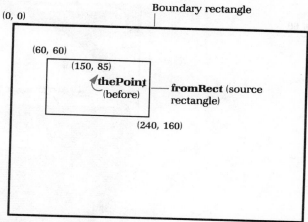

a. Source rectangle and point before mapping or scaling

MapPt (thePoint, fromRect, toRect)

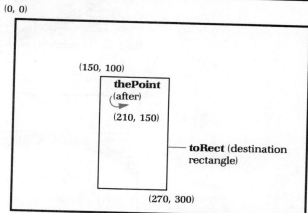

b. The new position of **thePoint** (210, 150) is mapped with reference to the origin of the destination rectangle (150, 100).

ScalePt (thePoint, fromRect, toRect)

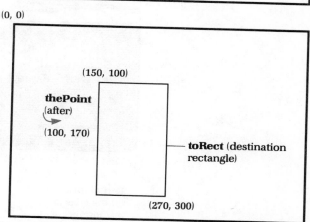

c. The new position of **thePoint** (100, 170) is scaled without reference to the origin of the destination rectangle.

Figure 5-10 Scaling and mapping a point

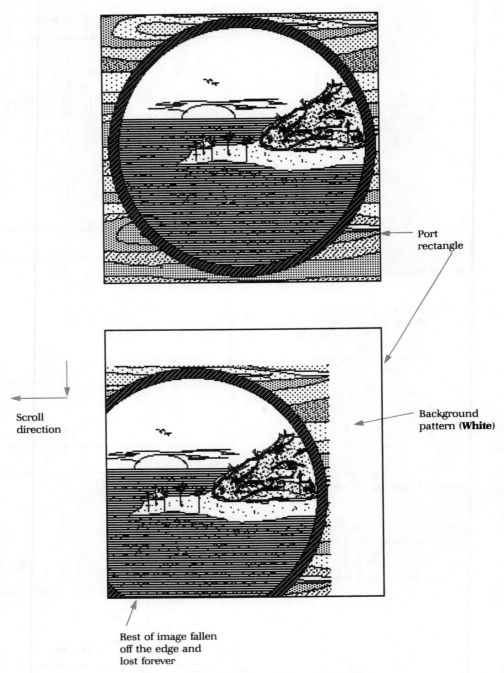

Port
rectangle

Scroll
direction

Background
pattern (**White**)

Rest of image fallen
off the edge and
lost forever

Figure 5-11 Scrolling a rectangle

It's then your responsibility to fill in this cleared area with whatever new information may have been scrolled into the window. As we'll see in the chapter on windows in Volume Two, this involves adding the area to the window's *update region.* **ScrollRect** supports this task by returning a handle to the affected region through its **updateRgn** parameter; you can then add the region to the window's update region with the window-management routine **InvalRgn** [II:3.4.2].

Icons

Icons are a particularly important category of bit image used extensively in the Macintosh user interface. These are images of a standard size, 32 pixels by 32, used (among other things) to represent objects on the Macintosh desktop. The user can manipulate the icons directly by using the mouse (see Figure 5-12). There isn't any special data type representing an icon; its simply a block of 1024 bits (128 bytes, or 64 words) that resides in the heap and is referred to by a handle.

Icons are commonly stored in resource files (Chapter 6) and read in with the Toolbox routine **GetIcon** [5.4.4], but you can also create one for yourself as an

    array [1..32] of LONGINT

and fill in its bits with **StuffHex** [2.2.4]. You can then draw the icon anywhere in the current port with **PlotIcon** [5.4.4].

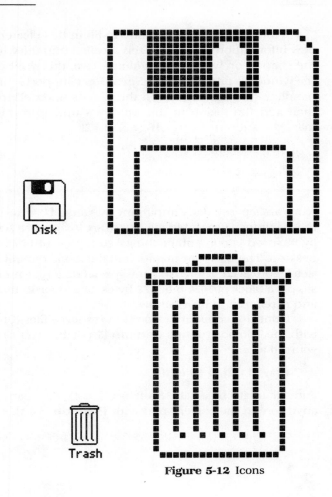

Figure 5-12 Icons

Drawing Shapes

In addition to simple line drawing and bit transfers, QuickDraw can also perform a range of drawing operations on a wide variety of standard shapes:

- Rectangles and squares, with both square and rounded corners
- Ovals and circles
- Arcs and wedges
- Polygons
- Regions of any shape

Shape-drawing operations are always performed in the current graphics port, and the shapes to be drawn must be specified in the coordinate system of that port. There are five standard drawing operations [5.3.1]:

- *Framing* the shape (drawing its outline)
- *Painting* the shape with the port's current pen pattern
- *Filling* the shape with any other designated pattern
- *Erasing* the shape (filling it with the port's background pattern)
- *Inverting* the shape (changing white pixels to black and vice versa)

Even though some of these operations (framing and painting) use the current pen characteristics, they're independent of the pen location and don't change at all. However, these operations *are* affected by the pen *level*, but have no effect on the bit map if the pen is hidden. As usual, all drawing operations are clipped to the port's boundary rectangle, port rectangle, clipping region, and visible region.

Rectangles

The simplest of all QuickDraw shapes is the rectangle, which we discussed in Chapter 4. To illustrate how the various shape-drawing operations work, let's look at how they apply to rectangles [5.3.2]. The equivalent operations on other shapes work in the same general way.

FrameRect (r)

Figure 5-13 Framing a rectangle

The **FrameRect** routine (Figure 5-13) draws the outline of a rectangle without affecting its interior. The outline is hollow: whatever was inside the rectangle before the operation will still show afterward. The outline is drawn with the port's graphics pen, so its appearance depends on the current pen size, pattern, and mode. The pen is then returned to wherever it was before, so the operation has no overall effect on its location.

In framing a shape, QuickDraw automatically adjusts for the current pen size to keep its drawing confined "within the lines." The outline that's drawn won't extend beyond the shape's boundary at the right and bottom, regardless of the pen's size. In general, QuickDraw drawing operations never affect any pixels outside the boundary of the shape being drawn. (The one exception to this rule, as we'll see later, occurs when you frame a polygon.)

PaintRect (r)

Figure 5-14 Painting a rectangle

FillRect (r, Gray)

Figure 5-15 Filling a rectangle

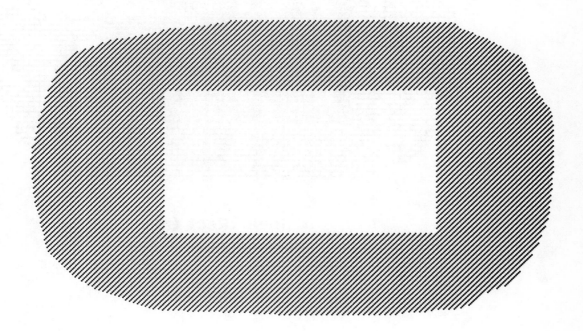

EraseRect (r)

Figure 5-16 Erasing a rectangle

PaintRect, FillRect, and **EraseRect** all fill a rectangle with a pattern. They fill both its outline and its interior. **PaintRect** (Figure 5-14) uses the port's current pen pattern and pen mode; **FillRect** (Figure 5-15) uses a pattern you supply as an argument, with a transfer mode of **PatCopy;** **EraseRect** (Figure 5-16) uses the port's background pattern and the **PatCopy** mode.

Finally, **InvertRect** (Figure 5-17) inverts all existing pixels within the rectangle, changing white to black and black to white. The entire rectangle is affected, both outline and interior.

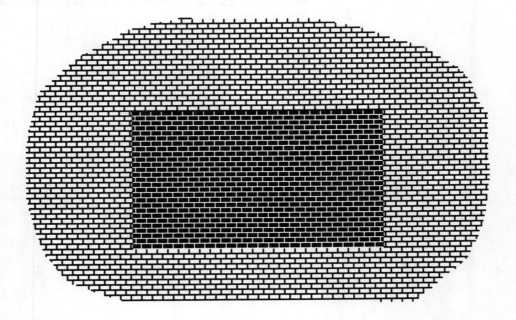

InvertRect (r)

Figure 5-17 Inverting a rectangle

```
procedure Mondrian;


  { Example of simple shape drawing using rectangles.  }


  const
     opRange      = 10;                      {Constant controlling degree of visual fragmentation}
     delayInterval = 500;                    {Length of delay between rectangles}


  var
     currentPort  : GrafPtr;                 {Pointer to current port [4.2.2]}
     oldOrigin    : Point;                   {Origin of port rectangle on entry [4.1.1]}
     windowWidth  : INTEGER;                 {Width of port rectangle}
     windowHeight : INTEGER;                 {Height of port rectangle}
     corner1      : Point;                   {First corner of rectangle to be drawn [4.1.1]}
     corner2      : Point;                   {Second corner of rectangle to be drawn [4.1.1]}
     randomRect   : Rect;                    {Rectangle to be drawn [4.1.2]}
     operation    : INTEGER;                 {Drawing operation to use}
     delayCount   : INTEGER;                 {Counter for delay between rectangles}


  begin {Mondrian}

     GetPort (currentPort);                  {Get pointer to current port [4.3.3]}
     with currentPort^.portRect do
        begin
           oldOrigin    := topLeft;          {Save old origin of port rectangle [4.1.2]}
           windowWidth  := right - left;     {Find dimensions of port rectangle [4.2.2]}
           windowHeight := bottom - top
        end;
     SetOrigin (0, 0);                       {Use origin of (0, 0) for convenience [4.3.4]}
```

Program 5-2 Drawing rectangles

```
repeat

    with corner1 do
        begin
            h := Randomize (windowWidth);        {Generate random coordinates     }
            v := Randomize (windowHeight)        {   for first corner [Prog. 2-1]}
        end;
    with corner2 do
        begin
            h := Randomize (windowWidth);        {Generate random coordinates     }
            v := Randomize (windowHeight)        {   for second corner [Prog. 2-1]}
        end;
    Pt2Rect (corner1, corner2, randomRect);      {Combine to form rectangle [4.1.2]}

    operation := Randomize (opRange);            {Generate random drawing operation [Prog. 2-1]}
    case operation of
        0:
            PaintRect  (randomRect);             {Fill with pen pattern (normally black) [5.3.2]}
        1:
            EraseRect  (randomRect);             {Fill with background pattern (normally white) [5.3.2]}
        otherwise
            InvertRect (randomRect)              {Invert colors [5.3.2]}
        end; {case}

    for delayCount := 1 to delayInterval do      {Wait a while . . . }
        {nothing}

until Button;                                    {Stop when mouse button is pressed [II:2.4.2]}

with oldOrigin do
    SetOrigin (h, v)                             {Restore old origin [4.3.4]}

end; {Mondrian}
```

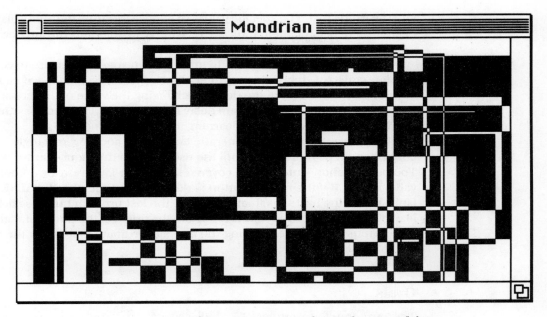

Figure 5-18 Output of procedure **Mondrian**

Program 5-2 illustrates the use of these rectangle-drawing operations to produce a dynamically changing work of "abstract art." The results (Figure 5-18) are reminiscent of the geometric style of the Dutch painter Piet Mondrian. To keep things simple, we adjust the origin of the current port's port rectangle (presumably a window on the screen) to coordinates (**0, 0**), after first saving the previous coordinates in variable **oldOrigin** for later restoration. Then we begin generating random rectangles based on the width and height of the port rectangle, using our earlier **Randomize** function (Program 2-1). Notice how we use **Pt2Rect** [4.1.2] to form the rectangle, so that we don't have to worry about the relative positions of the two points that define it: they can be any two diagonally opposite corners of the rectangle, not necessarily the top-left and bottom-right.

The most interesting graphical effects are produced by using the **InvertRect** operation to paint the rectangle on the screen. If we inverted all our rectangles, however, the image would soon become fragmented into tiny slivers of black and white with no discernible shape or pattern. The effect is more pleasing if we throw in a **PaintRect** or **EraseRect** every so often to restore part of the image to solid black or solid white (assuming those are the port's current fill and background patterns). To decide which drawing operation to use, we call **Randomize** again with a range determined by the constant **opRange.** On the average, out of every **opRange** rectangles we generate, we'll paint one black, erase one to white, and invert the rest. The specific value we choose for **opRange** controls the degree of visual fragmentation we're willing to tolerate: the higher the value, the more fragmentation.

To slow the operation down to mere human speed, we pause to count up to a constant **delayInterval** after drawing each rectangle; we can, of course, vary the length of the delay by changing the value of this constant. (A better way to control a program delay is with the Toolbox routines **Delay** or **TickCount,** which we'll be learning about in Volume Two.)

Then we go back to generate and draw another rectangle, and continue to repeat the cycle until the user presses the mouse button. (The Toolbox function **Button,** also covered in Volume Two, returns a Boolean value of **TRUE** if the mouse button is down at the time of call, **FALSE** if it isn't.) When the button is finally pressed, the last order of business before leaving procedure **Mondrian** is to restore the origin of the port rectangle to its previous coordinates, leaving the port's coordinate system set the way we found it.

Ovals

The oval-drawing routines [5.3.4] all accept a rectangle as a parameter. Instead of drawing the rectangle, however, they draw an oval inscribed *within* the rectangle (see Figure 5-19). The rectangle determines the oval's width and height (in proper mathematical terms, its major and minor axes); if the rectangle is a perfect square, the resulting oval will be a perfect circle.

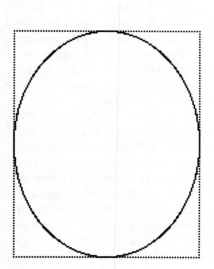
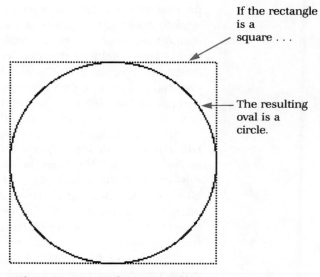

If the rectangle is a square . . .

The resulting oval is a circle.

Figure 5-19 Specifying an oval

```
procedure BigBrother (figureTop  : INTEGER        {Top edge of figure in local coordinates}
                      figureLeft : INTEGER;       {Left edge of figure in local coordinates}
                      scale      : INTEGER);      {Size of scale unit in pixels}


   { Example of simple shape drawing using ovals.  }


var
   currentPort : GrafPtr;                          {Pointer to current port [4.2.2]}
   oldOrigin   : Point;                            {Origin of port rectangle on entry [4.1.1]}
   ovalRect    : Rect;                             {Rectangle for defining ovals [4.1.2]}


begin {BigBrother}

   GetPort (currentPort);                          {Get pointer to current port [4.3.3]}
   oldOrigin := currentPort^.portRect.topLeft;     {Save old origin of port rectangle [4.2.2, 4.1.2]}
   with oldOrigin do
      SetOrigin (h - figureLeft, v - figureTop);   {Offset to origin of figure [4.3.4]}

   SetRect (ovalRect, 0, 0, 8 * scale, 6 * scale); {Set rectangle defining the outer oval [4.1.2]}
   FillOval (ovalRect, Black);                      {Fill outer oval with solid black [5.3.4, 5.1.2]}

   InsetRect (ovalRect, 1, scale);                 {Inset 1 pixel horizontally, 1 scale unit vertically}
   FillOval (ovalRect, White);                      {Fill inner oval with solid white [5.3.4, 5.1.2]}

   InsetRect (ovalRect, 2 * scale, 1);             {Inset 2 scale units horizontally, 1 pixel vertically}
   FillOval (ovalRect, Black);                      {Fill pupil with solid black [5.3.4, 5.1.2]}

   with oldOrigin do
      SetOrigin (h, v)                             {Restore old origin [4.3.4]}

end; {BigBrother}
```

Program 5-3 Drawing with ovals

Figure 5-20 Output of procedure **BigBrother**

Program 5-3 (**BigBrother**) uses ovals to draw the all-seeing eye of Figure 5-20. Just as we did with our stop sign in Program 5-1, we transform the top-left corner of the figure to coordinates (**0, 0**) and draw the figure in terms of a scale unit whose size is specified as a parameter. We draw the eye by first filling the outermost oval with black, then the next one with white, and finally the innermost with black again. The second oval, representing the inner edge of the eyelids, is derived from the outer one by insetting by one scale unit at the top and bottom; we also inset by 1 pixel at the left and right to leave a thin black outline visible. The innermost oval (actually a circle), representing the pupil of the eye, is inset again from there: two scale units at the left and right, 1 pixel to leave a little white space at the top and bottom. As usual, we carefully restore the port's coordinate system with **SetOrigin** before exiting.

Rounded Rectangles

In addition to ordinary rectangles, you can draw *rounded rectangles* [5.3.3] with curved corners instead of square ones. To specify a rounded rectangle, you supply the rectangle itself, along with the width and height of the ovals forming the corners. Each corner will be a quarter of an oval with the given dimensions (see Figure 5-21). QuickDraw won't allow the corner width or height to exceed those of the rectangle itself, even if you try to make them bigger.

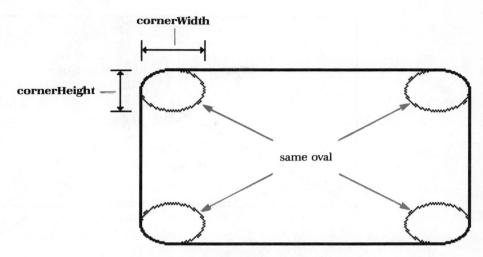

Figure 5-21 Specifying a rounded rectangle

Arcs and Wedges

There's also a set of routines for drawing arcs or wedges of an oval [5.3.5].
You supply a rectangle defining the oval, along with a pair of angles that tell
where the arc begins and how far it extends. The angles can be any whole
number of degrees, measured clockwise from the oval's center, with **0**
degrees at the top, **90** at the right, **180** at the bottom, and **270** at the left.
Negative angles are measured counterclockwise, with **−90** degrees at the
left and **−270** at the right. The arc in Figure 5-22, for instance, could be
specified with either a starting angle of **135** degrees and an arc angle of **90,**
or a starting angle of **225** (or **−135**) and an arc angle of **−90.**

An important point to notice is that the angles defining an arc aren't
necessarily expressed in true circular degrees; they're measured
relative to the oval's defining rectangle. The rectangle's top-right
corner, for instance, always corresponds to an angle of **45** degrees,
whether the rectangle (and hence the oval) is tall and skinny or short
and fat. Only if the rectangle is a perfect square (and the oval a circle)
will the angles be true.

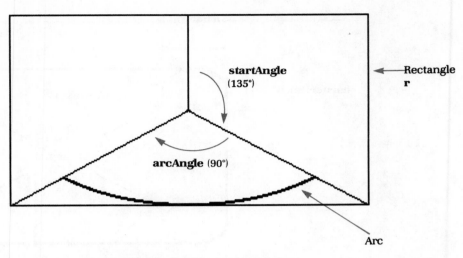

FrameArc (r, 135, 90)

Figure 5-22 Framing an arc

FrameArc draws the specified arc of the oval, as in Figure 5-22. All the remaining drawing operations, though they're called **PaintArc** and so on, actually draw a *wedge* (Figure 5-23) bounded by the arc itself and a pair of lines running from its endpoints to the center of the oval. (Sort of a slice of pi.)

A related utility routine is **PtToAngle** [5.3.5], which measures the angle of a given point from the center of a rectangle in the same kind of rectangle-relative degrees described above. In Figure 5-24, for example, the value of **PtToAngle(thePoint)** would be **135.**

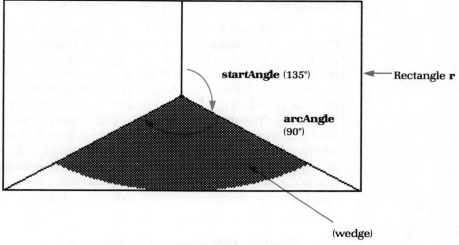

PaintArc (r, 135, 90)

Figure 5-23 Painting a wedge

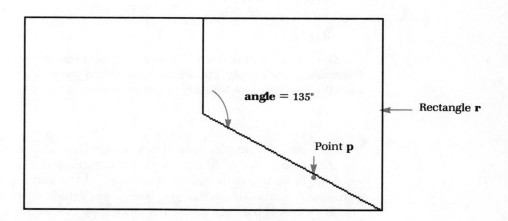

PtToAngle (r, p, angle)

Figure 5-24 Point to angle

Polygons

As we mentioned in Chapter 4, you define the shape of a polygon by drawing its outline with the line-drawing operations **Line** and **LineTo** [5.2.4]. First you have to open the polygon definition by calling **OpenPoly** [4.1.4]. This allocates a new **Polygon** data structure [4.1.3] from the heap and returns a handle you can use to refer to it. While the polygon is open, all your line-drawing operations will be accumulated into the polygon definition. (**OpenPoly** automatically hides the graphics pen, so that the lines defining the polygon won't be drawn into the current port.) When you're finished defining the polygon, you close it with **ClosePoly** [4.1.4], which reshows the pen, calculates the polygon's bounding box, and stores it into the **polyBBox** field of the **Polygon** record [4.1.3]. For example, you can define the polygon shown in Figure 5-25 with the following statements:

```
thePolygon := OpenPoly;

MoveTo ( 150,   50);
Line    (−100,   0);
Line    (   0, 100);
Line    ( 100,   0);
Line    ( −50, −50);
Line    (  50, −50);

ClosePoly
```

Once a polygon is defined, you can draw it into the current port with **FramePoly, PaintPoly,** and so on [5.3.6]. When you're completely through with the polygon, use **KillPoly** [4.1.4] to destroy it.

In framing a polygon, QuickDraw makes no adjustment for the current pen size; it simply traces the outline of the polygon, from vertex to vertex, with the top-left corner of the graphics pen. This means that the outline that gets drawn will extend beyond the polygon's edges at the right and bottom by the pen's width and height. As mentioned earlier, this is the exception to the rule that shape-drawing operations never go outside the boundaries of the shape being drawn.

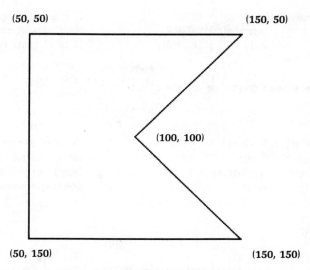

Figure 5-25 Defining a polygon

Program 5-4 (**StopPoly**) shows a version of our earlier stop sign procedure that illustrates how to define and use a polygon. Instead of only drawing the octagonal outline of the stop sign directly, we define it as a polygon by enclosing our line-drawing operations between calls to **OpenPoly** and **ClosePoly.** This prevents the lines from being drawn immediately, and accumulates them into the polygon definition instead.

Since we're now treating the octagon as a shape instead of a simple line drawing, we can use a fill pattern to produce the fancier version of the stop sign shown in Figure 5-26. First we use **FillPoly** to fill the entire octagon with gray; then we draw in its border with **FramePoly**. Next, to create the white background area around the letters, we define a rectangle representing the area, fill it with solid white, and frame it. Finally we use line drawing operations to draw the letters, just as before.

```
procedure StopPoly (figureTop  : INTEGER          {Top edge of figure in local coordinates}
                    figureLeft : INTEGER;         {Left edge of figure in local coordinates}
                    scale      : INTEGER);        {Size of scale unit in pixels}


{ Example showing definition and use of a polygon. }


var
    currentPort : GrafPtr;                        {Pointer to current port [4.2.2]}
    oldOrigin   : Point;                          {Origin of port rectangle on entry [4.1.1]}
    theOctagon  : PolyHandle;                      {Handle to polygon defining outline of sign [4.1.3]}
    theRect     : Rect;                           {Rectangle surrounding letters [4.1.2]}


begin {StopPoly}

    GetPort (currentPort);                        {Get pointer to current port [4.3.3]}
    oldOrigin := currentPort^.portRect.topLeft;   {Save old origin of port rectangle [4.2.2, 4.1.2]}
    with oldOrigin do
        SetOrigin (h - figureLeft, v - figureTop); {Offset to origin of figure [4.3.4]}

    theOctagon := OpenPoly;                        {Open polygon definition [4.1.4]}
        MoveTo ( 5 * scale, 0        );            {Draw the octagon [5.2.4]}
        Line   ( 8 * scale, 0        );
        Line   ( 5 * scale, 5 * scale);
        Line   ( 0        , 8 * scale);
        Line   (-5 * scale, 5 * scale);
        Line   (-8 * scale, 0        );
        Line   (-5 * scale, -5 * scale);
        Line   ( 0        , -8 * scale);
        Line   ( 5 * scale, -5 * scale);
    ClosePoly;                                     {Close polygon definition [4.1.4]}

    FillPoly  (theOctagon, Gray);                  {Fill polygon with gray [5.3.6]}
    FramePoly (theOctagon);                        {Outline the polygon [5.3.6]}
    KillPoly  (theOctagon);                        {Dispose of polygon record [4.1.4]}

    SetRect (theRect, 0, 5 * scale, 18 * scale, 13 * scale);
                                                   {Define rectangle surrounding letters [4.1.2]}
    FillRect  (theRect, White);                    {Clear rectangle to white [5.3.2]}
    FrameRect (theRect);                           {Outline the rectangle [5.3.2]}
```

Program 5-4 Defining and drawing a polygon

```
MoveTo ( 4 $ scale,  7 $ scale);                    {Draw the "S" [5.2.4]}
Line   (-2 $ scale,  0        );
Line   ( 0       ,  2 $ scale);
Line   ( 2 $ scale,  0        );
Line   ( 0       ,  2 $ scale);
Line   (-2 $ scale,  0        );


MoveTo ( 7 $ scale,  7 $ scale);                    {Draw the "T" [5.2.4]}
Line   ( 0       ,  4 $ scale);
Move   (-1 $ scale, -4 $ scale);
Line   ( 2 $ scale,  0        );


MoveTo (10 $ scale,  7 $ scale);                    {Draw the "O" [5.2.4]}
Line   ( 2 $ scale,  0        );
Line   ( 0       ,  4 $ scale);
Line   (-2 $ scale,  0        );
Line   ( 0       , -4 $ scale);


MoveTo (14 $ scale,  7 $ scale);                    {Draw the "P" [5.2.4]}
Line   ( 0       ,  4 $ scale);
Move   ( 0       , -4 $ scale);
Line   ( 2 $ scale,  0        );
Line   ( 0       ,  2 $ scale);
Line   (-2 $ scale,  0        );


with oldOrigin do
   SetOrigin (h, v)                                 {Restore old origin [4.3.4]}

end;  {StopPoly}
```

Program 5-4 (*continued*)

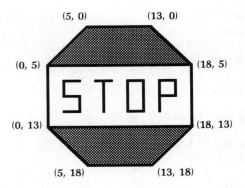

All coordinates are
expressed in scale units.

Figure 5-26 Output of procedure **StopPoly**

Regions

Defining a region is similar to defining a polygon, but it does differ in a few ways. Unlike **OpenPoly,** the analogous routine **OpenRgn** [4.1.6] doesn't create the **Region** data structure for you; you have to do that for yourself first with **NewRgn** [4.1.6]. **OpenRgn** simply begins a new, anonymous region definition in the current port and starts collecting your drawing operations into it. In addition to line-drawing operations, a region definition can also include shape-framing operations such as **FrameRect, FrameOval,** and so on; these operations add the boundary of the framed shape to the boundary of the region. When you close the region definition with **CloseRgn** [4.1.6], you supply the region handle you received from **NewRgn** and QuickDraw sets it to the shape you've specified. The region shown in Figure 5-27 might be defined with the statements

```
theRegion := NewRgn;

OpenRgn;

   SetRect        (theRect, 25, 50, 125, 150);
   FrameOval      (theRect);
   SetRect        (theRect, 75, 50, 175, 150);
   FrameOval      (theRect);

CloseRgn (theRegion)
```

and then drawn with **FrameRgn, PaintRgn,** and so on [5.3.7].

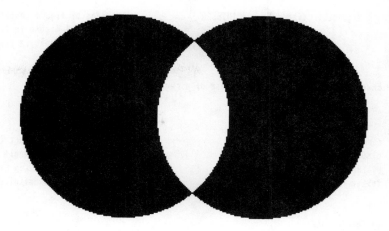

Shaded area is the region.

Figure 5-27 Defining a region

A given port can have only one polygon or region definition open at a time. Always be sure to close one definition (with **ClosePoly** or **CloseRgn**) before opening another.

There are special routines, **RectRgn** and **SetRectRgn** [4.1.7], for the common case of creating rectangular regions; one accepts a rectangle as an argument, the other accepts four separate integer coordinates. You can also copy one region to another with **CopyRgn** [4.1.7] or set a region to empty (erasing its existing structure, if any) with **SetEmptyRgn** [4.1.7]. All these routines merely set the shape of an existing region; you must always create the region for yourself first with **NewRgn.** To destroy a region when you're finished with it, use **DisposeRgn** [4.1.6].

Program 5-5 uses a region to define and draw Big Brother's watchful eye, shown earlier in Figure 5-20. The logic is essentially the same as in Program 5-3, except that the drawing operations that define the eye are enclosed within a region definition delimited by calls to **OpenRgn** and **CloseRgn.** Notice that we must draw the ovals with **FrameOval** instead of **FillOval** as in the earlier program, since framing is the only operation that accumulates a shape into the open region definition. After the definition is complete, a single drawing operation (in this case **FillRgn**) draws the entire region at once, even if it has holes and separate pieces like this one.

```
procedure BigBrother (figureTop  : INTEGER          {Top edge of figure in local coordinates}
                      figureLeft : INTEGER;         {Left edge of figure in local coordinates}
                      scale      : INTEGER);        {Size of scale unit in pixels}



    {  Example showing definition and use of a region.  }



var
    currentPort : GrafPtr;                          {Pointer to current port [4.2.2]}
    oldOrigin   : Point;                            {Origin of port rectangle on entry [4.1.1]}
    ovalRect    : Rect;                             {Rectangle for defining ovals [4.1.2]}
    theEye      : RgnHandle;                        {Handle to region defining the figure [4.1.5]}



begin {BigBrother}

    GetPort (currentPort);                          {Get pointer to current port [4.3.3]}
    oldOrigin := currentPort^.portRect.topLeft;     {Save old origin of port rectangle [4.2.2, 4.1.2]}
    with oldOrigin do
        SetOrigin (h - figureLeft, v - figureTop);  {Offset to origin of figure [4.3.4]}

    theEye := NewRgn;                               {Create a new region [4.1.6]}
    OpenRgn;                                        {Open region definition [4.1.6]}

        SetRect (ovalRect, 0, 0, 8 * scale, 6 * scale); {Set rectangle defining the outer oval [4.1.2]}
        FrameOval (ovalRect);                       {Draw outer oval [5.3.4]}

        InsetRect (ovalRect, 1, scale);             {Inset 1 pixel horizontally, 1 scale unit vertically}
        FrameOval (ovalRect);                       {Draw inner oval [5.3.4]}

        InsetRect (ovalRect, 2 * scale, 1);         {Inset 2 scale units horizontally, 1 pixel vertically}
        FrameOval (ovalRect);                       {Draw pupil [5.3.4]}

    CloseRgn (theEye);                              {Close region definition [4.1.6]}

    FillRgn    (theEye, Black);                     {Fill region with solid black [5.3.7]}
    DisposeRgn (theEye);                            {Dispose of region record [4.1.6]}

    with oldOrigin do
        SetOrigin (h, v)                            {Restore old origin [4.3.4]}

end;  {BigBrother}
```

Program 5-5 Defining and drawing a region

One use for region definitions is for setting a port's *clipping region,* one of the clipping boundaries we discussed in Chapter 4. Recall that the clipping region is a general-purpose clipping boundary that's available for you to use in any way you need. As an example, Program 5-6 uses the clipping region to draw the globe shown in Figure 5-28. Since the routine will change the current port's coordinate origin, pen width, and clipping region, we begin by saving the old values so we can restore them again later. Then we define a region **globeRgn** consisting of the globe's circular outline and install it as the port's clipping region with **SetClip** [4.3.6].

```
procedure Globe (figureTop  : INTEGER      {Top edge of figure in local coordinates}
                 figureLeft : INTEGER;     {Left edge of figure in local coordinates}
                 diameter   : INTEGER;     {Diameter of figure in pixels}
                 edgeWidth  : INTEGER;     {Pen width for drawing figure outline}
                 gridWidth  : INTEGER;     {Pen width for drawing grid lines}
                 nSteps     : INTEGER);    {Number of divisions in grid}


   { Example showing use of a port's clipping region. }


   var
      currentPort : GrafPtr;               {Pointer to current port [4.2.2]}
      oldOrigin   : Point;                 {Origin of port rectangle on entry [4.1.1]}
      oldState    : PenState;              {State of graphics pen on entry [5.2.1]}
      oldClip     : RgnHandle;             {Handle to old clipping region [4.1.5]}
      globeRgn    : RgnHandle;             {Handle to region defining figure outline [4.1.5]}
      ovalRect    : Rect;                  {Rectangle for defining ovals [4.1.2]}
      radius      : INTEGER;               {Radius of figure in pixels}
      stepNumber  : INTEGER;               {Counter for drawing grid}
      stepSize    : INTEGER;               {Size of grid unit in pixels}
      offset      : INTEGER;               {Offset from center for drawing grid lines}


   begin {Globe}

      GetPort (currentPort);               {Get pointer to current port [4.3.3]}
      oldOrigin := currentPort^.portRect.topLeft;  {Save old origin of port rectangle [4.2.2, 4.1.2]}
      with oldOrigin do
         SetOrigin (h - figureLeft, v - figureTop);  {Offset to origin of figure [4.3.4]}

      GetPenState (oldState);              {Save old pen state [5.2.1]}
      GetClip    (oldClip);                {Save old clipping region [4.2.2]}
```

Program 5-6 Using the clipping region

```
globeRgn := NewRgn;                              {Create a new region [4.1.6]}
OpenRgn;                                          {Open region definition [4.1.6]}
    SetRect (ovalRect, 0, 0, diameter, diameter); {Set rectangle defining the outer oval [4.1.2]}
    FrameOval (ovalRect);                        {Draw outline of figure [5.3.4]}
CloseRgn (globeRgn);                             {Close region definition [4.1.6]}
SetClip (globeRgn);                              {Set port's clipping region [4.3.6]}

PenSize  (edgeWidth, edgeWidth);                 {Set pen size for figure outline [5.2.2]}
FrameRgn (globeRgn);                             {Draw outline of figure [5.3.7]}

radius   := diameter div 2;                      {Find radius}
stepSize := diameter div nSteps;                 {Find size of grid unit}
PenSize (gridWidth, gridWidth);                  {Set pen size for grid [5.2.2]}

for stepNumber := 0 to (nSteps div 2) do         {Draw parallels of latitude}
   begin
       offset := stepNumber * stepSize;          {Find offset from center}

       MoveTo (  0   , radius - offset);         {Draw parallel north of equator [5.2.4]}
       Line   (diameter,        0    );

       MoveTo (  0   , radius + offset);         {Draw parallel south of equator [5.2.4]}
       Line   (diameter,        0    )
   end;

for stepNumber := (nSteps div 2) downto 0 do     {Draw meridians of longitude}
   begin
       offset := stepNumber * stepSize;          {Find offset from center}
       SetRect (ovalRect,                        {Set rectangle defining oval [4.1.2]: }
                    radius - offset,             {   from west of prime meridian     }
                    0,                           {       at north pole               }
                    radius + offset,             {   to east of prime meridian       }
                    diameter);                   {       at south pole               }
       FrameOval (ovalRect)                      {Draw the meridians [5.3.4]}
   end;
MoveTo (radius,    0  );                          {Draw prime meridian from north}
Line   (  0  , diameter);                         {   to south pole [5.2.4]         }

SetClip    (oldClip);                             {Restore old clipping region [4.3.6]}
SetPenState (oldState);                           {Restore old pen state [5.2.1]}
with oldOrigin do
   SetOrigin (h, v);                              {Restore old origin [4.3.4]}

DisposeRgn  (globeRgn)                            {Dispose of region record [4.1.6]}

end;  {Globe}
```

Program 5-6 (*continued*)

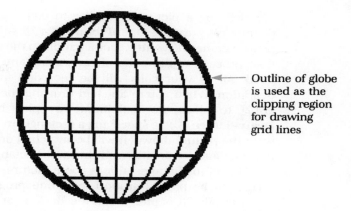

Outline of globe is used as the clipping region for drawing grid lines

Figure 5-28 Output of procedure **Globe**

After drawing the outline on the screen with **FrameRgn** [5.3.7], we proceed to draw in the parallels of latitude. This is where the circular clipping region comes in handy. Instead of calculating the endpoints where each parallel meets the circumference of the globe, we simply draw a series of horizontal lines straight across the full width of the figure, letting QuickDraw clip them to the right lengths for us. For the meridians of longitude, we use a series of ovals of decreasing widths running from north pole to south. A final straight line drawn vertically between the poles marks the prime meridian; then all that remains is to restore the port's original clipping region, pen size, and coordinate origin and dispose of the region **globeRgn.**

Pictures

Pictures is a very powerful, general mechanism for defining and using graphical images of arbitrary complexity. A picture is like a tape recording of a sequence of QuickDraw calls. Once you've defined it, you can "play back" the recording at any time, duplicating the original sequence of calls and redrawing the picture.

Like a polygon or a region, a picture is represented by a variable-length data structure (in this case, a record of type **Picture** [5.4.1]). It consists of a **picSize** field giving the overall length of the structure in bytes, a **picFrame** rectangle analogous to the polygon's or region's bounding box, and an indefinite amount of additional data defining the picture's contents. A picture differs conceptually from a polygon or region, however, in that it represents a dynamic sequence of QuickDraw operations, not just a static shape on the coordinate grid.

Defining a picture is similar to defining a polygon. You open the definition by calling **OpenPicture** [5.4.2], supplying a rectangle for the picture frame and getting back a handle to the new picture record. You can then proceed to draw the picture, using any QuickDraw operations you need. All of your calls will be recorded for posterity in the picture definition. When you're finished drawing the picture, call **ClosePicture** [5.4.2] to close the definition. To "play back" the calls later, use **DrawPicture** [5.4.3], specifying a rectangle in the current port where you want the picture drawn; it will be stretched or condensed, if necessary, to make its frame coincide with the given rectangle.

One of the handiest things about pictures is that they allow graphical images to be passed around from one program to another by way of resource files (Chapter 6), or the desk scrap (Chapter 7). The program drawing the picture doesn't have to know anything about its contents, where it came from, or what it represents; all that's necessary is to pass it to **DrawPicture** and the picture will "draw itself." This is what enables you to copy MacPaint pictures to the Scrapbook or paste them into a MacWrite document.

REFERENCE

5.1 Drawing Fundamentals

5.1.1 Patterns

Definitions

```
type
    PatHandle = ^PatPtr;
    PatPtr    = ^Pattern;

    Pattern   = packed array [0..7] of 0..255;    {8 rows of 8 bits each}

    GrafPort = record
                . . . ;
                bkPat    : Pattern;               {Background pattern}
                fillPat  : Pattern;               {Fill pattern for shape drawing}
                . . . ;
                pnPat    : Pattern;               {Pen pattern for line drawing [5.2.1]}
                . . .
              end;

procedure BackPat
            (newPattern : Pattern);               {New background pattern}

function   GetPattern
            (patternID : INTEGER)                 {Resource ID of desired pattern}
             : PatHandle;                         {Handle to pattern in memory}

procedure GetIndPattern
            (var thePattern : Pattern;            {Returns desired pattern}
             patListID      : INTEGER;            {Resource ID of pattern list}
             patIndex       : INTEGER);           {Index of pattern within list}
```

215

Notes

1. A pattern is an 8-by-8-bit "tile" that can be repeated indefinitely to draw lines or fill areas in a graphical image.

2. When drawn in a graphics port, a pattern is aligned with the coordinates of the port rectangle, so that adjacent patterned areas will blend continuously without creating "seams."

3. Use **StuffHex** [2.2.4] to fill in the bits defining a pattern, or read it from a resource file with **GetPattern** (notes 9–11, below).

4. Three patterns are associated with each graphics port [4.2.2]:

   - A *pen pattern* (**pnPat**) for drawing lines and shapes
   - A *fill pattern* (**fillPat**) for filling areas
   - A *background pattern* (**bkPat**) for erasing areas

5. The pen and fill patterns are initially solid black, the background pattern solid white.

6. **BackPat** sets the current port's background pattern.

7. To set a port's pen pattern, use **PenPat** [5.2.2].

8. The fill pattern is used privately by QuickDraw for shape-filling operations [5.3.1]. Don't store into a port's **fillPat** field yourself.

9. **GetPattern** gets a pattern from a resource file (Chapter 6), reads it into memory if necessary, and returns a handle to it.

10. **patternID** is the resource ID of the desired pattern; its resource type is '**PAT** ' [5.5.1].

11. **GetIndPattern** gets a pattern from a pattern list in a resource file (Chapter 6).

12. **patListID** is the resource ID of the pattern list (resource type '**PAT#**' [5.5.2]; **patIndex** is the index of the desired pattern within the list.

13. The pattern itself (not a handle) is returned via the variable parameter **thePattern.**

14. **GetIndPattern** is part of the Pascal Toolbox interface, not part of the Toolbox itself. It doesn't reside in ROM and can't be called from assembly language via the trap mechanism.

15. A set of standard patterns is available in the system resource file and as QuickDraw global variables: see [5.1.2].

Assembly Language Information

Field offsets in a graphics port:

(Pascal) Field name	(Assembly) Offset name	Offset in bytes
bkPat	**bkPat**	**32**
fillPat	**fillPat**	**40**
pnPat	**pnPat**	**58**

Trap macros:

(Pascal) Routine name	(Assembly) Trap macro	Trap word
BackPat	**_BackPat**	**$A87C**
GetPattern	**_GetPattern**	**$A9B8**

5.1.2 Standard Patterns

Definitions

```
var
   White  : Pattern;    {Solid white}
   LtGray : Pattern;    {Light gray}
   Gray   : Pattern;    {Medium gray}
   DkGray : Pattern;    {Dark gray}
   Black  : Pattern;    {Solid black}
const
   SysPatList = 0;      {Resource ID of standard pattern list}
```

Resource IDs for standard fill tones:

Resource ID	Pattern
0	Solid white
4	Light gray
8	Medium gray
12	Dark gray
15	Solid black

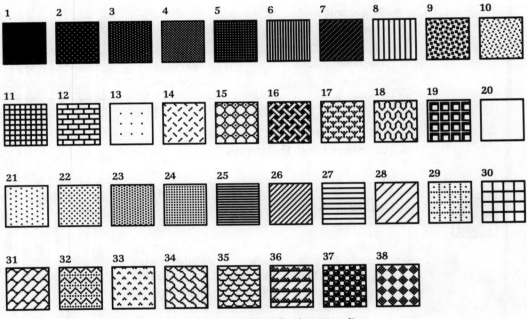

Standard pattern list

Notes

1. The Toolbox provides five standard patterns for fill tones ranging from solid white to solid black.

2. The standard fill tones are available both in QuickDraw global variables and as resources (Chapter 6) in the system resource file.

3. Use **GetPattern** [5.1.1] to load the standard fill tones from the system resource file. The table above shows their resource IDs; their resource type is **'Pat '** [5.5.1].

4. **SysPatListID** is the resource ID of the standard pattern list (see figure) in the system resource file; its resource type is **'PAT#'** [5.5.2]. Use **GetIndPattern** [5.1.1] to access individual patterns in this list.

5. To access the variables containing the standard fill tones in assembly language, find the pointer to QuickDraw's globals at the address contained in register **A5,** then locate the desired variable relative to that pointer using the offset constants given below. See [4.3.1] for further discussion.

Assembly Language Information

Assembly-language constant:

Name	Value	Meaning
DeskPatID	**16**	Resource ID of screen background pattern

Assembly-language global variable:

Name	Address	Meaning
DeskPattern	**$A3C**	Screen background pattern

QuickDraw global variables:

Name	Offset in bytes
White	**−8**
Black	**−16**
Gray	**−24**
LtGray	**−32**
DkGray	**−40**

5.1.3 Transfer Modes

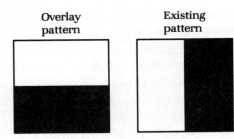

Overlay pattern   Existing pattern

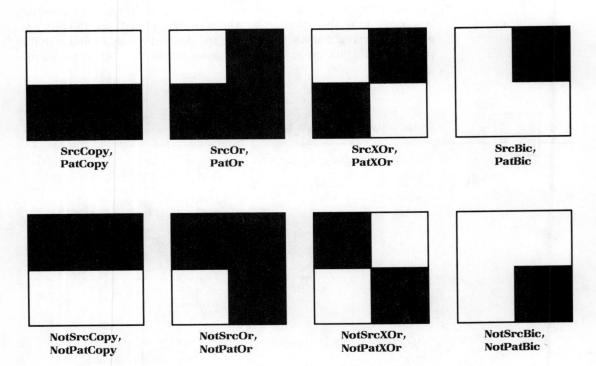

SrcCopy, PatCopy

SrcOr, PatOr

SrcXOr, PatXOr

SrcBic, PatBic

NotSrcCopy, NotPatCopy

NotSrcOr, NotPatOr

NotSrcXOr, NotPatXOr

NotSrcBic, NotPatBic

Transfer modes

Definitions

```
GrafPort = record
        . . . ;
            pnMode : INTEGER;        {Transfer mode for graphics pen [5.2.1]}
        . . . ;
            txMode : INTEGER;        {Transfer mode for text [8.3.1]}
        . . .
        end;
```

```
const
    SrcCopy    = 0;        {Copy source to destination}
    ScrOr      = 1;        {Set selected bits to black}
    SrcXOr     = 2;        {Invert selected bits}
    SrcBic     = 3;        {Clear selected bits to white}
    NotSrcCopy = 4;        {Copy inverted source to destination}
    NotSrcOr   = 5;        {Leave selected bits alone, set others to black}
    NotSrcXOr  = 6;        {Leave selected bits alone, invert others}
    NotSrcBic  = 7;        {Leave selected bits alone, clear others to white}

    PatCopy    = 8;        {Copy pattern to destination}
    PatOr      = 9;        {Set selected bits to black}
    PatXOr     = 10;       {Invert selected bits}
    PatBic     = 11;       {Clear selected bits to white}
    NotPatCopy = 12;       {Copy inverted pattern to destination}
    NotPatOr   = 13;       {Leave selected bits alone, set others to black}
    NotPatXOr  = 14;       {Leave selected bits alone, invert others}
    NotPatBic  = 15;       {Leave selected bits alone, clear others to white}
```

Notes

1. Transfer modes control the transfer of pixels between bit maps, or between a pattern and a bit map.

2. The source transfer modes (**SrcCopy** to **NotSrcBic**) are used for transfers from one bit map to another with **CopyBits** [5.1.4] and for drawing text characters into a bit map [8.3.3].

3. The pattern transfer modes (**PatCopy** to **NotPatBic**) are used for drawing lines and shapes and filling areas with a pattern [5.1.1].

4. Each transfer mode denotes a way of combining pixels from the source (bit map, character, or pattern) with the corresponding pixels from the destination bit map. The resulting pixels are then stored back into the destination.

5. **SrcCopy** and **PatCopy** copy pixels directly from the source to the destination, replacing whatever was there before. Black pixels in the source are set to black in the destination, white pixels to white:

Source pixel	Destination pixel	Result pixel
black	black	black
black	white	black
white	black	white
white	white	white

6. **SrcOr** and **PatOr** set selected pixels of the destination to black. Black pixels in the source select the destination pixels to be set; white source pixels leave the corresponding destination pixels unchanged:

Source pixel	Destination pixel	Result pixel
black	black	black
black	white	black
white	black	black
white	white	white

7. **SrcXOr** and **PatXOr** invert selected pixels of the destination, from white to black and vice versa. Black pixels in the source select the destination pixels to be inverted; white source pixels leave the corresponding destination pixels unchanged:

Source pixel	Destination pixel	Result pixel
black	black	white
black	white	black
white	black	black
white	white	white

8. **SrcBic** and **PatBic** ("bit clear") clear selected pixels of the destination to white. Black pixels in the source select the destination pixels to be cleared; white source pixels leave the corresponding destination pixels unchanged:

Source pixel	Destination pixel	Result pixel
black	black	white
black	white	white
white	black	black
white	white	white

9. The **NotSrc** and **NotPat** series of modes reverse the roles of black and white source pixels in the tables above.

10. Two transfer modes are associated with each graphics port [4.2.2]:

   • A *pen mode* (**pnMode**) for drawing lines and shapes [5.2.1]
   • A *text mode* (**txMode**) for drawing text characters [8.3.1]

11. The pen mode should be one of the pattern transfer modes, the text mode one of the source transfer modes.

12. To set a port's pen mode, use **PenMode** [5.2.2]; to set the text mode, use **TextMode** [8.3.2].

Assembly Language Information

Field offsets in a graphics port:

(Pascal) Field name	(Assembly) Offset name	Offset in bytes
pnMode	**pnMode**	**56**
txMode	**txMode**	**72**

Assembly-language constants:

Name	Value	Meaning
SrcCopy	**0**	Copy source to destination
SrcOr	**1**	Set selected bits to black
SrcXOr	**2**	Invert selected bits
SrcBic	**3**	Clear selected bits to white
NotSrcCopy	**4**	Copy inverted source to destination
NotSrcOr	**5**	Leave selected bits alone, set others to black
NotSrcXOr	**6**	Leave selected bits alone, invert others
NotSrcBic	**7**	Leave selected bits alone, clear others to white
PatCopy	**8**	Copy pattern to destination
PatOr	**9**	Set selected bits to black
PatXOr	**10**	Invert selected bits
PatBic	**11**	Clear selected bits to white
NotPatCopy	**12**	Copy inverted pattern to destination
NotPatOr	**13**	Leave selected bits alone, set others to black
NotPatXOr	**14**	Leave selected bits alone, invert others
NotPatBic	**15**	Leave selected bits alone, clear others to white

5.1.4 Low-Level Bit Transfer

Definitions

```
procedure CopyBits
          (fromBitMap : BitMap;        {Bit map to copy from}
           toBitMap   : BitMap;        {Bit map to copy to}
           fromRect   : Rect;          {Rectangle to copy from}
           toRect     : Rect;          {Rectangle to copy to}
           mode       : INTEGER;       {Transfer mode}
           clipTo     : RgnHandle);    {Region to clip to}
```

Notes

1. **CopyBits** transfers pixels from one bit map to another, in any transfer mode and with any specified scaling and clipping.

2. **fromBitMap** is the source bit map for the transfer, **toBitMap** the destination.

3. **mode** specifies the transfer mode, and should be one of the eight source transfer modes [5.1.3].

4. **fromRect** tells which pixels of the source bit map to transfer; **toRect** tells where in the destination bit map to transfer them to.

5. Each of the two rectangles is expressed in the local coordinate system of the corresponding bit map.

6. If the dimensions of the two rectangles don't match, the contents of the source rectangle are scaled to the width and height of the destination rectangle.

7. The transfer operation is clipped to the destination bit map's boundary rectangle. If the destination is the bit map belonging to the current port, the transfer is clipped to the port rectangle and the port's visible and clipping regions as well.

8. **clipTo** is an additional clipping region to be used for this transfer only, expressed in the destination bit map's coordinate system. If **clipTo** = **NIL,** no additional clipping region will be used.

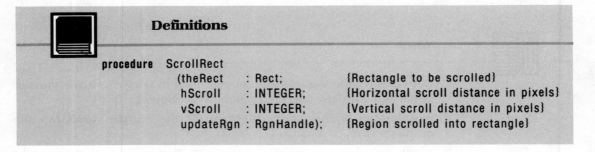

Assembly Language Information

Trap macros:

(Pascal) Routine name	(Assembly) Trap macro	Trap word
CopyBits	**_CopyBits**	**$A8EC**

5.1.5 Scrolling in a Bit Map

Definitions

```
procedure  ScrollRect
            (theRect   : Rect;          {Rectangle to be scrolled}
             hScroll   : INTEGER;       {Horizontal scroll distance in pixels}
             vScroll   : INTEGER;       {Vertical scroll distance in pixels}
             updateRgn : RgnHandle);    {Region scrolled into rectangle}
```

Notes

1. **ScrollRect** shifts pixels horizontally and vertically within the bit map of the current port.

2. **theRect** is a rectangle in the local coordinate system of the current port. The pixels affected will be those within the intersection of this rectangle with the port's boundary rectangle, port rectangle, visible region, and clipping region.

3. Pixels scrolled out of this region are lost irretrievably; the new space scrolled in at the other end is filled with the port's background pattern (**bkPat** [5.1.1]).

4. **hScroll** and **vScroll** give the horizontal and vertical scrolling distance, in pixels.

5. Positive values of **hScroll** scroll to the right, negative to the left; positive **vScroll** values scroll downward, negative values scroll upward.

6. Scrolling doesn't affect the port's coordinate system; it simply shifts the scrolled pixels to new coordinates within the port. To restore the pixels to their previous coordinates, follow **ScrollBits** with **SetOrigin** [4.3.4] to adjust the port's coordinate system.

7. The coordinates of the port's graphics pen [5.2.1] aren't affected by scrolling, so it remains at the same position in the port while the image scrolls away from it. Adjusting the coordinate system with **SetOrigin** will bring the pen back to its previous position relative to the image.

8. The region handle **updateRgn** is set to the area cleared to the background pattern as a result of scrolling. If the port is a window on the screen, this region can be added to the window's update region with **InvalRgn** [II:3.4.2], forcing the contents of the scrolled-in area to be drawn on the screen.

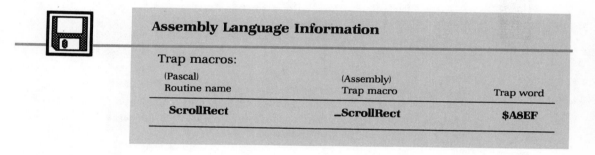

Assembly Language Information

Trap macros:

(Pascal) Routine name	(Assembly) Trap macro	Trap word
ScrollRect	**_ScrollRect**	**$A8EF**

5.2 Line Drawing

5.2.1 Pen Characteristics

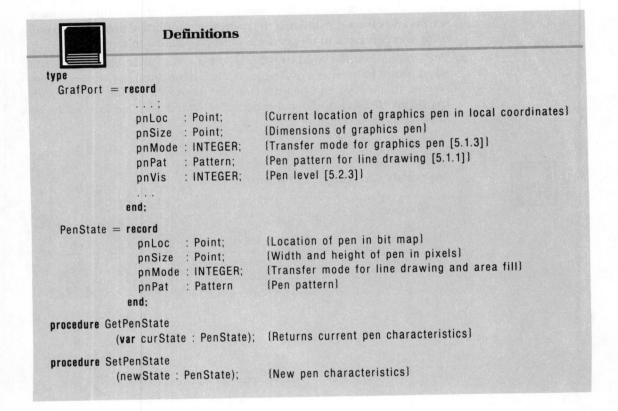

Definitions

```
type
  GrafPort = record
           . . . ;
              pnLoc    : Point;       {Current location of graphics pen in local coordinates}
              pnSize   : Point;       {Dimensions of graphics pen}
              pnMode   : INTEGER;     {Transfer mode for graphics pen [5.1.3]}
              pnPat    : Pattern;     {Pen pattern for line drawing [5.1.1]}
              pnVis    : INTEGER;     {Pen level [5.2.3]}
              . . .
           end;

  PenState = record
              pnLoc    : Point;       {Location of pen in bit map}
              pnSize   : Point;       {Width and height of pen in pixels}
              pnMode   : INTEGER;     {Transfer mode for line drawing and area fill}
              pnPat    : Pattern      {Pen pattern}
           end;

procedure GetPenState
          (var curState : PenState);  {Returns current pen characteristics}

procedure SetPenState
          (newState : PenState);      {New pen characteristics}
```

Notes

1. Each port has its own graphics pen, used for drawing lines and text characters.

2. The pen has a location, size, transfer mode, drawing pattern, and visibility level, kept in the **pnLoc, pnSize, pnMode, pnPat,** and **pnVis** fields of the graphics port [4.2.2].

3. **pnLoc** is the pen's location, a point on the coordinate grid expressed in the port's local coordinate system. The pen is a rectangle with its top-left corner at this point.

4. **pnSize** is a point whose horizontal and vertical coordinates define the width and height of the pen in pixels. If either coordinate is zero or negative, the pen shrinks to nothing and will not draw.

5. **pnMode** is the pen's transfer mode, which should be one of the eight pattern transfer modes [5.1.3].

6. **pnPat** is the pen pattern [5.1.1], used for drawing lines and outlining shapes.

7. **pnVis** is the pen's visibility level, which controls whether the pen is visible or hidden; see [5.2.3] for further information.

8. The pen is initially 1 pixel wide by 1 high, located at coordinates (**0, 0**), with transfer mode **PatCopy** and a solid black pen pattern, and is initially visible (visibility level = **0**).

9. A pen state record summarizes the pen's characteristics. It's used solely for manipulating the state of the pen with **GetPenState** and **SetPenState.**

10. **GetPenState** returns a pen state record describing the current pen characteristics of the current port.

11. **SetPenState** sets the current port's text characteristics as specified by a pen state record.

12. These routines are useful for saving and restoring the pen's characteristics to make a routine "transparent" to the state of the pen.

Assembly Language Information

Field offsets in a graphics port:

(Pascal) Field name	(Assembly) Offset name	Offset in bytes
pnLoc	**pnLoc**	**48**
pnSize	**pnSize**	**52**
pnMode	**pnMode**	**56**
pnPat	**pnPat**	**58**
pnVis	**pnVis**	**66**

Field offsets in a pen state record:

(Pascal) Field name	(Assembly) Offset name	Offset in bytes
pnLoc	**psLoc**	**0**
pnSize	**psSize**	**4**
pnMode	**psMode**	**8**
pnPat	**psPat**	**10**

Assembly-language constant:

Name	Value	Meaning
PSRec	**18**	Size of pen state record in bytes

Trap macros:

(Pascal) Routine name	(Assembly) Trap macro	Trap word
GetPenState	**_GetPenState**	**$A898**
SetPenState	**_SetPenState**	**$A899**

5.2.2 Setting Pen Characteristics

Definitions

```
procedure PenSize
            (newWidth  : INTEGER;    {New pen width}
             newHeight : INTEGER);   {New pen height}
procedure PenPat
            (newPat : Pattern);      {New pen pattern}
procedure PenMode
            (newMode : INTEGER);     {New pen transfer mode}
procedure PenNormal;
```

Notes

1. These routines set the pen characteristics of the current port.
2. **PenSize, PenPat,** and **PenMode** control individual pen characteristics.
3. The current pen size, pattern, and mode can be read from the **pnSize, pnPat,** and **pnMode** fields of the graphics port record [4.2.2].
4. If either **newWidth** or **newHeight** is zero or negative, both the pen's width and height are set to **0;** the pen will not draw in this state.
5. **newMode** should be one of the eight pattern transfer modes [5.1.3].
6. **PenNormal** resets the pen to its initial state: 1 pixel wide by 1 high, with a solid black pattern and transfer mode **PatCopy** [5.1.3].
7. None of these routines affects the pen's location.

Assembly Language Information

Trap macros:

(Pascal) Routine name	(Assembly) Trap macro	Trap word
PenSize	**_PenSize**	**$A89B**
PenPat	**_PenPat**	**$A89D**
PenMode	**_PenMode**	**$A89C**
PenNormal	**_PenNormal**	**$A89E**

5.2.3 Hiding and Showing the Pen

Definitions

```
type
   GrafPort = record
                . . . ;
                pnVis : INTEGER;        {Pen visibility level}
                . . . .
              end;
   procedure HidePen;
   procedure ShowPen;
```

Notes

1. These routines control the visibility of the current port's graphics pen by manipulating the *pen level*, an integer kept in the port's **pnVis** field [4.2.2].

2. The pen is visible if the pen level is zero or positive, hidden if it's negative.

3. Drawing operations have no effect when the pen is hidden.

4. The pen level is initialized to **0** (visible) by **OpenPort** or **InitPort** [4.3.2].

5. **HidePen** makes the pen invisible and decrements the pen level by **1.**

6. **ShowPen** undoes the effects of **HidePen** and restores the pen's visibility to its previous state. It increments the pen level by **1;** if the result is **0,** the pen becomes visible again.

7. Calls to **HidePen** and **ShowPen** may be nested to any depth. Every call to **HidePen** should be balanced by a corresponding call to **ShowPen.**

8. The QuickDraw routines **OpenPoly** [4.1.4], **OpenRgn** [4.1.6], and **OpenPicture** [5.4.2] call **HidePen** to prevent the drawing operations used to define a polygon, region, or picture from affecting the screen. When the definition is complete, **ClosePoly** [4.1.4], **CloseRgn** [4.1.6], and **ClosePicture** [5.4.2] restore the pen's previous visibility with **ShowPen.**

Assembly Language Information

Field offsets in a graphics port:

(Pascal) Field name	(Assembly) Offset name	Offset in bytes
pnVis	**pnVis**	**66**

Trap macros:

(Pascal) Routine name	(Assembly) Trap macro	Trap word
HidePen	**_HidePen**	**$A896**
ShowPen	**_ShowPen**	**$A897**

5.2.4 Drawing Lines

Definitions

```
procedure GetPen
          (var penLoc : Point);      {Returns current pen location}

procedure Move
          (horiz : INTEGER;          {Horizontal distance to move, in pixels}
           vert  : INTEGER);         {Vertical distance to move, in pixels}

procedure MoveTo
          (horiz : INTEGER;          {Horizontal coordinate to move to, in pixels}
           vert  : INTEGER);         {Vertical coordinate to move to, in pixels}

procedure Line
          (horiz : INTEGER;          {Horizontal distance to draw, in pixels}
           vert  : INTEGER);         {Vertical distance to draw, in pixels}

procedure LineTo
          (horiz : INTEGER;          {Horizontal coordinate to draw to, in pixels}
           vert  : INTEGER);         {Vertical coordinate to draw to, in pixels}
```

Notes

1. **GetPen** returns the current port's pen location, a point expressed in the port's local coordinate system.

2. The current pen location is kept in the **pnVis** field of the graphics port [4.2.2, 5.2.1].

3. **Move** and **MoveTo** move the current port's pen to a new location without drawing anything.

4. **Line** and **LineTo** move the pen and draw a straight line from the old pen location to the new one.

5. The thickness and appearance of the line are determined by the port's current pen size, pattern, and mode.

6. All drawing in a port is clipped to the intersection of its boundary rectangle, port rectangle, clipping region, and visible region. The pen can move freely outside these boundaries, but only those portions of lines that fall within the clipping boundaries will actually be drawn.

7. Drawing operations have no effect when the pen is hidden.

8. **MoveTo** and **LineTo** move the pen to a given absolute location, expressed in the local coordinate system of the current port.

9. **Move** and **Line** move the pen a given horizontal and vertical distance from its current location.

10. Positive values of **horiz** move the pen to the right, negative to the left; positive **vert** values move it downward, negative values move it upward.

Assembly Language Information

Trap macros:

(Pascal) Routine name	(Assembly) Trap macro	Trap word
GetPen	**_GetPen**	**$A89A**
Move	**_Move**	**$A894**
MoveTo	**_MoveTo**	**$A893**
Line	**_Line**	**$A892**
LineTo	**_LineTo**	**$A891**

5.3 Drawing Shapes

5.3.1 Basic Drawing Operations

Definitions

```
type
  GrafVerb = (Frame,    {Draw outline}
              Paint,    {Fill with current pen pattern}
              Erase,    {Fill with background pattern}
              Invert,   {Invert pixels}
              Fill);    {Fill with specified pattern}
```

Notes

1. The enumerated type **GrafVerb** represents the five basic shape-drawing operations. Its only actual use in a program is for customizing QuickDraw operations: see Apple's *Inside Macintosh* documentation for details.

2. Any of the five operations can be applied to rectangles [5.3.2], rounded rectangles [5.3.3], ovals [5.3.4], arcs and wedges [5.3.5], polygons [5.3.6], or regions [5.3.7].

3. Drawing always takes place in the current graphics port, and all shapes are defined in that port's local coordinate system.

4. *Framing* a shape draws its outline, using the port's current pen size, pattern, and mode [5.2.1]. Pixels in the shape's interior are left unchanged.

5. If a region definition [4.1.6] is open, framing any shape adds the shape's outline to the boundary of the region. (*Exception:* Arcs aren't added to the region definition when framed.)

6. *Painting* a shape fills it completely with the current port's pen pattern, using the current pen mode.

7. *Filling* a shape fills it completely with a specified pattern; the transfer mode is always **PatCopy** [5.1.3]. The current port's pen pattern and mode are unaffected.

8. *Erasing* a shape fills it completely with the current port's background pattern. The transfer mode is always **PatCopy** [5.1.3].

9. *Inverting* a shape reverses all pixels it encloses, from white to black and vice versa.

10. The location of the graphics pen is not changed by any shape-drawing operation; however, drawing operations have no effect if the pen is hidden.

11. All drawing operations are clipped to the intersection of the current port's boundary rectangle, port rectangle, clipping region, and visible region. Only those portions of shapes that fall within these boundaries will actually be drawn.

12. Drawing operations never affect pixels outside the boundaries of the shape being drawn.
    (*Exception:* Framing a polygon will draw outside the polygon's boundary; see [5.3.6].)

Assembly Language Information

Assembly-language constants:

Name	Value	Meaning
Frame	0	Draw outline
Paint	1	Fill with current pen pattern
Erase	2	Fill with background pattern
Invert	3	Invert pixels
Fill	4	Fill with specified pattern

5.3.2 Drawing Rectangles

Definitions

```
procedure FrameRect
          (theRect : Rect);        {Rectangle to be framed}
procedure PaintRect
          (theRect : Rect);        {Rectangle to be painted}
procedure FillRect
          (theRect : Rect;         {Rectangle to be filled}
           fillPat : Pattern);     {Pattern to fill it with}
procedure EraseRect
          (theRect : Rect);        {Rectangle to be erased}
procedure InvertRect
          (theRect : Rect);        {Rectangle to be inverted}
```

Notes

1. These routines perform the five basic drawing operations [5.3.1] on rectangles.

2. The trap macro for **InvertRect** is spelled **_InverRect**.

Assembly Language Information

Trap macros:

(Pascal) Routine name	(Assembly) Trap macro	Trap word
FrameRect	**_FrameRect**	**$A8A1**
PaintRect	**_PaintRect**	**$A8A2**
FillRect	**_FillRect**	**$A8A5**
EraseRect	**_EraseRect**	**$A8A3**
InvertRect	**_InverRect**	**$A8A4**

5.3.3 Drawing Rounded Rectangles

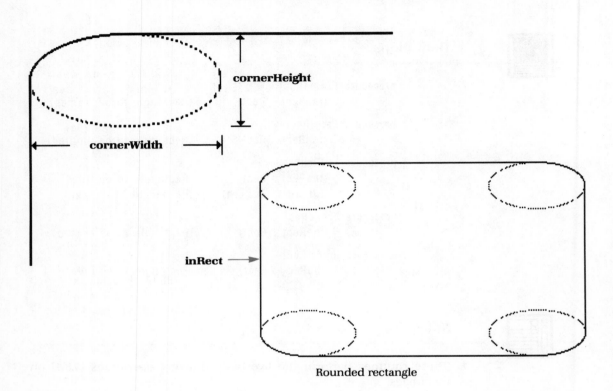

Rounded rectangle

Definitions

```
procedure FrameRoundRect
        (theRect      : Rect;          {Body of rectangle}
        cornerWidth  : INTEGER;       {Width of corner oval}
        cornerHeight : INTEGER);      {Height of corner oval}

procedure PaintRoundRect
        (theRect      : Rect;          {Body of rectangle}
        cornerWidth  : INTEGER;       {Width of corner oval}
        cornerHeight : INTEGER);      {Height of corner oval}

procedure FillRoundRect
        (theRect      : Rect;          {Body of rectangle}
        cornerWidth  : INTEGER;       {Width of corner oval}
        cornerHeight : INTEGER;       {Height of corner oval}
        fillPat      : Pattern);      {Pattern to fill with}

procedure EraseRoundRect
        (theRect      : Rect;          {Body of rectangle}
        cornerWidth  : INTEGER;       {Width of corner oval}
        cornerHeight : INTEGER);      {Height of corner oval}

procedure InvertRoundRect
        (theRect      : Rect;          {Body of rectangle}
        cornerWidth  : INTEGER;       {Width of corner oval}
        cornerHeight : INTEGER);      {Height of corner oval}
```

Notes

1. These routines perform the five basic drawing operations [5.3.1] on rounded rectangles.

2. **cornerWidth** and **cornerHeight** give the horizontal and vertical axes of the oval to be used for the rounded corners. Each corner will be a quarter of this oval (see figure).

3. **cornerWidth** and **cornerHeight** can never exceed the width and height of the body rectangle **theRect,** even if the values supplied are larger.

4. The trap macro for **InvertRoundRect** is spelled **_InverRoundRect.**

Assembly Language Information

Trap macros:

(Pascal) Routine name	(Assembly) Trap macro	Trap word
FrameRoundRect	**_FrameRoundRect**	**$A8B0**
PaintRoundRect	**_PaintRoundRect**	**$A8B1**
FillRoundRect	**_FillRoundRect**	**$A8B4**
EraseRoundRect	**_EraseRoundRect**	**$A8B2**
InvertRoundRect	**_InverRoundRect**	**$A8B3**

5.3.4 Drawing Ovals

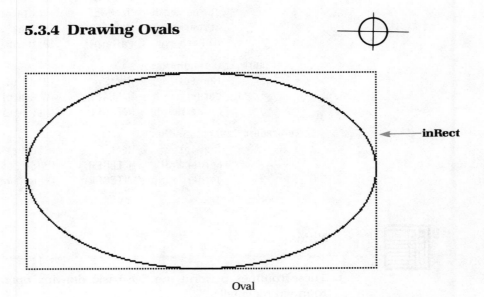

Oval

Definitions

```
procedure FrameOval
          (inRect : Rect);        {Rectangle defining oval}
procedure PaintOval
          (inRect : Rect);        {Rectangle defining oval}
procedure FillOval
          (inRect : Rect;         {Rectangle defining oval}
           fillPat : Pattern);    {Pattern to fill with}
procedure EraseOval
          (inRect : Rect);        {Rectangle defining oval}
procedure InvertOval
          (inRect : Rect);        {Rectangle defining oval}
```

Notes

1. These routines perform the five basic drawing operations [5.3.1] on ovals.
2. The oval is inscribed in rectangle **inRect.**
3. If the specified rectangle is a square, the resulting oval will be a circle.

Assembly Language Information

Trap macros:

(Pascal) Routine name	(Assembly) Trap macro	Trap word
FrameOval	**_FrameOval**	**$A8B7**
PaintOval	**_PaintOval**	**$A8B8**
FillOval	**_FillOval**	**$A8BB**
EraseOval	**_EraseOval**	**$A8B9**
InvertOval	**_InvertOval**	**$A8BA**

5.3.5 Drawing Arcs and Wedges

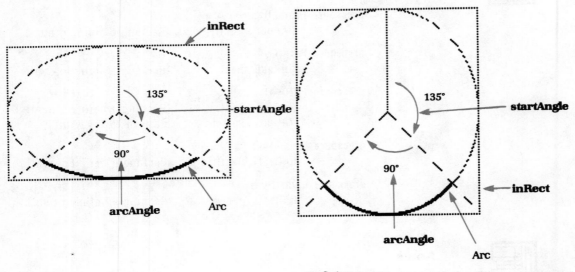

Defining an arc

Definitions

```
procedure FrameArc
        (inRect        : Rect;        {Rectangle defining oval}
        startAngle     : INTEGER;     {Starting angle}
        arcAngle       : INTEGER);    {Extent of arc}

procedure PaintArc
        (inRect        : Rect;        {Rectangle defining oval}
        startAngle     : INTEGER;     {Starting angle}
        arcAngle       : INTEGER);    {Extent of arc}

procedure FillArc
        (inRect        : Rect;        {Rectangle defining oval}
        startAngle     : INTEGER;     {Starting angle}
        arcAngle       : INTEGER;     {Extent of arc}
        fillPat        : Pattern);    {Pattern to fill with}

procedure EraseArc
        (inRect        : Rect;        {Rectangle defining oval}
        startAngle     : INTEGER;     {Starting angle}
        arcAngle       : INTEGER);    {Extent of arc}

procedure InvertArc
        (inRect        : Rect;        {Rectangle defining oval}
        startAngle     : INTEGER;     {Starting angle}
        arcAngle       : INTEGER);    {Extent of arc}

procedure PtToAngle
        (inRect        : Rect;        {Rectangle to measure in}
        thePoint       : Point;       {Point to be measured}
        var theAngle   : INTEGER);    {Returns angle of point, in degrees}
```

Notes

1. These routines perform the five basic drawing operations [5.3.1] on arcs and wedges.

2. The arc is a portion of the oval-inscribed rectangle **inRect**.

3. **startAngle** gives the angle at which the arc begins; **arcAngle** is the arc's angular extent (see figure).

4. All angles are expressed in degrees, *modulo* **360.**

5. Angles are measured from the center of the oval, with **0** degrees at the top.

6. Positive angles are measured clockwise, negative ones counterclockwise.

7. All angles are measured relative to the given rectangle: for instance, **45** degrees designates the rectangle's top-right corner. Unless the rectangle is square, the angles will not be in true circular degrees.

8. **FrameArc** just draws the specified arc, using the current pen size, pattern, and mode. All other drawing operations draw a wedge bounded by the arc itself and the lines joining its two endpoints to the center of the oval.

9. Unlike other framing operations, **FrameArc** doesn't add what it draws to any open region definition.

10. **PtToAngle** calculates the angle corresponding to a given point with respect to a given rectangle, according to the same conventions just given for specifying arcs.

11. The resulting angle is always between **0** and **359,** measured clockwise from **0** at the top.

Assembly Language Information

Trap macros:

(Pascal) Routine name	(Assembly) Trap macro	Trap word
FrameArc	**_FrameArc**	**$A8BE**
PaintArc	**_PaintArc**	**$A8BF**
FillArc	**_FillArc**	**$A8C2**
EraseArc	**_EraseArc**	**$A8C0**
InvertArc	**_InvertArc**	**$A8C1**
PtToAngle	**_PtToAngle**	**$A8C3**

5.3.6 Drawing Polygons

Definitions

procedure FramePoly
          (thePolygon : PolyHandle);   {Handle to polygon to be framed}

procedure PaintPoly
          (thePolygon : PolyHandle);   {Handle to polygon to be painted}

procedure FillPoly
          (thePolygon : PolyHandle;   {Handle to polygon to be filled}
           fillPat   : Pattern);   {Pattern to fill it with}

procedure ErasePoly
          (thePolygon : PolyHandle);   {Handle to polygon to be erased}

procedure InvertPoly
          (thePolygon : PolyHandle);   {Handle to polygon to be inverted}

Notes

1. These routines perform the five basic drawing operations [5.3.1] on polygons.

2. **FramePoly** uses the standard line-drawing operations [5.2.4] to draw the polygon's outline. This causes it to draw outside the actual outline at the right and bottom by the width and height of the graphics pen. This is the only shape-drawing operation that ever draws outside the boundary of a shape.

Assembly Language Information

Trap macros:

(Pascal) Routine name	(Assembly) Trap macro	Trap word
FramePoly	**_FramePoly**	**$A8C6**
PaintPoly	**_PaintPoly**	**$A8C7**
FillPoly	**_FillPoly**	**$A8CA**
ErasePoly	**_ErasePoly**	**$A8C8**
InvertPoly	**_InvertPoly**	**$A8C9**

5.3.7 Drawing Regions

Definitions

procedure FrameRgn
        (theRegion : RgnHandle);   {Handle to region to be framed}

procedure PaintRgn
        (theRegion : RgnHandle);   {Handle to region to be painted}

procedure FillRgn
        (theRegion : RgnHandle;   {Handle to region to be filled}
        fillPat   : Pattern);   {Pattern to fill it with}

procedure EraseRgn
        (theRegion : RgnHandle);   {Handle to region to be erased}

procedure InvertRgn
        (theRegion : RgnHandle);   {Handle to region to be inverted}

Notes

1. These routines perform the five basic drawing operations [5.3.1] on regions.
2. A region should always be drawn in the same graphics port in which it was defined.
3. The trap macro for **InvertRgn** is spelled **_InverRgn.**

Assembly Language Information

Trap macros:

(Pascal) Routine name	(Assembly) Trap macro	Trap word
FrameRgn	**_FrameRgn**	**$A8D2**
PaintRgn	**_PaintRgn**	**$A8D3**
FillRgn	**_FillRgn**	**$A8D6**
EraseRgn	**_EraseRgn**	**$A8D4**
InvertRgn	**_InverRgn**	**$A8D5**

5.4 Pictures and Icons

5.4.1 Picture Records

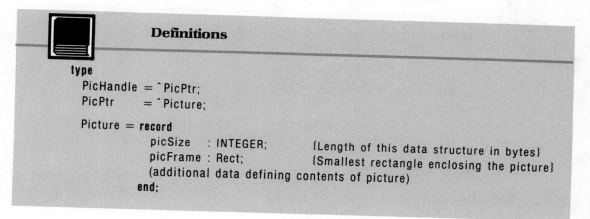

Definitions

```
type
    PicHandle = ^PicPtr;
    PicPtr    = ^Picture;

    Picture = record
            picSize   : INTEGER;        {Length of this data structure in bytes}
            picFrame  : Rect;           {Smallest rectangle enclosing the picture}
            (additional data defining contents of picture)
        end;
```

Notes

1. A **Picture** is a variable-length data structure representing an arbitrary sequence of QuickDraw operations for drawing an image.

2. At the end of the **Picture** record is variable-length data (not directly accessible in Pascal) describing the operations needed to draw the picture in compact, encoded form. The Toolbox maintains this data for you—you'll never need to access or store into it yourself.

3. **picSize** is the overall length of this **Picture** data structure in bytes, including the variable-length data describing the drawing operations.

4. **picFrame** is the *picture frame,* the rectangle within which the picture is drawn.

Assembly Language Information

Field offsets in a picture record:

(Pascal) Field name	(Assembly) Offset name	Offset in bytes
picSize	**picSize**	**0**
picFrame	**picFrame**	**2**
———	**picData**	**10**

5.4.2 Defining Pictures

Definitions

```
function    OpenPicture
                (picFrame : Rect);          {Frame for new picture}
                  : PicHandle;              {Handle to new picture}

procedure CloscPicture;

function    GetPicture
                (pictureID: INTEGER)        {Resource ID of desired picture}
                  : PicHandle;              {Handle to picture in memory}

procedure KillPicture
                (thePicture : PicHandle);   {Handle to picture to be destroyed}
```

Notes

1. **OpenPicture** creates a new **Picture** record [5.4.1], opens it for definition, and returns a handle to it.

2. **picFrame** is the frame for the new picture.

3. Subsequent drawing operations will be accumulated into the picture definition.

4. The graphics pen [5.2.1] is hidden while a picture is open; the drawing operations that define the picture will not appear on the screen.

5. Only one picture may be open for definition at a time; don't attempt to open another without closing the one that's already open.

6. **ClosePicture** closes the picture currently open for definition, if any.

7. The graphics pen is redisplayed on the screen; subsequent drawing operations will appear on the screen instead of being accumulated into the picture definition.

8. **GetPicture** gets a picture from a resource file (Chapter 6), reads it into memory if necessary, and returns a handle to it.

9. **pictureID** is the resource ID of the desired picture; its resource type is **'PICT'** [5.5.5].

10. **KillPicture** destroys a **Picture** record and deallocates the memory space it occupies. The picture is no longer usable after this operation.

(Pascal) Routine name	(Assembly) Trap macro	Trap word
OpenPicture	**_OpenPicture**	**$A8F3**
ClosePicture	**_ClosePicture**	**$A8F4**
GetPicture	**_GetPicture**	**$A9BC**
KillPicture	**_KillPicture**	**$A8F5**

5.4.3 Drawing Pictures

Definitions

```
procedure DrawPicture
          (thePicture : PicHandle;      {Picture to be drawn}
           inRect     : Rect);          {Rectangle to draw it in}
```

Notes

1. **DrawPicture** draws a specified picture in the current graphics port.
2. The picture will be scaled so that its picture frame coincides with the given rectangle **inRect.**

Assembly Language Information

Trap macro:

(Pascal) Routine name	(Assembly) Trap macro	Trap word
DrawPicture	**_DrawPicture**	**$A8F6**

5.4.4 Icons

Definitions

```
function   GetIcon
              (iconID : INTEGER)        {Resource ID of desired icon}
                : Handle;               {Handle to icon in memory}

procedure  PlotIcon
              (inRect    : Rect;        {Rectangle to plot in}
               iconHandle : Handle);    {Handle to icon}
```

Notes

1. An icon is a 32-by-32 bit image, commonly (but not necessarily) used to represent an object on the screen.

2. Icons reside in the heap and are referred to by handles.

3. There is no defined data type representing an icon. If you have to create one in your program, you can use an

   `array [1..32] of LONGINT`

4. Icons are usually stored in resource files and read in as resources (Chapter 6).

5. **GetIcon** gets an icon from a resource file (Chapter 6), reads it into memory if necessary, and returns a handle to it.

6. **iconID** is the resource ID of the desired icon; its resource type is '**ICON**' [5.5.3].

7. **PlotIcon** draws an icon in the current graphics port, scaled to a specified rectangle.

8. The rectangle **inRect** is expressed in the local coordinate system of the current port.

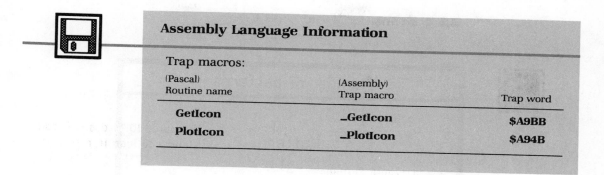

Assembly Language Information

Trap macros:

(Pascal) Routine name	(Assembly) Trap macro	Trap word
GetIcon	**_GetIcon**	**$A9BB**
PlotIcon	**_PlotIcon**	**$A94B**

5.5 QuickDraw-Related Resources

5.5.1 Resource Type 'PAT '

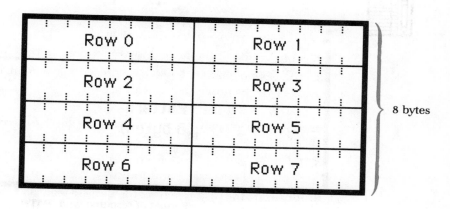

Format of resource type '**PAT** '

Notes

1. A resource of type '**PAT** ' contains a QuickDraw pattern.
2. The space in '**PAT** ' is required.
3. The resource data consists of the bits (pixels) of the pattern, 8 rows of 8 bits (1 byte) each.
4. Use **GetPattern** [5.1.1] to load a resource of this type.

5.5.2 Resource Type 'PAT#'

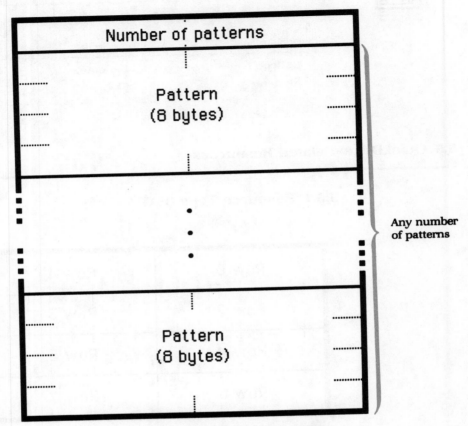

Format of resource type 'PAT#'

Notes

1. A resource of type '**PAT#**' contains a list of QuickDraw patterns.

2. The resource data consists of a 2-byte integer giving the number of patterns in the list, followed by the patterns themselves (8 bytes each, as described under '**PAT** ' [5.5.1]).

3. Use **GetIndPattern** [5.1.1] to access individual patterns in a pattern list.

4. The system resource file contains a standard pattern list [5.1.2] containing the 38 patterns in MacPaint's standard pattern palette. The resource ID for this standard pattern list is **0**.

5.5.3 Resource Type 'ICON'

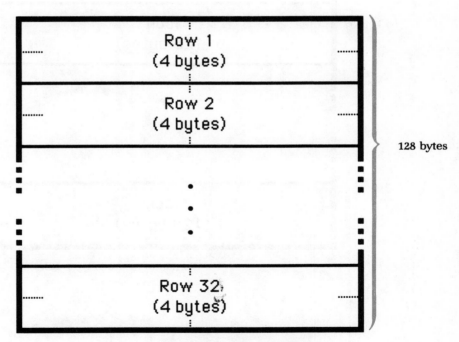

Format of resource type '**ICON**'

Notes

1. A resource of type '**ICON**' contains an icon to be displayed on the screen.
2. The resource data consists of the bits (pixels) of the icon, 32 rows of 32 bits (4 bytes) each.
3. Use **GetIcon** [5.4.4] to load a resource of this type.

5.5.4 Resource Type 'ICN#'

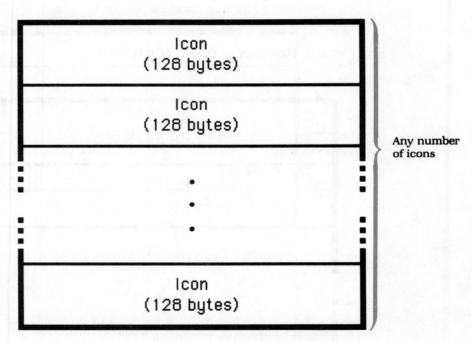

Format of resource type '**ICN#**'

Notes

1. A resource of type **'ICN#'** contains a list of icons.
2. The resource data consists of any number of icons, **128** bytes each (**32** rows of 4 bytes, as described under **'ICON'** [5.5.3]).
3. Resources of this type are commonly used to hold a file icon and its mask for use by the Finder [7.5.3].

5.5.5 Resource Type 'PICT'

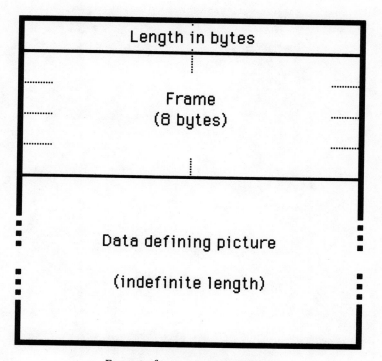

Format of resource type **'PICT'**

Notes

1. A resource of type '**PICT**' contains a QuickDraw picture.
2. The resource data consists of a QuickDraw picture record [5.4.1], with a 2-byte **picSize** field and an 8-byte **picFrame** rectangle, followed by any number of bytes of the picture definition.
3. Use **GetPicture** [5.4.2] to load a resource of this type.

CHAPTER

6

Summoning Your Resources

One of the brightest of the bright ideas in the Macintosh Toolbox is the concept of *resources*. A program's resources can include all the odds and ends it needs to do its job: the menus it offers in the menu bar, the icons and character fonts it uses to display information on the screen, the layout and contents of its dialog and alert boxes. Resources are even found in the program code; each of its code segments is a resource. Looked at in a certain way, a Macintosh program is nothing but a bundle of resources.

Resources were originally invented to help convert (the in word is "localize") Macintosh software for use in foreign countries. From the start, Apple designed Macintosh to be an international product. The idea behind resources was to isolate those aspects of a program's behavior that could vary from one country to another. That way you could translate all the menus and error messages into Dutch, or reconfigure the keyboard to the standard French layout, or display text in a Japanese Katakana font, without changing the basic program. By using resources to their fullest, you could write programs that would work just as well in Brussels or Buenos Aires as they would in Boston or Boise.

Resources were soon recognized, though, as a powerful general mechanism that could be useful for much more than just foreign localization. Separating the text of menus and dialogs from the rest of the program makes it easy to correct misspellings or change terminology. By designating as a resource the code that draws windows on the screen, you can experiment with windows of different shapes and styles without affecting either the code of a particular program or the general window-management code built into the Macintosh ROM. Not only application programs but the individual data files they work on can have their own resources. That means a text document, for instance, can carry its own font information and illustrations with it even when it's copied from one disk to another.

Resources have another important advantage as well: they allow descriptive information about a program's behavior to be separated into bite-sized "chunks" rather than embedded in the program code. Because they're identified as separate entities, not all the "chunks" must be in memory at once. They can be read in from the disk on demand and then purged from memory when no longer needed. This allows great flexibility in managing the Macintosh's precious memory space. In particular, it provides a natural mechanism for breaking up a program's code into segments that can be loaded into memory as needed and "swapped out" when they're not being executed. We'll be discussing this subject again in the next chapter.

In fact, resources are so useful that they've become a pervasive part of the whole Macintosh software design. Because just about every part of the Toolbox uses them, they'll be coming up repeatedly in the following chapters. Any program you write will use resources extensively through the Toolbox, even if you never explicitly refer to them yourself.

As this book is being written, no software is officially available from Apple for defining a program's resources directly on the Macintosh. Apple's own programmers and licensed software developers use a program named **RMaker**, a "resource compiler" that reads a coded text file describing the resources to be defined and produces an equivalent Macintosh resource file. A version of this program that runs under the Lisa Workshop software development system is included in the Macintosh Software Supplement mentioned in Chapter 2. So far, the Macintosh version has not been released as an official product available to the general public.

Unofficially, a variety of resource-handling software is already available in the public domain through Macintosh clubs, user groups, and "bulletin boards." Among the programs in wide circulation are a resource editor that allows you to define resources of various types directly on your Macintosh screen with the mouse and keyboard, and a resource mover for copying existing resources from one file to another. There are also specialized tools for handling specific types of resources, such as a font editor, menu editor, and desk accessory mover. Some of these programs are only preliminary versions and are still infested with bugs; the entire risk as to their quality or performance is with you, the user.

Help is on the way, however. Apple's planned software development system for the Macintosh will include fully supported versions of the resource editor, resource mover, and possibly other resource-handling tools as well. Until such tools become available, you'll either have to be content with the public-domain software described above, or else write your own *ad hoc* programs to create the resources you need, using the Toolbox facilities described in this chapter, the information on resource formats given in the rest of the book, and your own ingenuity.

Identifying Resources

Every resource has a *resource type* and a *resource ID*. The resource type is a four-character string denoting the kind of information the resource represents, such as '**ICON**' or '**MENU**'. The resource ID is an identifying number to distinguish one resource from another of the same type. Together, the resource type and resource ID make up a *resource specification* that uniquely identifies a particular resource.

A resource's type determines what kind of information it contains (the *resource data*) and how that information is structured internally. A resource type's name must have four characters. The contents and structure of resources of that type can follow any conventions agreed on between the program that creates them and the one that uses them (which may or may not be the same program). Certain standard resource types are built into the Toolbox [6.1.1]. You can also invent your own resource types, provided that their four-character names don't conflict with the standard ones.

A resource type's name must always be exactly four characters long. If it's shorter, it must include trailing spaces to fill it out to four characters, as in '**STR** ' or '**PAT** '. Upper- and lowercase letters are distinguished, so '**BLOB**', '**Blob**', and '**blob**' would be considered three different resource types. Notice also that the Pascal string quotes (') enclosing the type name are merely delimiters, not part of the name.

A resource ID can be any 16-bit signed integer, as long as it doesn't conflict with another resource of the same type. (It's OK for different resources to have the same ID number. In fact, this can be a convenient way of indicating that the resources are related—such as a font resource of type '**FONT**' [8.4.5] and the corresponding character width table of type '**FWID**' [8.4.6].) However, all negative ID numbers and positive ones up to **127** are reserved for system use. Resources that you create must have positive IDs between **128** and **32767.**

In addition to a type and an ID number, a resource may also have a *resource name*, which can be any string up to 255 characters long. Resource names are optional, and are generally used only for resources that will be listed on a menu, such as fonts or desk accessories. A named resource can be identified by type and name instead of type and ID number. To make sure the identification is unique, like resources must always have different names. (Again, it's OK—although not necessarily advisable—to have two distinct resources with the same name, as long as they're different types.)

Resource Files

Resources reside in *resource files* on the disk. A single resource file can contain any number of resources of any types. The file's contents are summarized in a table called the *resource map*, stored as part of the file. Each entry in the resource map holds all the pertinent information about one resource in the file: its type, ID number, name (if any), attributes, and the location of its data within the resource file (see Figure 6-1). The resource map is read into memory from the disk when you open the file, and remains in memory as long as the file remains open.

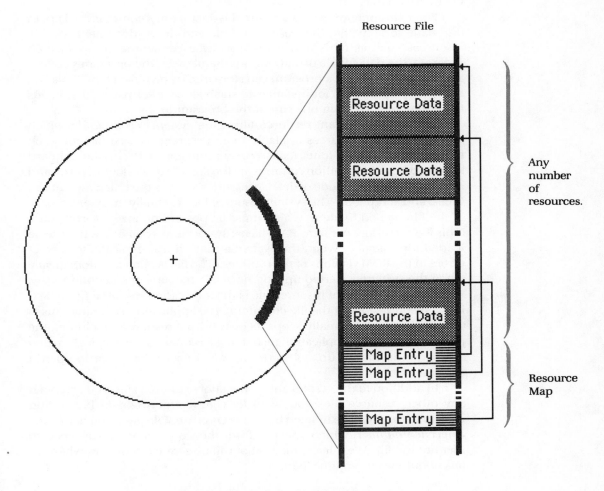

Resources reside in *resource files* on disk.

Figure 6-1 Resource map

Strictly speaking, there's no such thing as a resource file as such. Or, put another way, every file on the disk is (at least potentially) a resource file. Each file has two parts, or "forks": a *data fork* and a *resource fork*. It's almost as if there were two separate files with the same name, which are inseparably linked and always travel as a unit (for instance, when copied from one disk to another with the Finder). To read or write a file's data fork, you use the ordinary input/output operations that we'll be discussing in Volume Two, Chapter 8; to read or write the resource fork, you use the resource operations described in this chapter. The term "resource file" is simply convenient fiction: when we speak of a resource file named, say, **Rumpelstiltskin,** what we're really referring to is the resource fork of the file by that name.

For a file containing a document, the document's contents are kept in the data fork, while the resource fork can hold document-specific resources such as fonts and icons. For a file containing an application program, the data fork is usually empty. (Remember, the program's code is a resource.) Of course, a program can store into its own data fork—this can be a convenient place, for instance, to stash global information that needs to be remembered from one run of the program to the next.

The most important resource file is the *system resource file*, which contains shared resources available to all programs. These include such things as the standard fonts, icons, cursors, and gray patterns; the standard keyboard layout; definition routines for the standard window, control, and menu types; and the code of desk accessories such as the Calculator, Alarm Clock, and Scrapbook. The system resource file is actually the resource fork of the file named **System**, which must be present on every startup disk. (This file's data fork contains RAM-based system and Toolbox routines to be loaded into memory when the system is started up—typically to correct errors in the ROM versions of the routines.) The file is opened automatically when the system is started up, and normally remains open continuously.

Another important resource file is the *application resource file*, which is the resource fork of the file containing the application program. This is where a program normally keeps its own private resources (including the program code). The application resource file is opened automatically when a program is started up, so there's no need for the program to open it explicitly.

In addition to the system and application resource files, you can open any other resource files you need by calling **OpenResFile** [6.2.1]. You designate the file to be opened by name; **OpenResFile** gives you back a *file reference number*, which you use from then on whenever you need to identify the file. We'll learn more about file reference numbers when we talk about files in Volume Two.

All resource-related Toolbox routines that deal with file reference numbers interpret a reference number of **0** to denote the system resource file. This is merely a convention, however; the file actually has a true reference number different from **0.**

All the open resource files are kept in a list, linked together through a field of their resource maps in memory. When a new file is opened, it's linked to the front of this list. So the files are listed in reverse order chronologically, with the most recently opened resource file first in the list, and the system resource file last.

When you ask for a resource, the Toolbox searches each file in the list until it finds a resource with the specified type and ID (or type and name). The search always begins with the *current resource file* and proceeds from there to the end of the list (see Figure 6-2). Opening a new resource file makes it current, so normally the current file is the first one in the list. If necessary, you can change this by calling **UseResFile** or find out which file is current with **CurResFile** [6.2.2]. Changing the current resource file causes some files at the beginning of the list to be bypassed; you can't change the order of the list itself.

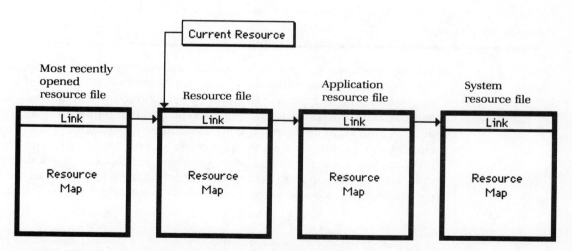

When a resource file is opened, the map is read into memory, but the resource data remains on the disk. The open resource files are linked through a field of their resource maps.

Figure 6-2 Current resource file

Notice that the system resource file is always the last to be searched. This makes it easy to override any of the standard resources simply by redefining it in another resource file under the same type and ID number (and name, if any) as in the system file.

Closing a resource file removes it from the list and deallocates the space occupied by its resource map. It also deallocates any of the file's resources that may have been read into memory. All open resource files (except the system file) are closed automatically when a program terminates, but if you need space you may want to close a file explicitly while your program is running. You can do this by calling **CloseResFile** [6.2.1], and giving the reference number of the file you want to close.

Closing the system resource file automatically closes all other open resource files as well. This isn't something you would normally want to do, since other parts of the system depend on the system resource file.

Access to Resources

To use a resource, you first have to read it into memory from its resource file. The usual way of doing this is with **GetResource** [6.3.1], identifying the resource by its type and ID number. For resources with names, you can use **GetNamedResource,** giving a type and name instead of a type and ID. Both routines search the list of resource files beginning with the current file, as described in the preceding section. When they find the resource you asked for, they allocate space in the heap for the resource's data, read the data in from the file, and return a handle to it. You can then use this handle to do whatever you need to do with the resource's data.

A copy of the handle is also saved in the file's resource map in memory. If the resource is still in memory the next time you ask for it, you'll just get back this same handle; the resource won't have to be read in again from the disk.

```
{ Skeleton code showing the use of a purgeable resource. }

var
    theHandle : Handle;
    thePointer : Ptr;

begin

    . . . ;

    LoadResource (theHandle);                  {Make sure resource is in memory [6.3.4]}

    HLock (theHandle);                         {Lock before dereferencing [3.2.4]}
        thePointer := theHandle^;              {Dereference handle}
        ...thePointer^...;                     {Use simple pointer}
    HUnlock (theHandle);                       {Unlock when through [3.2.4]}

    . . .

end
```

Program 6-1 Using a purgeable resource

Like any other relocatable block, a resource in the heap can be locked or unlocked, and is purgeable or unpurgeable. The resource's attributes (discussed in the next section) determine the initial settings of these properties when the resource is first read in from the disk. After that, you can change them as needed with **HLock** and **HUnlock, HPurge** and **HNoPurge** [3.2.4].

If you make a resource purgeable, of course, then each time you use it you have to check first to make sure it's still in memory. The best way to do this is to call **LoadResource** [6.3.4] before each use of the resource's handle. If the handle is empty (the resource has been purged), **LoadResource** will reload the resource from the disk; if it isn't empty (the resource is still in memory), **LoadResource** does nothing. You might then want to make the resource temporarily unpurgeable while it's in use (see Program 6-1).

Whether to make a given resource purgeable or unpurgeable depends on a number of factors, including the size of the resource, how often you'll be referring to it, and how much you need heap space. In general, you'll probably want to make larger resources (such as fonts) purgeable and smaller ones (such as patterns) unpurgeable.

When you're finished with a resource, you can free the memory space it occupies with **ReleaseResource** [6.3.2]. As usual, this makes all handles to the resource invalid; it also sets the resource's handle in the resource map to **NIL,** so that the resource will be reloaded from the disk the next time you ask for it. All the resources in a resource file are released automatically when you close the file.

Sometimes, though, you may want to hold onto a resource even after the file it came from is closed. For instance, suppose you need a single resource from a particular resource file. Once you have the resource, there's no need to keep the file open and allow its resource map to take up space in memory. To keep the resource from being deallocated when you close the file, you can *detach* it first with **DetachResource** [6.3.2]. This clears the resource's handle in the resource map but doesn't deallocate the resource itself. The resource isn't removed from the file; your copy of it in memory is just decoupled from the file's resource map, so that it won't go away when you close the file (see Figure 6-3). Even after the file is closed, your own copy of the resource's handle remains valid and you can continue to use it to refer to the resource data, as in Program 6-2.

You may sometimes want to perform an operation on all available resources of a given type, or of every type. Program 6-3 shows how. The function **CountTypes** [6.3.3] returns the total number of distinct resource types contained in all open resource files. You can then call **GetIndType** [6.3.3] once for each value of its **index** parameter from **1** to the number of types. Each time it will return a different resource type. For each of these types, **CountResources** [6.3.3] will return the total number of available resources of that type in all open files; you can get each of the resources in turn by calling **GetIndResource** [6.3.3] once for each value from **1** to the number of resources. We'll see a further example of this technique in Chapter 8.

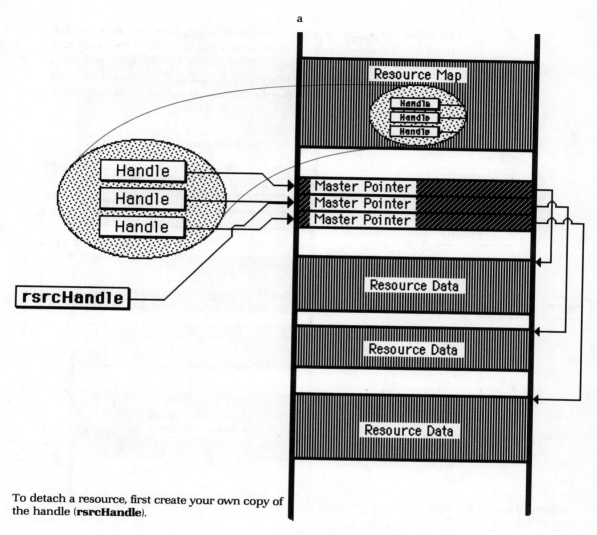

To detach a resource, first create your own copy of the handle (**rsrcHandle**).

Figure 6-3 Detaching a resource

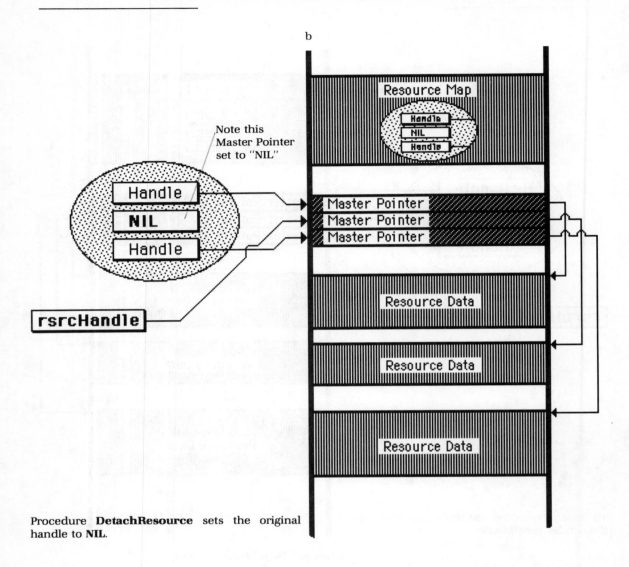

b

Note this
Master Pointer
set to "NIL"

Procedure **DetachResource** sets the original
handle to **NIL**.

DetachResource (rsrchandle)

Figure 6-3 (continued)

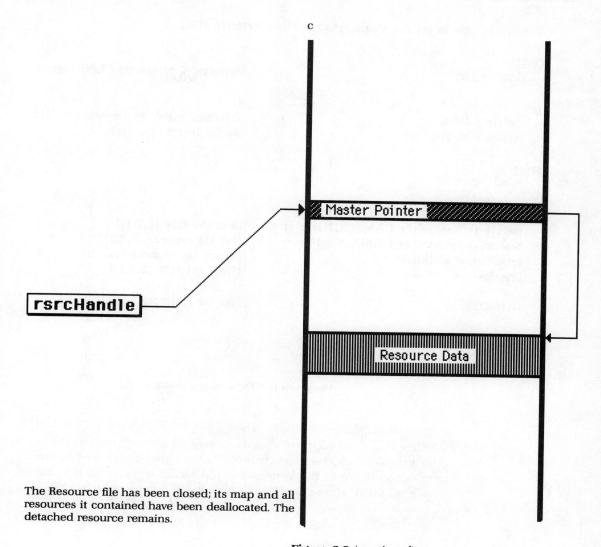

The Resource file has been closed; its map and all resources it contained have been deallocated. The detached resource remains.

Figure 6-3 (*continued*)

```
{ Skeleton code to get one single resource from a resource file. }

const
    blobID = 128;                                    {Resource ID of desired 'BLOB' resource}

var
    theFile : INTEGER;                               {Reference number of the resource file}
    theBlob : Handle;                                {Handle to the resource}

begin

    . . . ;

    theFile := OpenResFile ('Rumpelstiltskin');      {Open the file [6.2.1]}
    theBlob := GetResource ('BLOB', blobID);         {Get the resource [6.3.1]}
    DetachResource (theBlob);                        {Detach the resource [6.3.2]}
    CloseResFile    (theFile);                       {Close the file [6.2.1]}

    ...theBlob...;                                   {Use the resource}

    . . .

end
```

Program 6-2 Detaching a resource

Notice that these routines always operate on *all* open resource files, regardless of which one is current. To limit your operations to one particular resource file, generate all the available resources and test each one with **HomeResFile** [6.4.3] to see if it belongs to the file of interest.

```
{ Skeleton code to generate all available resources. }

var
   typeIndex  : INTEGER;                              {Index of resource type}
   rsrcIndex  : INTEGER;                              {Index of individual resource}
   theType    : ResType;                              {Resource type}
   rsrcHandle : Handle;                               {Handle to resource}

begin

   . . . ;

   for typeIndex := 1 to CountTypes do                {Loop over all resource types [6.3.3]}
      begin
         GetIndType (theType, typeIndex);             {Get next type [6.3.3]}
         for rsrcIndex := 1 to CountResources (theType) do   {Loop over all resources of this type [6.3.3]}
            begin
               rsrcHandle := GetIndResource (theType, rsrcIndex);  {Get handle to next resource [6.3.3]}
               ...rsrcHandle...                        {Use the handle}
            end
      end;

   . . .

end
```

Program 6-3 Generating all resources

Resource Attributes

In addition to its resource data, every resource has extra information associated with it. These additional items are kept in the resource's entry in its file's resource map. They fall into two categories: identifying information and resource attributes.

The *identifying information* for a resource consists of its resource type, ID number, and (optional) name. Given a handle to the resource, you can find out its identifying information with **GetResInfo** or change it with **SetResInfo** [6.4.1]. (You can't change a resource's type, just its ID and name.) To find out the size of a resource's data, in bytes, use **SizeResource** [6.4.3].

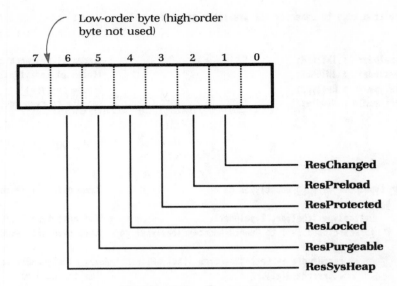

Figure 6-4 Resource attributes

A resource's *attributes* are a set of 1-bit flags describing the resource's properties. They're collected in a single "attribute byte" of the resource map entry, with the format shown in Figure 6-4. The Toolbox provides the routines **GetResAttrs** and **SetResAttrs** [6.4.2] for reading and changing a resource's attributes, as well as constants for referring to each of the attribute bits. In every case, the constant's name tells the meaning of the corresponding attribute bit when set to **1**; a bit value of **0** has the opposite meaning. (For instance, a resource is protected if its **ResProtected** bit is set to **1**, unprotected if it is **0**.)

You can use these attribute constants along with the bit-manipulation routines **BitAnd, BitOr, BitXOr,** and **BitNot** [2.2.2] to operate on the individual attribute bits of a resource. For example, if **theResource** is a handle to a resource, you might turn on its **ResProtected** attribute as follows:

```
attrs := GetResAttrs (theResource);
attrs := BitOr (attrs, ResProtected);
SetResAttrs (theResource, attrs)
```

The **ResSysHeap** attribute tells whether the space for a resource's data is allocated from the system heap or the application heap. **ResLocked** and **ResPurgeable** control whether the resource is initially locked and made purgeable respectively, when it's loaded from the disk. Changing these attributes does *not* immediately lock or unlock the resource or change is purgeability—you still have to do that in the usual way, with **HLock** and **HUnlock, HPurge** and **HNoPurge** [3.2.4]. Changing the **ResLocked** and **ResPurgeable** attributes affects only what will happen the next time the resource is read in from the disk.

The **ResProtected** attribute prevents you from removing a resource from its resource file or changing its name or ID. (You still can change the resource's attributes. If you couldn't, there would be no way to turn off the **ResProtected** attribute itself.) **ResPreload** causes the resource to be read into memory immediately when its resource file is opened, instead of waiting for you to get or load it explicitly. Finally, **ResChanged** means that the resource has been changed since the last time it was read in from the disk, and must be written back out before the file is closed. (We'll have more to say about this process in the next section.) The first and last bits of the attribute byte are reserved for private use by the Toolbox.

Not only individual resources but whole resource files have their own attributes, which you can access and change with **GetResFileAttrs** and **SetResFileAttrs** [6.6.2]. You'll rarely have to deal with resource file attributes, but there are a few cases when they're useful. Some examples are given in the "Nuts and Bolts" section at the end of this chapter.

Modifying Resources

So far, we've assumed that all you want is to read and use existing resources from existing resource files. In most applications that's all you'll need to do, but occasionally you may want to add new resources to a resource file, remove files, change them, or even create new resource files.

When you change a resource and you want that change to be on the disk permanently, you must take special measures. Simply changing the resource in memory isn't enough—you must also mark it as changed by setting its **ResChanged** attribute. When the file is later *updated*, all resources that have been marked as changed will be written out to the disk. A resource file is automatically updated when it's closed (and recall that all except the system resource file are closed automatically when your program terminates). If you want to update a resource file without closing it, use **UpdateResFile** [6.5.4].

You can add resources to the current resource file with **AddResource** and remove them with **RmveResource** [6.5.3]. Both these routines make the appropriate changes in the resource map of the current file; **AddResource** also marks the new resource as changed, so it will automatically be written out to the disk when the file is updated. When you add a resource, you can use **UniqueID** [6.5.3] to make sure the ID number you give it doesn't conflict with another resource of the same type. To create a brand-new resource file, use **CreateResFile** [6.5.1] and then add whatever resources and system references the new file is to contain.

When you change any data of an existing resource in memory (or change its resource map information with **SetResInfo** or **SetResAttrs** [6.4.2]), you can choose whether to permanently change the disk, or do it temporarily for as long as the resource remains in memory. To make the change permanent, you must call **ChangedResource** [6.5.2] to mark the resource as changed. This ensures that it'll be written out when the resource file is updated. (Always use **ChangedResource** for this purpose; never directly change a resource's **ResChanged** attribute yourself.)

If any resource in a file is marked as changed, the entire resource map will always be written out when the file is updated. This means that changes in some other resource's identifying information or attributes may be written back to the disk even though you haven't marked that specific resource as changed. If you want such a change to be temporary, it's up to you to undo the change before the file is updated.

The situation is especially tricky when the resource you're modifying is purgeable. First of all, you have to make sure the resource isn't purged from the heap while you're in the middle of changing it. To prevent this, always use **HNoPurge** to make the resource temporarily unpurgeable while you're modifying it, then **HPurge** to make it purgeable again when you're through. But even if you take this precaution, there's still the danger that the resource may be purged after you've changed it and before its resource file is updated. In that case your changes will be lost, and empty (zero-length) data will be written to the file for that resource.

One way to make sure your changes aren't accidentally lost is to write the resource out explicitly with **WriteResource** [6.5.4] as soon as you finish changing it, and before you make it purgeable again. Another way to do it is with **SetResPurge** [6.5.5]. The call

```
SetResPurge(TRUE)
```

tells the Toolbox to check every time it purges a block from the heap, to see if the block is a changed resource. If it is, the Toolbox will write it out to its resource file before purging it. This guarantees that all your changes will be saved eventually, although you have no control over exactly when.

```
SetResPurge(FALSE)
```

turns off this feature, so that blocks are again purged from the heap without any checking. You must turn on automatic purge checking with **SetResPurge** if you want to use it because it isn't on unless you do.

Error Reporting

The routines dealing with resources use an error-reporting mechanism similar to the one in memory management, which we discussed in Chapter 3. The function **ResError** [6.6.1] is analogous to **MemError** [3.1.3]: after a call to any resource-related routine, this function returns an integer result code. A code of **0** (**NoErr**) means that all is well; a nonzero code reports an error. If the routine reporting the error is a function, it generally returns a special value, such as **NIL** or **−1,** to alert you that an error has occurred; if it's a procedure, it typically posts the error and returns without doing anything.

In assembly language, you can find the result code from the last resource-related operation in the global variable **ResErr.**

The list given in [6.6.1] includes only those error codes that deal specifically with resources. It's also possible for **ResError** to return error codes related to other parts of the Toolbox. For instance, you may get a code of **MemFullErr** [3.1.2] if you try to load a resource from the disk when there isn't enough room for it in the heap. See Appendix E for a complete list of possible error codes.

Nuts and Bolts

Since a resource's identifying information and attributes reside in the resource map, it's unnecessary to load the resource into memory to work with them. A routine called **SetResLoad** [6.3.4] allows you to get a handle to a resource without loading its data from the resource file. The call

```
SetResLoad(FALSE)
```

turns off the automatic loading of resources by **GetResource** [6.3.1], **GetNamedResource** [6.3.1], and **GetIndResource** [6.3.3]. If the resource you ask for is already in memory, these routines will still return a handle to it, as usual; but if it isn't, they'll return to you an empty handle instead of loading the resource from the file. This empty handle identifies the resource well enough for those routines that operate on its resource map entry (**GetResInfo** and **SetResInfo** [6.4.1], **GetResAttrs** and **SetResAttrs** [6.4.2], and **HomeResFile** [6.4.3]). If you later need to refer to the resource's data, you can read it in explicitly with **LoadResource** [6.3.4].

Be careful, though. Turning off automatic resource loading is tricky, and can lead to many subtle problems if you don't watch your step. For one thing, some parts of the Toolbox rely on automatic loading and won't work properly without it. So if you do turn it off, be sure to turn it back on again as soon as possible with

```
SetResLoad(TRUE)
```

And remember too that if any resource in a resource file is marked as changed, the entire resource map will be written out when the file is updated. Changes you make to a resource's identifying information or attributes in the resource map (even if you intend them to be temporary) may accidentally be incorporated into the permanent disk copy of the file because of changes made to other resources. If you've made any other changes, you must be careful to undo the temporary ones and restore the resource's map entry to its original state before the file is updated.

Yet another trap awaits you if you *do* want permanent changes. **SetResInfo** and **SetResAttrs** don't automatically mark the affected resource as changed; to make sure your changes are written out when the file is updated, you must mark the resource explicitly with **Changed-Resource** [6.5.2]. But if you've turned off automatic resource loading with **SetResLoad** to get a handle to the resource without loading its data from the disk, the resource map will now contain an empty handle for that resource. When the file is updated, the empty handle will cause the existing resource data to be replaced with empty (zero-length) data.

One way to prevent this from happening is to turn on the resource file's **MapChanged** attribute with **SetResFileAttrs** [6.6.2] instead of marking the resource itself with **ChangedResource.** This will cause the resource map to be written out when the file is updated (making your changes permanent), but since the resource isn't marked as changed, the empty handle in the resource map won't replace the existing resource data in the file with empty data.

Another occasional use for **SetResFileAttrs** has to do with the file's **MapCompact** attribute. Certain changes that you make in a resource file create "holes" in the file: areas of the file's contents that are no longer in use and can be closed up by compaction when the file is written back to the disk. The **MapCompact** attribute tells the Toolbox to compact the file's contents the next time it's updated.

Some operations that create holes in the file, such as **RmveResource** [6.5.3], cause this attribute to be set automatically. Similarly, if you increase the length of a resource's data, the new data has to be written at the end when the file is updated, since it will no longer fit at its original location within the file. This leaves a hole where the resource used to be. So again, the file's **MapCompact** attribute is set automatically whenever you lengthen the data of any resource. For some reason, however, **MapCompact** is *not* set automatically when you *shorten* a resource, even though this also creates a hole that could be closed up by compaction. So in this case you can use **SetResFileAttrs** to turn on the **MapCompact** attribute yourself and force a compaction when the file is updated.

One final use for **SetResFileAttrs** is to "protect" a resource file by turning on its **MapReadOnly** attribute. This prevents the file from being updated at all, ensuring that any and all changes you make will be temporary and will never be written out to the disk.

REFERENCE

6.1 Resource Types

6.1.1 Resource Types

Definitions

```
type
   ResType = packed array [1..4] of CHAR;        {Resource type}
```

Resource type	Meaning	See Section
'PAT '	QuickDraw pattern	[5.5.1]
'PAT#'	Pattern list	[5.5.2]
'ICON'	Icon	[5.5.3]
'ICN#'	Icon list	[5.5.4]
'PICT'	QuickDraw picture	[5.5.5]
'CODE'	Code segment	[7.5.1]
'PACK'	Package	[7.5.2]
'FREF'	Finder file reference	[7.5.3]
'BNDL'	Finder bundle	[7.5.4]
'DRVR'	I/O driver (including desk accessories)	[7.5.5]
'TEXT'	Any text	[8.4.1]
'STR '	String	[8.4.2]
'STR#'	String list	[8.4.3]
'INIT'	Initialization resource	[8.4.4]
'FONT'	Font	[8.4.5]
'FWID'	Font width table	[8.4.6]
'CURS'	Cursor	[II:2.9.1]
'WIND'	Window template	[II:3.7.1]
'MENU'	Menu	[II:4.8.1]
'MBAR'	Menu bar	[II:4.8.2]
'CNTL'	Control template	[II:6.6.1]
'LART'	Alert template	[II:7.6.1]
'DLOG'	Dialog template	[II:7.6.2]
'DITL'	Dialog or alert item list	[II:7.6.3]
'WDEF'	Window definition function	
'MDEF'	Menu definition procedure	
'CDEF'	Control definition function	
'PDEF'	Printing code	
'PREC'	Print record	
'FKEY'	Low-level keyboard routine	
'INTL'	International resource	
'FRSV'	Reserved system font	
'DSAT'	"Dire straits" alert table	

Notes

1. Resource types for which no section number is given above are covered in the *Inside Macintosh* manual.

6.2 Resource Files

6.2.1 Opening and Closing Resource Files

Definitions

```
function  OpenResFile
             (fileName : Str255)        {Name of resource file to be opened}
                : INTEGER;              {Reference number of file}

procedure CloseResFile
             (refNum : INTEGER);        {Reference number of resource file to be closed}
```

Notes

1. **OpenResFile** opens a resource file; **CloseResFile** closes it.

2. **OpenResFile** accepts the name of the resource file to be opened and returns the file's reference number. Thereafter, the reference number is used whenever you want to refer to the file.

3. The file's resource map is read into memory and remains there for as long as the file remains open.

4. The designated file becomes the current resource file.

5. If the designated resource file is already open, **OpenResFile** returns its reference number.

6. In case of an error opening the file, **OpenResFile** returns −1.

7. The system resource file is opened automatically at system startup and the application resource file when the application is started. These files need not be explicitly opened within the program itself.

8. **CloseResFile** releases the space occupied by the file's resource map and all its resources.

9. If the file or any of its resources have been changed, the file is updated on the disk before closing.

10. A reference number of **0** denotes the system resource file.

11. Closing the system resource file causes all other open resource files to be closed as well.

12. All open resource files except the system resource file are closed automatically when a program terminates.

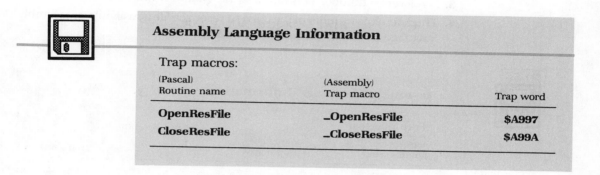

Assembly Language Information

Trap macros:

(Pascal) Routine name	(Assembly) Trap macro	Trap word
OpenResFile	**_OpenResFile**	**$A997**
CloseResFile	**_CloseResFile**	**$A99A**

6.2.2 Current Resource File

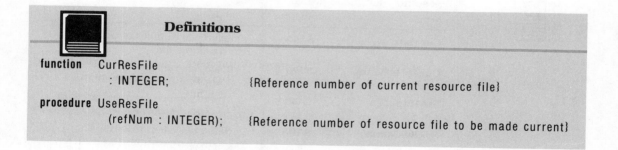

Definitions

```
function   CurResFile
             : INTEGER;            {Reference number of current resource file}
procedure UseResFile
             (refNum : INTEGER);   {Reference number of resource file to be made current}
```

Notes

1. **CurResFile** returns the reference number of the current resource file; **UseResFile** makes a designated file the current resource file.
2. The search for a requested resource begins with the current resource file and proceeds backward chronologically through all resource files opened earlier.
3. A reference number of **0** denotes the system resource file.
4. The reference number of the current resource file is available in assembly language in the global variable **CurMap.**

Assembly Language Information

Trap macros:

(Pascal) Routine name	(Assembly) Trap macro	Trap word
CurResFile	**_CurResFile**	**$A994**
UseResFile	**_UseResFile**	**$A998**

Assembly-language global variables:

Name	Address	Meaning
CurMap	**$A5A**	Reference number of current resource file
CurApRefNum	**$900**	Reference number of application resource file
SysMap	**$A58**	True reference number (not **0**) of system resource file
SysResName	**$AD8**	Name of system resource file (string, maximum 19 characters)
SysMapHndl	**$A54**	Handle to resource map of system resource file
TopMapHndl	**$A50**	Handle to resource map of most recently opened (not necessarily current) resource file

6.3 Access to Resources

6.3.1 Getting Resources

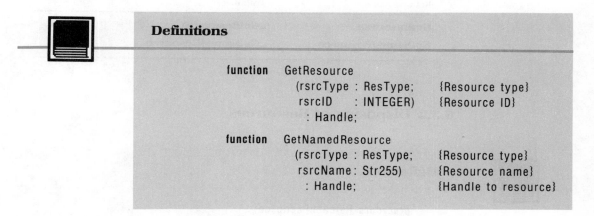

Definitions

```
function  GetResource
              (rsrcType : ResType;      {Resource type}
               rsrcID   : INTEGER)      {Resource ID}
               : Handle;

function  GetNamedResource
              (rsrcType : ResType;      {Resource type}
               rsrcName : Str255)       {Resource name}
               : Handle;                {Handle to resource}
```

Notes

1. These routines search the list of open resource files for a designated resource, read it into memory if necessary, and return a handle to it.

2. The resource is identified by type and ID number (**GetResource**) or type and name (**GetNamedResource**).

3. The search for the resource begins with the current resource file and proceeds backward chronologically through all resource files opened earlier.

4. The resource's handle is saved in the file's resource map in memory for future use.

5. If the resource is already in memory, its existing handle is returned.

6. In case of an error, the handle returned is **NIL.**

7. Automatic loading of resources into memory can be suppressed with **SetResLoad** [6.3.4]. In this case, **GetResource** and **GetNamedResource** return an empty handle if the requested resource isn't already in memory. This empty handle is sufficient to identify the resource for routines that operate only on the resource map, such as **GetResInfo, SetResInfo, GetResAttrs, SetResAttrs,** and **HomeResFile** [6.4.3]. It can also be used to load the resource into memory later with **LoadResource** [6.3.4].

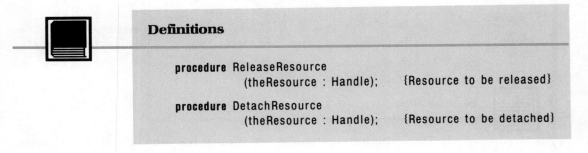

Assembly Language Information

Trap macros:

(Pascal) Routine name	(Assembly) Trap macro	Trap word
GetResource	**_GetResource**	**$A9A0**
GetNamedResource	**_GetNamedResource**	**$A9A1**

6.3.2 Disposing of Resources

Definitions

```
procedure ReleaseResource
          (theResource : Handle);    {Resource to be released}

procedure DetachResource
          (theResource : Handle);    {Resource to be detached}
```

Notes

1. **ReleaseResource** deallocates the space occupied by a resource and removes its handle from its file's resource map in memory. All existing handles to the resource become invalid.

2. **DetachResource** removes the resource's handle from the resource map, but doesn't deallocate the resource itself. Existing handles remain valid, but are no longer recognized as referring to a resource.

3. In both cases, later attempts to get the resource with **GetResource** [6.3.1], **GetNamedResource** [6.3.1], or **GetIndResource** [6.3.3] will cause it to be reread into memory from its resource file and a new handle allocated.

4. Detaching a resource prevents it from being deallocated when its resource file is closed.

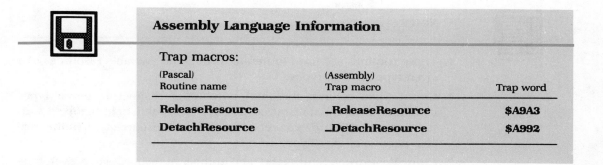

Assembly Language Information

Trap macros:

(Pascal) Routine name	(Assembly) Trap macro	Trap word
ReleaseResource	_ReleaseResource	$A9A3
DetachResource	_DetachResource	$A992

6.3.3 Generating All Resources

Definitions

```
function   CountTypes
              : INTEGER;                    {Total number of resource types}

procedure  GetIndType
              (var rsrcType : ResType;      {Returns next resource type}
               index        : INTEGER);     {Index of desired resource type}

function   CountResources
              (rsrcType : ResType)          {Resource type}
                 : INTEGER);                {Total number of resources of this type}

function   GetIndResource
              (rsrcType : ResType;          {Resource type}
               index    : INTEGER)          {Index (not ID) of desired resource}
                 : Handle;                  {Handle to resource}
```

Notes

1. These routines are used to iterate through all available resources of a given type or of all types.

2. **CountTypes** returns the total number of distinct resource types contained in all open resource files. For each value of **index** from **1** up to this count, **GetIndType** returns a different resource type in the variable parameter **rsrcType**.

3. **CountResources** returns the total number of resources of a given type contained in all open resource files. For each value of **index** from **1** up to this count, **GetIndResource** returns a different resource of the designated type.

4. These routines always operate on *all* open resource files, regardless of which one is current.

5. In case of an error, **GetIndResource** returns **NIL.**

Assembly Language Information

Trap macros:

(Pascal) Routine name	(Assembly) Trap macro	Trap word
CountTypes	**_CountTypes**	**$A99E**
GetIndType	**_GetIndType**	**$A99F**
CountResources	**_CountResources**	**$A99C**
GetIndResource	**_GetIndResource**	**$A99D**

6.3.4 Loading Resources

Definitions

```
procedure SetResLoad
        (onOrOff : BOOLEAN);          {Turn automatic loading on or off?}
procedure LoadResource
        (theResource : Handle);       {Resource to be loaded}
```

Notes

1. **SetResLoad** controls whether resources are automatically loaded into memory from their resource files by **GetResource** [6.3.1], **GetNamedResource** [6.3.1], and **GetIndResource** [6.3.3].

2. When automatic loading of resources is on, the "get" routines automatically load any requested resource into memory if it isn't already there. When automatic loading is off, they just return an empty handle if the requested resource isn't already in memory.

3. Automatic loading is initially off.

4. Automatic loading is overridden by the **ResPreload** attribute of an individual resource [6.4.2]. Resources with this attribute are always preloaded when their resource file is opened, regardless of whether automatic loading is on or off.

5. The flag that controls automatic loading is accessible in machine language as the global variable **ResLoad.**

6. Don't turn off automatic loading for any longer than is absolutely necessary, since some parts of the Toolbox depend on it.

7. **LoadResource** accepts an empty handle to a resource and loads the resource into memory from its resource file. If the handle isn't empty, **LoadResource** does nothing.

8. The empty handle may have been returned by **GetResource, GetNamedResource,** or **GetIndResource** when automatic loading was off, or it may have become empty because the resource it refers to was purged from memory.

9. Call **LoadResource** before using any handle to a purgeable resource, to make sure the resource is in memory.

Assembly Language Information

Trap macros:

(Pascal) Routine name	(Assembly) Trap macro	Trap word
SetResLoad	**_SetResLoad**	**$A99B**
LoadResource	**_LoadResource**	**$A9A2**

Assembly-language global variable:

Name	Address	Meaning
ResLoad	**$A5E**	Load resources automatically?

6.4 Properties of Resources

6.4.1 Identifying Information

Definitions

```
procedure GetResInfo
            (theResource : Handle;        {Handle to resource}
            var rsrcID    : INTEGER;      {Returns resource ID}
            var rsrcType  : ResType;      {Returns resource type}
            var rsrcName  : Str255);      {Returns resource name}

procedure SetResInfo
            (theResource : Handle;        {Handle to resource}
            rsrcID       : INTEGER;       {New resource ID}
            rsrcName     : Str255);       {New resource name}
```

Notes

1. **GetResInfo** returns the identifying information of a resource (resource type, ID number, and name) via its *var* parameters.
2. **SetResInfo** sets a resource's ID and name; the resource type can't be changed.
3. The identifying information of a protected resource can't be changed.
4. An empty string as the **rsrcName** parameter to **SetResInfo** removes the resource's name, if any; a **NIL** value leaves the existing name unchanged.
5. Changing the name or ID number of a resource in the system resource file is dangerous, since the Toolbox or other programs may depend on them.

Assembly Language Information

Trap macros:

(Pascal) Routine name	(Assembly) Trap macro	Trap word
GetResInfo	**_GetResInfo**	**$A9A8**
SetResInfo	**_SetResInfo**	**$A9A9**

6.4.2 Resource Attributes

Definitions

```
function  GetResAttrs
            (theResource : Handle)        {Handle to resource}
              : INTEGER;                  {Current resource attributes}

procedure SetResAttrs
            (theResource : Handle;        {Handle to resource}
             newAttrs    : INTEGER);      {New resource attributes}

const
  ResSysHeap   = $0040;                   {Resides in system heap}
  ResPurgeable = $0020;                   {Purgeable from heap}
  ResLocked    = $0010;                   {Locked during heap compaction}
  ResProtected = $0008;                   {Protected from change}
  ResPreload   = $0004;                   {Preload when file opened}
  ResChanged   = $0002;                   {Has been changed in memory}
```

Notes

1. **GetResAttrs** returns the attributes of a resource; **SetResAttrs** sets them.

2. The constants for the individual attribute bits can be combined with **BitAnd, BitOr, BitXOr,** and **BitNot** [2.2.2] to form any combination of attributes you need.

3. The **ResSysHeap** attribute tells whether the resource data resides in the system (**1**) or application (**0**) heap.

4. The **ResPurgeable** and **ResLocked** attributes define the initial settings of these properties when the resource is loaded from the disk—*not* their current settings. To change these properties for a resource in memory, you must use **HLock** and **HUnlock, HPurge** and **HNoPurge** [3.2.4].

5. A protected resource (**ResProtected** = **1**) can't be removed from its resource file or have its identifying information changed. Unlike other attributes, changes in the **ResProtected** attribute take effect immediately.

6. The **ResPreload** attribute causes a resource to be loaded into memory immediately when its resource file is opened, instead of waiting to be loaded explicitly with **GetResource** [6.3.1], **GetNamedResource** [6.3.1], **GetIndResource** [6.3.3], or **LoadResource** [6.3.4].

7. The **ResPreload** attribute overrides **SetResLoad** [6.3.4]. Resources with this attribute are always preloaded when their resource file is opened, regardless of whether automatic loading is on or off.

8. The **ResChanged** attribute tells whether a resource has been changed in memory and so must be written out to the disk when its resource file is updated.

9. The assembly-language constants **ResSysHeap, ResPurgeable**, etc. (below) are bit numbers for use with the **BTST, BSET, BCLR,** and **BCHG** instructions.

10. Always use **ChangedResource** [6.5.2] to mark a resource as changed, never **SetResAttrs.** Make sure all calls to **SetResAttrs** preserve the existing value of the **ResChanged** attribute.

Assembly Language Information

Trap macros:

(Pascal) Routine name	(Assembly) Trap macro	Trap word
GetResAttrs	**_GetResAttrs**	**$A9A6**
SetResAttrs	**_SetResAttrs**	**$A9A7**

Bit numbers of resource attributes:

Name	Value	Meaning
ResSysHeap	**6**	Resides in system heap
ResPurgeable	**5**	Purgeable from heap
ResLocked	**4**	Locked during compaction
ResProtected	**3**	Protected from change
ResPreload	**2**	Preload when file opened
ResChanged	**1**	Has been changed in memory

6.4.3 Other Properties

Definitions

function SizeResource
      (theResource : Handle)   {Handle to resource}
        : LONGINT;   {Size of resource data, in bytes}

function HomeResFile
      (theResource : Handle)   {Handle to resource}
        : INTEGER;   {Reference number of home resource file}

Notes

1. **SizeResource** returns the size of a resource's data, in bytes.
2. The resource need not be in memory; its size will be read from the resource file if necessary.
3. The trap macro for **SizeResource** is spelled **_SizeRsrc.**
4. **HomeResFile** returns the reference number of the resource file that contains a given resource.
5. A reference number of **0** denotes the system resource file.
6. In case of an error, both functions return **−1**.

Assembly Language Information

Trap macros:

(Pascal) Routine name	(Assembly) Trap macro	Trap word
SizeResource	**_SizeRsrc**	**$A9A5**
HomeResFile	**_HomeResFile**	**$A9A4**

6.5 Modifying Resources

6.5.1 Creating Resource Files

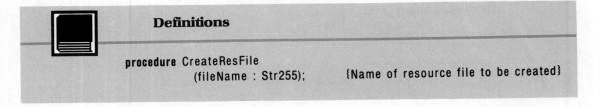

Definitions

procedure CreateResFile
      (fileName : Str255);   {Name of resource file to be created}

Notes

1. **CreateResFile** creates a new, empty resource file with the given name.
2. The new file is not opened and no reference number is returned; call **OpenResFile** [6.2.1] to get a reference number for the file.
3. If no file of the specified name exists, a new one is created with both its data and resource forks empty.
4. If there's already a file of this name with no resource fork, it is given one.
5. If there's already a file of this name with a nonempty resource fork, an error is signaled.

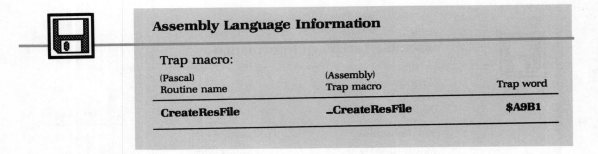

Assembly Language Information

Trap macro:

(Pascal) Routine name	(Assembly) Trap macro	Trap word
CreateResFile	**_CreateResFile**	**$A9B1**

6.5.2 Marking Changed Resources

Definitions

procedure ChangedResource
            (theResource : Handle);   {Resource to be marked as changed}

Notes

1. **ChangedResource** marks a resource as changed, so that it will be written out to its resource file the next time the file is updated.

2. Always use **ChangedResource** to mark a resource as changed; never change the **ResChanged** attribute yourself with **SetResAttrs** [6.4.2].

3. **Changed Resource** checks to see whether there's enough disk space to write out the new version of the resource to its file. If not, it will post the error code **DskFulErr** [6.6.1] and will not set the resource's **ResChanged** attribute. Consequently, when the resource file is later updated, the resource will not be written out; no error will be reported at that time. To detect this problem, you must check for an error at the time you mark the resource as changed, by following **ChangedResource** with a call to **ResError** [6.6.1].

Assembly Language Information

Trap macro:

(Pascal) Routine name	(Assembly) Trap macro	Trap word
ChangedResource	**_ChangedResource**	**$A9AA**

6.5.3 Adding and Removing Resources

Definitions

```
procedure AddResource
          (rsrcData  : Handle;        {Handle to data of new resource}
           rsrcType  : ResType;       {Type of new resource}
           rsrcID    : INTEGER;       {ID number of new resource}
           rsrcName  : Str255);       {Name of new resource}

procedure RmveResource
          (theResource : Handle);     {Resource to be removed}

function   UniqueID
          (rsrcType : ResType);       {Resource type}
             : INTEGER                {Unique ID number for this type}
```

Notes

1. **AddResource** adds a new resource to the current resource file; **RmveResource** removes an existing resource.

2. The resource affected is automatically marked as changed, so that the change will be incorporated permanently on the disk the next time the resource file is updated.

3. **RmveResource** doesn't deallocate the resource's data from the heap; do it yourself with **DisposHandle** [3.2.2].

4. **AddResource** adds a new resource to the current resource file, with the resource data given by **rsrcData** and the identifying information given by **rsrcType, rsrcID,** and **rsrcName.** It's an error if **rsrcData** is already a handle to an existing resource.

5. **RmveResource** removes an existing resource from the current resource file. It's an error if **theResource** doesn't belong to the current file.

6. Removing a resource from the system resource file is dangerous, since other programs and parts of the Toolbox may depend on it.

7. **UniqueID** returns a positive ID number for a new resource that doesn't conflict with that of any existing resource of the given type in any open resource file.

Assembly Language Information

Trap macros:

(Pascal) Routine name	(Assembly) Trap macro	Trap word
AddResource	**_AddResource**	**$A9AB**
RmveResource	**_RmveResource**	**$A9AD**
UniqueID	**_UniqueID**	**$A9C1**

6.5.4 Updating Resource Files

Definitions

```
procedure UpdateResFile
          (refNum : INTEGER);        {Reference number of resource file to be updated}
procedure WriteResource
          (theResource : Handle);    {Resource file to be written out}
```

Notes

1. **UpdateResFile** writes out a new version of the designated resource file on the disk, incorporating all changes since the file was last opened or updated.

2. All resources marked as changed (**ResChanged** = **1**) are written out.

3. If at least one resource is marked as changed, the file's entire resource map is written out.

4. The updated version of the file is compacted to remove empty space resulting from changes in the file.

5. A reference number of **0** designates the system resource file.

6. Closing a resource file updates it automatically.

7. **WriteResource** writes out a single resource to the disk if the resource has been changed.

8. If the resource's **ResChanged** attribute [6.4.2] is **1**, the resource data is written to its file and **ResChanged** is cleared to **0**; if **ResChanged** is already **0, WriteResource** does nothing.

9. Protected resources are never written out to the disk by either **UpdateResFile** or **WriteResource.**

10. If a resource to be written out by either **UpdateResFile** or **WriteResource** has been purged, the resource data written to the file will be empty (zero-length).

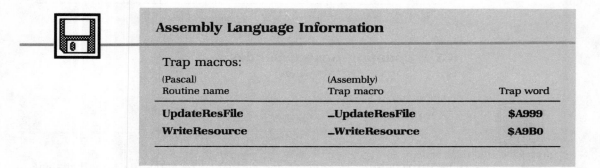

Assembly Language Information

Trap macros:

(Pascal) Routine name	(Assembly) Trap macro	Trap word
UpdateResFile	**_UpdateResFile**	**$A999**
WriteResource	**_WriteResource**	**$A9B0**

6.5.5 Purge Checking

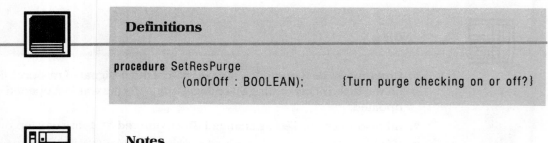

Definitions

```
procedure SetResPurge
          (onOrOff : BOOLEAN);        {Turn purge checking on or off?}
```

Notes

1. **SetResPurge** is used to turn purge checking on or off.

2. When purge checking is on, any block about to be purged from the heap is checked to see if it's a changed resource; if so, it's written out to its resource file before being purged.

3. When purge checking is off, no special checking is performed when a block is purged.

4. Purge checking is initially off.

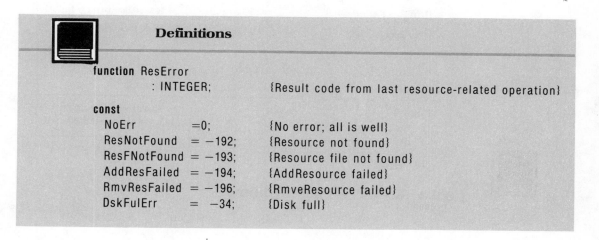

Assembly Language Information

Trap macro:

(Pascal) Routine name	(Assembly) Trap macro	Trap word
SetResPurge	**_SetResPurge**	**$A993**

6.6 Nuts and Bolts

6.6.1 Error Reporting

Definitions

```
function ResError
            : INTEGER;           {Result code from last resource-related operation}

const
   NoErr          =0;           {No error; all is well}
   ResNotFound  = −192;         {Resource not found}
   ResFNotFound = −193;         {Resource file not found}
   AddResFailed = −194;         {AddResource failed}
   RmvResFailed = −196;         {RmveResource failed}
   DskFulErr    =  −34;         {Disk full}
```

Notes

1. **ResError** returns the result code from the last resource-related procedure or function call.

2. The result code returned in the normal case is **0** (**NoErr**). Any nonzero result code denotes an error.

3. Error codes listed here are only those directly related to resources. Errors from other parts of the Toolbox can also occur in the course of resource-related operations, and will be reported by **ResError.**

4. In assembly language, the result code is also available in the global variable **ResErr.**

Assembly Language Information

Trap macro:

(Pascal) Routine name	(Assembly) Trap macro	Trap word
ResError	**_ResError**	**$A9AF**

Result codes:

Name	Value	Meaning
NoErr	**0**	No error
ResNotFound	**−192**	Resource not found
ResFNotFound	**−193**	Resource file not found
AddResFailed	**−194**	**AddResource** failed
RmvResFailed	**−196**	**RmveResource** failed
DskFulErr	**−34**	Disk full

Assembly-language global variable:

Name	Address	Meaning
ResErr	**$A60**	Result code from last resource-related call

6.6.2 Resource File Attributes

Definitions

```
function   GetResFileAttrs
              (refNum : INTEGER)        {Reference number of resource file}
                  : INTEGER;            {Current resource file attributes}

procedure  SetResFileAttrs
              (refNum   : INTEGER;      {Reference number of resource file}
               newAttrs : INTEGER);     {New resource file attributes}

const
   MapReadOnly = 128;                   {No changes allowed}
   MapCompact  =  64;                   {Compact file when updated}
   MapChanged  =  32;                   {Write resource map when updated}
```

Notes

1. **GetResFileAttrs** returns the current attributes of a resource file; **SetResFileAttrs** changes them.

2. The **MapReadOnly** attribute prevents the file from being updated. No changes made to the file or its resources in memory will be written out to the disk.

3. **MapCompact** tells the Toolbox to compact the file when it's updated in order to squeeze out unused space.

4. The **MapCompact** attribute is set automatically when a resource is removed from the file or when the data of a resource is lengthened, but not when it's shortened.

5. **MapChanged** tells the Toolbox to write out the file's resource map when the file is updated.

6. The **MapChanged** attribute is set automatically when a resource is added to or removed from the file or when any resource is marked as changed.

7. The assembly-language constants **MapReadOnly, MapCompact**, and **MapChanged** (below) are bit numbers for use with the **BTST, BSET, BCLR**, and **BCHG** instructions.

Assembly Language Information

Trap macros:

(Pascal) Routine name	(Assembly) Trap macro	Trap word
GetResFileAttrs	**_GetResFileAttrs**	**$A9F6**
SetResFileAttrs	**_SetResFileAttrs**	**$A9F7**

Bit numbers of resource file attributes:

Name	Value	Meaning
MapReadOnly	**7**	No changes allowed
MapCompact	**6**	Compact file when updated
MapChanged	**5**	Write resource map when updated

C H A P T E R
7
Getting Loaded

Now that we know something about resources, we're ready to discuss the way programs are started up and how code is loaded into memory for execution. Most of this chapter's information is offered as "curriculum enrichment"; you don't really need to know it to write short and straightforward application programs. You'll find it useful, however, if you want to produce "stand-alone" programs that can be started directly from the Finder, or define your own icons to stand for your program and its files on the Finder desktop, or support cut-and-paste editing between your program and other programs or desk accessories. If you're in a hurry and want to skip most of this chapter, you should at least read the section on packages, because you'll need it to understand certain other topics discussed elsewhere in the book, such as the MiniFinder (Volume Two, Chapter 8).

Code Segments

We mentioned in the last chapter that the application program's code is stored in the application's resource file. The resources containing it are called *code segments*, and have resource type **'CODE'** [7.5.1]. Their resource data consists mainly of executable machine-language code, ready to be loaded into memory and run. (There's also a short *segment header* that we'll be discussing later.) The entire program can be contained in a single code segment, or it can be divided into as many separate segments as you like.

301

Code segments are meaningful only for programs that are assembled or compiled directly into executable machine language. If you're programming in an interpreter-based system, the program has no machine code as such, so there aren't any code segments.

The main advantage of code segments is that they allow you to divide a program into separate pieces that don't all have to be in memory at once. Like any resource, a code segment can be read into memory from the disk when needed and then purged when you're finished with it, thereby freeing the space for another use. This means you can isolate seldom-used portions of your program in segments, so that they won't take up precious memory space when not being used. It also means you can write programs bigger than the Macintosh's available memory, by breaking them into segments that can be "swapped" in and out as needed.

Exactly how you break your program into segments depends on the language you're writing in; you'll need to consult your language documentation for details. Typically you give each segment a name, and switch from one segment to another with a compilation-time directive. Code will then be compiled (or assembled) into the segment you name until you switch to another. Such segment names are meaningful only at compilation time, however; the Toolbox simply identifies each segment by its resource ID, known as a *segment number*. The compiler will assign a number to correspond to each segment name, then place the segment code in a '**CODE**' resource with that number as its resource ID. (If you never use segments, the whole program will be placed in a single segment by default.)

The Jump Table

Calls from one code segment to another are made through a *jump table* in RAM. The jump table is part of your program's application global space, or "**A5** world," which we discussed in Chapter 3. The contents and organization of the application global space are repeated for reference in Figure 7-1.

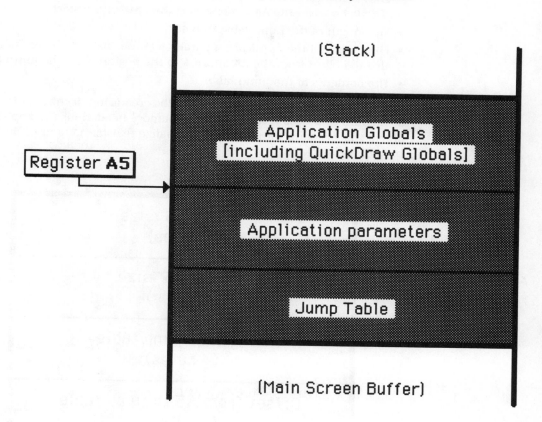

Low memory addresses

(Stack)

Application Globals
[including QuickDraw Globals]

Register **A5**

Application parameters

Jump Table

(Main Screen Buffer)

High memory addresses

Figure 7-1 Application global space

The information needed to set up the application global space is stored in a special 'CODE' resource with ID number 0, created by the language software when the program is compiled or assembled. Every stand-alone program must have a segment 0 in addition to the one or more segments holding the actual code. Figure 7-2 shows the format of this special segment, which includes the following information:

- The "above A5" size: the total number of bytes to be reserved between the beginning of the screen buffer (or the alternate sound buffer) and the base address in register **A5,** including both the application parameters and the jump table

- The "below **A5**" size: the number of bytes to be reserved for application globals between the **A5** address and the base of the stack
- The length of the jump table in bytes
- The length of the application parameters (normally 32 bytes), which is also the offset from the **A5** address to the beginning of the jump table
- The contents of the jump table

When a program is started, the Toolbox reads in this information from segment **0** and uses it to reserve the memory needed for the application global space, set up the jump table, initialize register **A5,** and position the base of the stack.

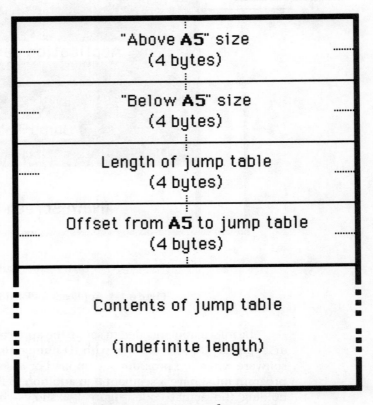

Figure 7-2 Contents of segment **0**

a. Unloaded state

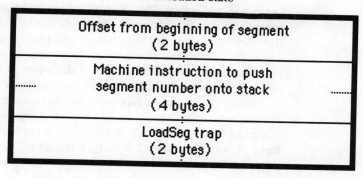

b. Loaded state

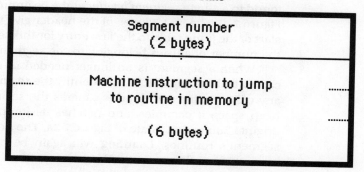

Figure 7-3 Jump table entry

The jump table handles routine calls from one segment to another. It contains one 8-byte entry for every routine in the program that can be called from a segment other than the one it's in; routines that are called only from within the same segment are not included. The first entry in the table corresponds to the program's *main entry point*, where execution begins when the program is first started up. Initially only the segment containing this main entry point (the *main segment*) is loaded into memory; other segments will be read in only when needed.

When a segment is not in memory, the jump table entry for each of its routines has the form shown in Figure 7-3a. The first 2 bytes give the relative location of the routine's entry point within the segment, as an offset from the beginning of the segment's code. This is followed by 6 bytes of actual machine instructions that push the segment number onto the stack as a parameter and then trap to the Toolbox routine **LoadSeg** [7.1.2]. Each "external reference" to this routine from another segment will be represented in machine code by a subroutine jump to these instructions in the jump table entry. They in turn call **LoadSeg,** which reads in the code segment containing the routine from the application resource file and locks it into the heap. Then it uses the offset in the first 2 bytes of the table entry to locate the routine within the segment and jump to it.

Once the segment has been loaded into memory, there's no need to load it again the next time. So before jumping to the routine, **LoadSeg** "patches" the jump table entries for all routines in the segment into the form shown in Figure 7-3b. Here the first 2 bytes of the entry hold the segment number and the last 6 contain a direct jump instruction to the beginning of the routine in memory. Subsequent calls to any routine in the segment will be directed straight to the proper memory address, bypassing the **LoadSeg** call.

The information about which entries in the jump table belong to a given segment (and so much be patched when the segment is loaded) is found in a 4-byte *segment header* at the beginning of the segment itself (see Figure 7-4). The first 2 bytes of the header give the offset in bytes from the start of the jump table to the first entry for this segment; the last 2 bytes give the number of entries belonging to the segment.

When a segment is no longer needed in memory, you release it by calling **UnloadSeg** [7.1.2]. You identify the segment by passing a pointer to any of its routines; **UnloadSeg** marks the segment purgeable to free the heap space it occupies, and patches its jump table entries back to the original "unloaded" state of Figure 7-3a. The next time you call one of the segment's routines, **LoadSeg** will again be called to load it back into memory from the resource file.

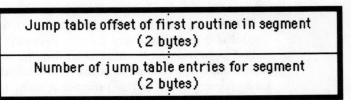

Figure 7-4 Segment header

Notice that you have to call **UnloadSeg** for yourself, whereas **LoadSeg** is always called implicitly. It is called through the instructions in a jump table entry, when you try to call a routine in an unloaded segment. In fact, **LoadSeg** won't work properly *unless* it's called through the jump table; you should never try to call it explicitly from within your own program.

Packages

Another kind of code-containing resource, similar in some ways to a code segment, is a *package*. Like a code segment, a package is a collection of routines grouped together. These routines reside in a resource file and are loaded into memory only when needed. It differs from a code segment, however, in that it isn't a part of any particular program: it's a set of general-purpose routines that are available for any program to use, and normally resides in the system resource file rather than in a program's own application resource file.

The main reason for packages is to serve as extensions to the Toolbox. In general, they provide additional facilities that either require too much code or are not used frequently enough to justify taking up precious ROM space. The Toolbox can accommodate as many as eight separate packages, referred to by *package numbers* from **0** to **7.** The package number is simply the resource ID of the package in the system resource file; its resource type is 'PACK' [7.5.2].

The standard **System** file found on Macintosh software disks includes the following standard packages:

- The Disk Initialization Package (package number **2**) takes corrective action when an unreadable disk is inserted into the disk drive, usually by initializing the disk.

- The Standard File Package (package number **3**), also called the MiniFinder, provides a convenient, standard way for the user to supply file names for input/output operations.

- The Floating-Point Arithmetic Package (package number **4**) performs arithmetic on floating-point numbers in accordance with the "IEEE standard" published by the Institute of Electrical and Electronic Engineers, using the Standard Apple Numeric Environment (SANE).

- The Transcendental Functions Package (package number **5**) calculates various transcendental functions on floating-point numbers, such as logarithms, exponentials, trigonometric functions, compound interest, and discounted value.

- The International Utilities Package (package number **6**) helps a program conform to the prevailing conventions of different countries in such matters as formatting of numbers, dates, times, and currency; use of metric units; and alphabetization of foreign-language accents, diacriticals, and ligatures.
- The Binary/Decimal Conversion Package (package number **7**) converts numbers between their internal binary format and their external representation as strings of decimal digits.

Only the Disk Initialization [II:8.4], Standard File [II:8.3], and Binary/Decimal Conversion [2.3.4] Packages are covered in this book; for information on the others, see Apple's *Inside Macintosh* manual. Package numbers **0** and **1** are reserved for future expansion.

At the machine-language level, packages are called via the Toolbox "package traps," **_Pack0** to **_Pack7** [7.2.1]. To call a routine that belongs to a package, you push the routine's parameters onto the stack, then push an integer *routine selector* to identify the particular routine you want within the package, and finally execute the trap corresponding to the package the routine belongs to (for instance, **_Pack7** for the Binary/Decimal Conversion Package). If the package isn't already in memory, the Toolbox reads it in from the resource file and locks it into the heap. Then it jumps to the routine, using the routine selector to look up its address within the package in a small table at the beginning of the package.

Ordinarily, though, you needn't worry about routine selectors and package traps. The Pascal interface to the Toolbox includes a unit named **PackIntf** for calling the routines in the standard packages. This unit contains "glue routines" to convert your Pascal calls into the proper low-level trap sequences, as described above. By including **PackIntf** in your program with a *uses* declaration, you can call all the package routines in the normal way, as if they were part of the Toolbox proper. Thus you needn't ever think about whether a given routine resides in ROM or in a package on the disk. Similarly in assembly language, the interface file **PackMacs** defines macros for calling all the standard package routines. You simply push the routine's parameters onto the stack and execute the macro for that routine; the macro pushes the routine selector and executes the package trap for you.

Signatures and File Types

Generally, a user starts up an application program by opening a file in the Finder, either by selecting the file's icon with the mouse and choosing the **Open** command from the Finder's **File** menu or by the equivalent shortcut of double-clicking the icon. At this point one of three things may happen:

- If the selected file contains an application program, the Finder starts up the program.

- If the file contains a document belonging to some application program, the Finder starts up that program.

- If the file isn't identified as belonging to a particular application program, or if the program it belongs to is unavailable on the disk, the Finder displays an alert message: **An application can't be found to open this file.**

The Finder decides what to do by looking at two special pieces of information that are associated with every file on the disk, the *file type* and *creator signature* [7.3.1]. Both of these are four-character strings, just like a resource type. Whenever a program creates a new file, it must supply a file type and creator signature.

The Finder keeps track of each file's type and creator (along with other items such as the location of the file's icon on the screen) in a special *desktop file* for each disk. The desktop file is invisible to the user: the Finder never displays an icon for it on the screen, so there's no danger of the user's destroying or damaging it. The Toolbox routine **GetFInfo** [7.3.3] returns all the Finder information associated with a given file, summarized as a *Finder information record* [7.3.2]. **SetFInfo** [7.3.3] accepts a Finder information record as a parameter and sets the file's Finder information accordingly.

The creator signature attached to a file tells the Finder what program the file belongs to, so it can start up that program when the user opens the file. Every application program has its own four-character signature: for example, the signature of the MacPaint graphics editor is '**MPNT**'. If you were writing an interactive music editor named Allegro, you might give it the signature '**CLEF**'.

A program ordinarily puts its signature on any file it creates, but in some cases you may want to use another program's signature instead. For instance, a program that creates a MacPaint drawing should put MacPaint's signature on it, so that the Finder will start up MacPaint when the user opens the file. A file that is not to be opened at all from the Finder should carry the creator signature '**????**'.

The data files that a program works on are called *document files,* or simply *documents.* Most programs deal with a particular type of document, although it's possible to support several distinct document types in the same program, containing varied information to be used for different purposes. Each kind of document is identified by its own four-character file type. For instance, MacPaint documents have file type '**PNTG**' (for "painting"); a document produced by our hypothetical music editor Allegro, representing a musical score, might have file type '**SCOR**'. In Volume Two, we'll learn how the MiniFinder can offer the user a scrollable list of files to select from, using the mouse. In doing this, you can select file types to be listed. Thus you can use different file types to restrict the user's choice to only those that are relevant to the situation.

To avoid conflicts, all "serious" Macintosh applications are supposed to be registered with Apple's Macintosh Technical Support group so they can be assigned unique signatures and file types. Unless you're a professional software developer, you probably won't want to go to this extreme. You should, though, still take care not to use a signature or file type that's already used by another program or that conflicts with resource type.

There are two standard file types of particular interest. A file containing a stand-alone program to be started from the Finder should be of type '**APPL**' (for "application") and carry the program's own signature as its creator. File type '**TEXT**' identifies a *text file* consisting of a stream of "raw" text characters, without additional formatting or other information. This type of file is useful for exchanging pure text between different programs: for instance, MacWrite writes a text file when it's asked to save a document with the **Text Only** option, and will accept text files written by another program.

Finder Startup Information

When the user selects and opens one or more document files, the Finder examines their creator signatures to find out what application program they belong to. If the signatures aren't all the same, it just puts up an alert message (**Please open only documents of the same kind**); otherwise it starts up the designated application, passing it a handle to a table of *startup information* [7.3.4] identifying which documents were selected.

Recall from Chapter 3 that this *startup handle* is one of the program's application parameters, located at address **16(A5)** in the application global space (that is, at an offset of 16 bytes from the base address kept in register **A5**). The program then can use the startup handle to find out which document files to open on first starting up.

One way to access the startup information is with the Toolbox routine **GetAppParms** [7.3.4]. This returns a copy of the startup handle, along with the name and file reference number of your program's application resource file. However, you're then faced with the problem of deciphering the startup information to find out which documents to open—an awkward task in Pascal, since the startup information is a variable-length data structure that can't be properly described in a Pascal type declaration.

It's generally more convenient to use **CountAppFiles** and **GetAppFiles**, letting the Toolbox parse the startup information for you. **CountAppFiles** [7.3.4] tells you the number of document files to be opened. It also returns an integer "message" telling whether the user chose the Finder's **Open** command after selecting the documents (in which case you should open them for work in the usual way) or whether they were opened with the Finder's **Print** command (in which case you should just print each of the selected documents and then exit back to the Finder). The subject of printing is covered in Apple's *Inside Macintosh* manual.

Once you know how many documents there are, you use **GetAppFiles** [7.3.4] to find out their names. **GetAppFiles** accepts an index number as a parameter, ranging from **1** up to the number of documents reported by **CountAppFiles**. For each index value, it returns an information record of type **AppFile** [7.3.4] giving the document's file name, file type, and other identifying information. After opening (or printing) each file, you should call **ClrAppFiles** [7.3.4] to notify the Finder that the file has been duly processed. Putting all this together, your startup code should run something like this:

```
CountAppFiles (openOrPrint, nFiles);
for index := 1 to nFiles do
  begin
    GetAppFiles (index, infoRecord);
    if openOrPrint = AppOpen then
      with infoRecord do
        {Open document for work}
    else
      with infoRecord do
        {Open and print document};
    ClrAppFiles (index)
  end;
if openOrPrint = AppPrint then
  ExitToShell
```

(**ExitToShell** [7.1.3] terminates the program and starts up the Finder in its place. This routine is needed only for taking an immediate exit from somewhere in the middle of the program, as in this example; there's no need to call it when the program terminates in the normal way, by "falling out the bottom" of its main program body.)

Finder Resources

A program can provide its icons to stand for its files on the Finder desktop. There can be a separate icon for each distinct file type the program works with, as well as one for the application file (file type '**APPL**') containing the program itself. The icons and their association with the various file types are defined by a set of *Finder resources* in the program's application resource file. If a program doesn't provide its own file icons, the Finder will use the standard ones shown in Figure 7-5 for the application file and its documents.

Every stand-alone program, whether it defines its own file icons or not, must have a special resource called an *autograph* in its resource file. The resource type of the autograph is always the same as the program's own signature; by convention, its resource ID should be **0.** Whenever the program is copied from one disk to another, the Finder will copy its autograph resource into the desktop file on the new disk. The sole purpose of the autograph is to serve as the program's representative in the desktop file.

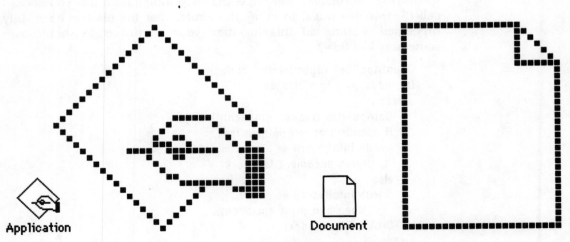

Figure 7-5 Standard file icons

The Finder never looks at the autograph's resource data, so you can use it for any purpose. Typically it's used to hold a string identifying the version of the program, such as

Allegro version 2.0, 8 November 1984

(For this reason, the autograph is sometimes referred to as the program's "version data" resource.) Notice that an autograph resource is *required* for every stand-alone application file; the rest of the Finder resources discussed in this section are optional.

Every file icon that a program defines is represented in the application resource file by an *icon list* resource of type '**ICN#**' [5.5.4]. The icon list must contain exactly two icons of 32 by 32 bits each. The first is the file icon itself and the second is a mask telling the Finder how to draw the icon against the screen background. A white (**0**) bit in the mask means to leave the background pixel unchanged at that position; a black (**1**) bit means to replace it with the corresponding pixel of the file icon. The mask usually consists of the icon's outline, filled in with solid black: for example, Figure 7-6 shows a possible application and document icon and their masks for our music editor.

The connection between a file type and its icon is established by a *file reference* resource of type '**FREF**' [7.5.3]. The resource data consists of the four-character file type and the resource ID of the corresponding icon list. (For the icon representing the application file itself, the file type would of course be '**APPL**').

Actually, the ID number of the icon list as given in a file reference isn't necessarily the same as its true resource ID in the application resource file. The translation from this "local ID" to the actual resource ID is given by yet another Finder resource called a *bundle* (resource type '**BNDL**' [7.5.4]). Any program that defines its own file icons must include a bundle resource to tie all of its other Finder resources together. The bundle gives the program's signature and the ID number of its autograph resource, then goes on to define a series of correspondences between local and actual resource IDs for any number of resource types. The other Finder resources can then refer to each other by their IDs; the bundle tells the Finder the actual IDs under which to look for them in the application file.

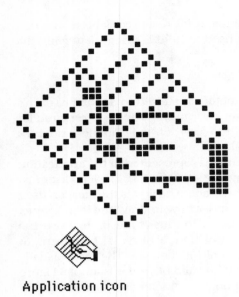

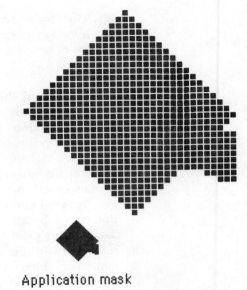

Application icon

Application mask

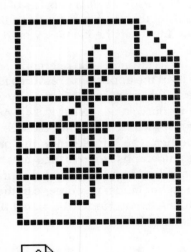

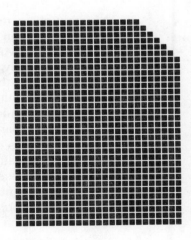

Document icon

Document mask

Figure 7-6 File icons and masks

When a program is copied from one disk to another, its Finder-related resources have to travel along with it. The program's *bundle bit* tells the Finder whether there are any such resources that need to be copied (other than the autograph, which must always be present). The bundle bit is one of the bits in the **fdFlags** field of the Finder information record [7.3.2]. If it's set, the Finder will copy the program's bundle resource to the desktop file on the new disk, along with any other Finder resources that are identified in the bundle. If the bundle bit isn't set, none of the program's Finder resources will be copied to the new disk.

Using local IDs allows the Finder to resolve ("arbitrate") conflicts among different programs. If two programs use the same IDs for their file icons or other Finder resources, the Finder can avoid a conflict by changing the actual IDs for one of the programs when it copies the resources to a disk's desktop file. It can then adjust the actual IDs given in the bundle resource to reflect the change, without affecting the local IDs that the resources use to refer to one another.

A bundle resource's format is general enough to define local IDs for many resource types. At present they're useful only for file references ('**FREF**') and icon lists ('**ICN#**'), but the same mechanism may eventually be used for other purposes as well.

As an example, suppose the music editor **Allegro** has a satellite file named **WaveForms**, of type 'WAVE', containing wave-form definitions for a variety of instruments. Recall that the program's signature is '**CLEF**' and that it works with document files of type '**SCOR**'. The program might then have the following Finder resources in its application resource file:

- An autograph resource (resource type '**CLEF**', ID **0**) containing a string identifying the program version and date.
- Three file references (resource type '**FREF**', IDs **1000**, **1001**, and **1002**) associating file types '**APPL**', '**SCOR**', and '**WAVE**' with icon lists **0**, **1**, and **2**, respectively.

- Three icon lists (resource type 'ICN#', IDs **1000**, **1001**, and **1002**) containing the icons and associated masks for the three file types.
- A bundle (resource type 'BNDL', ID **0**) giving the type and ID of the autograph resource ('CLEF', **0**) and associating the local icon list IDs **0**, **1**, and **2** with actual IDs **1000**, **1001**, and **1002**.

Drivers and Desk Accessories

The Macintosh can communicate with many input/output devices, some of them built in (screen, speaker, disk drive), others peripheral and connected via cables (printer, modem, hard disk). Since each device has its own characteristics and peculiarities, you need some specialized knowledge to communicate with it. This "expertise" about a particular device is isolated in a piece of low-level software called a *device driver*. Each different kind of I/O device has its own driver; the rest of the system communicates with the device through the driver.

The drivers for devices that are built into the Macintosh are stored permanently in ROM, where they're always available. These include the *sound driver*, the *disk driver* for the standard Sony disk drive, and the *serial driver* for communicating through the serial ports on the back of the machine. Other drivers are stored in resource files under resource type 'DRVR' [7.5.5], and are loaded into RAM only when needed; one important example of such a RAM-based driver is the *printer driver*.

Every driver, whether ROM- or RAM-based, has a name, which conventionally begins with a period (.), and a *unit number* from **0** to **31**. For drivers that reside in resource files, the driver name and unit number are also the resource name and resource ID. When a driver is opened for use, it is also given a *driver reference number* by which it is always referred to. The driver reference number is always a negative number from **−1** to **−32**, and comes from the unit number by the formula

$$refNum = -(unitNum + 1)$$

For example, the sound driver has a unit number of **3** and a reference number of **−4.** The names and numbers of the standard device drivers are summarized in [7.5.5].

A very important special class of drivers are *desk accessories* like the Calculator, Scrapbook, and Control Panel. These behave like device drivers from the Toolbox's point of view, but they're actually "mini-applications" that can coexist on the screen with an ordinary application program (and with each other). Desk accessories are stored under resource type 'DRVR', just like bona fide device drivers, and are supposed to have unit numbers (resource IDs) of **12** and above.

Unlike the names of ordinary drivers, those of desk accessories *don't* begin with a period. We'll see in Volume Two that this allows them to be listed by name on a menu; ordinary drivers begin with a period so that they will be suppressed from the menu.

The Toolbox includes all the facilities needed to give the user access to desk accessories while running a program. The program itself doesn't need to know what accessories are available, what they do, or how they work. In Volume Two we'll learn how to offer a menu of available desk accessories for the user to choose from, how to open, close, and manipulate the system windows they appear in, and how to pass them the user's mouse and keyboard actions for processing. See the *Inside Macintosh* manual if you're interested in writing your own desk accessories.

The Desk Scrap

The *desk scrap* is what allows the user to cut and paste between application programs, between a program and a desk accessory, or between accessories. It corresponds to what Macintosh user manuals call the Clipboard: the place to which the standard editing commands **Cut** and **Copy** transfer information, and from which **Paste** retrieves it. When you cut or copy a picture from MacPaint and paste it into a MacWrite document, or transfer text from MacWrite to MacPaint, the information travels via the desk scrap. Similarly pictures can be moved to or from the Scrapbook desk accessory, and text to or from the Scrapbook, Note Pad, Key Caps, or even the Calculator. In each case the desk scrap serves as the intermediary vehicle for transferring the information from one program or accessory to another.

Programs that perform cut-and-paste editing typically keep their scrap for that purpose. As we'll see in Volume Two, the Toolbox text editing routines maintain an internal text scrap of their own. The desk scrap is only for transferring information *between* programs (including desk accessories). If your program is to exchange information with other programs, it's up to you to transfer the information between the desk scrap and your internal scrap at the appropriate times: on entry and exit, and whenever control passes to or from a desk accessory.

For instance, you might copy the desk scrap to the internal scrap as part of your normal startup sequence; or you might want to be more clever and fetch only the contents of the desk scrap if the user issues a **Paste** command before the first **Cut** or **Copy** within the program itself. Another possibility is to use the desk scrap in lieu of an internal scrap, and read or write it directly on every editing command. We'll see an example of one way to handle the desk scrap when we talk about text editing in Volume Two.

The scrap is designed to hold a single item, the last to be cut or copied, but in reality, it may contain several different forms of that item [7.4.1]. This allows the scrap's contents to be handled differently depending on what program they're passed to. Each separate representation is stored as a resource; if there are more than one, they should all be different resource types.

Two resource types in particular are considered standard: **'TEXT'** [8.4.1], consisting of straight ASCII text characters, and **'PICT'** [5.5.5], containing a QuickDraw picture definition. These standard types serve as a "lingua franca" for exchanging text and graphics among programs. Every application or desk accessory that uses the desk scrap is expected to deliver at least one of the standard types as output, and to accept at least one, and preferably both, as input. In addition, a program may use the desk scrap for any other data. For instance, our music editor might write the same musical fragment to the scrap both in its own private data format and also as a QuickDraw picture for displaying the notes graphically on the screen or printing them in a hard copy.

The contents of the desk scrap normally reside in the application heap, and are located through a handle kept in a system global named **ScrapHandle.** You can get a copy of this handle by calling the Toolbox function **InfoScrap** [7.4.2]. This returns a *scrap information record* that includes the scrap handle, the scrap's current size in bytes, and other descriptive information.

Usually, though, you'll want to use **GetScrap** [7.4.3] to access the scrap's contents. You specify the particular resource type you're interested in, and supply a handle (normally empty) to be filled with an item from the scrap. Like most of the Toolbox routines dealing with the scrap, **GetScrap** is a function that returns an Operating System result code similar to those we discussed in Chapters 3 and 6 on memory management and resources. If the scrap contains an item of the requested type, **GetScrap** will *copy* the item's resource data and set the handle you supply to point to the copy; if there's no such item, **GetScrap** will return the result code **NoTypeErr.**

To transfer an item *to* the desk scrap, use **PutScrap** [7.4.3]. You supply a *pointer* (not a handle) to the item's resource data, along with its resource type and length in bytes. **PutScrap** simply adds the new item to the existing contents of the scrap; it doesn't delete any other items already there. It's up to you to make sure the scrap doesn't already contain the same resource type. To replace the scrap's contents, clear the old contents with **ZeroScrap** [7.4.3] before storing the new contents with **PutScrap.**

Any call to **ZeroScrap** also changes the value of the *scrap count.* This is an integer maintained by the Toolbox, whose value is always available as one of the fields in the information record returned by **InfoScrap** [7.4.2]. The numerical value of the scrap count has no intrinsic meaning; its sole purpose is to tell you when the scrap's contents have been changed. When the user activates a system window (one that contains a desk accessory), you can save the old value of the scrap count before passing control to the accessory, then compare it with the new value when control returns to your program. If the scrap count has changed, then the accessory must have called **ZeroScrap,** and has presumably replaced the scrap's previous contents. You can then copy the desk scrap to your own private scrap, or take whatever other action is appropriate. If the scrap count is the same on return from the accessory as it was before, then the scrap hasn't changed and no special action is needed. Again, we'll see an example of how this works in the chapter on text editing in Volume Two.

The contents of the desk scrap normally reside in the application heap. However, if heap space is scarce or the scrap is large, you may want to keep it in a disk file instead. The Toolbox routines **LoadScrap** and **UnloadScrap** [7.4.4] transfer the scrap between a file and the heap. The scrap file's usual name is **ClipboardFile**. The Toolbox keeps a pointer to this file name in the system global **ScrapName**; in assembly language, you can change the scrap file's name by storing a new string pointer into this global. There's no way to change the scrap file name in Pascal, but you can find out the current name via the **ScrapName** field of the information record returned by **InfoScrap** [7.4.2].

Nuts and Bolts

The Toolbox routine that the Finder uses to start up an application program is called **Launch** [7.1.1]. This routine reinitializes the application heap, the application global space, and the stack for the new program, destroying their previous contents. (However, it leaves the system heap intact from one application to the next.) It opens the new program's application resource file and reads in the contents of segment **0,** which it then uses to allocate the application global space, set up the program's jump table, and initialize register **A5.** Finally, it starts up the program by transferring control to its main entry point through the first entry in the jump table.

The only thing in the old application heap that gets preserved across the launch of a new program is, of course, the desk scrap. The **Launch** routine locates the scrap through the system scrap handle in low memory and copies it temporarily into the stack. Then, after reinitializing the application heap, it retrieves the scrap from the stack, reinstalls it in the new heap, and fixes the system scrap handle to point to it at its new location. Thus the scrap is preserved even though everything else in the heap is lost.

Ordinarily the Finder is the only program that should ever call the **Launch** routine; however, there's a related routine named **Chain** [7.1.1] that you may find useful sometimes. Like **Launch, Chain** terminates the program that called it and starts up another in its place. The difference is that **Chain** doesn't reinitialize the application heap; it leaves it intact, so that the first program can leave information there for the second program to use. Neither **Launch** nor **Chain** can be called through the Pascal interface to the Toolbox; they're available only from assembly language via the trap mechanism. See [7.1.1] for details.

REFERENCE

7.1 Starting and Ending a Program

7.1.1 Starting a Program

Definitions

procedure Launch   {Assembly language only}

procedure Chain   {Assembly language only}

Notes

1. Both of these routines start up a new application program.

2. The previous program's application resource file is closed and the new one's is opened.

3. The information given in segment **0** in the application resource file is used to allocate the program's application global space, set up its segment jump table, initialize register **A5,** and position the base of the stack.

4. **Launch** reinitializes the application heap, destroying its previous contents, before starting the new program.

5. The contents of the desk scrap [7.4] are preserved by copying them temporarily to the stack. After initialization, the scrap is retrieved from the stack and reinstalled in the new heap, and the global scrap handle is updated to point to it.

6. **Launch** is normally used only by the Finder, not by a running program.

7. **Chain** leaves the entire application heap intact, and can be used to pass information from one application program to the next.

8. Both routines can be called from assembly language only, via the trap macros **_Launch** and **_Chain.**

9. On entry to either routine, register **A0** contains the address of a 4-byte pointer, which in turn points to a string giving the name of the file containing the application program to be started.

10. Following the file name pointer in memory is a 2-byte integer telling which screen and sound buffers the program will use:

Value	Screen buffer	Sound buffer
Zero	Main	Main
Positive	Main	Alternate
Negative	Alternate	Alternate

The value passed for this integer is kept in the assembly-language global **CurPageOption**.

Assembly Language Information

Trap macros:

(Assembly) Trap macro	Trap word
_Launch	$A9F2
_Chain	$A9F3

Register usage:

Routine	Register	Contents
Launch	A0.L (in)	pointer to parameter block:
	0(A0)	pointer to name of application file
	4(A0)	coded integer specifying sound and screen buffers (see note 10)
Chain	A0.L (in)	pointer to parameter block:
	0(A0)	pointer to name of application file
	4(A0)	coded integer specifying sound and screen buffers (see note 10)

Assembly-language global variable:

Name	Address	Meaning
CurPageOption	$936	Integer specifying screen and sound buffers

7.1.2 Loading and Unloading Segments

Definitions

```
procedure LoadSeg                          {Assembly language only}
procedure UnloadSeg
          (anyRoutine : Ptr);              {Pointer to any routine in the segment}
```

Notes

1. **LoadSeg** loads a code segment from the application resource file on the disk and locks it into the application heap.
2. The segment isn't reloaded if it's already in memory.
3. The segment to be loaded is identified by a segment number passed on the stack.
4. After the segment is loaded, all of its jump table entries are patched to jump directly to the corresponding routines in memory.
5. **LoadSeg** can be called only at the machine-language level, and only from within a jump table entry. It will not work properly if called from within the program's body.
6. **UnloadSeg** unloads a segment from memory, freeing its space for some other purpose.
7. The parameter **anyRoutine** is a pointer to any routine in the segment. The segment number is obtained from the jump table entry for this routine.
8. The unloaded segment is made purgeable, but is not immediately purged from the heap.
9. All jump table entries for the segment are restored to the "unloaded" state, so that they will reload the segment the next time it's needed.

Assembly Language Information

Trap macros:

(Pascal) Routine name	(Assembly) Trap macro	Trap word
	_LoadSeg	$A9F0
UnloadSeg	_UnloadSeg	$A9F1

7.1.3 Ending a Program

Definitions

procedure ExitToShell;

Notes

1. **ExitToShell** terminates a program and immediately returns control to the Finder.
2. The application heap is reinitialized, destroying its previous contents.
3. The contents of the desk scrap [7.4] are preserved. After initialization, the scrap is reinstalled in the new heap and the global scrap handle is updated to point to it.
4. A Pascal program need not call **ExitToShell** when it terminates in the normal way, by "falling out" of its main program body.

Assembly Language Information

Trap macro:

(Pascal) Routine name	(Assembly) Trap macro	Trap word
ExitToShell	**_ExitToShell**	**$A9F4**

Assembly-language global variable:

Name	Address	Meaning
FinderName	**$2E0**	Name of program to exit to (maximum 15 characters)

7.2 Packages

7.2.1 Standard Packages

Definitions

```
const
   DskInit = 2;     {Disk Initialization Package}
   StdFile = 3;     {Standard File Package (MiniFinder)}
   FlPoint = 4;     {Floating-Point Arithmetic Package}
   TrFunc  = 5;     {Transcendental Functions Package}
   IntUtil = 6;     {International Utilities Package}
   BDConv  = 7;     {Binary/Decimal Conversion Package}
```

Notes

1. Code packages are stored as resources of type **'PACK'** [7.5.2].

2. The resource ID is the same as the *package number,* which must be between **0** and **7.** The Toolbox can accommodate no more than eight packages at a time, including the standard ones.

3. The standard packages are included in the system resource file provided on Macintosh software disks.

4. Package numbers **0** and **1** are reserved for future expansion.

5. The Disk Initialization Package [II:8.4] takes corrective action when an unreadable disk is inserted into the disk drive, usually by initializing the disk.

6. The Standard File Package [II:8.3], also called the MiniFinder, provides a convenient, standard way for the user to supply file names for input/output operations.

7. The Floating-Point Arithmetic Package performs arithmetic on floating-point numbers in accordance with the "IEEE standard" published by the Institute of Electrical and Electronic Engineers, using the Standard Apple Numeric Environment (SANE). See *Inside Macintosh* for details.

8. The Transcendental Functions Package calculates various transcendental functions on floating-point numbers, such as logarithms, exponentials, trigonometric functions, compound interest, and discounted value. See *Inside Macintosh* for details.

9. The International Utilities Package helps a program conform to the prevailing conventions of different countries in such matters as formatting of numbers, dates, times, and currency; use of metric units; and alphabetization of foreign-language accents, diacriticals, and ligatures. See [2.4.4] and *Inside Macintosh* for more information.

10. The Binary/Decimal Conversion Package [2.3.4] converts numbers between their internal binary format and their external representation as strings of decimal digits.

11. Each routine within a package is identified by an integer *routine selector;* see sections on individual routines for specific values. To call such a routine in assembly language, push the selector onto the stack and execute the appropriate trap (**_Pack0** to **_Pack 7**) for the package it belongs to. The Pascal interface routines in unit **PackIntf** and the assembly-language macros in file **PackMacs** do this automatically for all routines in the standard packages.

Assembly Language Information

Trap macros:

(Assembly) Trap macro	Trap word
_Pack0	**$A9E7**
_Pack1	**$A9E8**
_Pack2	**$A9E9**
_Pack3	**$A9EA**
_Pack4	**$A9EB**
_Pack5	**$A9EC**
_Pack6	**$A9ED**
_Pack7	**$A9EE**

Standard package numbers:

Name	Number	Meaning
DskInit	2	Disk Initialization Package
StdFile	3	Standard File Package (MiniFinder)
FlPoint	4	Floating-Point Arithmetic Package
TrFunc	5	Transcendental Functions Package
IntUtil	6	International Utilities Package
BDConv	7	Binary/Decimal Conversion Package

7.2.2 Initializing Packages

Definitions

```
procedure InitPack
          (packNumber : INTEGER);        {Package number}
procedure InitAllPacks;
```

Notes

1. These routines initialize the standard packages, making them available for use in a program.
2. **InitPack** initializes a single package; **InitAllPacks** initializes all of the standard packages at once.
3. **InitAllPacks** is called automatically at program startup; there's normally no need to call either of these routines from within a running program.

Assembly Language Information

Trap macros:

(Pascal) Routine name	(Assembly) Trap macro	Trap word
InitPack	**_InitPack**	**$A9E5**
InitAllPacks	**_InitAllPacks**	**$A9E6**

7.3 Finder Information

7.3.1 Signatures and File Types

Definitions

```
type
   OSType = packed array [1..4] of CHAR;      {Create signature or file type}
```

Notes

1. Every file has a *file type* and a *creator signature,* assigned when the file is first created [II:8.2.1].

2. The creator signature identifies the application program to be started up when the file is opened from the Finder.

3. The signature '**????**' denotes a file that is not to be opened from the Finder.

4. The file type determines the icon the Finder uses to represent the file on the screen, and controls the user's access to the file via the MiniFinder [II:8.3].

5. File type '**APPL**' identifies a file containing an application program to be run from the Finder. Such a file should carry the program's own signature as its creator.

6. File type '**TEXT**' denotes a file consisting of pure text characters, with no additional formatting or other information.

7. Serious commercial applications should have their signatures and associated file types registered for uniqueness with Apple's Macintosh Technical Support.

7.3.2 Finder Information Records

Definitions

```
type
  FInfo = record
            fdType     : OSType;      {File type}
            fdCreator  : OSType;      {Creator signature}
            fdFlags    : INTEGER;     {Finder flags}
            fdLocation : Point;       {Top-left corner of file's icon in local (window) coordinates}
            fdFldr     : INTEGER      {Folder or window containing icon}
          end;

const
  FHasBundle = $2000;                 {Application has Finder resources}
  FInvisible = $4000;                 {File not visible on desktop}

  FDisk    =  0;                      {Icon is in main disk window}
  FDesktop = -2;                      {Icon is on desktop}
  FTrash   = -3;                      {Icon is in trash window}
```

Notes

1. A Finder information record summarizes a file's Finder-related properties.

2. **fdType** and **fdCreator** are the file type and creator signature [7.3.1], respectively.

3. **fdFlags** is a word of flags representing Finder-related attributes of the file.

4. Bit **13** of the flag word is the *bundle bit*; a **1** in this bit means that the file has a "bundle" of Finder-related resources [7.5.4] to be installed in the Finder's desktop file. The constant **FHasBundle** is a mask for manipulating this bit.

5. Bit **14** of the flag word is the *invisible bit;* a **1** in this bit means that the file's icon is not to be displayed on the screen by the Finder. The constant **FInvisible** is a mask for manipulating this bit.

6. The assembly-language mask constants for the bundle and invisible bits are byte-length masks and apply to the high-order byte of the flag word.

7. The remaining bits of the flag word are used internally by the Finder.

8. **fdFldr** specifies the location of the file's icon on the Finder screen. Common locations are the main window for the disk the file resides on (**FDisk**), out on the desktop (**FDesktop**), or in the trash window (**FTrash**). Any positive, nonzero value is a *folder number* assigned by the Finder to designate a subsidiary folder on the disk.

9. **fdLocation** gives the position of the top-left corner of the file's icon, in the local coordinate system of the window designated by **fdFldr.**

10. If the icon is on the desktop (**fdFldr = FDesktop**), **fdLocation** is in global (screen) coordinates.

Assembly Language Information

Field offsets in a Finder information record:

(Pascal) Field name	(Assembly) Offset name	Offset in bytes
fdType	fdType	0
fdCreator	fdCreator	4
fdFlags	fdFlags	8
fdLocation	fdLocation	10
fdFldr	fdFldr	14

Assembly-language constants:

Name	Value	Meaning
FHasBundle	$20	Mask for bundle bit
FInvisible	$40	Mask for invisible bit

7.3.3 Accessing Finder Properties

Definitions

```
function GetFInfo
          (fName      : Str255;        {File name}
          vRefNum     : INTEGER;       {Volume reference number}
          var finderInfo : FInfo)      {Returns current finder information [7.3.2]}
          : OSErr;                     {Result code}

function SetFInfo
          (fName      : Str255;        {File name}
          vRefNum     : INTEGER;       {Volume reference number}
          finderInfo : FInfo)          {New finder information [7.3.2]}
          : OSErr;                     {Result code}
```

Notes

1. These routines return or change a file's Finder-related properties [7.3.2].

2. The file is identified by its name and the reference number of the volume it resides on. Volumes and volume reference numbers are discussed in Volume Two, Chapter 8.

3. A file needn't be open in order to get or set its Finder information.

4. These routines are part of the high-level file system and are not directly available from assembly language. The trap macros correspond to the low-level file routines **PBGetFInfo** and **PGSetFInfo.** (See Volume Two, Chapter 8 for the distinction between high- and low-level file systems, and *Inside Macintosh* for details on **PBGetFInfo** and **PBSetFInfo.**)

5. The trap macros are spelled **_GetFileInto** and **_SetFileInfo.**

Assembly Language Information

Trap macros:

(Pascal) Routine name	(Assembly) Trap macro	Trap word
PBGetFInfo	**_GetFileInfo**	**$A00C**
PBSetFInfo	**_SetFileInfo**	**$A00D**

7.3.4 Startup Information

```
┌──────────────────────────────────────────┐
│            Message (2 bytes)             │
├──────────────────────────────────────────┤
│         Number of files (2 bytes)        │
├──────────────────────────────────────────┤
│  First volume reference number (2 bytes) │
├──────────────────────────────────────────┤
│               File type                  │
│               (4 bytes)                  │
├───────────────────────┬──────────────────┤
│ Version number (1 byte)│    Not used     │
├───────────────────────┤                  │
│Length of file name (1 byte)│             │
├───────────────────────┴──────────────────┤
│                File name                 │
│            (indefinite length)           │
│                                          │
└──────────────────────────────────────────┘

┌──────────────────────────────────────────┐
│  Last volume reference number (2 bytes)  │
├──────────────────────────────────────────┤
│               File type                  │
│               (4 bytes)                  │
├───────────────────────┬──────────────────┤
│ Version number (1 byte)│    Not used     │
├───────────────────────┤                  │
│Length of file name (1 byte)│             │
├───────────────────────┴──────────────────┤
│                File name                 │
│            (indefinite length)           │
└──────────────────────────────────────────┘
```

Finder startup information

Definitions

```
procedure CountAppFiles
           (var message : INTEGER;        {Open or print?}
            var count   : INTEGER);       {Returns number of files selected}

procedure GetAppFiles
           (index     : INTEGER;          {Index number of desired file}
            var theFile : AppFile);       {Returns identifying information about file}

procedure ClrAppFiles
           (index : INTEGER);             {Index number of file to be cleared}

procedure GetAppParms
           (var appName    : Str255;      {Returns name of application file}
            var appResFile : INTEGER;     {Returns reference number of application resource file}
            var startHandle : Handle);    {Returns handle to startup information}

const
   AppOpen = 0;                           {Open document file}
   AppPrint = 1;                          {Print document file}

type
   AppFile = record
             vRefNum : INTEGER;           {Volume reference number}
             fType   : OSType;            {File type}
             versNum : INTEGER;           {Version number}
             fName   : Str255             {Name of file}
           end;
```

Notes

1. These routines are used for accessing a program's Finder startup information, which identifies those document files the user selected in the Finder when starting up the program.

2. **CountAppFiles** returns the number of documents selected by the user.

3. The value returned in the **message** parameter tells whether the documents are to be opened for work (**AppOpen**) or for printing (**AppPrint**). See *Inside Macintosh* for information on printing.

4. **GetAppFiles** returns identifying information for one of the documents selected by the user.

5. The **index** parameter is an integer ranging from **1** to the **count** value returned by **CountAppFiles**.

6. The identifying information is returned as a record of type **AppFile**, giving the volume reference number, file name, file type [7.3.1], and version number. Volume reference numbers and version numbers are discussed in Volume Two, Chapter 8.

7. After opening or printing a document identified by **GetAppFiles**, call **ClrAppFiles** to notify the Finder that the document has been processed.

8. These routines are not available in assembly language via the trap mechanism. Instead, you can access the Finder startup information directly via the *startup handle* at address **16(A5)** in the application global space; a copy of the startup handle is also kept in the system global variable **AppParmHandle**. The internal structure of the startup information is shown in the previous figure.

9. **GetAppParms** returns the name of the program's application file, the reference number of its application resource file, and a handle to its "raw" startup information.

10. In assembly language, the same information is available directly in the system globals **CurApName**, **CurApRefNum**, and **AppParmHandle**.

Assembly Language Information

Trap macro:

(Pascal) Routine name	(Assembly) Trap macro	Trap word
GetAppParms	**_GetAppParms**	**$A9F5**

Assembly-language global variables:

Name	Address	Meaning
CurApName	**$910**	Name of current application (maximum 31 characters)
CurApRefNum	**$900**	Reference number of application resource file
AppParmHandle	**$AEC**	Handle to Finder startup information

7.4 Desk Scrap

7.4.1 Scrap Format

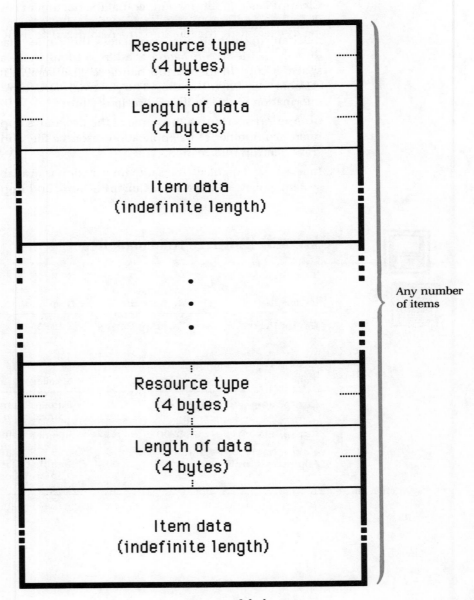

Format of desk scrap

Notes

1. The desk scrap may contain any number of separate items, each of which is a single resource of any type. They should all represent the same underlying information in different forms.

2. For each item, the scrap contains a four-character resource type and a long integer giving the length of the resource data in bytes, followed by the actual resource data.

3. The data must physically consist of an even number of bytes. If the specified length count is odd, there must be an extra byte of "padding" at the end to keep the physical length to a whole number of 16-bit words.

4. Two resource types are considered standard for the scrap. **'TEXT'** [8.4.1], consisting of plain, unformatted ASCII text, and **'PICT'** [5.5.5], representing a QuickDraw picture. Any program that uses the scrap at all should deliver at least one of these types to the scrap, and should be able to accept at least one and preferably both.

7.4.2 Scrap Information

Definitions

type

```
        PScrapStuff = ^ScrapStuff

    ScrapStuff = record
                scrapSize    : LONGINT;      {Overall size of scrap in bytes}
                scrapHandle  : Handle;       {Handle to scrap in memory}
                scrapCount   : INTEGER;      {Current scrap count}
                scrapState   : INTEGER;      {Is scrap in memory?}
                scrapName    : StringPtr     {Pointer to name of scrap file}
            end;

    function InfoScrap
                : PScrapStuff;               {Pointer to current scrap information}
```

Notes

1. **InfoScrap** returns a *scrap information record* summarizing the current contents and properties of the desk scrap.

2. **scrapSize** is the overall length of the scrap in bytes, including all items.

3. **scrapHandle** is a handle to the contents of the scrap in memory. If the scrap is on the disk, this field is **NIL.**

4. **scrapCount** is the current value of the scrap count, which is changed whenever **ZeroScrap** [7.4.3] is called. This number has no intrinsic meaning; its sole purpose is to enable a program to tell whether the scrap's contents have been changed on regaining control from a desk accessory.

5. **scrapState** is zero if the scrap currently resides on the disk, nonzero if it's in memory.

6. **scrapName** is a pointer to the name of the scrap file.

7. In assembly language, the contents of the scrap information record are accessible directly in the global variables listed below.

Assembly Language Information

Trap macro:

(Pascal) Routine name	(Assembly) Trap macro	Trap word
InfoScrap	**_InfoScrap**	**$A9F9**

Assembly-language global variables:

Name	Address	Meaning
ScrapSize	**$960**	Current scrap size
ScrapHandle	**$964**	Handle to scrap contents
ScrapCount	**$968**	Current scrap count
ScrapState	**$96A**	Current scrap state
ScrapName	**$96C**	Pointer to scrap file name

7.4.3 Reading and Writing the Scrap

Definitions

```
function GetScrap
        (theItem    : Handle;      {Handle to be set to requested item}
         itemType   : ResType;     {Resource type of desired item}
         var offset : LONGINT)     {Returns byte offset of item data within scrap contents}
                    : LONGINT;     {Length of item data in bytes, or error code}

function PutScrap
        (itemLength : LONGINT;     {Length of item data in bytes}
         itemType   : ResType;     {Resource type of item}
         theItem    : Ptr)         {Pointer to item data}
                    : LONGINT;     {Result code}

function ZeroScrap
                    : LONGINT;     {Result code}

const
   NoScrapErr = −100;             {Desk scrap not initialized}
   NoTypeErr  = −102;             {No item of requested type}
```

Notes

1. **GetScrap** reads an item from the desk scrap; **PutScrap** writes one; **ZeroScrap** empties the scrap.

2. The **itemType** parameter to **GetScrap** identifies the resource type of the desired item.

3. If the scrap contains an item of the requested type, a copy of the item is made and the handle **theItem** is set to point to the copy. The **offset** parameter returns the offset in bytes from the beginning of the scrap to the beginning of the item's data; the function result gives the (logical) length of the item's data in bytes.

4. If the scrap doesn't contain an item of the requested type, **GetScrap** returns the error code **NoTypeErr. theItem** and **offset** are undefined.

5. Pass **NIL** for **theItem** to get an item's length and offset, but no handle to its data. This allows you to check whether an item of a given type is present, or find out its length, without making a copy of the item itself.

6. **PutScrap** doesn't replace the existing contents of the scrap; it merely *adds* an item. To replace the scrap completely, call **ZeroScrap** first, to clear its previous contents.

7. **PutScrap** doesn't check for an existing item of the same type you're adding. It's up to you to avoid placing two items of the same type in the scrap.

8. Notice that **PutScrap** accepts a *pointer* to the data of the new item, not a handle.

9. In addition to emptying the scrap, **ZeroScrap** changes the value of the scrap count [7.4.2]. This enables you to detect when the scrap's contents have been changed by a desk accessory.

Assembly Language Information

Trap macros:

(Pascal) Routine name	(Assembly) Trap macro	Trap word
GetScrap	_GetScrap	$A9FD
PutScrap	_PutScrap	$A9FE
ZeroScrap	_ZeroScrap	$A9FC

7.4.4 Loading and Unloading the Scrap

Definitions

```
function LoadScrap
            : LONGINT;        {Result code}

function UnloadScrap
            : LONGINT;        {Result code}
```

Notes

1. These routines transfer the desk scrap between memory and the disk. **LoadScrap** reads the scrap into memory from the scrap file; **Unload-Scrap** writes the scrap out to the scrap file.
2. A pointer to the name of the scrap file is kept in the system global **ScrapName,** and is accessible via the **InfoScrap** routine [7.4.2].
3. The usual name of the scrap file is **ClipboardFile.**
4. The trap macros are spelled **_LodeScrap** and **_UnlodeScrap.**

Assembly Language Information

Trap macros:

(Pascal) Routine name	(Assembly) Trap macro	Trap word
LoadScrap	**_LodeScrap**	**$A9FB**
UnloadScrap	**_UnlodeScrap**	**$A9FA**

7.5 Resource Formats

7.5.1 Resource Type 'CODE'

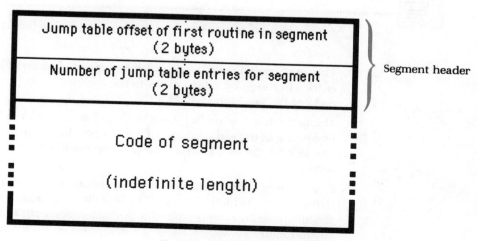

Format of resource type 'CODE'

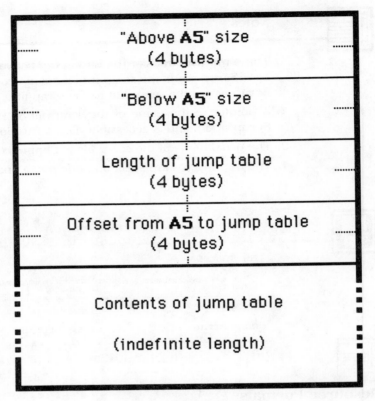

Format of segment **0**

Notes

1. A resource of type 'CODE' contains executable machine-language code.

2. The resource ID is called the *segment number*.

3. The resource data begins with a 4-byte *segment header* identifying which entries in the jump table belong to this segment; this is followed by the code of the segment itself.

4. The first 2 bytes of the segment header give the offset in bytes from the beginning of the jump table to the first entry belonging to this segment. The last 2 bytes give the number of jump table entries belonging to this segment.

5. Every application program has one special segment, resource ID **0**, containing information needed to initialize the program's application global space and jump table. The format of segment **0** is shown in the second figure above.

7.5.2 Resource Type 'PACK'

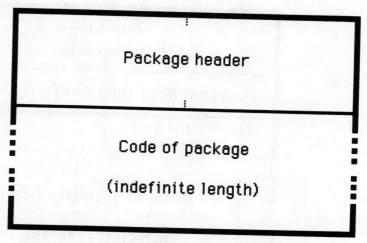

Format of resource type '**PACK**'

Notes

1. A resource of type '**PACK**' contains a *package* of predefined machine-language routines.

2. The resource data begins with a header used internally by the Toolbox to find the starting addresses of routines within the package; this is followed by the code of the routines themselves.

3. Resource IDs of packages, called *package numbers*, must be between **0** and **7**.

4. The standard packages [7.2.1] are included in the system resource file.

7.5.3 Resource Type 'FREF'

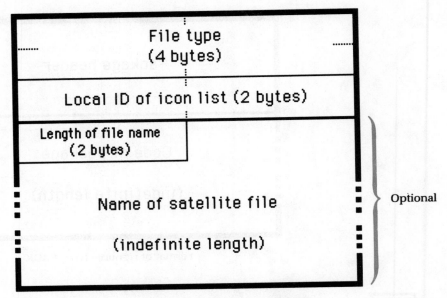

Format of resource type **'FREF'**

Notes

1. A resource of type **'FREF'** ("file reference") establishes a correspondence between a file type associated with an application program and the icon to be used by the Finder to represent files of that type on the screen.

2. The icon is defined by an *icon list* of resource type **'ICN#'** [5.5.4]. The list contains two icon definitions: the first representing the actual icon, the second a mask to be used for drawing it on the screen. The mask is normally the outline of the icon, filled in with solid black.

3. The resource data of a file reference consists of the four-character file type [7.3.1], followed by the "local ID" of the corresponding icon list. The translation from this local ID to the true resource ID is defined by a bundle resource [7.5.4].

7.5.4 Resource Type 'BNDL'

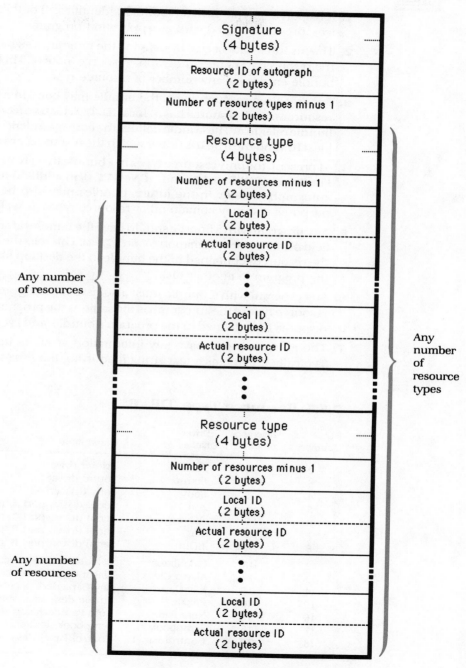

Format of resource type **'BNDL'**

Notes

1. A resource of type **'BNDL'** ("bundle") identifies all of the Finder-related rresources associated with an application program.

2. The resource data begins by defining the program's signature [7.3.1] and the resource ID of its "autograph" resource (note 6). This is followed by bundle entries for any number of resource types.

3. For any given resource type, the bundle may contain many individual resources. Each resource has a "local ID" by which other resources in the bundle refer to it. The bundle defines the correspondence between these local IDs and the true IDs under which the resources are actually stored.

4. At present, the only resource types in a bundle that are meaningful to the Finder are **'FREF'** [7.5.3] and **'ICN#'** [5.5.4], in addition to the program's autograph (note 6). In the future, bundles may also be used for other purposes and may contain other resource types as well.

5. Any program with a bundle should have the bundle bit set in the **fdFlags** field of its Finder information record [7.3.2]. This tells the Finder to install the resources contained in the bundle in the desktop file when copying the program to another disk.

6. Any program with a bundle must also have an *autograph* resource. The resource type of the autograph is the same as the program's signature; its resource ID is defined in the program's bundle, and is conventionally **0.**

7. The autograph can have any information at all as its resource data. Typically it contains a text string identifying the program and version.

7.5.5 Resource Type 'DRVR'

Unit number	Reference number	Driver name	Description
2	-3	.Print	Printer driver
3	-4	.Sound	Sound driver
4	-5	.Sony	Sony disk driver
5	-6	.AIn	Serial driver, port A (modem port) in
6	-7	.AOut	Serial driver, port A (modem port) out
7	-8	.BIn	Serial driver, port B (printer port) in
8	-9	.BOut	Serial driver, port B (printer port) out
12	-13	Calculator	Calculator desk accessory
13	-14	Alarm Clock	Alarm Clock desk accessory
14	-15	Key Caps	Key Caps desk accessory
15	-16	Puzzle	Puzzle desk accessory
16	-17	Note Pad	Note Pad desk accessory
17	-18	Scrapbook	Scrapbook desk accessory
18	-19	Control Panel	Control Panel desk accessory

Notes

1. A resource of type '**DRVR**' contains the code of an input/output device driver or a desk accessory.

2. A driver's resource ID is the same as its *unit number*, and must be between **0** and **31.**

3. The unit number also determines the *driver reference number*, by the formula

    refNum = (unitNum + 1)

4. Every driver resource must have a resource name as well as a resource ID. For true device drivers, the name begins with a period (**.**); for desk accessories, it must not.

5. The table lists the standard device drivers and desk accessories. The sound, disk, and serial drivers are permanently resident in ROM; the printer driver and desk accessories are resources included in the standard system resource file.

6. See the *Inside Macintosh* manual for further information on devices and drivers.

CHAPTER

8

Upstanding Characters

The Macintosh can display text on the screen in a seemingly endless variety of typefaces, sizes, and styles. In this chapter we'll learn how text is represented internally and how to display it and control its appearance on the screen.

The Macintosh Character Set

Every text character is represented by an 8-bit *character code* [8.1.1]. The Macintosh character set is based on the 7-bit ASCII code (American Standard Code for Information Interchange) widely used throughout the computer industry. Character codes from **0** to **127** (**$7F**) correspond to the standard ASCII characters; the remaining 128 codes are used for additional, non-ASCII characters available only on the Macintosh.

In the standard ASCII character set, the first 32 character codes, from **0** to **31** (**$1F**), along with **127** (**$7F**), stand for "control characters" with no direct visual representation. These were devised in early medieval times (circa 1940) to control teletype transmission, and many have outmoded or arcane meanings such as "end of tape," "negative acknowledge," and "synchronous idle." The Macintosh has no use for most of them; in fact, there isn't any way to type them, since the Macintosh keyboard doesn't have the control key found on most other computers. The only control characters that have their standard meanings on the Macintosh are backspace (ASCII code **$08**), tab (**$09**), and RETURN (**$0D**). A few more can be typed from the Macintosh keyboard but have nonstandard meanings: the ENTER key produces the ASCII Control-**C** or "end-of-text" character

($03), and others are generated by the clear (key) and arrow keys on the optional numeric keypad [8.1.1].

There also are a few control characters that can't be typed from the keyboard but have special graphical representations on the Macintosh screen, including the "cloverleaf" command symbol, the check mark for marking menu items, and the Apple symbol used for the menu title of desk accessories. The character codes for these screen-only characters are defined as Toolbox constants for your programs [8.1.1]. For instance, you can refer to the Apple character as **CHR(AppleMark)**.

Character codes of **128** (**$80**) and above denote extra characters added to the Macintosh character set for business and scientific purposes, as well as accents and other special characters used in foreign languages. Most of these special characters can be typed from the keyboard by holding down the option key in combination with some other character. If you are proficient in Dutch or Italian, Norwegian or Portuguese (or Albanian, Basque, or Rhaeto-Romansch, for that matter), you'll find the Macintosh provides all the characters needed to type your grocery list in those languages; if you haven't a clue what some of these characters are good for, don't lose any sleep over it.

As we learned in Chapter 2, the Toolbox uses an internal format for character strings consisting of a 1-byte character count followed by a series of bytes containing the character codes themselves. Strings of this form can be stored in resource files under resource type 'STR ' [8.4.2] and read into memory with **GetString** [8.1.2]. (Notice that the space in 'STR ' is required.) There also are utility routines [8.1.2] for copying strings within the heap: **NewString** simply returns a brand-new handle to the copy, while **SetString** accepts a handle and sets it to point to the copy.

Notice, though, that since the character count for such "Pascal-format" strings is limited to 1 byte, they can be no more than 255 characters long. For longer blocks of text there's resource type 'TEXT' [8.4.1], which has no count byte and unlimited length. (You can learn its length by using **SizeResource** [6.4.3].) It's recommended that you use string and text resources for all text your program displays on the screen, such as window titles and error or prompting messages. This makes it easy to reword messages, change terminology, correct misspellings, or translate your messages into alien tongues (such as English) without having to change the program itself.

Keyboard Configurations

Not only is the Macintosh character set designed for international use, but even the physical arrangement of characters on the keyboard can be tailored to the needs of different countries. The Macintosh keyboard is *configurable* to any desired layout. The correspondence between physical keys and the characters they stand for is defined by a *keyboard configuration* that's read from the system resource file (under resource type 'INIT' [8.4.4]) each time the system is started up. On software disks for use in a foreign country, the system file will include that country's preferred keyboard configuration. Starting the machine with such a disk transforms the keyboard into a German QWERTZ or a French AZERTY instead of the familiar American QWERTY layout. Fans of the more efficient Dvorak arrangement can reconfigure their keyboards that way also. (Of course, they'll have to rearrange the keycaps for themselves.)

When reporting the user's keystrokes to your program, the Toolbox gives both a *key code* and a *character code*. A program that uses this information properly will work the same way no matter how the user's keyboard is laid out. The key code [8.1.3] identifies the physical key that was pressed, and is unaffected by the keyboard configuration being used; the character code [8.1.1] tells what character the key stands for, as determined by the keyboard configuration. The shift, caps lock, option, and command keys are *modifier keys* that don't generate any characters of their own, but may change the meanings of the remaining *character keys*. (For instance, the shift key normally changes lowercase letters to capitals.) Exactly what effect the modifier keys have on the character keys depends on the keyboard configuration in effect; for details on the standard American configuration, see [8.1.4].

> You'll probably never have to define your own keyboard configuration, but if you do—or if you're simply curious about how the mechanism works—you'll find further information in [8.4.4] and in the "Nuts and Bolts" section at the end of this chapter.

Graphical Representation of Text

You can control the appearance of text on the screen by specifying its typeface, size, and style. The term *typeface* (or just "face") refers to the overall form or design of the characters, independent of size or style. Macintosh typefaces are conventionally named after world cities, such as **NewYork**, **Geneva**, or **Athens**. The type size is theoretically measured in printer's points; 72 points equal approximately one inch. (In practice this is more of a fiction than a reality: the actual type sizes aren't exact enough to satisfy a professional typographer, but nevertheless they're often called "point sizes.") *Type style* (or "text style" or "character style") refers to variations in the basic form of the characters such as bold, italic, underline, outline, or shadow. Together, the typeface, size, and style determine a character's form as it appears on the screen.

What we're calling typefaces are commonly referred to as "fonts," but that term also has another, more restricted meaning, as we'll discuss later. This unfortunate double use of the same term leads to some confusion. To try and minimize the ambiguity, we'll use *typeface* as defined here and reserve *font* for the second meaning to be introduced later.

The graphical representation of a character on the screen (or on a printer or other output device) is an array of pixels called a *character image* (Figure 8-1). The image is defined relative to a reference line called the *baseline* and a point on the baseline called the *character origin*. The character origin marks the position of the QuickDraw graphics pen when the character is drawn; the *character width* tells QuickDraw how far to advance the pen after drawing the character.

The character image isn't confined to these boundaries, however. The second character in Figure 8-1, for example, extends to the left of the character origin, causing it to jut slightly below the preceding character. In printer's lingo this is known as a *kern* (in this case, a backward kern). A character can also kern forward, if its image extends beyond the character width to the right. The actual width of the character image, in pixels, is called the *image width*. The character's *ascent* and *descent* measure how far it extends above and below the baseline.

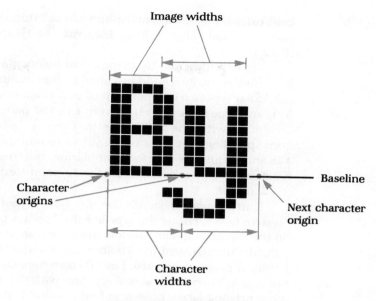

Figure 8-1 Character images

Notice that the character width and the image width aren't the same thing. The character width controls the positioning of the graphics pen as text is drawn, and is always measured from the character origin of one character to that of the next. It includes not only the width of the character itself, but also the extra space separating it from the next character. The image width measures the actual width of the character image itself. Either of the two may be **0**: a space character, for instance, has a zero image width but a nonzero character width. A zero character width produces a "dead" character that doesn't advance the pen, such as an accent that combines with the letter following it.

Fonts and Font Numbers

The collection of all the character images of a given typeface and size is called a *font*. Fonts are kept in resource files and are read into memory as needed; their resource type, reasonably enough, is **'FONT'** [8.4.5]. You don't normally have to deal with fonts directly: you specify the typeface, size, and style you want and let the Toolbox take care of the details. Before the Toolbox can do so, though, you have to initialize it for font handling with

InitFonts [8.2.4]. Always make sure you call this routine at the beginning of your program, after calling **InitGraf** [4.3.1] and before **InitWindows** [II:3.2.1].

You identify a font by giving a *font number* [8.2.1] and a type size. The font number really should be called a "face number," since it designates a particular typeface independent of size. Legal font numbers run from **0** to **511,** and type sizes can range from **1** to **127** points. The 9-bit font number combines with the 7-bit size to form a 16-bit resource ID for the corresponding font. This is equivalent to multiplying the font number by **128** and adding the size: for example, font number **3** stands for the **Geneva** typeface, so the resource ID for the 12-point **Geneva** font would be 3∗**128** + **12**, or **396.**

Font number **0** stands for the *system font* (it should really be the "system face"). This is the typeface the Toolbox uses for all text it displays on the screen, such as window titles and menu items. The system font is named **Chicago,** and the Toolbox always uses it in a standard size of 12 points. A program can also have its own *application font*, denoted by font number **1.** There is no actual typeface with this number; it refers to some other existing face whose true font number is found in the system global **ApFontID.** The application font is initialized to **Geneva** by default, but you can change it to any other typeface you wish (in assembly language, anyway) by storing the desired font number into this variable. (There's no easy way to change the application font in a high-level language like Pascal.)

Font numbers from **2** to **127** are reserved for typefaces provided by Apple. So far there are 10 such faces available in addition to the **Chicago** system font; their font numbers are included in the Toolbox interface as predefined constants [8.2.1]. Licensed Macintosh software developers can register their own typefaces with Apple and have assigned to them font numbers from **128** to **383.** Unregistered typefaces should have numbers between **384** and **511.**

The Toolbox routines **GetFontName** and **GetFNum** [8.2.5] convert between a font number and the corresponding typeface name. The Toolbox finds the name by looking for a font resource with the given font number and a point size of **0.** This resource name is the typeface name: for example, font resource number **384** (3∗**128** + **0**) has the resource name '**Geneva'.** This "0-point" font has no resource data; it exists solely to carry the typeface's name. The real fonts, those with nonzero point sizes, have no resource names.

Not every point size exists for a given typeface. If you ask to use a face and size that can't be found in any open resource file, the Toolbox will automatically choose a suitable existing font in that typeface and scale it to the requested size. The results aren't always pleasing to the eye, however, as you can see by looking at, say, 12-point **Athens** in MacWrite or MacPaint. To find out if a given combination exists, use **RealFont** [8.2.5].

Structure of a Font

A font's complete definition is contained in a *font record* [8.2.2]. This is a complex data structure that includes the character images themselves along with additional information about the font's overall characteristics. The Toolbox normally handles font records, so you don't really need to know their internal structure. The following discussion is for enhancing your background understanding, and you can safely skip it if you're in a hurry.

Do keep in mind, though, that because font records are lengthy they use a lot of space in memory or on the disk. It takes a great many bits to define all the character images, and since the images are two-dimensional, they grow with the square of the point size. Besides the actual character images, there's also a sizable fixed overhead for every font record. A typical 9-point font occupies about 2K bytes, an 18-point font about 5K, and a 24-point font about 8K.

A program that uses many fonts will find that it can't keep them all in memory at once. Such a program tends to become "disk-bound," spending most of its time waiting for fonts to be read in from the disk. To see this effect for yourself, try making up a MacWrite document that uses 10 or 12 different fonts on the same line of text, and listen to the disk spin when you try to select an insertion point on that line with the mouse.

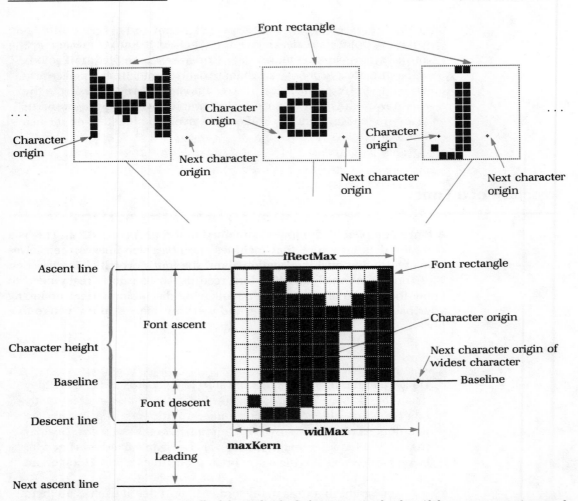

The font rectangle would enclose all of the individual characters in the font if they were superimposed with their character origins coinciding. **fRectMax,** the width of the font rectangle, is the font's maximum image width; **widMax** is the maximum character width.

Figure 8-2 Font characteristics

Figure 8-2 shows some font characteristics defined in the font record. If all the individual character images in the font are superimposed with their character origins coinciding, the *font rectangle* will be the smallest rectangle, relative to the baseline and character origin, that encloses them all. Its width, **fRectMax,** encloses the image widths of all the characters. (Don't forget that the image width isn't the same as the character width; the font's maximum character width, from character origin to character origin, is given by the **widMax** field.) The maximum ascent and descent for any individual character determine the overall ascent and descent of the font, and thus establish its *ascent line* and *descent line* with respect to the baseline. Together, the ascent and descent give the font's *character height*, the overall height of the font rectangle from ascent line to descent line. *Leading* (rhymes with "heading," not "heeding") is the amount of extra vertical space between lines of text, from the descent line of one to the ascent line of the next.

The font record's heart is the *font image* [8.2.3], which defines every character's appearance. This is a rectangular bit image made up of all the individual character images laid end to end in one long horizontal row, often called a "strike" of the font (see Figure 8-3). The font image's height is simply the font's character height; its row width is given by the **rowWords** field of the font record. (Notice that the row width is given in *words*, not in bytes as in a QuickDraw bit map [4.2.1].)

The character images are arranged within the strike by ascending character code. There needn't be an image for every possible character; characters that aren't included in the strike are said to be *missing* from the font. Every font includes a special *missing symbol* (typically a hollow square) to be used in place of all missing characters. The missing symbol is

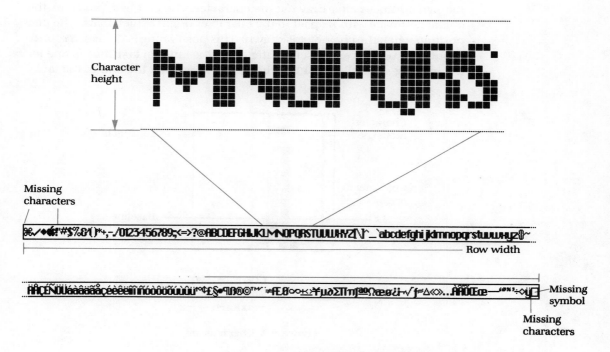

Figure 8-3 A font image

always the last character image in the strike. The font record's **firstChar** and **lastChar** fields give the character codes of the first and last character actually defined. Characters outside this range are understood to be missing, and some of those within the range may be missing as well.

To locate each individual character within the strike, there's a *location table* [8.2.3] with an entry for each character from **firstChar** to **lastChar.** The location table entry gives the horizontal offset, in pixels, from the beginning of the strike to the left edge of the character.

The character's image width is found by subtracting this offset from that of the next character, taken from the next entry in the location table. (Notice that for this to work properly, the location table entry for a missing character must always be the same as that of the next defined character.) At the end of the location table are two extra entries, one for the missing symbol and another to mark the end of the strike; this last entry is simply the total width of the strike in pixels.

Following the location table is the *offset/width table* [8.2.3], which controls the positioning of the graphics pen as text is drawn. Like the location table, the offset/width table is indexed from **firstChar** to **lastChar + 2.** An entry of **−1** in this table marks a character as missing. Otherwise, the second byte of the 2-byte table entry gives the character width, the distance the pen advances after drawing the character. The first byte positions the character image with respect to the character origin (which marks the pen position when the character is drawn). This positioning is done in a round-about way, which we'll discuss later. After the entry of **lastChar** is one for the missing symbol, then a final entry of **−1** marking the end of the table.

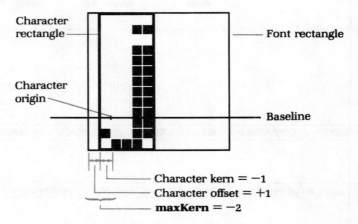

Figure 8-4 Character offset

Returning to the font rectangle shown in Figure 8-2, notice that it extends to the left of the character origin by an amount equal to the font's **maxKern** field, the maximum leftward kern of any character in the font. Because it's measured from right to left, **maxKern** always has a negative (or zero) value; in the figure, it would be −**2**. Now suppose that a given character kerns by less than the maximum—say by one pixel instead of two (see Figure 8-4). Then the left edge of the character lies one pixel in from the left edge of the overall font rectangle. This *character offset* is what's kept in the high-order byte of an offset/width table entry. Adding the character offset (**1** in the figure) to the font's maximum kern (−**2**) gives the kern for the individual character (−**1**). For a character with no kern at all, the character offset is the negative of **maxKern** (+**2** in the example) so when they're added together they cancel and produce a character kern of **0**.

Because the font image, location table, and offset/width table all vary in length from one font to another, they can't be included in a valid Pascal declaration for the font record. (Notice that they're shown in comment brackets in [8.2.2].) The Toolbox has no trouble accessing them, of course, since it's written in assembly language; they can even be reached in Pascal if you're willing to do some (ugh!) pointer arithmetic. The **owTLoc** field of the font record serves as a guidepost by giving the distance in words (not bytes!) from itself to the beginning of the offset/width table.

QuickDraw Text Characteristics

Like anything you put on the screen, text gets drawn through the medium of a QuickDraw graphics port. The **GrafPort** record includes six fields that control the way text is drawn in that port [8.3.1]. The QuickDraw routines to set these fields, as well as those that draw and measure text, operate implicitly on the current port—so before using them you must "get into" the right port with **SetPort** [4.3.3].

Unfortunately, the names of the port's text-related fields suffer from the inconsistent terminology mentioned earlier. The **txFont** field doesn't really identify a font, but a typeface (that is, a "font number"); the field named **txFace** doesn't refer to the typeface at all, but to what we're calling the character style, such as bold or italic. Please make the appropriate mental annotations on your conceptual map.

A newly created graphics port is initially set up to display text in the system font (font number **0**) at the standard size of 12 points, with plain character style. You can change the typeface for the current port with **TextFont,** the point size with **TextSize,** the character style with **TextFace,** or the transfer mode used for drawing text with **TextMode** [8.3.2]. Character styles are expressed as Pascal sets containing values of the enumerated type **StyleItem** [8.3.1]. For instance, the set [**Underline**] denotes underlining, [**Bold, Underline**] denotes bold and underline in combination, and the empty set [] stands for plain character style, with none of the fancy variations. You can also do "set arithmetic" to turn individual style variations on or off without affecting the others: for example, the statement

```
TextFace (ThePort^.txFace + [Underline])
```

turns on underlining without affecting the remaining settings, and

```
TextFace (ThePort^.txFace — [Underline])
```

turns it off.

QuickDraw produces the style variations by applying transformations to the character images it gets from the font. For instance, it produces boldface by thickening the character horizontally a suitable number of pixels, and creates italic by skewing the pixels horizontally depending on their height above or below the baseline. These style transformations aren't normally reflected in the font itself.

The **spExtra** field of the graphics port (set with **SpaceExtra** [8.3.2]) is useful mainly for justifying text to both a left and a right margin. Although this field is nominally defined as a long integer [4.2.2], it's actually interpreted as a fixed-point number [2.3.1] with a 16-bit integer part and a 16-bit fraction. When drawing text, QuickDraw uses this information to widen the space characters to make the text come out even at both margins. To find the proper **spExtra** value for a line of text, divide the excess line width (the width between margins minus the measured width of the text) by the number of spaces in the line, using the utility function **FixRatio** [2.3.2] to produce a fixed-point result.

Finally, there's a **device** field that tells what output device the port is intended to draw on, such as the screen or a printer. The Toolbox uses this information to select the appropriate fonts for that particular device. When you create a port, its **device** field is initialized to **0,** representing the Macintosh screen, and for most ordinary purposes you'll want to leave this setting alone.

Drawing and Measuring Text

To draw text in the current graphics port, you use the QuickDraw routines **DrawChar, DrawString,** and **DrawText** [8.3.3]. **DrawChar** is the basic routine, which draws a single character; the other two routines call it repeatedly to draw the text a character at a time. **DrawString** accepts a Pascal string, which is expected to begin with a 1-byte character count. **DrawText** accepts a pointer to an arbitrary data structure, which *doesn't* start with a character count; the text to be drawn can be any specified sequence of bytes from within the structure.

> **DrawText** is useful for displaying the contents of '**TEXT**' resources [8.4.1], but notice that you have to convert the handle you get from **GetResource** [6.3.1] into a simple pointer to pass to **DrawText.** To be safe, you had better lock the text into the heap before dereferencing the handle and don't forget to unlock it again when you've finished drawing it.

Text is always drawn in the port's current typeface, size, style, and text mode. Each character is drawn with its character origin at the port's current pen position (**pnLoc** [5.2.1]); the pen then advances to the right by the character width, adjusted for style variations if necessary. The operation leaves the pen positioned on the baseline just after the last character drawn. ASCII control characters such as carriage return, line feed, tab, and backspace have no special meaning to QuickDraw; if you want to use these characters for formatting purposes, you must test for them and reposition the pen yourself with **Move** or **MoveTo** [5.2.4].

```
procedure ShowFonts;


   { Display samples of all available fonts.  }


   const
      leftMargin = 10;                          {Margin from left edge of window, in pixels}
      topMargin  = 10;                          {Margin from top edge of window, in pixels}


   var
      currentPort : GrafPtr;                    {Pointer to current port [4.2.2]}

      oldOrigin   : Point;                      {Previous origin of port rectangle [4.1.1]}
      oldPenLoc   : Point;                      {Previous position of graphics pen [4.1.1]}

      oldFont     : INTEGER;                    {Previous typeface ("font number") [8.3.1]}
      oldSize     : INTEGER;                    {Previous point size [8.3.1]}
      oldFace     : Style;                      {Previous text style ("face") [8.3.1]}

      baseline    : INTEGER;                    {Vertical position of baseline in pixels}

      nFonts      : INTEGER;                    {Total number of font resources available}
      thisFont    : INTEGER;                    {Index for accessing individual fonts}

      rsrcHandle  : Handle;                     {Handle to font resource [3.1.1]}
      rsrcID      : INTEGER;                    {Resource ID of font}
      rsrcType    : ResType;                    {Resource type of font [6.1.1]}
      rsrcName    : Str255;                     {Resource name of font [2.1.1]}

      faceNumber  : INTEGER;                    {"Font number" for typeface}
      faceName    : Str255;                     {Name of typeface [2.1.1]}

      pointSize   : INTEGER;                    {Type size in points}
      pointString : Str255;                     {Type size as character string [2.1.1]}

      theInfo     : FontInfo;                   {Font information record [8.2.6]}


   begin {ShowFonts}

      GetPort (currentPort);                    {Get pointer to current port [4.3.3]}
      with currentPort^ do
         begin
            oldOrigin := portRect.topLeft;      {Save old origin of port rectangle [4.2.2, 4.1.2]}
            GetPen (oldPenLoc);                 {Save old pen position [5.2.4]}
```

Program 8-1 Display available fonts

```
      oldFont   := txFont;               {Save old typeface ("font number") [8.3.1]}
      oldSize   := txSize;               {Save old point size [8.3.1]}
      oldFace   := txFace                {Save old text style ("face") [8.3.1]}
   end;

SetOrigin (-leftMargin, -topMargin);     {Offset to origin of text [4.3.4]}
baseline := 0;                           {Start text at top margin}
TextFace ([ ]);                          {Use plain text style [8.3.2]}

nFonts := CountResources ('FONT');       {Get total number of available fonts [6.3.3]}
for thisFont := 1 to nFonts do           {Iterate through available fonts}
   begin

      rsrcHandle := GetIndResource ('FONT', thisFont);      {Get next font [6.3.3]}
      GetResInfo (rsrcHandle, rsrcID, rsrcType, rsrcName);  {Get resource information [6.4.1]}

      faceNumber := rsrcID div 128;      {Isolate typeface number}
      pointSize  := rsrcID mod 128;      {   and point size       }

      if pointSize <> 0 then             {Ignore dummy "font name" resources}
         begin

            TextFont (faceNumber);       {Set port's typeface [8.3.2]}
            TextSize (pointSize);        {Set port's type size [8.3.2]}

            GetFontInfo (theInfo);                    {Get font measurements [8.2.6]}
            baseline := baseline + theInfo.ascent;    {Advance baseline by font ascent [8.2.6]}
            MoveTo (0, baseline);                     {Position pen at start of line [5.2.4]}

            GetFontName (faceNumber, faceName);  {Get name of typeface [8.2.5]}
            DrawString (faceName);               {Display typeface name [8.3.3]}
            DrawChar   (' ');                    {Insert space character for separation [8.3.3]}

            NumToString (pointSize, pointString); {Convert type size to string [2.3.4]}
            DrawString  (pointString);            {Display type size [8.3.3]}

            with theInfo do              {Advance to next ascent line [8.2.6]}
               baseline := baseline + descent + leading

         end {if}

   end; {for}
```

Program 8-1 (*continued*)

```
TextFont (oldFont);              {Restore previous typeface ("font number") [8.3.2]}
TextSize (oldSize);              {Restore previous point size [8.3.2]}
TextFace (oldFace);              {Restore previous text style ("face") [8.3.2]}


with oldOrigin do                {Restore previous origin [4.3.4]}
    SetOrigin (h, v);


with oldPenLoc do                {Restore previous pen position [5.2.4]}
    MoveTo (h, v)

end;   {ShowFonts}
```

Program 8-1 (*continued*)

Program 8-1 (**ShowFonts**) shows an example of text drawing. This routine finds every available font in all open resource files and displays a sample of each in the current graphics port, as in Figure 8-5. (Of course, if the current port is a window on the screen, it may not have room to display this much text all at once. In that case, some of the text will fall outside the window's port rectangle and won't be drawn: QuickDraw will suppress it automatically, as it always does when you try to draw anything outside a port's clipping boundaries.)

We begin by saving various properties of the current port that we'll be changing within the routine (the coordinate origin, pen position, typeface, type size, and type style), so we can restore their previous settings before returning. For convenience, we transform the coordinate origin to the top-left corner of the area where the font samples will be displayed, as defined by the pair of constants **leftMargin** and **topMargin**. The baseline for text drawing is initialized to the very top of this area; we'll be advancing it downward by the appropriate distance as we draw each line of text.

After setting the port's type style with **TextFace** [8.3.2] to plain text (no bold, italic, or other variations), we're ready to start generating the available font resources, using the Toolbox routines **CountResources** and **GetIndResource** [6.3.3]. As we learned in Chapter 6, **CountResources** tells how many resources there are of a given type (in this case 'FONT') in all open resource files. By calling **GetIndResource** with an index number (**thisFont**) ranging from 1 up to this total number, we can get a handle to each individual font resource in turn.

For each font resource, we call **GetResInfo** [6.4.1] to find out the resource ID, which we then break down with the Pascal *div* and *mod* operators into a 9-bit typeface number and a 7-bit point size. Remember, though, that some of the fonts in a resource file are "dummy" fonts with a point size of **0**, which exist solely to carry the typeface name; these "0-point" fonts have no character images to display text with, so we just ignore them.

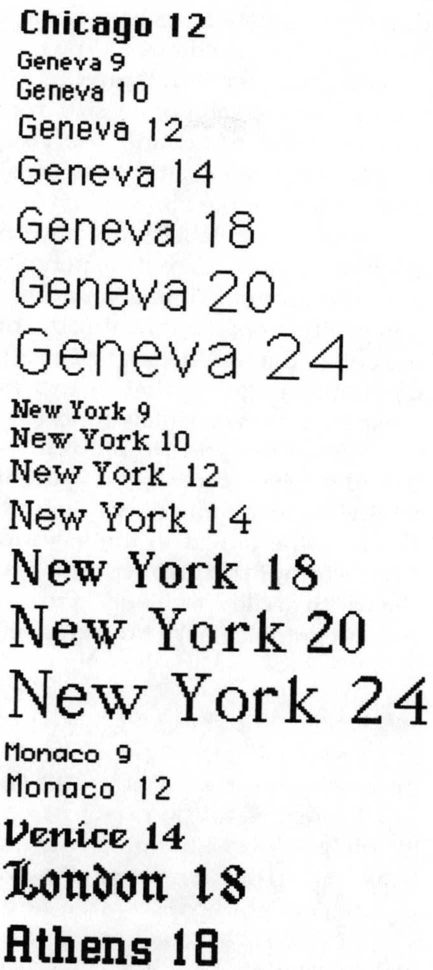

Chicago 12
Geneva 9
Geneva 10
Geneva 12
Geneva 14
Geneva 18
Geneva 20
Geneva 24
New York 9
New York 10
New York 12
New York 14
New York 18
New York 20
New York 24
Monaco 9
Monaco 12
Venice 14
𝕷ondon 18
Athens 18

Figure 8-5 Output of procedure **ShowFonts**

For every font with a nonzero point size, we set the current port's text characteristics to the font's typeface and size with **TextFont** and **TextSize** [8.3.2], then call **GetFontInfo** [8.2.6] to get the font's ascent, descent, and leading measurements.

The ascent value tells us how far to lower our baseline to position it for the line of text we're about to display. Then we move the graphics pen to the beginning of the new baseline to get ready to display the characters. We get the name of the font's typeface by calling **GetFontName** [8.2.5] and display it with **DrawString** [8.3.3]. (Notice that we can't simply use the resource name we received earlier from **GetResInfo**, since only the dummy "0-point" fonts have resource names; the resource representing a "real" font has no name of its own.) Following the typeface name, we insert a space character with **DrawChar** [8.3.3] to separate it from the point size; then we convert the point size from an integer to a character string with **NumToString** [2.3.4] and use **DrawString** again to display the result. Finally we advance the baseline by the font's descent and leading to prepare for the next line of text and repeat the loop.

After all available fonts have been generated, we restore the port's original typeface, size, style, pen position, and coordinate origin, then exit from the routine. Notice that at the beginning of the routine we saved the pen position *before* adjusting the port's coordinate origin. When we got to the end of the routine, we had to restore the original pen position *after* the coordinate origin, so that it's expressed in the same system of coordinates in which it was originally reported.

Sometimes you simply want to measure how wide a piece of text would be *if* you drew it, but without actually drawing it. (For instance, you might be calculating how much extra space you need between words to justify a line of text to the left and right margins.) For this, you can use **CharWidth, StringWidth,** and **TextWidth** [8.3.4]. These routines measure the width of the specified text in pixels, using the text characteristics of the current graphics port. No text is actually drawn and the pen is not moved.

QuickDraw doesn't need a font's actual character images to measure text, just the character widths given in the font's offset/width table. So to conserve heap space, there's a special, abbreviated form of font record especially for measuring text, called a *font-width table.* It's identified by the constant **FontWid** in the font's **fontType** field [8.2.2], and contains no font image, location table, or **rowWords** field. Width tables are stored in resource files under resource type **'FWID'** [8.4.6]; the resource ID is the same as for the corresponding font. If such a resource is available for a given font, the Toolbox will use it for text-measuring operations. If no **'FWID'** resource is available, the full font is used instead.

Nuts and Bolts

"Dead" Characters

Some of the accented foreign letters in the Macintosh character set have no direct keyboard equivalents, even when using the option key. Instead, they're typed as two-character sequences: first the accent, followed by the letter it applies to. For instance, to type a circumflex "e" (ê, character code **$90**), you must type the circumflex (^) first, then the letter **e.**

The Macintosh keyboard driver—the part of the system software that reads characters typed from the keyboard and feeds them to the running program by way of the Toolbox—automatically detects such sequences and converts them into the corresponding accented letters. By the time the program sees them, it receives the single accented letter instead of the two-character sequence that was actually typed. In effect, the accents (acute, grave, circumflex, umlaut, and tilde) function as "dead keys": typing them doesn't advance the insertion point, so the next letter is combined with the accent instead of following it separately.

Actually, the accents combine with the following letter only if the resulting combination exists as a distinct single character in the Macintosh character set. Otherwise, the accent and the letter remain two separate characters. For instance, although the circumflex accent combines with a following **e** to form the character ê (**$90**) as described above, a circumflex followed by an **f** would remain two separate characters.

Notice, also, that three of the accents are included in the standard ASCII character set, with character codes below **$7F:** grave (**'**, code **$60**), circumflex (**^**, **$5E**), and tilde (**~**, **$7E**). Each of these characters can be typed in two different ways, on different keys, one with and one without the option key. When typed without the option, the accent always stands alone as a separate character. With the option, it becomes a "dead" character and will combine with the following letter if appropriate (for instance, the tilde will combine with a following **n**). If you find this discussion hard to follow, try experimenting for yourself with the Key Caps desk accessory.

Details of Keyboard Configurations

The job of translating the "raw" keystrokes typed by the user into characters to be sent to the program is performed by a pair of low-level machine language routines, one for the keyboard and another for the numeric keypad. Pointers to these routines are kept in the system globals **Key1Trans** and **Key2Trans.** The configuration routines are loaded from the system resource file each time the system is started up; they have resource type '**INIT**' [8.4.4] and resource IDs **1** (keyboard) and **2** (keypad). The resource data is simply the routine's machine-language code.

The configuration routines receive their arguments and return their results directly in the processor's registers, so they can only be written in and called from assembly language. They receive a key code in register **D2** and a word giving the state of the modifier keys in **D1,** and return a character code in **D0** (or **0** for no character). See [8.4.4] for further details.

REFERENCE

8.1 Keys and Characters

8.1.1 Character Set

Definitions

```
const
  CommandMark = $11;    {Character code of command mark}
  CheckMark    = $12;    {Character code of check mark}
  DiamondMark  = $13;    {Character code of diamond mark}
  AppleMark    = $14;    {Character code of Apple mark}
```

First hex digit

	$0	$1	$2	$3	$4	$5	$6	$7	$8	$9	$A	$B	$C	$D	$E	$F
0	NUL	□	Space	0	@	P	`	p	Ä	ê	†	∞	¿	–	□	□
1	□	⌘	!	1	A	Q	a	q	Å	ë	°	±	¡	—	□	□
2	□	✓	"	2	B	R	b	r	Ç	í	¢	≤	¬	"	□	□
3	□	◆	#	3	C	S	c	s	É	ì	£	≥	√	"	□	□
4	□	🍎	$	4	D	T	d	t	Ñ	î	§	¥	ƒ	'	□	□
5	□	□	%	5	E	U	e	u	Ö	ï	•	µ	≈	'	□	□
6	□	□	&	6	F	V	f	v	Ü	ñ	¶	∂	∆	÷	□	□
7	□	□	'	7	G	W	g	w	á	ó	ß	Σ	«	◊	□	□
8	□	□	(	8	H	X	h	x	à	ò	®	Π	»	ÿ	□	□
9	TAB	□	)	9	I	Y	i	y	â	ô	©	π	…	□	□	□
A	□	□	*	:	J	Z	j	z	ä	ö	™	∫	non-break space	□	□	□
B	□	□	+	;	K	[	k	{	ã	õ	´	ª	Â	□	□	□
C	□	□	,	<	L	\	l	|	å	ú	¨	º	Ã	□	□	□
D	CR	□	-	=	M	]	m	}	ç	ù	≠	Ω	Õ	□	□	
E	□	□	.	>	N	^	n	~	é	û	Æ	æ	Œ	□	□	
F	□	□	/	?	O	_	o		è	ü	Ø	ø	œ	□	□	□

Second hex digit

Characters with shading are typed
as two-character combinations.

Character codes

Notes

1. Character codes stand for the characters themselves, not the keys that produce them. The character produced by a given key depends on which modifier keys were held down along with it and on the keyboard configuration in effect.

2. Character codes from **$00** to **$7F** follow the standard ASCII character set (American Standard Code for Information Interchange).

3. Most ASCII control characters (character codes **$00** to **$1F**, as well as **$7F**) can't be generated from the Macintosh keyboard. Exceptions are:

Keyboard:

Character code	Key
$03	Enter
$08	Backspace
$09	Tab
$0D	Return

Keypad:

Character code	Key
$03	Enter
$1B	Clear
$1C	Left arrow
$1D	Right arrow
$1E	Up arrow
$1F	Down arrow

4. The following ASCII control characters are redefined as special symbols for use on the Macintosh screen:

Character code	Symbol	Name
$11	⌘	Command mark
$12	✓	Check mark
$13	◆	Diamond mark
$14	🍎	Apple mark

These characters are intended only for display on the screen, and can't be typed from the keyboard.

5. The command mark is used for displaying Command-key equivalents of items on a menu; the check mark for marking menu items [II:4.6.4]; the Apple mark for the title of the menu of desk accessories.

6. The diamond mark is a vestige of earlier versions of the Macintosh user interface and no longer has any specific use.

7. Character codes of **$80** and above denote special characters added to the Macintosh character set for international, business, and scientific use.

8. Characters shaded in the figure aren't generated directly from the keyboard. Instead they're typed as two-character combinations, a diacritical (accent) mark followed by the letter it is combined with. The Toolbox automatically converts such two-character combinations into the corresponding single accented characters.

Assembly-Language Information

Assembly language constants:

Name	Value	Meaning
CommandMark	$11	Character code of command mark
CheckMark	$12	Character code of check mark
DiamondMark	$13	Character code of diamond mark
AppleMark	$14	Character code of Apple mark

8.1.2 Character Strings

Definitions

```
type
  StringPtr    = ^Str255;              {Pointer to a string}
  StringHandle = ^StringPtr;           {Handle to a string}

function  NewString
              (oldString : Str255)     {String to be copied}
                : StringHandle;        {Handle to copy}

function  GetString
              (stringID: INTEGER)      {Resource ID of desired string}
                : StringHandle;        {Handle to string in memory}

procedure SetString
              (theString : StringHandle;   {Handle to be set}
               setTo     : Str255);        {String to set it to}
```

Notes

1. **StringPtr** and **StringHandle** are a pointer and a handle to a string, respectively.
2. **NewString** allocates heap space for a new, relocatable copy of a given string and returns a handle to the copy.
3. **GetString** gets a string from a resource file, reads it into memory if necessary, and returns a handle to it.
4. **stringID** is the resource ID of the desired string; its resource type is 'STR ' [8.4.2].
5. **SetString** makes a copy of a given string and sets an existing string handle to point to the copy.

Assembly Language Information

Trap macros:

(Pascal) Routine name	(Assembly) Trap macro	Trap word
NewString	**_NewString**	**$A906**
GetString	**_GetString**	**$A9BA**
SetString	**_SetString**	**$A907**

8.1.3 Key Codes

Notes

1. Key codes stand for physical keys on the Macintosh keyboard, not the characters the keys represent. They're independent of any particular keyboard configuration and are not affected by modifier keys.

2. The modifier keys (Shift, Caps Lock, Option, Command) have no key codes, since they don't generate characters by themselves.

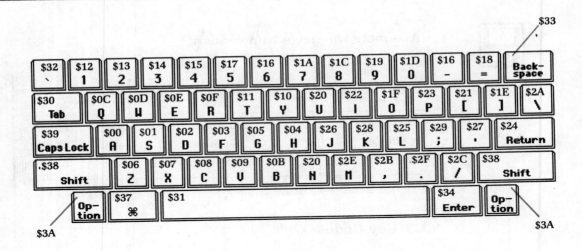

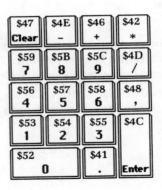

Small hexadecimal numbers are key codes.

Key codes

8.1.4 Standard Keyboard Layout

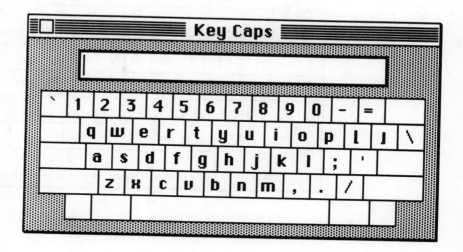

Unshifted.

Standard keyboard layout (unshifted)

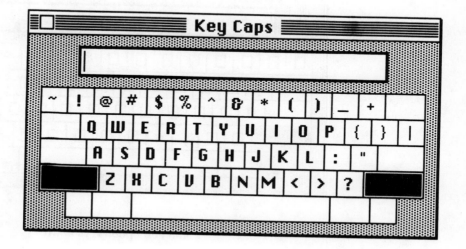

Shift key down.

Standard keyboard layout (with Shift)

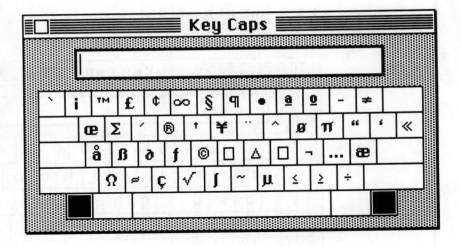

Option key down.

Standard keyboard layout (with Option)

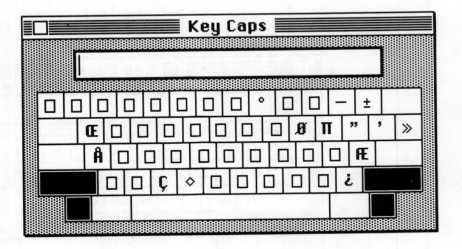

Shift and option keys down.

Standard keyboard layout (with Option-Shift)

Notes

1. The keyboard layouts shown are for the standard (American) keyboard configuration.
2. Keys left blank in the diagrams have no character assignment for that modifier combination.
3. The Caps Lock key has the same effect as Shift, but for letter keys only; it has no effect on other keys.

8.2 Fonts

8.2.1 Standard Font Numbers

Definitions

```
const
    SystemFont  =  0;
    ApplFont    =  1;
    NewYork     =  2;
    Geneva      =  3;
    Monaco      =  4;
    Venice      =  5;
    London      =  6;
    Athens      =  7;
    SanFran     =  8;
    Toronto     =  9;
    Cairo       = 11;
    LosAngeles  = 12;
```

Notes

1. A font number identifies a typeface, independent of size or style.

2. Font numbers must not exceed **511.**

3. To get the resource ID of the font for a given typeface and size, multiply the font number by 128 and add the type size in points.

4. Font number **0** refers to the *system font,* used for menu items, window titles, and other text displayed on the screen by the system.

5. The system font is named **Chicago,** and is always displayed in a standard size of 12 points. The system font cannot be changed.

6. The assembly-language global variable **ROMFont0** holds a handle to the font record [8.2.2] for the system font.

7. Font number **1** refers to the *application font,* which is always some other existing typeface with a (true) font number of its own. There is no actual typeface with this number.

8. By default, the application font is **Geneva**; the number of the default application font is kept in the global variable **SPFont.**

9. To change the application font in assembly language, store the desired font number into the global variable **ApFontID.** There is no straightforward way to change this setting in Pascal.

10. Font numbers from **2** to **383** are reserved for official assignment by Apple. Numbers **2** to **127** are for Apple's own typefaces, **128** to **383** for those formally registered with Apple by licensed Macintosh software developers. Unregistered typefaces should have numbers from **384** to **511.**

Assembly Language Information

Standard font numbers:

Name	Value
SysFont	**0**
ApplFont	**1**
NewYork	**2**
Geneva	**3**
Monaco	**4**
Venice	**5**
London	**6**
Athens	**7**
SanFran	**8**
Toronto	**9**
Cairo	**11**
LosAngeles	**12**

Assembly-language global variables:

Name	Address	Meaning
ROMFont0	**$980**	Handle to system font
ApFontID	**$984**	True font number of current application font
SPFont	**$204**	True font number of default application font

8.2.2 Font Records

Definitions

```
type
  FontRecord = record
                fontType  : INTEGER;  {Font type (proportional or fixed-width)}
                firstChar : INTEGER;  {Character code of first defined character}
                lastChar  : INTEGER;  {Character code of last defined character}
                widMax    : INTEGER;  {Maximum character width in pixels}
                kernMax   : INTEGER;  {Maximum backward kern in pixels}
                nDescent  : INTEGER;  {Negative of descent in pixels}
                fRectMax  : INTEGER;  {Maximum image width in pixels}
                chHeight  : INTEGER;  {Character height in pixels (ascent + descent)}
                owTLoc    : INTEGER;  {Offset to owTable in words}
                ascent    : INTEGER;  {Ascent in pixels}
                descent   : INTEGER;  {Descent in pixels}
                leading   : INTEGER;  {Leading in pixels}
                rowWords  : INTEGER;  {Row width of bitImage in words}
                {bitImage : array [1..rowWords, 1..chHeight] of INTEGER;}
                                      {Font image [8.2.3]}
                {locTable : array [firstChar..lastChar+2] of INTEGER;}
                                      {Location table [8.2.3]}
                {owTable  : array [firstChar..lastChar+2] of INTEGER;}
                                      {Offset/width table [8.2.3]}
              end;

const
  PropFont  = $9000;              {Font type for proportional font}
  FixedFont = $B000;              {Font type for fixed-width font}
  FontWid   = $ACB0;              {Font type for font width table}
```

Notes

1. A font record defines the character images and other characteristics of a single font.

2. Font records are used internally by the Toolbox; there's normally no need for an application program to refer to them directly.

3. Font records are stored in resource files under resource type 'FONT' [8.4.5] and read into the heap with **GetResource** [6.3.1].

4. **fontType** should be **PropFont** for a proportional font (character widths vary), **FixedFont** for a fixed-width font (all characters same width), **FontWid** for a font width table [8.4.6].

5. A font width table has no **rowWords, bitImage,** and **locTable** fields.

6. **firstChar** and **lastChar** are the character codes of the first and last characters defined in this font.

7. **fRectMax** and **chHeight** give the dimensions of the *font rectangle.* If all the individual character images in the font are superimposed with their character origins coinciding, the font rectangle is the smallest rectangle enclosing them all.

8. **widMax** is the maximum character width for any single character in the font; **fRectMax** is the width of the font rectangle, enclosing all the individual image widths.

9. **ascent** and **descent** define the font's vertical extent relative to the baseline. Their sum gives the overall character height, **chHeight.**

10. **nDescent** should always equal the negative of **descent.**

11. **kernMax** is the maximum negative (leftward) kern of any character in the font, and should never be greater than **0.** This value determines the position of the character origin within the font rectangle.

12. **leading** is the amount of extra vertical space in pixels between lines of text, from the descent line of one to the ascent line of the next.

13. The leading value given in the font record is merely recommended, and is not binding on the application program. Some parts of the Toolbox, notably the TextEdit routines for cut-and-paste editing (Volume Two, Chapter 5) will use this value by default, but you can override it to produce whatever vertical spacing you like.

14. The remaining fields (**owTLoc, rowWords, bitImage, locTable, owTable**) are discussed in [8.2.3].

Assembly Language Information

Field offsets in a font record:

(Pascal) Field name	(Assembly) Offset name	Size in bytes
fontType	**FFormat**	**0**
firstChar	**FMinChar**	**2**
lastChar	**FMaxChar**	**4**
widMax	**FMaxWd**	**6**
kernMax	**FBBOX**	**8**
nDescent	**FBBOY**	**10**
fRectMax	**FBBDX**	**12**
chHeight	**FBBDY**	**14**
owTLoc	**FLength**	**16**
ascent	**FAscent**	**18**
descent	**FDescent**	**20**
leading	**FLeading**	**22**
rowWords	**FRaster**	**24**

Assembly-language constants:

Name	Value	Meaning
PropFont	**$9000**	Font type for proportional font
FixedFont	**$B000**	Font type for fixed-width font
FontWid	**$ACB0**	Font type for font width table

8.2.3 The Font Image

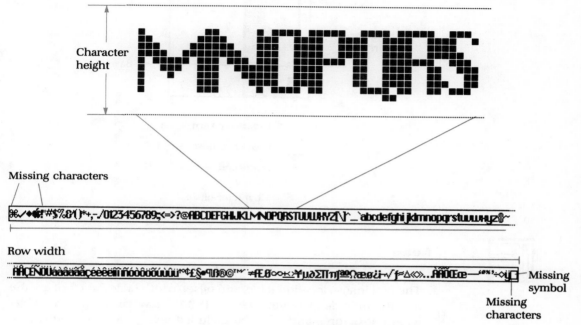

Font image

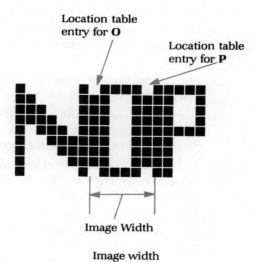

Image width

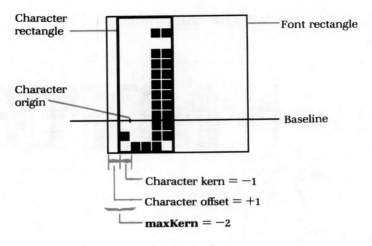

Character offset

Notes

1. The font image, location table, and offset/width table for a font are the last three fields of its font record [8.2.2]. However, they're variable-length structures and can't be included (except as comments) in a valid Pascal type declaration for the font record. They're accessible in assembly language, or in Pascal via pointer manipulation with **POINTER, ORD**, and @ (Chapter 2).

2. The *font image* (**bitImage**) is a bit image containing all the font's character images arranged consecutively in a single horizontal "strike."

3. The row width of the font image (**rowWords**) is given in *words,* not in bytes as in a QuickDraw bit map [4.2.1].

4. Every font has a *missing symbol* to be used for drawing characters that are missing from the font. The missing symbol is always the last character in the font image, following the last defined character.

5. A character is considered missing if its character code is less than **firstChar** or greater than **lastChar** [8.2.2], or if its entry in the offset/width table is −1.

6. The ASCII null character (character code **$00**), horizontal tab (**$09**), and carriage return (**$0D**) must not be missing; they must be defined in the font image, even if only with zero image width. The tab character, in particular, is commonly defined to be equivalent to an ordinary space.

7. The location table (**locTable**) gives the horizontal offset, in pixels, from the beginning of the font image to the beginning of each character image.

8. A character's image width is found by subtracting its location table entry from that of the next character. The entry for a missing character should be the same as that of the next defined character in the font.

9. The next-to-last entry in the location table, **locTable[lastChar+1]**, gives the location of the missing symbol within the font image. The last entry, **locTable[lastChar+2]**, contains the total width of the font image (strike) in pixels.

10. The offset/width table (**owTable**) is located within the font record by means of the **owTLoc** field, which gives the offset in words from itself to the beginning of the table.

11. The low-order byte of an offset/width table entry gives the character width in pixels.

12. The high-order byte gives the *character offset,* the difference between this character's leftward kern and **maxKern**. This determines the position of the character rectangle relative to the overall font rectangle, and thus locates the character origin (QuickDraw pen position) within the character image.

13. Missing characters have an offset/width table entry of −**1.**

14. The next-to-last entry in the offset/width table, **owTable[lastChar+1]**, gives the offset and width of the font's missing symbol. The last entry, **owTable[lastChar+2]**, is always −**1.**

8.2.4 Initializing the Toolbox for Fonts

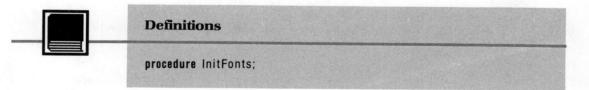

Definitions

procedure InitFonts;

Notes

1. **InitFonts** must be called before any other operation involving fonts directly, such as drawing or measuring text [8.3.3, 8.3.4], or indirectly, such as displaying windows, menus, and so forth.
2. It initializes the Toolbox's font-related data structures, reads the system font into memory if necessary, and initializes the application font to its default setting [8.2.1].
3. **InitFonts** should be called after **InitGraf** [4.3.1] and before **InitWindows** [II:3.2.1].

Assembly Language Information

Trap macro:

(Pascal) Routine name	(Assembly) Trap macro	Trap word
InitFonts	**_InitFonts**	**$A8FE**

8.2.5 Access to Fonts

Definitions

```
procedure GetFontName
         (fontNumber : INTEGER;          {Font number}
          var name   : Str255);          {Returns name of typeface}

procedure GetFNum
         (name            : Str255;      {Name of typeface}
          var fontNumber : INTEGER);     {Returns font number}

function  RealFont
         (fontNumber : INTEGER;          {Desired font number}
          pointSize  : INTEGER);         {Desired point size}
           : BOOLEAN;                    {Does font exist?}
```

Notes

1. **GetFontName** returns the typeface name with a given font number; **GetFNum** returns the font number of the face with a given name.

2. The typeface is found by searching all open resource files for a named resource of type **'FONT'** [8.4.5] with a resource ID corresponding to a point size of **0.**

3. If no such resource exists, **GetFontName** returns the empty string and **GetFNum** returns **0.**

4. **RealFont** returns a Boolean result telling whether a **'FONT'** resource exists for a given combination of typeface (font number) and point size. If this result is **FALSE,** requests to draw or measure text in that face and size will be carried out by substituting (and usually scaling) a suitable existing font; see [8.3.1, notes 4 and 5].

5. The trap macro for **GetFontName** is spelled **_GetFName.**

Assembly Language Information

Trap macros:

(Pascal) Routine name	(Assembly) Trap macro	Trap word
GetFontName	**_GetFName**	**$A8FF**
GetFNum	**_GetFNum**	**$A900**
RealFont	**_RealFont**	**$A902**

8.2.6 Requesting Font Information

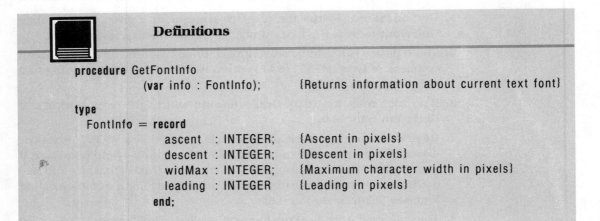

Definitions

```
procedure GetFontInfo
        (var info : FontInfo);          {Returns information about current text font}

type
   FontInfo = record
            ascent  : INTEGER;          {Ascent in pixels}
            descent : INTEGER;          {Descent in pixels}
            widMax  : INTEGER;          {Maximum character width in pixels}
            leading : INTEGER           {Leading in pixels}
          end;
```

Notes

1. **GetFontInfo** returns information on the characteristics of a font.
2. The information returned is for the font identified by the **txFont** and **txSize** fields [8.3.1] of the current graphics port, and is adjusted for the character style specified in the **txFace** field.

Assembly Language Information

Trap macro:

(Pascal) Routine name	(Assembly) Trap macro	Trap word
GetFontInfo	**_GetFontInfo**	**$A88B**

Field offsets in a font information record:

(Pascal) Field name	(Assembly) Offset name	Offset in bytes
ascent	**ascent**	**0**
descent	**descent**	**2**
widMax	**widMax**	**4**
leading	**leading**	**6**

8.2.7 Locking a Font

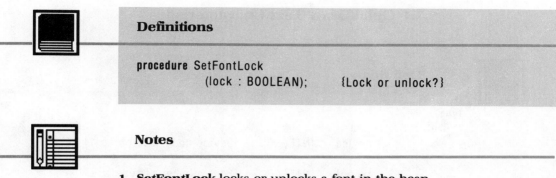

Definitions

```
procedure SetFontLock
         (lock : BOOLEAN);        {Lock or unlock?}
```

Notes

1. **SetFontLock** locks or unlocks a font in the heap.
2. A locked font can't be moved or purged.
3. The font affected is the last one used in any text-drawing operation [8.3.3].

Assembly Language Information

Trap macro:

(Pascal) Routine name	(Assembly) Trap macro	Trap word
SetFontLock	**_SetFontLock**	**$A903**

8.3 Text and QuickDraw

8.3.1 QuickDraw Text Characteristics

Definitions

```
type
   GrafPort = record
                 device  : INTEGER;      {Device code (see notes 11-13)}
                 . . . ;
                 txFont  : INTEGER;      {Font number of typeface}
                 txFace  : Style;        {Type style}
                 txMode  : INTEGER;      {Transfer mode for text}
                 txSize  : INTEGER;      {Type size in points}
                 spExtra : LONGINT;      {Extra space between words, in pixels}
                 . . .
              end;

   StyleItem = (Bold, Italic, Underline, Outline, Shadow, Condense, Extend);

   Style     = set of StyleItem;
```

Notes

1. These fields of the **GrafPort** record [4.2.2] pertain to the drawing of text in a given graphics port.

2. **txFont** is a font number identifying the typeface to be used; **0** designates the system font.

3. **txSize** is the type size in points; **0** specifies 12 points or the nearest size available in the requested typeface.

4. If no font exists for the requested combination of typeface and size, another size of the same face will be substituted. If the requested typeface isn't available in any size, the application font [8.2.1] will be used; if the application font isn't available in any size, the system font [8.2.1] will be used.

5. If a font of a different size is substituted, it will ordinarily be scaled to the size requested. However, no scaling will be performed if the assembly-language global **FScaleDisable** is nonzero; in this case the substituted font will be used in its original size. (There is no straightforward way to disable font scaling in Pascal.)

6. **txFace** identifies the text style as a Pascal set of type **Style.** The set can include any combination of individual style properties of type **StyleItem.**

7. The assembly-language constants **BoldBit, ItalicBit,** etc. (below) are bit numbers within the byte representing a **Style** set, for use with the **BTST, BSET, BCLR,** and **BCHG** instructions.

8. **txMode** is the transfer mode for text in this graphics port, and should be one of the eight source transfer modes [5.1.3].

9. **spExtra** is the extra width, in pixels, to be added to each space character for text justification.

10. Although nominally a long integer, **spExtra** is actually interpreted as a fixed-point number [2.3.1] consisting of a 16-bit integer part and a 16-bit fraction.

11. **device** identifies the output device on which text will be drawn. This information is used in choosing the appropriate fonts for use on the device.

12. The high-order byte of the device code is the reference number of the device driver, which is always negative; the low-order byte is a device-dependent modifier controlling the way the device is to be used (for example, the dot resolution on a printer with a choice of resolutions).

13. A device code of **0** denotes the Macintosh screen.

14. A newly created graphics port is initialized to draw text on the screen, using the system font at the standard size of 12 points, with a transfer mode of **SrcOr** [5.1.3], plain character style, and no extra width for spaces.

Assembly Language Information

Field offsets in a graphics port:

(Pascal) Field name	(Assembly) Offset name	Size in bytes
device	device	0
txFont	txFont	68
txFace	txFace	70
txMode	txMode	72
txSize	txSize	74
spExtra	spExtra	76

Assembly-language global variable:

Name	Address	Meaning
FScaleDisable	$A63	Disable font scaling if nonzero

Bit numbers in a **Style** byte:

Name	Bit number	Meaning
BoldBit	0	Bold
ItalicBit	1	Italic
UlineBit	2	Underline
OutlineBit	3	Outline
ShadowBit	4	Shadow
CondenseBit	5	Condense
ExtendBit	6	Extend

8.3.2 Setting Text Characteristics

Definitions

procedure GrafDevice
    (deviceCode : INTEGER);   {Device code [8.3.1]}

procedure TextFont
    (fontNumber : INTEGER);   {Font number of desired typeface [8.2.1]}

procedure TextSize
    (pointSize : INTEGER);   {Type size in points}

procedure TextFace
    (typeStyle : Style);   {Type style [8.3.1]}

procedure TextMode
    (mode : INTEGER);   {Transfer mode for text [5.1.3]}

procedure SpaceExtra
    (extraSpace : Fixed);   {Extra space between words, in pixels [2.3.1]}

Notes

1. These routines set the text characteristics of the current graphics port [8.3.1]. All subsequent text will be drawn with the specified characteristics.

2. If the point size specified to **TextSize** isn't available in the current typeface, another size will be substituted and (usually) scaled to match; see [8.3.1, notes 4 and 5].

3. **mode** should be one of the eight source transfer modes [5.1.3].

4. **extraSpace** is a fixed-point number [2.3.1] consisting of a 16-bit integer part and a 16-bit fraction, specifying the amount of extra space to be added between words.

5. To obtain the proper value of **extraSpace** for a line of justified text, use **FixRatio** [2.3.2] to divide the excess line width in pixels by the number of spaces in the line.

Assembly Language Information

Trap macros:

(Pascal) Routine name	(Assembly) Trap macro	Trap word
GrafDevice	**_GrafDevice**	**$A872**
TextFont	**_TextFont**	**$A887**
TextSize	**_TextSize**	**$A88A**
TextFace	**_TextFace**	**$A888**
TextMode	**_TextMode**	**$A889**
SpaceExtra	**_SpaceExtra**	**$A88E**

8.3.3 Drawing Text

Definitions

```
procedure DrawChar
        (theChar : CHAR);           {Character to be drawn}

procedure DrawString
        (theString : Str255);       {String to be drawn}

procedure DrawText
        (theText    : Ptr;          {Pointer to text to be drawn}
         firstChar  : INTEGER;      {Index of first character within text}
         charCount  : INTEGER);     {Number of characters to be drawn}
```

Notes

1. These routines draw text in the current graphics port, using the port's current typeface, size, style, and other text characteristics [8.3.2].

2. Each character is drawn with its character origin at the current pen position; the pen is then advanced to the right by the character width.

3. Characters not defined in the port's current font are replaced with the font's missing symbol.

4. Space characters include any extra space called for by the port's **spExtra** field [8.3.2].

5. ASCII control characters such as carriage return, line feed, tab, and backspace have no special meaning; if these characters are to be used for formatting, their effects must be simulated by explicitly moving the pen with **Move** and **MoveTo** [5.2.4].

6. The pen is left positioned beyond the last character drawn, ready for the next drawing operation.

Assembly Language Information

Trap macros:

(Pascal) Routine name	(Assembly) Trap macro	Trap word
DrawChar	**_DrawChar**	**$A883**
DrawString	**_DrawString**	**$A884**
DrawText	**_DrawText**	**$A885**

8.3.4 Measuring Text

Definitions

```
function CharWidth
        (theChar : CHAR)          {Character to be measured}
        : INTEGER;                {Width of character}

function StringWidth
        (theString : Str255)      {String to be measured}
        : INTEGER;                {Width of string}

function TextWidth
        (theText    : Ptr;        {Pointer of text to be measured}
        firstChar   : INTEGER;    {Index of first character within text}
        charCount   : INTEGER)    {Number of characters to be measured}
        : INTEGER;                {Width of text}
```

Notes

1. These routines measure the width of the specified text without drawing it.

2. The result is the distance in pixels that the pen would be advanced if the text were drawn in the current graphics port, using the port's current typeface, size, style, and other text characteristics [8.3.2].

3. Characters not defined in the port's current font are considered to have the same width as the font's missing symbol.

4. Space characters include any extra space called for by the port's **spExtra** field [8.3.2].

5. ASCII control characters such as carriage return, line feed, tab, and backspace have no special meaning, but are treated as ordinary characters.

6. The port's graphics pen is not moved in any way.

Assembly Language Information

Trap macros:

(Pascal) Routine name	(Assembly) Trap macro	Trap word
CharWidth	**_CharWidth**	**$A88D**
StringWidth	**_StringWidth**	**$A88C**
TextWidth	**_TextWidth**	**$A886**

8.4 Text-Related Resources

8.4.1 Resource Type 'TEXT'

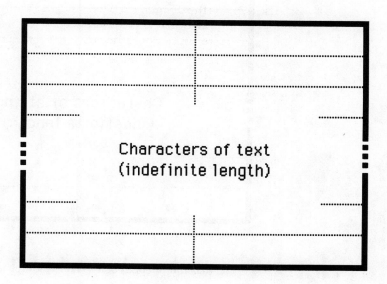

Characters of text
(indefinite length)

A 'TEXT' resource does *not* begin with a length byte.

Format of resource type 'TEXT'

Notes

1. A resource of type 'TEXT' contains any number of characters of "raw" text.

2. The resource data doesn't include a character count. The length of the text can be found with **SizeResource** [6.4.3].

8.4.2 Resource Type 'STR '

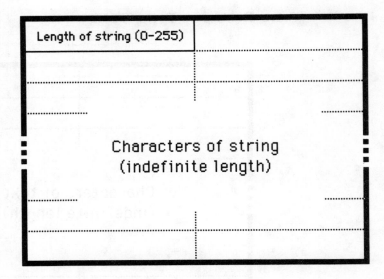

The maximum length of a 'STR ' resource is 255 characters.

Format of resource type 'STR '

Notes

1. A resource of type 'STR ' contains a character string in internal Pascal format.

2. The space in 'STR ' is required.

3. The first byte of resource data gives the length of the string, which cannot exceed 255 characters. The rest of the data consists of the characters themselves.

8.4.3 Resource Type 'STR#'

Format of resource type **'STR#'**

Notes

1. A resource of type '**STR#**' contains a list of character strings.
2. The resource data consists of a 2-byte integer giving the number of strings in the list, followed by the strings themselves in internal Pascal format (1-byte character count, 0 to 255 characters), as described under '**STR** ' [8.4.2]).

8.4.4 Resource Type 'INIT'

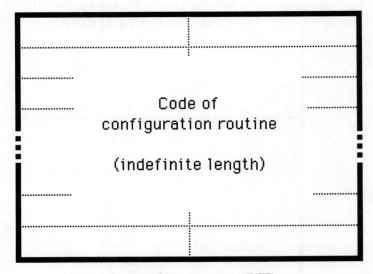

Format of resource type '**INIT**'

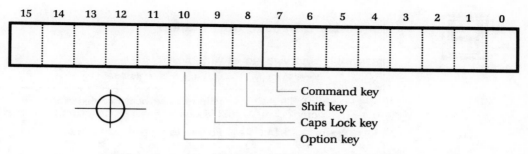

Register **D1** contains the fourth word of the system key map which includes the state of the four modifier keys.

Modifier bits for configuration routines

Notes

1. A resource of type 'INIT' contains a keyboard configuration routine. The resource data is simply the machine-language code of the routine.

2. Two configuration routines are loaded from the system resource file when the system is started up, both with resource type 'INIT'. The keyboard configuration routine has resource ID **1;** resource ID **2** is the configuration routine for the (optional) numeric keypad.

3. Pointers to the two configuration routines are kept in the system globals **Key1Trans** and **Key2Trans.**

4. The configuration routines must be written in assembly language, since they accept their arguments and return their results directly in the processor's registers.

5. On entry to the configuration routine, register **D2** contains the key code [8.1.3] for the key to be translated. **D1** contains the fourth word of the system key map [II:2.6.1], which includes the state of the four modifier keys (see figure). The routine can use this modifier information any way it wishes.

6. The entry point for executing the configuration routine must be at the first byte of the resource data.

7. The routine returns the character code corresponding to the given key and modifiers in the low-order byte of register **D0.**

8. The routine should preserve the contents of all registers except **D0.**

Assembly Language Information

Assembly-language global variables:

Name	Address	Meaning
Key1Trans	$29E	Pointer to keyboard configuration routine
Key2Trans	$2A2	Pointer to keypad configuration routine

8.4.5 Resource Type 'FONT'

Notes

1. A resource of type '**FONT**' contains a complete font record [8.2.2], including the variable-length fields **bitImage, locTable,** and **owTable** [8.2.3].

2. The resource ID for a font consists of a 9-bit font number [8.2.1] identifying the typeface, and a 7-bit point size. Thus the resource ID is equal to the font number times 128, plus the point size.

3. For each typeface, the '**FONT**' resource corresponding to a point size of **0** is a dummy resource with no data, which exists solely to carry the name of the typeface as its resource name. "Real" fonts with nonzero point sizes have no resource name.

fontType (2 bytes)
firstChar (2 bytes)
lastChar (2 bytes)
widMax (2 bytes)
kernMax (2 bytes)
nDescent (2 bytes)
fRectWid (2 bytes)
chHeight (2 bytes)
owTloc (2 bytes)
ascent (2 bytes)
descent (2 bytes)
leading (2 bytes)
rowWords (2 bytes)
bitImage (indefinite length)
locTable (indefinite length)
owTable (indefinite length)

Format of resource type 'FONT'

Resource ID of a font

8.4.6 Resource Type 'FWID'

fontType (2 bytes)
firstChar (2 bytes)
lastChar (2 bytes)
widMax (2 bytes)
kernMax (2 bytes)
nDescent (2 bytes)
fRectWid (2 bytes)
chHeight (2 bytes)
owTloc (2 bytes)
ascent (2 bytes)
descent (2 bytes)
leading (2 bytes)
owTable (indefinite length)

Format of resource type 'FWID'

Notes

1. A resource of type '**FWID**' contains a font width table.

2. The resource data consists of an abbreviated font record [8.2.2] with no **rowWords, bitImage,** and **locTable** fields [8.2.3].

3. The **fontType** field always contains the constant **FontWid** [8.2.2].

4. The **owTLoc** field is always set to **4.**

5. The resource ID for a font width table is the same as for the corresponding font [8.4.5].

A P P E N D I X

A

Toolbox Summary

Chapter 2 General Utilities

2.1 Elementary Data Structures

2.1.1 Strings and Procedures

type

    Str255   = STRING[255];   {Any text string, maximum 255 characters}

    ProcPtr = Ptr;   {Pointer to a procedure or function}

2.1.2 String Operations

function EqualString

            (string1   : Str255;   {First string to be compared}
            string2   : Str255;   {Second string to be compared}
            caseCounts   : BOOLEAN;   {Distinguished upper- and lowercase?}
            ignoreMarks : BOOLEAN)   {Ignore diacritical marks?}
             : BOOLEAN;   {Are the two strings equivalent?}

procedure UprString

            (var theString : Str255;   {String to be converted}
            stripMarks   : BOOLEAN);   {Eliminate diacritical marks?}

2.2 Bit-Level Operations

2.2.1 Single Bit Access

```
procedure BitSet
        (bitsPtr    : Ptr;           {Pointer to bits}
         bitNumber : LONGINT);       {Number of bit to be set to 1}

procedure BitClr
        (bitsPtr    : Ptr;           {Pointer to bits}
         bitNumber : LONGINT);       {Number of bit to be cleared to 0}

function   BitTst
        (bitsPtr    : Ptr;           {pointer to bits}
         bitNumber : LONGINT);       {Number of bit to be tested}
          : BOOLEAN;                 {Is bit set to 1?}
```

2.2.2 Logical Operations

```
function BitAnd
        (bits1 : LONGINT;            {First operand}
         bits2 : LONGINT)            {Second operand}
          : LONGINT;                 {Bitwise "and"}

function BitOr
        (bits1 : LONGINT;            {First operand}
         bits2 : LONGINT)            {Second operand}
          : LONGINT;                 {Bitwise "or"}

function BitXOr
        (bits1 : LONGINT;            {First operand}
         bits2 : LONGINT)            {Second operand}
          : LONGINT;                 {Bitwise "exclusive or"}

function BitNot
        (bits   : LONGINT)           {Bits to be complemented}
          : LONGINT;                 {Bitwise complement}

function BitShift
        (bits        : LONGINT;      {Bits to be shifted}
         shiftCount : INTEGER)       {Number of places to shift}
          : LONGINT;                 {Result of shift}
```

2.2.3 Word Access

function HiWord
        (longWord : LONGINT)   {32-bit operand}
          : INTEGER;   {High-order 16 bits}

function LoWord
        (longWord : LONGINT)   {32-bit operand}
          : INTEGER;   {Low-order 16 bits}

2.2.4 Direct Storage

procedure StuffHex
        (destPtr : Ptr;   {Pointer to data structure to be stuffed}
         hexString : Str255);   {String representing data in hexadecimal}

2.3 Arithmetic Operations

2.3.1 Fixed-Point Numbers

type
  Fixed = LONGINT;   {Fixed-point number}

function FixRound
        (theNumber : Fixed)   {Fixed-point number to be rounded}
          : INTEGER;   {Number rounded to an integer}

2.3.2 Fixed-Point Arithmetic

function FixMul
        (number1 : Fixed;   {First fixed-point operand}
         number2 : Fixed)   {Second fixed-point operand}
          : Fixed;   {Fixed-point product}

function FixRatio
        (numerator   : INTEGER; {Integer numerator}
         denominator : INTEGER) {Integer denominator}
          : Fixed;   {Fixed-point quotient}

2.3.3 Long Multiplication

```
type
  Int64Bit = record
                hiLong : LONGINT;        {High-order 32 bits}
                loLong : LONGINT         {Low-order 32 bits}
             end;

procedure LongMul
             (number1     : LONGINT;     {First 32-bit operand}
              number2     : LONGINT;     {Second 32-bit operand}
              var product : Int64Bit);   {Returns 64-bit product}
```

2.3.4 Binary/Decimal Conversion

```
procedure NumToString
             (theNumber     : LONGINT;     {Number to be converted}
              var theString : Str255);     {Returns equivalent string}

procedure StringToNum
             (theString     : Str255;      {String to be converted}
              var theNumber : LONGINT);     {Returns equivalent number}
```

2.3.5 Random Numbers

```
function Random
             : INTEGER;       {Random number}

var
  RandSeed : LONGINT;     {"Seed" for random number generation}
```

2.4 Date and Time

2.4.1 Date and Time in Seconds

```
procedure GetDateTime
             (var seconds : LONGINT);     {Returns current date and time in "raw" seconds}

function  SetDateTime
             (seconds : LONGINT)          {New date and time in "raw" seconds}
             : OSErr;                      {Result code}

const
  ClkRdErr = −85;                          {Unable to read clock}
  ClkWrErr = −86;                          {Clock not written correctly}
```

2.4.2 Date and Time Records

type
   DateTimeRec = **record**

year	: INTEGER;	{Year}
month	: INTEGER;	{Month: 1 (January) to 12 (December)}
day	: INTEGER;	{Day of month: 1 to 31}
hour	: INTEGER;	{Hour: 0 to 23}
minute	: INTEGER;	{Minute: 0 to 59}
second	: INTEGER;	{Second: 0 to 59}
dayOfWeek	: INTEGER	{Day of week: 1 (Sunday) to 7 (Saturday)}

        end;

procedure GetTime
    (**var** dateAndTime : DateTimeRec);   {Returns current date and time}

procedure SetTime
    (dateAndTime : DateTimeRec);   {Current date and time}

2.4.3 Date and Time Conversion

procedure Secs2Date
    (seconds   : LONGINT;   {Date and time in "raw" seconds}
    var dateAndTime : DateTimeRec);   {Returns equivalent date and time record}

procedure Date2Secs
    (dateAndTime : DateTimeRec;   {Date and time record}
    var seconds : LONGINT);   {Returns equivalent in "raw" seconds}

2.4.4 Date and Time Strings

type
  DateForm = (ShortDate, LongDate, AbbrevDate);

procedure IUDateString
    (seconds   : LONGINT;   {Date and time in "raw" seconds}
    format   : DateForm;   {Format desired for date}
    var theString : Str255);   {Returns equivalent character string}

procedure IUTimeString
    (seconds   : LONGINT;   {Date and time in "raw" seconds}
    withSeconds : BOOLEAN;   {Include seconds in string?}
    var theString : Str255);   {Returns equivalent character string}

Chapter 3 Memory

3.1 Elementary Data Types

3.1.1 Pointers and Handles

```
type
  Byte       =    0..255;        {Any byte in memory}
  SignedByte = −128..127;        {Any byte in memory}

  Ptr        = ˆSignedByte;      {General pointer}
  Handle     = ˆPtr;             {General handle}

  Size       = LONGINT;          {Size of a heap block in bytes}
```

3.1.2 Error Reporting

```
type
  OSErr      = INTEGER;          {Operating System result (error) code}

const
  NoErr       =    0;            {No error; all is well}
  MemFullErr  = −108;            {No room; heap is full}
  NilHandleErr = −109;           {Illegal operation on empty handle}
  MemWZErr    = −111;            {Illegal operation on free block}
  MemPurErr   = −112;            {Illegal operation on locked block}

function MemError
            : OSErr;             {Result code of last memory operation}
```

3.2 Heap Allocation

3.2.1 Allocating Blocks

function	NewHandle	
	(blockSize : Size)	{Size of needed block in bytes}
	: Handle;	{Handle to new relocatable block}
function	NewPtr	
	(blockSize : Size)	{Size of needed block in bytes}
	: Ptr;	{Pointer to new nonrelocatable block}
procedure	ResrvMem	
	(blockSize : Size);	{Size of needed block in bytes}
function	RecoverHandle	
	(masterPtr : Ptr)	{Master pointer to relocatable block}
	: Handle;	{Handle to block}

3.2.2 Releasing Blocks

procedure	DisposHandle	
	(theHandle : Handle);	{Handle to relocatable block to be deallocated}
procedure	DisposPtr	
	(thePtr : Ptr);	{Pointer to nonrelocatable block to be deallocated}

3.2.3 Size of Blocks

function	GetHandleSize	
	(theHandle : Handle)	{Handle to a relocatable block}
	: Size;	{Size of block in bytes}
function	GetPtrSize	
	(thePtr : Ptr)	{Pointer to a nonrelocatable block}
	: Size;	{Size of block in bytes}
procedure	SetHandleSize	
	(theHandle : Handle;	{Handle to a relocatable block}
	newSize : Size);	{New size of block in bytes}
procedure	SetPtrSize	
	(thePtr : Ptr;	{Pointer to a nonrelocatable block}
	newSize : Size);	{New size of block in bytes}

3.2.4 Properties of Blocks

procedure HLock
  (theHandle : Handle); {Handle to a relocatable block}

procedure HUnlock
  (theHandle : Handle); {Handle to a relocatable block}

procedure HPurge
  (theHandle : Handle); {Handle to a relocatable block}

procedure HNoPurge
  (theHandle : Handle); {Handle to a relocatable block}

3.2.5 Copying Blocks

function HandToHand
  (**var** theHandle : Handle) {Handle to relocatable block to be copied}
   : OSErr; {Result code}

function PtrToHand
  (fromPtr : Ptr; {Pointer to nonrelocatable block to be copied}
  var toHandle : Handle; {Returns handle to relocatable copy}
  byteCount : LONGINT) {Number of bytes to be copied}
   : OSErr; {Result code}

function PtrToXHand
  (fromPtr : Ptr; {Pointer to nonrelocatable block to be copied}
  toHandle : Handle; {Handle to be set to relocatable copy}
  byteCount : LONGINT) {Number of bytes to be copied}
   : OSErr; {Result code}

procedure BlockMove
  (fromPtr : Ptr; {Pointer to data to be copied}
  toPtr : Ptr; {Pointer to destination location}
  byteCount : Size); {Number of bytes to be copied}

3.2.6 Combining Blocks

```
function HandAndHand
        (appendHandle : Handle;        {Handle to relocatable block to be appended}
         afterHandle   : Handle)       {Handle to relocatable block to append to}
         : OSErr;                      {Result code}

function PtrAndHand
        (appendPtr   : Ptr;           {Pointer to nonrelocatable block to be appended}
         afterHandle : Handle;        {Handle to relocatable block to append to}
         byteCount   : LONGINT)       {Number of bytes to append}
         : OSErr;                     {Result code}
```

3.3 Reclaiming Heap Space

3.3.1 Free Space

```
function FreeMem
        : LONGINT;                    {Total free bytes in the heap}

function MaxMem
        (var growBytes : Size)        {Returns maximum bytes by which heap can grow}
        : Size;                       {Size of largest free block in heap}

function TopMem
        : Ptr;                        {Pointer to end of memory}
```

3.3.2 Heap Compaction

```
function CompactMem
        (sizeNeeded : Size)           {Size of needed block in bytes}
        : Size;                       {Size of largest free block after compaction}
```

3.3.3 Purging Blocks

```
procedure EmptyHandle
        (theHandle : Handle);         {Handle to relocatable block to be purged}

procedure ReallocHandle
        (theHandle : Handle;          {Empty handle to be reallocated}
         sizeNeeded : Size);          {Size of block to be allocated in bytes}

procedure PurgeMem
        (sizeNeeded : Size);          {Size of needed block in bytes}
```

3.3.4 Heap Expansion

procedure SetApplLimit
        (newLimit : Ptr);   {Pointer to new application heap limit}

procedure MaxApplZone;

Chapter 4 QuickDraw Fundamentals

4.1 Mathematical Foundations

4.1.1 Points

type
  VHSelect = (V, H);   {Selector for coordinates of a point}

  Point   = **record**
                    case INTEGER **of**
                        0: (v : INTEGER;   {Vertical coordinate}
                            h : INTEGER);   {Horizontal coordinate}

                        1: (vh : **array** [VHSelect] **of** INTEGER)   {Coordinates as a two-element array}

            end;

procedure SetPt
            (**var** thePoint : Point;   {Point to be set}
              hCoord   : INTEGER;   {Horizontal coordinate}
              vCoord   : INTEGER);   {Vertical coordinate}

4.1.2 Rectangles

type
```
    Rect = record
            case INTEGER of

            0: (top     : INTEGER;        {Top coordinate}
                left    : INTEGER;        {Left coordinate}
                bottom  : INTEGER;        {Bottom coordinate}
                right   : INTEGER);       {Right coordinate}

            1: (topLeft  : Point;         {Top-left corner}
                botRight : Point)         {Bottom-right corner}

        end;
```

procedure SetRect
```
        (var theRect : Rect;         {Rectangle to be set}
        left        : INTEGER;       {Left coordinate}
        top         : INTEGER;       {Top coordinate}
        right       : INTEGER;       {Right coordinate}
        bottom      : INTEGER);      {Bottom coordinate}
```

procedure Pt2Rect
```
        (point1      : Point;        {First corner}
        point2      : Point;         {Diagonally opposite corner}
        var theRect : Rect);         {Rectangle to be set}
```

4.1.3 Polygons

type
```
    PolyHandle = ^PolyPtr;
    PolyPtr    = ^Polygon;

    Polygon    = record
                polySize   : INTEGER;              {Length of this data structure in bytes}
                polyBBox   : Rect;                 {Bounding box}
                polyPoints : array [0..0] of Point {Variable-length array of vertices}
            end;
```

4.1.4 Defining Polygons

function OpenPoly
: PolyHandle;   {Handle to new polygon}

procedure ClosePoly;

procedure KillPoly
(thePolygon : PolyHandle);   {Handle to polygon to be destroyed}

4.1.5 Regions

type
RgnHandle = ^RgnPtr;
RgnPtr   = ^Region;

Region   = **record**
rgnSize : INTEGER;   {Length of this data structure in bytes}
rgnBBox : Rect;   {Bounding box}
(additional data defining shape of region)
end;

4.1.6 Defining Regions

function NewRgn
: RgnHandle;   {Handle to new region}

procedure OpenRgn;

procedure CloseRgn
(theRegion : RgnHandle);   {Handle to be set to defined region}

procedure DisposeRgn
(theRegion : RgnHandle);   {Handle to region to be destroyed}

4.1.7 Setting Regions

procedure SetEmptyRgn
      (theRegion : RgnHandle);   {Handle to region to be set empty}

procedure RectRgn
      (theRegion : RgnHandle;   {Handle to region to be set}
      theRect   : Rect);   {Rectangle to set it to}

procedure SetRectRgn
      (theRegion : RgnHandle;   {Handle to region to be set}
      left   : INTEGER;   {Left coordinate of rectangle to set it to}
      top   : INTEGER;   {Top coordinate of rectangle to set it to}
      right   : INTEGER;   {Right coordinate of rectangle to set it to}
      bottom   : INTEGER); {Bottom coordinate of rectangle to set it to}

procedure CopyRgn
      (fromRegion : RgnHandle;   {Region to be copied}
      toRegion   : RgnHandle); {Region to copy it to}

4.2 Graphical Foundations

4.2.1 Bit Maps

  BitMap = **record**
          baseAddr : Ptr;   {Pointer to bit image}
          rowBytes : INTEGER; {Row width in bytes}
          bounds : Rect   {Boundary rectangle}
       end;

var
  ScreenBits : BitMap;   {Bit map for Macintosh screen}

4.2.2 Graphics Ports

type
```
  GrafPtr   = ^GrafPort;

  GrafPort = record
```

device	: INTEGER;	{Device code for font selection}
portBits	: BitMap;	{Bit map for this port}
portRect	: Rect;	{Port rectangle}
visRgn	: RgnHandle;	{Visible region}
clipRgn	: RgnHandle;	{Clipping region}
bkPat	: Pattern;	{Background pattern}
fillPat	: Pattern;	{Fill pattern for shape drawing}
pnLoc	: Point;	{Current pen location in local coordinates}
pnSize	: Point;	{Dimensions of graphics pen}
pnMode	: INTEGER;	{Transfer mode for graphics pen}
pnPat	: Pattern;	{Pen pattern for line drawing}
pnVis	: INTEGER;	{Pen visibility level}
txFont	: INTEGER;	{Font number for text}
txFace	: Style;	{Type style for text}
txMode	: INTEGER;	{Transfer mode for text}
txSize	: INTEGER;	{Type size for text}
spExtra	: LONGINT;	{Extra space between words}
fgColor	: LONGINT;	{Foreground color}
bkColor	: LONGINT;	{Background color}
colrBit	: INTEGER;	{Color plane}
patStretch	: INTEGER;	{Private}
picSave	: Handle;	{Private}
rgnSave	: Handle;	{Private}
polySave	: Handle;	{Private}
grafProcs	: QDProcsPtr	{Pointer to bottleneck procedures}

```
            end;
```

4.2.3 Pixel Access

function GetPixel

(hCoord : INTEGER;	{Horizontal coordinate of pixel}
vCoord : INTEGER)	{Vertical coordinate of pixel}
: BOOLEAN;	{Is it a black pixel?}

4.3 Operations on Graphics Ports

4.3.1 Initializing QuickDraw

procedure InitGraf
      (globalVars : Ptr);   {Pointer to QuickDraw global variables}

var
  ThePort   : GrafPtr;   {Pointer to current port}
  White   : Pattern;   {Solid white pattern}
  Black   : Pattern;   {Solid black pattern}
  Gray   : Pattern;   {Medium gray pattern}
  LtGray   : Pattern;   {Light gray pattern}
  DkGray   : Pattern;   {Dark gray pattern}
  Arrow   : Cursor;   {Standard arrow cursor}
  ScreenBits : BitMap;   {Bit map for Macintosh screen}
  RandSeed : LONGINT;   {Seed for random number generation}

4.3.2 Creating and Destroying Ports

procedure OpenPort
      (whichPort : GrafPtr);   {Pointer to port to open}

procedure InitPort
      (whichPort : GrafPtr);   {Pointer to port to initialize}

procedure ClosePort
      (whichPort : GrafPtr);   {Pointer to port to close}

4.3.3 Current Port

procedure SetPort
      (newPort : GrafPtr);   {Pointer to port to be made current}

procedure GetPort
      (**var** curPort : GrafPtr);   {Returns pointer to current port}

var
  ThePort : GrafPtr;   {Pointer to current port}

4.3.4 Bit Map and Coordinate System

procedure SetPortBits
      (theBits : BitMap);   {New bit map for current port}

procedure SetOrigin
      (hOrigin : INTEGER;   {New horizontal coordinate of port rectangle}
       vOrigin : INTEGER);   {New vertical coordinate of port rectangle}

4.3.5 Port Rectangle

procedure MovePortTo
      (leftGlobal : INTEGER;   {New left edge of port rectangle in global coordinates}
       topGlobal : INTEGER);   {New top edge of port rectangle in global coordinates}

procedure PortSize
      (portWidth : INTEGER;   {New width of port rectangle}
       portHeight : INTEGER);   {New height of port rectangle}

4.3.6 Clipping Region

procedure SetClip
      (newClip : RgnHandle);   {Handle to new clipping region}

procedure ClipRect
      (clipRect : Rect);   {Rectangle defining new clipping region}

procedure GetClip
      (curClip : RgnHandle);   {Handle to current clipping region}

4.4 Calculations on Graphical Entities

4.4.1 Calculations on Points

procedure AddPt
      (addPoint   : Point;   {Point to be added}
      var toPoint   : Point);   {Point to add it to}

procedure SubPt
      (subPoint   : Point;   {Point to be subtracted}
      var fromPoint : Point);   {Point to subtract it from}

function EqualPt
      (point1   : Point;   {First point to be compared}
       point2   : Point);   {Second point to be compared}
        : BOOLEAN;   {Are they equal?}

4.4.2 Coordinate Conversion

procedure LocalToGlobal
        (**var** thePoint : Point);   {Point to be converted}

procedure GlobalToLocal
        (**var** thePoint : Point);   {Point to be converted}

4.4.3 Testing for Inclusion

function PtInRect
        (thePoint   : Point;   {Point to be tested}
         theRect   : Rect)   {Rectangle to test it against}
          : BOOLEAN;   {Is the point in the rectangle?}

function PtInRgn
        (thePoint   : Point;   {Point to be tested}
         theRegion : RgnHandle)   {Handle to region to test it against}
          : BOOLEAN;   {Is the point in the region?}

function RectInRgn
        (theRect   : Rect;   {Rectangle to be tested}
         theRegion : RgnHandle)   {Handle to region to test it against}
          : BOOLEAN;   {Does the rectangle intersect the rectangle?}

function PinRect
        (theRect   : Rect;   {Rectangle to pin to}
         thePoint   : Point)   {Point to be pinned}
          : LONGINT;   {Point pinned to rectangle}

4.4.4 Calculations on One Rectangle

procedure OffsetRect
        (**var** theRect : Rect;   {Rectangle to be offset}
         hOffset   : INTEGER;   {Horizontal offset in pixels}
         vOffset   : INTEGER);   {Vertical offset in pixels}

procedure InsetRect
        (**var** theRect : Rect;   {Rectangle to be inset}
         hInset   : INTEGER;   {Horizontal inset in pixels}
         vInset   : INTEGER);   {Vertical inset in pixels}

function   EmptyRect
        (theRect : Rect);   {Rectangle to be tested}
          : BOOLEAN;   {Is the rectangle empty?}

4.4.5 Calculations on Two Rectangles

procedure UnionRect
        (rect1   : Rect;   {First rectangle}
        rect2   : Rect;   {Second rectangle}
        var resultRect : Rect);   {Returns union of two rectangles}

function SectRect
        (rect1   : Rect;   {First rectangle}
        rect2   : Rect;   {Second rectangle}
        var resultRect : Rect)   {Returns intersection of two rectangles}
         : BOOLEAN;   {Do the rectangles intersect?}

function EqualRect
        (rect1 : Rect;   {First rectangle}
        rect2 : Rect)   {Second rectangle}
         : BOOLEAN;   {Are the rectangles equal?}

4.4.6 Calculations on Polygons

procedure OffsetPoly
        (thePolygon : PolyHandle;   {Polygon to be offset}
        hOffset   : INTEGER;   {Horizontal offset in pixels}
        vOffset   : INTEGER);   {Vertical offset in pixels}

4.4.7 Calculations on One Region

procedure OffsetRgn
        (theRegion : RgnHandle;   {Handle to region to be offset}
        hOffset   : INTEGER;   {Horizontal offset in pixels}
        vOffset   : INTEGER);   {Vertical offset in pixels}

procedure InsetRgn
        (theRegion : RgnHandle;   {Handle to region to be inset}
        hInset   : INTEGER;   {Horizontal inset in pixels}
        vInset   : INTEGER);   {Vertical inset in pixels}

function EmptyRgn
        (theRegion : RgnHandle)   {Handle to region to be tested}
         : BOOLEAN;   {Is the region empty?}

4.4.8 Calculations on Two Regions

procedure UnionRgn
   (region1 : RgnHandle; {Handle to first region}
   region2 : RgnHandle; {Handle to second region}
   resultRegion : RgnHandle); {Handle to be set to union of two regions}

procedure SectRgn
   (region1 : RgnHandle; {Handle to first region}
   region2 : RgnHandle; {Handle to second region}
   resultRegion : RgnHandle); {Handle to be set to intersection of two regions}

procedure DiffRgn
   (region1 : RgnHandle; {Handle to region to be subtracted from}
   region2 : RgnHandle; {Handle to region to subtract from it}
   resultRegion : RgnHandle); {Handle to be set to difference of two regions}

procedure XOrRgn
   (region1 : RgnHandle; {Handle to first region}
   region2 : RgnHandle; {Handle to second region}
   resultRegion : RgnHandle); {Handle to be set to "exclusive or" of two regions}

function EqualRgn
   (region1 : RgnHandle; {Handle to first region}
   region2 : RgnHandle) {Handle to second region}
   : BOOLEAN; {Are the regions equal?}

4.4.9 Scaling and Mapping

procedure ScalePt

(**var** thePoint	: Point;	{Point to be scaled}
fromRect	: Rect;	{Rectangle to scale it from}
toRect	: Rect);	{Rectangle to scale it to}

procedure MapPt

(**var** thePoint	: Point;	{Point to be mapped}
fromRect	: Rect;	{Rectangle to map it from}
toRect	: Rect);	{Rectangle to map it to}

procedure MapRect

(**var** theRect	: Rect;	{Rectangle to be mapped}
fromRect	: Rect;	{Rectangle to map it from}
toRect	: Rect);	{Rectangle to map it to}

procedure MapPoly

(thePolygon	: PolyHandle;	{Polygon to be mapped}
fromRect	: Rect;	{Rectangle to map it from}
toRect	: Rect);	{Rectangle to map it to}

procedure MapRgn

(theRegion	: RgnHandle;	{Region to be mapped}
fromRect	: Rect;	{Rectangle to map it from}
toRect	: Rect);	{Rectangle to map it to}

Chapter 5 Drawing

5.1 Drawing Fundamentals

5.1.1 Patterns

```
type
  PatHandle  = ˆPatPtr;
  PatPtr     = ˆPattern;

  Pattern    = packed array [0..7] of 0..255;   {8 rows of 8 bits each}

  GrafPort   = record
                  . . . ;
                  bkPat   : Pattern;        {Background pattern}
                  fillPat : Pattern;        {Fill pattern for shape drawing}
                  . . . ;
                  pnPat   : Pattern;        {Pen pattern for line drawing}
                  . . .
               end;

procedure BackPat
          (newPattern : Pattern);           {New background pattern}

function  GetPattern
          (patternID : INTEGER)             {Resource ID of desired pattern}
            : PatHandle;                     {Handle to pattern in memory}

procedure GetIndPattern
          (var thePattern : Pattern;         {Returns desired pattern}
           patListID      : INTEGER;         {Resource ID of pattern list}
           patIndex       : INTEGER);        {Index of pattern within list}
```

5.1.2 Standard Patterns

```
var
  White   : Pattern;      {Solid white}
  LtGray  : Pattern;      {Light gray}
  Gray    : Pattern;      {Medium gray}
  DkGray  : Pattern;      {Dark gray}
  Black   : Pattern;      {Solid black}
const
  SysPatList = 0;         {Resource ID of standard pattern list}
```

5.1.3 Transfer Modes

```
GrafPort = record
            . . . ;
            pnMode : INTEGER;        {Transfer mode for graphics pen}
            . . . ;
            txMode : INTEGER;        {Transfer mode for text}
            . . .
          end;

const
  SrcCopy    =  0;        {Copy source to destination}
  SrcOr      =  1;        {Set selected bits to black}
  SrcXOr     =  2;        {Invert selected bits}
  SrcBic     =  3;        {Clear selected bits to white}
  NotSrcCopy =  4;        {Copy inverted source to destination}
  NotSrcOr   =  5;        {Leave selected bits alone, set others to black}
  NotSrcXOr  =  6;        {Leave selected bits alone, invert others}
  NotSrcBic  =  7;        {Leave selected bits alone, clear others to white}

  PatCopy    =  8;        {Copy pattern to destination}
  PatOr      =  9;        {Set selected bits to black}
  PatXOr     = 10;        {Invert selected bits}
  PatBic     = 11;        {Clear selected bits to white}
  NotPatCopy = 12;        {Copy inverted pattern to destination}
  NotPatOr   = 13;        {Leave selected bits alone, set others to black}
  NotPatXOr  = 14;        {Leave selected bits alone, invert others}
  NotPatBic  = 15;        {Leave selected bits alone, clear others to white}
```

5.1.4 Low-Level Bit Transfer

```
procedure CopyBits
          (fromBitMap : BitMap;        {Bit map to copy from}
           toBitMap   : BitMap;        {Bit map to copy to}
           fromRect   : Rect;          {Rectangle to copy from}
           toRect     : Rect;          {Rectangle to copy to}
           mode       : INTEGER;       {Transfer mode}
           clipTo     : RgnHandle);    {Region to clip to}
```

5.1.5 Scrolling in a Bit Map

```
procedure ScrollRect
          (theRect   : Rect;          {Rectangle to be scrolled}
           hScroll   : INTEGER;       {Horizontal scroll distance in pixels}
           vScroll   : INTEGER;       {Vertical scroll distance in pixels}
           updateRgn : RgnHandle);    {Region scrolled into rectangle}
```

5.2 Line Drawing

5.2.1 Pen Characteristics

```
type
  GrafPort  = record
            . . . ;
                pnLoc    : Point;          {Current location of graphics pen in local coordinates}
                pnSize   : Point;          {Dimensions of graphics pen}
                pnMode : INTEGER;          {Transfer mode for graphics pen}
                pnPat    : Pattern;        {Pen pattern for line drawing}
                pnVis    : INTEGER;        {Pen level}
            . . .
          end;

  PenState = record
                pnLoc    : Point;          {Location of pen in bit map}
                pnSize   : Point;          {Width and height of pen in pixels}
                pnMode : INTEGER;          {Transfer mode for line drawing and area fill}
                pnPat    : Pattern         {Pen pattern}
          end;

procedure GetPenState
          (var curState : PenState);       {Returns current pen characteristics}

procedure SetPenState
          (newState : PenState);           {New pen characteristics}
```

5.2.2 Setting Pen Characteristics

```
procedure PenSize
          (newWidth  : INTEGER;            {New pen width}
           newHeight : INTEGER);           {New pen height}

procedure PenPat
          (newPat : Pattern);              {New pen pattern}

procedure PenMode
          (newMode : INTEGER);             {New pen transfer mode}

procedure PenNormal;
```

5.2.3 Hiding and Showing the Pen

```
type
  GrafPort = record
            . . . ;
              pnVis : INTEGER;        {Pen visibility level}
            . . . .
          end;

procedure HidePen;

procedure ShowPen;
```

5.2.4 Drawing Lines

```
procedure GetPen
          (var penLoc : Point);       {Returns current pen location}

procedure Move
          (horiz : INTEGER;           {Horizontal distance to move, in pixels}
           vert  : INTEGER);          {Vertical distance to move, in pixels}

procedure MoveTo
          (horiz : INTEGER;           {Horizontal coordinate to move to, in pixels}
           vert  : INTEGER);          {Vertical coordinate to move to, in pixels}

procedure Line
          (horiz : INTEGER;           {Horizontal distance to draw, in pixels}
           vert  : INTEGER);          {Vertical distance to draw, in pixels}

procedure LineTo
          (horiz : INTEGER;           {Horizontal coordinate to draw to, in pixels}
           vert  : INTEGER);          {Vertical coordinate to draw to, in pixels}
```

5.3 Drawing Shapes

5.3.1 Basic Drawing Operations

```
type
  GrafVerb = (Frame,      {Draw outline}
              Paint,      {Fill with current pen pattern}
              Erase,      {Fill with background pattern}
              Invert,     {Invert pixels}
              Fill);      {Fill with specified pattern}
```

5.3.2 Drawing Rectangles

procedure FrameRect
       (theRect : Rect);   {Rectangle to be framed}

procedure PaintRect
       (theRect : Rect);   {Rectangle to be painted}

procedure FillRect
       (theRect : Rect;   {Rectangle to be filled}
       fillPat : Pattern);   {Pattern to fill it with}

procedure EraseRect
       (theRect : Rect);   {Rectangle to be erased}

procedure InvertRect
       (theRect : Rect);   {Rectangle to be inverted}

5.3.3 Drawing Rounded Rectangles

procedure FrameRoundRect
       (theRect   : Rect;   {Body of rectangle}
       cornerWidth : INTEGER;   {Width of corner oval}
       cornerHeight : INTEGER);   {Height of corner oval}

procedure PaintRoundRect
       (theRect   : Rect;   {Body of rectangle}
       cornerWidth : INTEGER;   {Width of corner oval}
       cornerHeight : INTEGER);   {Height of corner oval}

procedure FillRoundRect
       (theRect   : Rect;   {Body of rectangle}
       cornerWidth : INTEGER;   {Width of corner oval}
       cornerHeight : INTEGER;   {Height of corner oval}
       fillPat   : Pattern);   {Pattern to fill with}

procedure EraseRoundRect
       (theRect   : Rect;   {Body of rectangle}
       cornerWidth : INTEGER;   {Width of corner oval}
       cornerHeight : INTEGER);   {Height of corner oval}

procedure InvertRoundRect
       (theRect   : Rect;   {Body of rectangle}
       cornerWidth : INTEGER;   {Width of corner oval}
       cornerHeight : INTEGER);   {Height of corner oval}

5.3.4 Drawing Ovals

procedure FrameOval
        (inRect : Rect);   {Rectangle defining oval}

procedure PaintOval
        (inRect : Rect);   {Rectangle defining oval}

procedure FillOval
        (inRect : Rect;   {Rectangle defining oval}
        fillPat : Pattern);   {Pattern to fill with}

procedure EraseOval
        (inRect : Rect);   {Rectangle defining oval}

procedure InvertOval
        (inRect : Rect);   {Rectangle defining oval}

5.3.5 Drawing Arcs and Wedges

procedure FrameArc
        (inRect   : Rect;   {Rectangle defining oval}
        startAngle : INTEGER; {Starting angle}
        arcAngle   : INTEGER); {Extent of arc}

procedure PaintArc
        (inRect   : Rect;   {Rectangle defining oval}
        startAngle : INTEGER; {Starting angle}
        arcAngle   : INTEGER); {Extent of arc}

procedure FillArc
        (inRect   : Rect;   {Rectangle defining oval}
        startAngle : INTEGER; {Starting angle}
        arcAngle   : INTEGER; {Extent of arc}
        fillPat   : Pattern); {Pattern to fill with}

procedure EraseArc
        (inRect   : Rect;   {Rectangle defining oval}
        startAngle : INTEGER; {Starting angle}
        arcAngle   : INTEGER); {Extent of arc}

procedure InvertArc
        (inRect   : Rect;   {Rectangle defining oval}
        startAngle : INTEGER; {Starting angle}
        arcAngle   : INTEGER); {Extent of arc}

procedure PtToAngle
        (inRect   : Rect;   {Rectangle to measure in}
        thePoint   : Point;   {Point to be measured}
        var theAngle : INTEGER); {Returns angle of point, in degrees}

5.3.6 Drawing Polygons

procedure FramePoly
      (thePolygon : PolyHandle);   {Handle to polygon to be framed}

procedure PaintPoly
      (thePolygon : PolyHandle);   {Handle to polygon to be painted}

procedure FillPoly
      (thePolygon : PolyHandle;   {Handle to polygon to be filled}
       fillPat   : Pattern);   {Pattern to fill it with}

procedure ErasePoly
      (thePolygon : PolyHandle);   {Handle to polygon to be erased}

procedure InvertPoly
      (thePolygon : PolyHandle);   {Handle to polygon to be inverted}

5.3.7 Drawing Regions

procedure FrameRgn
      (theRegion : RgnHandle);   {Handle to region to be framed}

procedure PaintRgn
      (theRegion : RgnHandle);   {Handle to region to be painted}

procedure FillRgn
      (theRegion : RgnHandle;   {Handle to region to be filled}
       fillPat   : Pattern);   {Pattern to fill it with}

procedure EraseRgn
      (theRegion : RgnHandle);   {Handle to region to be erased}

procedure InvertRgn
      (theRegion : RgnHandle);   {Handle to region to be inverted}

5.4 Pictures and Icons

5.4.1 Picture Records

type
```
  PicHandle = ˆPicPtr;
  PicPtr    = ˆPicture;

  Picture = record
              picSize  : INTEGER;      {Length of this data structure in bytes}
              picFrame : Rect;         {Smallest rectangle enclosing the picture}
              {additional data defining contents of picture}
            end;
```

5.4.2 Defining Pictures

function   OpenPicture
        (picFrame : Rect);   {Frame for new picture}
        : PicHandle;   {Handle to new picture}

procedure ClosePicture;

function   GetPicture
        (pictureID: INTEGER)   {Resource ID of desired picture}
        : PicHandle;   {Handle to picture in memory}

procedure KillPicture
        (thePicture : PicHandle);   {Handle to picture to be destroyed}

5.4.3 Drawing Pictures

procedure DrawPicture
        (thePicture : PicHandle;   {Picture to be drawn}
        inRect   : Rect);   {Rectangle to draw it in}

5.4.4 Icons

function   GetIcon
        (iconID : INTEGER)   {Resource ID of desired icon}
        : Handle;   {Handle to icon in memory}

procedure PlotIcon
        (inRect   : Rect;   {Rectangle to plot in}
        iconHandle : Handle);   {Handle to icon}

Chapter 6 Resources

6.1 Resource Types

6.1.1 Resource Types

type
  ResType = **packed array** [1..4] **of** CHAR;   {Resource type}

6.2 Resource Files

6.2.1 Opening and Closing Resource Files

function OpenResFile
        (fileName : Str255)   {Name of resource file to be opened}
          : INTEGER;   {Reference number of file}

procedure CloseResFile
        (refNum : INTEGER);   {Reference number of resource file to be closed}

6.2.2 Current Resource File

function CurResFile
          : INTEGER;   {Reference number of current resource file}

procedure UseResFile
        (refNum : INTEGER);   {Reference number of resource file to be made current}

6.3 Access to Resources

6.3.1 Getting Resources

function	GetResource	
	(rsrcType : ResType;	{Resource type}
	rsrcID : INTEGER)	{Resource ID}
	: Handle;	{Handle to resource}

function	GetNamedResource	
	(rsrcType : ResType;	{Resource type}
	rsrcName: Str255)	{Resource name}
	: Handle;	{Handle to resource}

6.3.2 Disposing of Resources

procedure	ReleaseResource	
	(theResource : Handle);	{Resource to be released}

procedure	DetachResource	
	(theResource : Handle);	{Resource to be detached}

6.3.3 Generating All Resources

function	CountTypes	
	: INTEGER;	{Total number of resource types}

procedure	GetIndType	
	(**var** rsrcType : ResType;	{Returns next resource type}
	index : INTEGER);	{Index of desired resource type}

function	CountResources	
	(rsrcType : ResType)	{Resource type}
	: INTEGER;	{Total number of resources of this type}

function	GetIndResource	
	(rsrcType : ResType;	{Resource type}
	index : INTEGER)	{Index (not ID) of desired resource}
	: Handle;	{Handle to resource}

6.3.4 Loading Resources

procedure SetResLoad
       (onOrOff : BOOLEAN);   {Turn automatic loading on or off?}

procedure LoadResource
       (theResource : Handle);   {Resource to be loaded}

6.4 Properties of Resources

6.4.1 Identifying Information

procedure GetResInfo
       (theResource : Handle;   {Handle to resource}
       var rsrcID   : INTEGER;   {Returns resource ID}
       var rsrcType : ResType;   {Returns resource type}
       var rsrcName : Str255);   {Returns resource name}

procedure SetResInfo
       (theResource : Handle;   {Handle to resource}
       rsrcID   : INTEGER;   {New resource ID}
       rsrcName   : Str255);   {New resource name}

6.4.2 Resource Attributes

function   GetResAttrs
       (theResource : Handle)   {Handle to resource}
        : INTEGER;   {Current resource attributes}

procedure SetResAttrs
       (theResource : Handle;   {Handle to resource}
       newAttrs   : INTEGER);   {New resource attributes}

const
  ResSysHeap   = $0040;   {Resides in system heap}
  ResPurgeable = $0020;   {Purgeable from heap}
  ResLocked   = $0010;   {Locked during heap compaction}
  ResProtected = $0008;   {Protected from change}
  ResPreload   = $0004;   {Preload when file opened}
  ResChanged = $0002;   {Has been changed in memory}

6.4.3 Other Properties

```
function SizeResource
        (theResource : Handle)        {Handle to resources}
            : LONGINT;                {Size of resource data, in bytes}

function HomeResFile
        (theResource : Handle)        {Handle to resource}
            : INTEGER;                {Reference number of home resource file}
```

6.5 Modifying Resources

6.5.1 Creating Resource Files

```
procedure CreateResFile
        (fileName : Str255);          {Name of resource file to be created}
```

6.5.2 Marking Changed Resources

```
procedure ChangedResource
        (theResource : Handle);       {Resource to be marked as changed}
```

6.5.3 Adding and Removing Resources

```
procedure AddResource
        (rsrcData   : Handle;         {Handle to data of new resource}
         rsrcType   : ResType;        {Type of new resource}
         rsrcID     : INTEGER;        {ID number of new resource}
         rsrcName   : Str255);        {Name of new resource}

procedure RmveResource
        (theResource : Handle);       {Resource to be removed}

function   UniqueID
        (rsrcType : ResType);         {Resource type}
            : INTEGER                 {Unique ID number for this type}
```

6.5.4 Updating Resource Files

procedure UpdateResFile
    (refNum : INTEGER);   {Reference number of resource file to be updated}

procedure WriteResource
    (theResource : Handle);   {Resource file to be written out}

6.5.5 Purge Checking

procedure SetResPurge
    (onOrOff : BOOLEAN);   {Turn purge checking on or off?}

6.6 Nuts and Bolts

6.6.1 Error Reporting

function ResError
    : INTEGER;   {Result code from last resource-related operation}

const
  ResNotFound   = −192;   {Resource not found}
  ResFNotFound = −193;   {Resource file not found}
  AddResFailed = −194;   {AddResource failed}
  RmvResFailed = −196;   {RmveResource failed}
  DskFulErr   = −34;   {Disk full}

6.6.2 Resource File Attributes

function   GetResFileAttrs
      (refNum : INTEGER)   {Reference number of resource file}
        : INTEGER;   {Current resource file attributes}

procedure SetResFileAttrs
      (refNum   : INTEGER;   {Reference number of resource file}
       newAttrs : INTEGER);   {New resource file attributes}

const
  MapReadOnly = 128;   {No changes allowed}
  MapCompact = 64;   {Compact file when updated}
  MapChanged = 32;   {Write resource map when updated}

Chapter 7 Program Startup

7.1 Starting and Ending a Program

7.1.1 Starting a Program

procedure Launch   {Assembly language only}

procedure Chain   {Assembly language only}

7.1.2 Loading and Unloading Segments

procedure LoadSeg   {Assembly language only}

procedure UnloadSeg
        (anyRoutine : Ptr);   {Pointer to any routine in the segment}

7.1.3 Ending a Program

procedure ExitToShell;

7.2 Packages

7.2.1 Standard Packages

const
  DskInit = 2;   {Disk Initialization Package}
  StdFile = 3;   {Standard File Package (MiniFinder)}
  FlPoint = 4;   {Floating-Point Arithmetic Package}
  TrFunc   = 5;   {Transcendental Functions Package}
  IntUtil = 6;   {International Utilities Package}
  BDConv   = 7;   {Binary/Decimal Conversion Package}

7.2.2 Initializing Packages

procedure InitPack
        (packNumber : INTEGER);   {Package number}

procedure InitAllPacks;

7.3 Finder Information

7.3.1 Signatures and File Types

type
```
OSType = packed array [1..4] of CHAR;      {Creator signature or file type}
```

7.3.2 Finder Information Records

type
```
FInfo = record
            fdType     : OSType;     {File type}
            fdCreator  : OSType;     {Creator signature}
            fdFlags    : INTEGER;    {Finder flags}
            fdLocation : Point;      {Top-left corner of file's icon in local (window) coordinates}
            fdFldr     : INTEGER     {Folder or window containing icon}
        end;
```

const
```
FHasBundle = $2000;      {Application has Finder resources}
FInvisible  = $4000;     {File not visible on desktop}

FDisk    =  0;           {Icon is in main disk window}
FDesktop = −2;           {Icon is on desktop}
FTrash   = −3;           {Icon is in trash window}
```

7.3.3 Accessing Finder Properties

function GetFInfo
```
        (fName        : Str255;      {File name}
         vRefNum      : INTEGER;     {Volume reference number}
     var finderInfo : FInfo)         {Returns current finder information}
         : OSErr;                    {Result code}
```

function SetFInfo
```
        (fName       : Str255;       {File name}
         vRefNum     : INTEGER;       {Volume reference number}
         finderInfo : FInfo)          {New finder information}
         : OSErr;                     {Result code}
```

7.3.4 Startup Information

```
procedure CountAppFiles
            (var message : INTEGER;          {Open or print?}
             var count   : INTEGER);         {Returns number of files selected}

procedure GetAppFiles
            (index       : INTEGER;          {Index number of desired file}
             var theFile : AppFile);         {Returns identifying information about file}

procedure ClrAppFiles
            (index : INTEGER);               {Index number of file to be cleared}

procedure GetAppParms
            (var appName    : Str255;        {Returns name of application file}
             var appResFile : INTEGER;       {Returns reference number of application resource file}
             var startHandle : Handle);      {Returns handle to startup information}

const
  AppOpen = 0;                               {Open document file}
  AppPrint = 1;                              {Print document file}

type
  AppFile = record
              vRefNum : INTEGER;             {Volume reference number}
              fType   : OSType;              {File type}
              versNum : INTEGER;             {Version number}
              fName   : Str255               {Name of file}
            end;
```

7.4 Desk Scrap

7.4.2 Scrap Information

```
type
  PScrapStuff = ^ScrapStuff

  ScrapStuff = record
                 scrapSize   : LONGINT;      {Overall size of scrap in bytes}
                 scrapHandle : Handle;       {Handle to scrap in memory}
                 scrapCount  : INTEGER;      {Current scrap count}
                 scrapState  : INTEGER;      {Is scrap in memory?}
                 scrapName   : StringPtr     {Pointer to name of scrap file}
               end;

function InfoScrap
            : PScrapStuff;                   {Pointer to current scrap information}
```

7.4.3 Reading and Writing the Scrap

```
function GetScrap
        (theItem      : Handle;      {Handle to be set to requested item}
         itemType     : ResType;     {Resource type of desired item}
     var offset       : LONGINT)     {Returns byte offset of item data within scrap contents}
                      : LONGINT;     {Length of item data in bytes, or error code}

function PutScrap
        (itemLength : LONGINT;       {Length of item data in bytes}
         itemType   : ResType;       {Resource type of item}
         theItem        : Ptr)       {Pointer to item data}
                    : LONGINT;       {Result code}

function ZeroScrap
                    : LONGINT;       {Result code}

const
  NoScrapErr = −100;               {Desk scrap not initialized}
  NoTypeErr  = −102;               {No item of requested type}
```

7.4.4 Loading and Unloading the Scrap

```
function LoadScrap
                : LONGINT;         {Result code}

function UnloadScrap
                : LONGINT;         {Result code}
```

Chapter 8 Text

8.1 Keys and Characters

8.1.1 Character Set

```
const
  CommandMark = $11;    {Character code of command mark}
  CheckMark   = $12;    {Character code of check mark}
  DiamondMark = $13;    {Character code of diamond mark}
  AppleMark   = $14;    {Character code of Apple mark}
```

8.1.2 Character Strings

```
type
  StringPtr    = ^Str255;              {Pointer to a string}
  StringHandle = ^StringPtr;           {Handle to a string}

function   NewString
           (oldString : Str255)        {String to be copied}
           : StringHandle;             {Handle to copy}

function   GetString
           (stringID: INTEGER)         {Resource ID of desired string}
           : StringHandle;             {Handle to string in memory}

procedure  SetString
           (theString : StringHandle;  {Handle to be set}
           setTo      : Str255);       {String to set it to}
```

8.2 Fonts

8.2.1 Standard Font Numbers

```
const
  SystemFont  =  0;
  ApplFont    =  1;
  NewYork     =  2;
  Geneva      =  3;
  Monaco      =  4;
  Venice      =  5;
  London      =  6;
  Athens      =  7;
  SanFran     =  8;
  Toronto     =  9;
  Cairo       = 11;
  LosAngeles  = 12;
```

8.2.2 Font Records

type
  FontRec = **record**
            fontType : INTEGER; {Font type (proportional or fixed-width)}
            firstChar : INTEGER; {Character code of first defined character}
            lastChar : INTEGER; {Character code of last defined character}
            widMax   : INTEGER; {Maximum character width in pixels}
            kernMax : INTEGER; {Maximum backward kern in pixels}
            nDescent : INTEGER; {Negative of descent in pixels}
            fRectMax : INTEGER; {Maximum image width in pixels}
            chHeight : INTEGER; {Character height in pixels (ascent + descent)}
            owTLoc   : INTEGER; {Offset to owTable in words}
            ascent   : INTEGER; {Ascent in pixels}
            descent : INTEGER; {Descent in pixels}
            leading   : INTEGER; {Leading in pixels}
            rowWords: INTEGER; {Row width of bitImage in words}
         {bitImage : array [1..rowWords, 1..chHeight] of INTEGER;}
                            {Font image}
         {locTable : array [firstChar..lastChar+2] of INTEGER;}
                            {Location table}
         {owTable : array [firstChar..lastChar+2] of INTEGER;}
                            {Offset/width table}
      end;

const
  PropFont = $9000;   {Font type for proportional font}
  FixedFont = $B000;   {Font type for fixed-width font}
  FontWid   = $ACB0;   {Font type for font width table}

8.2.4 Initializing the Toolbox for Fonts

procedure InitFonts;

8.2.5 Access to Fonts

procedure GetFontName

             (fontNumber : INTEGER;   {Font number}

             var name   : Str255);   {Returns name of typeface}

procedure GetFNum

             (name   : Str255;   {Name of typeface}

             var fontNumber : INTEGER);   {Returns font number}

function RealFont

             (fontNumber : INTEGER;   {Desired font number}

             pointSize   : INTEGER);   {Desired point size}

              : BOOLEAN;   {Does font exist?}

8.2.6 Requesting Font Information

procedure GetFontInfo

             (**var** info : FontInfo);   {Returns information about current text font}

type

  FontInfo = **record**

             ascent   : INTEGER;   {Ascent in pixels}

             descent : INTEGER;   {Descent in pixels}

             widMax : INTEGER;   {Maximum character width in pixels}

             leading : INTEGER   {Leading in pixels}

         end;

8.2.7 Locking a Font

procedure SetFontLock

             (lock : BOOLEAN);   {Lock or unlock?}

8.3 Text and QuickDraw

8.3.1 QuickDraw Test Characteristics

```
type
  GrafPort = record
              device  : INTEGER;    {Device code}
              . . . ;
              txFont  : INTEGER;    {Font number of typeface}
              txFace  : Style;      {Type style}
              txMode  : INTEGER;    {Transfer mode for text}
              txSize  : INTEGER;    {Type size in points}
              spExtra : LONGINT;    {Extra space between words, in pixels}
              . . .
            end;

StyleItem = (Bold, Italic, Underline, Outline, Shadow, Condense, Extend);

Style     = set of StyleItem;
```

8.3.2 Setting Text Characteristics

```
procedure GrafDevice
          (deviceCode : INTEGER);    {Device code}

procedure TextFont
          (fontNumber : INTEGER);    {Font number of desired typeface}

procedure TextSize
          (pointSize : INTEGER);     {Type size in points}

procedure TextFace
          (typeStyle : Style);       {Type style}

procedure TextMode
          (mode : INTEGER);          {Transfer mode for text}

procedure SpaceExtra
          (extraSpace : Fixed);      {Extra space between words, in pixels}
```

8.3.3 Drawing Text

procedure DrawChar
      (theChar : CHAR);   {Character to be drawn}

procedure DrawString
      (theString : Str255);   {String to be drawn}

procedure DrawText
      (theText   : Ptr;   {Pointer to text to be drawn}
       firstChar : INTEGER; {Index of first character within text}
       charCount : INTEGER); {Number of characters to be drawn}

8.3.4 Measuring Text

function CharWidth
      (theChar : CHAR)   {Character to be measured}
       : INTEGER;   {Width of character}

function StringWidth
      (theString : Str255)   {String to be measured}
       : INTEGER;   {Width of string}

function TextWidth
      (theText   : Ptr;   {Pointer to text to be measured}
       firstChar : INTEGER; {Index of first character within text}
       charCount : INTEGER) {Number of characters to be measured}
       : INTEGER;   {Width of text}

APPENDIX

B
Resource Formats

Resource Type 'BNDL'

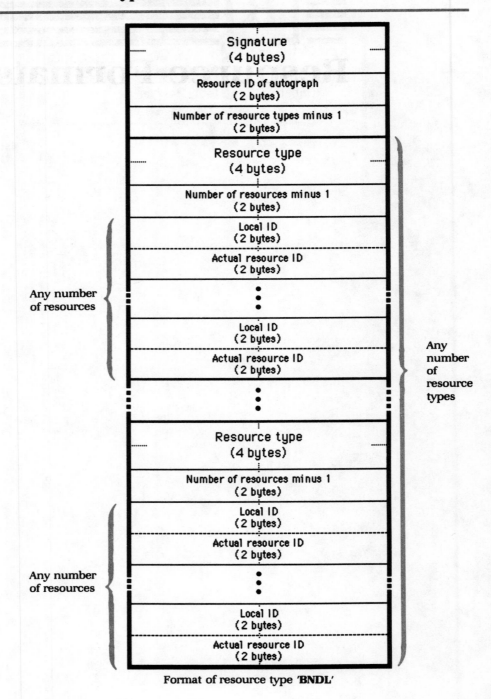

Format of resource type **'BNDL'**

Resource Type 'CODE'

Format of resource type '**CODE**'

Resource Type 'FONT'

fontType (2 bytes)
firstChar (2 bytes)
lastChar (2 bytes)
widMax (2 bytes)
kernMax (2 bytes)
nDescent (2 bytes)
fRectWid (2 bytes)
chHeight (2 bytes)
owTloc (2 bytes)
ascent (2 bytes)
descent (2 bytes)
leading (2 bytes)
rowWords (2 bytes)
bitImage (indefinite length)
locTable (indefinite length)
owTable (indefinite length)

Format of resource type **'FONT'**

Resource Type 'FREF'

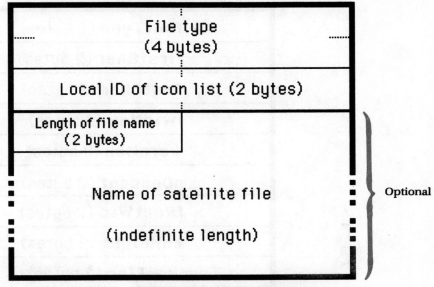

Format of resource type 'FREF'

Resource Type 'FWID'

fontType (2 bytes)
firstChar (2 bytes)
lastChar (2 bytes)
widMax (2 bytes)
kernMax (2 bytes)
nDescent (2 bytes)
fRectWid (2 bytes)
chHeight (2 bytes)
owTloc (2 bytes)
ascent (2 bytes)
descent (2 bytes)
leading (2 bytes)
owTable (indefinite length)

Format of resource type **'FWID'**

Resource Type 'ICN#'

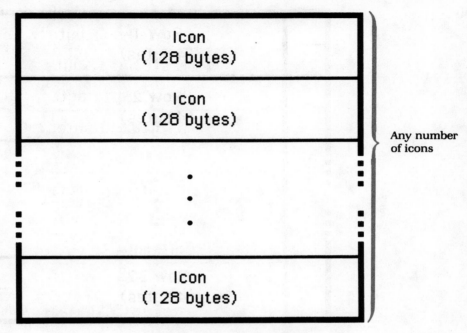

Format of resource type 'ICN#'

Resource Type 'ICON'

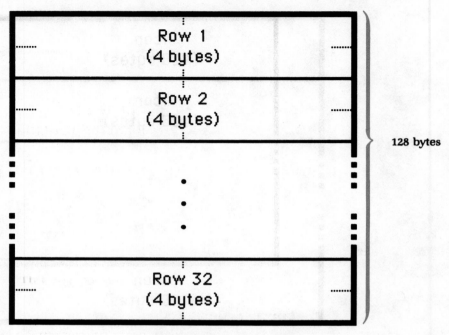

Format of resource type '**ICON**'

Resource Type 'INIT'

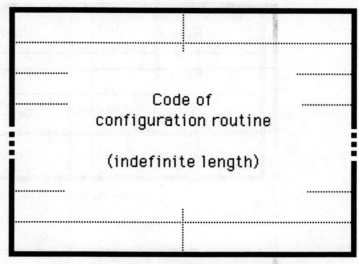

Format of resource type '**INIT**'

Resource Type 'PACK'

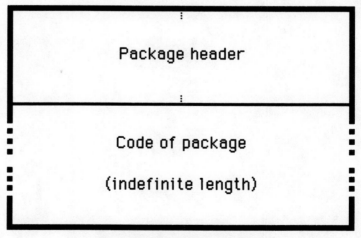

Format of resource type '**PACK**'

Resource Type 'PAT '

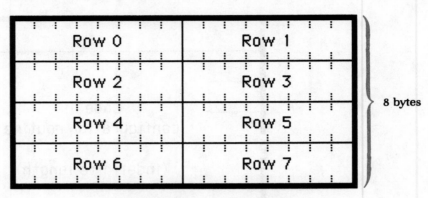

Format of resource type **'PAT '**

Resource Type 'PAT#'

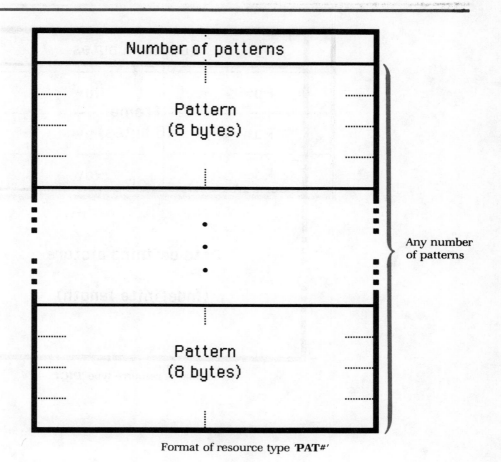

Format of resource type **'PAT#'**

Resource Type 'PICT'

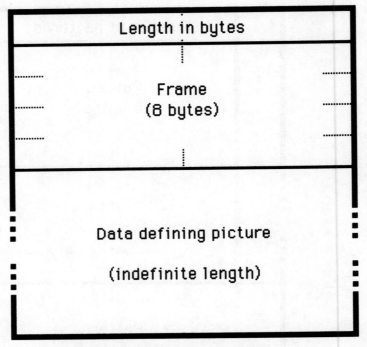

Format of resource type **'PICT'**

Resource Type 'STR '

Length of string (0-255)	
Characters of string (indefinite length)	

The maximum length of a 'STR ' resource is 255 characters.

Format of resource type 'STR '

Resource Type 'STR#'

Format of resource type '**STR#**'

Resource Type 'TEXT'

A '**TEXT**' resource does *not* begin with a length byte.

Format of resource type '**TEXT**'

A P P E N D I X

Macintosh Memory Layouts

128K Macintosh

128K
Macintosh

$00	Trap Vectors
$100	System Globals
$400	Dispatch Table
$800	System Globals
$B00	System Heap
$4E00	Application Heap
	Stack
	Application Global Space
$1A700	Main Screen Buffer
$1FC7F	
$1FD00	
$1FFE3	Main Sound Buffer
$1FFFF	

KEY

 System Use

Arrows show direction of
growth of stack and
application heap.

Memory layout for 128K Macintosh

512K "Fat Mac"

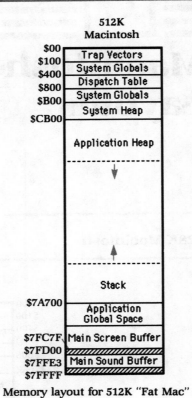

512K
Macintosh

$00	Trap Vectors
$100	System Globals
$400	Dispatch Table
$800	System Globals
$B00	System Heap
$CB00	Application Heap
	Stack
$7A700	Application Global Space
$7FC7F	Main Screen Buffer
$7FD00	
$7FFE3	Main Sound Buffer
$7FFFF	

Memory layout for 512K "Fat Mac"

512K Macintosh XL (Lisa)

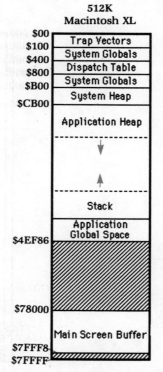

Memory layout for 512K Macintosh XL

1M Macintosh XL (Lisa)

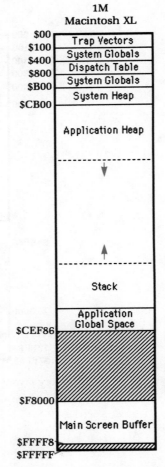

Memory layout for 1M Macintosh XL

Key Codes and Character Codes

Key Codes

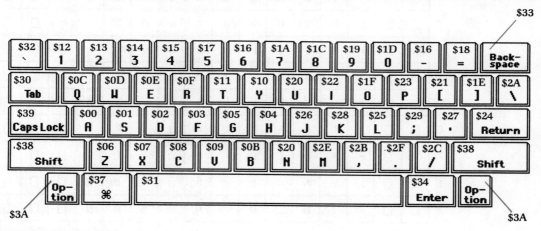

Small hexadecimal numbers are key codes.

Key codes

Character Codes

First Hex digit

	$0	$1	$2	$3	$4	$5	$6	$7	$8	$9	$A	$B	$C	$D	$E	$F
0	NUL	□	Space	0	@	P	`	p	Ä	ê	†	∞	¿	–	□	□
1	□	⌘	!	1	A	Q	a	q	Å	ë	°	±	¡	—	□	□
2	□	✓	"	2	B	R	b	r	Ç	í	¢	≤	¬	"	□	□
3	□	◆	#	3	C	S	c	s	É	ì	£	≥	√	"	□	□
4	□		$	4	D	T	d	t	Ñ	î	§	¥	ƒ	'	□	□
5	□	□	%	5	E	U	e	u	Ö	ï	•	µ	≈	'	□	□
6	□	□	&	6	F	V	f	v	Ü	ñ	¶	∂	Δ	÷	□	□
7	□	□	'	7	G	W	g	w	á	ó	ß	Σ	«	◊	□	□
8	□	□	(	8	H	X	h	x	à	ò	®	∏	»	ÿ	□	□
9	TAB	□	)	9	I	Y	i	y	â	ô	©	π	…	□	□	□
A	□	□	*	:	J	Z	j	z	ä	ö	™	∫	non-break space	□	□	□
B	□	□	+	;	K	[	k	{	ã	õ	´	ª	À	□	□	□
C	□	□	,	<	L	\	l	|	å	ú	¨	º	Ã	□	□	□
D	CR	□	–	=	M	]	m	}	ç	ù	≠	Ω	Õ·	□	□	
E	□	□	.	>	N	^	n	~	é	û	Æ	æ	Œ	□	□	
F	□	□	/	?	O	_	o	□	è	ü	Ø	ø	œ	□	□	□

Second hex digit

Characters with shading are typed
as two-character combinations.

Character codes

Error Codes

Operating System Errors

The following is a complete list of Operating System error codes. Not all are covered in this book, and some of the meanings may be obscure. For the errors you're most likely to encounter, see sections [3.1.2, 6.6.1, II:8.2.8] of the Reference Handbook.

Number	Name	Meaning
0	NoErr	No error; all is well
−1	QErr	Queue element not found during deletion
−2	VTypErr	Invalid queue element
−3	CorErr	Trap ("core routine") number out of range
−4	UnimpErr	Unimplemented trap
−17	ControlErr	Driver error during Control operation
−18	StatusErr	Driver error during Status operation
−19	ReadErr	Driver error during Read operation
−20	WritErr	Driver error during Write operation
−21	BadUnitErr	Bad unit number
−22	UnitEmptyErr	No such entry in unit table
−23	OpenErr	Driver error during Open operation
−24	CloseErr	Driver error during Close operation
−25	DRemovErr	Attempt to remove an open driver
−26	DInstErr	Attempt to install nonexistent driver
−27	AbortErr	Driver operation aborted
−28	NotOpenErr	Driver not open
−33	DirFulErr	Directory full
−34	DskFulErr	Disk full
−35	NSVErr	No such volume

Number	Name	Meaning
−36	IOErr	Disk I/O error
−37	BdNamErr	Bad name
−38	FNOpnErr	File not open
−39	EOFErr	Attempt to read past end of file
−40	PosErr	Attempt to position before start of file
−41	MFulErr	Memory (system heap) full
−42	TMFOErr	Too many files open (more than 12)
−43	FNFErr	File not found
−44	WPrErr	Disk is write-protected
−45	FLckdErr	File locked
−46	VLckdErr	Volume locked
−47	FBsyErr	File busy
−48	DupFNErr	Duplicate file name
−49	OpWrErr	File already open for writing
−50	ParamErr	Invalid parameter list
−51	RfNumErr	Invalid reference number
−52	GFPErr	Error during **GetFPos**
−53	VolOffLinErr	Volume off-line
−54	PermErr	Permission violation
−55	VolOnLinErr	Volume already on-line
−56	NSDrvErr	No such drive
−57	NoMacDskErr	Non-Macintosh disk
−58	ExtFSErr	External file system
−59	FSRnErr	Unable to rename file
−60	BadMDBErr	Bad master directory block
−61	WrPermErr	No write permission
−64	NoDriveErr	No such drive
−65	OffLinErr	Drive off-line
−66	NoNybErr	Can't find 5 nybbles
−67	NoAdrMkErr	No address mark
−68	DataVerErr	Data read doesn't verify
−69	BadCksmErr	Bad checksum (address mark)
−70	BadBtSlpErr	Bad bit-slip nybbles (address mark)
−71	NoDtaMkErr	No data mark
−72	BadDCksumErr	Bad checksum (data mark)
−73	BadDBtSlpErr	Bad bit-slip nybbles (data mark)
−74	WrUnderrun	Write underrun
−75	CantStepErr	Can't step disk drive
−76	TkOBadErr	Track O bad
−77	InitIWMErr	Can't initialize disk drip ("Integrated Wozniak Machine")
−78	TwoSideErr	Two-sided operation on one-sided drive
−79	SpdAdjErr	Can't adjust disk speed
−80	SeekErr	Seek to wrong track
−81	SectNFErr	Sector not found
−85	ClkRdErr	Error reading clock
−86	ClkWrErr	Error writing clock
−87	PRWrErr	Error writing parameter RAM
−88	PRInitErr	Parameter RAM uninitialized

Number	Name	Meaning
−89	**RcvrErr**	Receiver error (serial communications)
−90	**BreakRecd**	Break received (serial communications)
−100	**NoScrapErr**	No desk scrap
−102	**NoTypeErr**	No item in scrap of requested type
−108	**MemFullErr**	No room; heap is full
−109	**NilHandleErr**	Illegal operation on empty handle
−110	**MemAdrErr**	Bad memory address
−111	**MemWZErr**	Illegal operation on free block
−112	**MemPurErr**	Illegal operation on locked block
−113	**MemAZErr**	Address not in heap zone
−114	**MemPCErr**	Pointer check failed
−115	**MemBCErr**	Block check failed
−116	**MemSCErr**	Size check failed
−192	**ResNotFound**	Resource not found
−193	**ResFNotFound**	Resource file not found
−194	**AddResFailed**	**AddResource** failed
−195	**AddRefFailed**	**AddReference** failed
−196	**RmvResFailed**	**RmveResource** failed
−197	**RmvRefFailed**	**RmveReference** failed

"Dire Straits" Errors

The following errors are reported directly to the user—not to the running program—by the "Dire Straits" Manager (officially called the System Error Handler). Errors in this category are considered so serious that recovery is impossible: the Toolbox simply displays a "dire straits" alert box (the one with the bomb icon) on the screen, forcing the user to restart the system.

Number	Name	Meaning
1	**DSBusErr**	Bus error
2	**DSAddressErr**	Address error
3	**DSIllInstErr**	Illegal instruction
4	**DSZeroDivErr**	Attempt to divide by zero
5	**DSChkErr**	Check trap
6	**DSOvflowErr**	Overflow trap
7	**DSPrivErr**	Privilege violation
8	**DSTraceErr**	Trace trap
9	**DSLineAErr**	"A emulator" trap
10	**DSLineFErr**	"F emulator" trap
11	**DSMiscErr**	Miscellaneous hardware exception
12	**DSCoreErr**	Unimplemented core routine
13	**DSIRQErr**	Uninstalled interrupt
14	**DSIOCoreErr**	I/O core error
15	**DSLoadErr**	Segment Loader error
16	**DSFPErr**	Floating-point error

Number	Name	Meaning
17	**DSNoPackErr**	Package 0 not present
18	**DSNoPk1**	Package 1 not present
19	**DSNoPk2**	Package 2 not present
20	**DSNoPk3**	Package 3 not present
21	**DSNoPk4**	Package 4 not present
22	**DSNoPk5**	Package 5 not present
23	**DSNoPk6**	Package 6 not present
24	**DSNoPk7**	Package 7 not present
25	**DSMemFullErr**	Out of memory
26	**DSBadLaunch**	Can't launch program
27	**DSFSErr**	File system error
28	**DSStkNHeap**	Stack/heap collision
30	**DSReinsert**	Ask user to reinsert disk
31	**DSNotTheOne**	Wront disk inserted

Summary of Trap Macros and Trap Words

Trap Macros

The following is an alphabetical list of assembly-language trap macros covered in this volume, with their corresponding trap words. For routines belonging to the standard packages, the trap word shown is one of the eight package traps (_Pack0 to _Pack7) and is followed by a routine selector in parentheses.

Trap macro name	Trap word	Handbook section
_AddPt	$A87E	[4.4.1]
_AddResource	$A9AB	[6.5.3]
_BackPat	$A87C	[5.1.1]
_BitAnd	$A858	[2.2.2]
_BitClr	$A85F	[2.2.1]
_BitNot	$A85A	[2.2.2]
_BitOr	$A85B	[2.2.2]
_BitSet	$A85E	[2.2.1]
_BitShift	$A85C	[2.2.2]
_BitTst	$A85D	[2.2.1]
_BitXOr	$A859	[2.2.2]
_BlockMove	$A02E	[3.2.5]
_Chain	$A9F3	[7.1.1]
_ChangedResource	$A9AA	[6.5.2]
_CharWidth	$A88D	[8.3.4]
_ClipRect	$A87B	[4.3.6]
_ClosePgon	$A8CC	[4.1.4]
_ClosePicture	$A8F4	[5.4.2]
_ClosePort	$A87D	[4.3.2]

Trap macro name	Trap word	Handbook section
_CloseResFile	$A99A	[6.2.1]
_CloseRgn	$A8DB	[4.1.6]
_CmpString	$A03C	[2.1.2]
_CompactMem	$A04C	[3.3.2]
_CopyBits	$A8EC	[5.1.2]
_CopyRgn	$A8DC	[4.1.7]
_CountResources	$A99C	[6.3.3]
_CountTypes	$A99E	[6.3.3]
_CreateResFile	$A9B1	[6.5.1]
_CurResFile	$A994	[6.2.2]
_Date2Secs	$A9C7	[2.4.3]
_DetachResource	$A992	[6.3.2]
_DiffRgn	$A8E6	[4.4.8]
_DisposHandle	$A023	[3.2.2]
_DisposPtr	$A01F	[3.2.2]
_DisposRgn	$A8D9	[4.1.6]
_DrawChar	$A883	[8.3.3]
_DrawPicture	$A8F6	[5.4.3]
_DrawString	$A884	[8.3.3]
_DrawText	$A885	[8.3.3]
_EmptyHandle	$A02B	[3.3.3]
_EmptyRect	$A8AE	[4.4.4]
_EmptyRgn	$A8E2	[4.4.7]
_EqualPt	$A881	[4.4.1]
_EqualRect	$A8A6	[4.4.5]
_EqualRgn	$A8E3	[4.4.8]
_EraseArc	$A8C0	[5.3.5]
_EraseOval	$A8B9	[5.3.4]
_ErasePoly	$A8C8	[5.3.6]
_EraseRect	$A8A3	[5.3.2]
_EraseRgn	$A8D4	[5.3.7]
_EraseRoundRect	$A8B2	[5.3.3]
_ExitToShell	$A9F4	[7.1.3]
_FillArc	$A8C2	[5.3.5]
_FillOval	$A8BB	[5.3.4]
_FillPoly	$A8CA	[5.3.6]
_FillRect	$A8A5	[5.3.2]
_FillRgn	$A8D6	[5.3.7]
_FillRoundRect	$A8B4	[5.3.3]
_FixMul	$A868	[2.3.2]
_FixRatio	$A869	[2.3.2]
_FixRound	$A86C	[2.3.1]
_FrameArc	$A8BE	[5.3.5]
_FrameOval	$A8B7	[5.3.4]
_FramePoly	$A8C6	[5.3.6]
_FrameRect	$A8A1	[5.3.2]
_FrameRgn	$A8D2	[5.3.7]
_FrameRoundRect	$A8B0	[5.3.3]
_FreeMem	$A01C	[3.3.1]

Trap macro name	Trap word	Handbook section
_GetAppParms	$A9F5	[7.3.4]
_GetClip	$A87A	[4.3.6]
_GetFileInfo	$A00C	[7.3.3]
_GetFName	$A8FF	[8.2.5]
_GetFNum	$A900	[8.2.5]
_GetFontInfo	$A88B	[8.2.6]
_GetHandleSize	$A025	[3.2.3]
_GetIndResource	$A99D	[6.3.3]
_GetIndType	$A99F	[6.3.3]
_GetNamedResource	$A9A1	[6.3.1]
_GetPattern	$A9B8	[5.1.1]
_GetPen	$A89A	[5.2.4]
_GetPenState	$A898	[5.2.1]
_GetPicture	$A9BC	[5.4.2]
_GetPixel	$A865	[4.2.3]
_GetPort	$A874	[4.3.3]
_GetPtrSize	$A021	[3.2.3]
_GetResAttrs	$A9A6	[6.4.2]
_GetResFileAttrs	$A9F6	[6.6.2]
_GetResInfo	$A9A8	[6.4.1]
_GetResource	$A9A0	[6.3.1]
_GetScrap	$A9FD	[7.4.3]
_GetString	$A9BA	[8.1.2]
_GlobalToLocal	$A871	[4.4.2]
_GrafDevice	$A872	[8.3.2]
_HandAndHand	$A9E4	[3.2.6]
_HandToHand	$A9E1	[3.2.5]
_HidePen	$A896	[5.2.3]
_HiWord	$A86A	[2.2.3]
_HLock	$A029	[3.2.4]
_HNoPurge	$A04A	[3.2.4]
_HomeResFile	$A9A4	[6.4.3]
_HPurge	$A049	[3.2.4]
_HUnlock	$A02A	[3.2.4]
_InfoScrap	$A9F9	[7.4.2]
_InitAllPacks	$A9E6	[7.2.2]
_InitFonts	$A8FE	[8.2.4]
_InitGraf	$A86E	[4.3.1]
_InitPack	$A9E5	[7.2.2]
_InitPort	$A86D	[4.3.2]
_InsetRect	$A8A9	[4.4.4]
_InsetRgn	$A8E1	[4.4.7]
_InverRect	$A8A4	[5.3.2]
_InverRgn	$A8D5	[5.3.7]
_InverRoundRect	$A8B3	[5.3.3]
_InvertArc	$A8C1	[5.3.5]
_InvertOval	$A8BA	[5.3.4]
_InvertPoly	$A8C9	[5.3.6]
_IUDateString	$A9ED (0)	[2.4.4]

Trap macro name	Trap word	Handbook section
_IUTimeString	$A9ED (2)	[2.4.4]
_KillPicture	$A8F5	[5.4.2]
_KillPoly	$A8CD	[4.1.4]
_Launch	$A9F2	[7.1.1]
_Line	$A892	[5.2.4]
_LineTo	$A891	[5.2.4]
_LoadSeg	$A9F0	[7.1.2]
_LocalToGlobal	$A870	[4.4.2]
_LodeScrap	$A9FB	[7.4.4]
_LongMul	$A867	[2.3.3]
_LoWord	$A86B	[2.2.3]
_MapPoly	$A8FC	[4.4.9]
_MapPt	$A8F9	[4.4.9]
_MapRect	$A8FA	[4.4.9]
_MapRgn	$A8FB	[4.4.9]
_MaxMem	$A11D	[3.3.1]
_Move	$A894	[5.2.4]
_MovePortTo	$A877	[4.3.5]
_MoveTo	$A893	[5.2.4]
_NewHandle	$A122	[3.2.1]
_NewPtr	$A11E	[3.2.1]
_NewRgn	$A8D8	[4.1.6]
_NewString	$A906	[8.1.2]
_NumToString	$A9EE (0)	[2.3.4]
_OffsetPoly	$A8CE	[4.4.6]
_OffsetRect	$A8A8	[4.4.4]
_OfsetRgn	$A8E0	[4.4.7]
_OpenPicture	$A8F3	[5.4.2]
_OpenPoly	$A8CB	[4.1.4]
_OpenPort	$A86F	[4.3.2]
_OpenResFile	$A997	[6.2.1]
_OpenRgn	$A8DA	[4.1.6]
_Pack0	$A9E7	[7.2.1]
_Pack1	$A9E8	[7.2.1]
_Pack2	$A9E9	[7.2.1]
_Pack3	$A9EA	[7.2.1]
_Pack4	$A9EB	[7.2.1]
_Pack5	$A9EC	[7.2.1]
_Pack6	$A9ED	[7.2.1]
_Pack7	$A9EE	[7.2.1]
_PaintArc	$A8BF	[5.3.5]
_PaintOval	$A8B8	[5.3.4]
_PaintPoly	$A8C7	[5.3.6]
_PaintRect	$A8A2	[5.3.2]
_PaintRgn	$A8D3	[5.3.7]
_PaintRoundRect	$A8B1	[5.3.3]
_PenMode	$A89C	[5.2.2]
_PenNormal	$A89E	[5.2.2]

Trap macro name	Trap word	Handbook section
_PenPat	$A89D	[5.2.2]
_PenSize	$A89B	[5.2.2]
_PinRect	$A94E	[4.4.3]
_PortSize	$A876	[4.3.5]
_Pt2Rect	$A8AC	[4.1.2]
_PtInRect	$A8AD	[4.4.3]
_PtInRgn	$A8E8	[4.4.3]
_PtrAndHand	$A9EF	[3.2.6]
_PtrToHand	$A9E3	[3.2.5]
_PtrToXHand	$A9E2	[3.2.5]
_PtToAngle	$A8C3	[5.3.5]
_PurgeMem	$A04D	[3.3.3]
_PutScrap	$A9FE	[7.4.3]
_Random	$A861	[2.3.5]
_RealFont	$A902	[8.2.5]
_ReallocHandle	$A027	[3.3.3]
_RecoverHandle	$A128	[3.2.1]
_RectInRgn	$A8E9	[4.4.3]
_RectRgn	$A8DF	[4.1.7]
_ReleaseResource	$A9A3	[6.3.2]
_ResError	$A9AF	[6.6.1]
_ResrvMem	$A040	[3.2.1]
_RmveResource	$A9AD	[6.5.3]
_ScalePt	$A8F8	[4.4.9]
_ScrollRect	$A8EF	[5.1.5]
_Secs2Date	$A9C6	[2.4.3]
_SectRect	$A8AA	[4.4.5]
_SectRgn	$A8E4	[4.4.8]
_SetApplLimit	$A02D	[3.3.4]
_SetClip	$A879	[4.3.6]
_SetDateTime	$A03A	[2.4.1]
_SetEmptyRgn	$A8DD	[4.1.7]
_SetFileInfo	$A00D	[7.3.3]
_SetFontLock	$A903	[8.2.7]
_SetHandleSize	$A024	[3.2.3]
_SetOrigin	$A878	[4.3.4]
_SetPBits	$A875	[4.3.4]
_SetPenState	$A899	[5.2.1]
_SetPort	$A873	[4.3.3]
_SetPt	$A880	[4.1.1]
_SetPtrSize	$A020	[3.2.3]
_SetRecRgn	$A8DE	[4.1.7]
_SetRect	$A8A7	[4.1.2]
_SetResAttrs	$A9A7	[6.4.2]
_SetResFileAttrs	$A9F7	[6.6.2]
_SetResInfo	$A9A9	[6.4.1]
_SetResPurge	$A993	[6.5.5]
_SetString	$A907	[8.1.2]
_ShowPen	$A897	[5.2.3]
_SizeRsrc	$A9A5	[6.4.3]

Trap macro name	Trap word	Handbook section
_SpaceExtra	$A88E	[8.3.2]
_StringToNum	$A9EE (1)	[2.3.4]
_StringWidth	$A88C	[8.3.4]
_StuffHex	$A866	[2.2.4]
_SubPt	$A87F	[4.4.1]
_TextFace	$A888	[8.3.2]
_TextFont	$A887	[8.3.2]
_TextMode	$A889	[8.3.2]
_TextSize	$A88A	[8.3.2]
_TextWidth	$A886	[8.3.4]
_UnionRect	$A8AB	[4.4.5]
_UnionRgn	$A8E5	[4.4.8]
_UniqueID	$A9C1	[6.5.3]
_UnloadSeg	$A9F1	[7.1.2]
_UnlodeScrap	$A9FA	[7.4.4]
_UpdateResFile	$A999	[6.5.4]
_UprString	$A854	[2.1.2]
_UseResFile	$A998	[6.2.2]
_WriteResource	$A9B0	[6.5.4]
_XOrRgn	$A8E7	[4.4.8]
_ZeroScrap	$A9FC	[7.4.3]

Trap Words

Here is the same list sorted numerically by trap word. Again, routine selectors are given in parentheses following the trap word for routines belonging to the standard packages.

Trap word	Trap macro name	Handbook section
$A00C	_GetFileInfo	[7.3.3]
$A00D	_SetFileInfo	[7.3.3]
$A01C	_FreeMem	[3.3.1]
$A01F	_DisposPtr	[3.2.2]
$A020	_SetPtrSize	[3.2.3]
$A021	_GetPtrSize	[3.2.3]
$A023	_DisposHandle	[3.2.2]
$A024	_SetHandleSize	[3.2.3]
$A025	_GetHandleSize	[3.2.3]
$A027	_ReallocHandle	[3.3.3]
$A029	_HLock	[3.2.4]
$A02A	_HUnlock	[3.2.4]
$A02B	_EmptyHandle	[3.3.3]

Trap word	Trap macro name	Handbook section
$A02D	_SetApplLimit	[3.3.4]
$A02E	_BlockMove	[3.2.5]
$A03A	_SetDateTime	[2.4.1]
$A03C	_CmpString	[2.1.2]
$A040	_ResrvMem	[3.2.1]
$A049	_HPurge	[3.2.4]
$A04A	_HNoPurge	[3.2.4]
$A04C	_CompactMem	[3.3.2]
$A04D	_PurgeMem	[3.3.3]
$A11D	_MaxMem	[3.3.1]
$A11E	_NewPtr	[3.2.1]
$A122	_NewHandle	[3.2.1]
$A128	_RecoverHandle	[3.2.1]
$A854	_UprString	[2.1.2]
$A858	_BitAnd	[2.2.2]
$A859	_BitXOr	[2.2.2]
$A85A	_BitNot	[2.2.2]
$A85B	_BitOr	[2.2.2]
$A85C	_BitShift	[2.2.2]
$A85D	_BitTst	[2.2.1]
$A85E	_BitSet	[2.2.1]
$A85F	_BitClr	[2.2.1]
$A861	_Random	[2.3.5]
$A865	_GetPixel	[4.2.3]
$A866	_StuffHex	[2.2.4]
$A867	_LongMul	[2.3.3]
$A868	_FixMul	[2.3.2]
$A869	_FixRatio	[2.3.2]
$A86A	_HiWord	[2.2.3]
$A86B	_LoWord	[2.2.3]
$A86C	_FixRound	[2.3.1]
$A86D	_InitPort	[4.3.2]
$A86E	_InitGraf	[4.3.1]
$A86F	_OpenPort	[4.3.2]
$A870	_LocalToGlobal	[4.4.2]
$A871	_GlobalToLocal	[4.4.2]
$A872	_GrafDevice	[8.3.2]
$A873	_SetPort	[4.3.3]
$A874	_GetPort	[4.3.3]
$A875	_SetPBits	[4.3.4]
$A876	_PortSize	[4.3.5]
$A877	_MovePortTo	[4.3.5]
$A878	_SetOrigin	[4.3.4]
$A879	_SetClip	[4.3.6]
$A87A	_GetClip	[4.3.6]
$A87B	_ClipRect	[4.3.6]
$A87C	_BackPat	[5.1.1]
$A87D	_ClosePort	[4.3.2]

Trap word	Trap macro name	Handbook section
$A87E	_AddPt	[4.4.1]
$A87F	_SubPt	[4.1.1]
$A880	_SetPt	[4.1.1]
$A881	_EqualPt	[4.4.1]
$A883	_DrawChar	[8.3.3]
$A884	_DrawString	[8.3.3]
$A885	_DrawText	[8.3.3]
$A886	_TextWidth	[8.3.4]
$A887	_TextFont	[8.3.2]
$A888	_TextFace	[8.3.2]
$A889	_TextMode	[8.3.2]
$A88A	_TextSize	[8.3.2]
$A88B	_GetFontInfo	[8.2.6]
$A88C	_StringWidth	[8.3.4]
$A88D	_CharWidth	[8.3.4]
$A88E	_SpaceExtra	[8.3.2]
$A891	_LineTo	[5.2.4]
$A892	_Line	[5.2.4]
$A893	_MoveTo	[5.2.4]
$A894	_Move	[5.2.4]
$A896	_HidePen	[5.2.3]
$A897	_ShowPen	[5.2.3]
$A898	_GetPenState	[5.2.1]
$A899	_SetPenState	[5.2.1]
$A89A	_GetPen	[5.2.4]
$A89B	_PenSize	[5.2.2]
$A89C	_PenMode	[5.2.2]
$A89D	_PenPat	[5.2.2]
$A89E	_PenNormal	[5.2.2]
$A8A1	_FrameRect	[5.3.2]
$A8A2	_PaintRect	[5.3.2]
$A8A3	_EraseRect	[5.3.2]
$A8A4	_InverRect	[5.3.2]
$A8A5	_FillRect	[5.3.2]
$A8A6	_EqualRect	[4.4.5]
$A8A7	_SetRect	[4.1.2]
$A8A8	_OffsetRect	[4.4.4]
$A8A9	_InsetRect	[4.4.4]
$A8AA	_SectRect	[4.4.5]
$A8AB	_UnionRect	[4.4.5]
$A8AC	_Pt2Rect	[4.1.2]
$A8AD	_PtInRect	[4.4.3]
$A8AE	_EmptyRect	[4.4.4]
$A8B0	_FrameRoundRect	[5.3.3]
$A8B1	_PaintRoundRect	[5.3.3]
$A8B2	_EraseRoundRect	[5.3.3]
$A8B3	_InverRoundRect	[5.3.3]
$A8B4	_FillRoundRect	[5.3.3]
$A8B7	_FrameOval	[5.3.4]

Trap word	Trap macro name	Handbook section
$A8B8	_PaintOval	[5.3.4]
$A8B9	_EraseOval	[5.3.4]
$A8BA	_InvertOval	[5.3.4]
$A8BB	_FillOval	[5.3.4]
$A8BE	_FrameArc	[5.3.5]
$A8BF	_PaintArc	[5.3.5]
$A8C0	_EraseArc	[5.3.5]
$A8C1	_InvertArc	[5.3.5]
$A8C2	_FillArc	[5.3.5]
$A8C3	_PtToAngle	[5.3.5]
$A8C6	_FramePoly	[5.3.6]
$A8C7	_PaintPoly	[5.3.6]
$A8C8	_ErasePoly	[5.3.6]
$A8C9	_InvertPoly	[5.3.6]
$A8CA	_FillPoly	[5.3.6]
$A8CB	_OpenPoly	[4.1.4]
$A8CC	_ClosePgon	[4.1.4]
$A8CD	_KillPoly	[4.1.4]
$A8CE	_OffsetPoly	[4.4.6]
$A8D2	_FrameRgn	[5.3.7]
$A8D3	_PaintRgn	[5.3.7]
$A8D4	_EraseRgn	[5.3.7]
$A8D5	_InverRgn	[5.3.7]
$A8D6	_FillRgn	[5.3.7]
$A8D8	_NewRgn	[4.1.6]
$A8D9	_DisposRgn	[4.1.6]
$A8DA	_OpenRgn	[4.1.6]
$A8DB	_CloseRgn	[4.1.6]
$A8DC	_CopyRgn	[4.1.7]
$A8DD	_SetEmptyRgn	[4.1.7]
$A8DE	_SetRecRgn	[4.1.7]
$A8DF	_RectRgn	[4.1.7]
$A8E0	_OfsetRgn	[4.4.7]
$A8E1	_InsetRgn	[4.4.7]
$A8E2	_EmptyRgn	[4.4.7]
$A8E3	_EqualRgn	[4.4.8]
$A8E4	_SectRgn	[4.4.8]
$A8E5	_UnionRgn	[4.4.8]
$A8E6	_DiffRgn	[4.4.8]
$A8E7	_XOrRgn	[4.4.8]
$A8E8	_PtInRgn	[4.4.3]
$A8E9	_RectInRgn	[4.4.3]
$A8EC	_CopyBits	[5.1.2]
$A8EF	_ScrollRect	[5.1.5]
$A8F3	_OpenPicture	[5.4.2]
$A8F4	_ClosePicture	[5.4.2]
$A8F5	_KillPicture	[5.4.2]
$A8F6	_DrawPicture	[5.4.3]
$A8F8	_ScalePt	[4.4.9]

Trap word	Trap macro name	Handbook section
$A8F9	_MapPt	[4.4.9]
$A8FA	_MapRect	[4.4.9]
$A8FB	_MapRgn	[4.4.9]
$A8FC	_MapPoly	[4.4.9]
$A8FE	_InitFonts	[8.2.4]
$A8FF	_GetFName	[8.2.5]
$A900	_GetFNum	[8.2.5]
$A902	_RealFont	[8.2.5]
$A903	_SetFontLock	[8.2.7]
$A906	_NewString	[8.1.2]
$A907	_SetString	[8.1.2]
$A94E	_PinRect	[4.4.3]
$A992	_DetachResource	[6.3.2]
$A993	_SetResPurge	[6.5.5]
$A994	_CurResFile	[6.2.2]
$A997	_OpenResFile	[6.2.1]
$A998	_UseResFile	[6.2.2]
$A999	_UpdateResFile	[6.5.4]
$A99A	_CloseResFile	[6.2.1]
$A99C	_CountResources	[6.3.3]
$A99D	_GetIndResource	[6.3.3]
$A99E	_CountTypes	[6.3.3]
$A99F	_GetIndType	[6.3.3]
$A9A0	_GetResource	[6.3.1]
$A9A1	_GetNamedResource	[6.3.1]
$A9A3	_ReleaseResource	[6.3.2]
$A9A4	_HomeResFile	[6.4.3]
$A9A5	_SizeRsrc	[6.4.3]
$A9A6	_GetResAttrs	[6.4.2]
$A9A7	_SetResAttrs	[6.4.2]
$A9A8	_GetResInfo	[6.4.1]
$A9A9	_SetResInfo	[6.4.1]
$A9AA	_ChangedResource	[6.5.2]
$A9AB	_AddResource	[6.5.3]
$A9AD	_RmveResource	[6.5.3]
$A9AF	_ResError	[6.6.1]
$A9B0	_WriteResource	[6.5.4]
$A9B1	_CreateResFile	[6.5.1]
$A9B8	_GetPattern	[5.1.1]
$A9BA	_GetString	[8.1.2]
$A9BC	_GetPicture	[5.4.2]
$A9C1	_UniqueID	[6.5.3]
$A9C6	_Secs2Date	[2.4.3]
$A9C7	_Date2Secs	[2.4.3]
$A9E1	_HandToHand	[3.2.5]
$A9E2	_PtrToXHand	[3.2.5]
$A9E3	_PtrToHand	[3.2.5]

Trap word	Trap macro name	Handbook section
$A9E4	_HandAndHand	[3.2.6]
$A9E5	_InitPack	[7.2.2]
$A9E6	_InitAllPacks	[7.2.2]
$A9E7	_Pack0	[7.2.1]
$A9E8	_Pack1	[7.2.1]
$A9E9	_Pack2	[7.2.1]
$A9EA	_Pack3	[7.2.1]
$A9EB	_Pack4	[7.2.1]
$A9EC	_Pack5	[7.2.1]
$A9ED (0)	_IUDateString	[2.4.4]
$A9ED (2)	_IUTimeString	[2.4.4]
$A9ED	_Pack6	[7.2.1]
$A9EE	_Pack7	[7.2.1]
$A9EE (0)	_NumToString	[2.3.4]
$A9EE (1)	_StringToNum	[2.3.4]
$A9EF	_PtrAndHand	[3.2.6]
$A9F0	_LoadSeg	[7.1.2]
$A9F1	_UnloadSeg	[7.1.2]
$A9F2	_Launch	[7.1.1]
$A9F3	_Chain	[7.1.1]
$A9F4	_ExitToShell	[7.1.3]
$A9F5	_GetAppParms	[7.3.4]
$A9F6	_GetResFileAttrs	[6.6.2]
$A9F7	_SetResFileAttrs	[6.6.2]
$A9F9	_InfoScrap	[7.4.2]
$A9FA	_UnlodeScrap	[7.4.4]
$A9FB	_LodeScrap	[7.4.4]
$A9FC	_ZeroScrap	[7.4.3]
$A9FD	_GetScrap	[7.4.3]
$A9FE	_PutScrap	[7.4.3]

Summary of Assembly-Language Variables

System Globals

Listed below are all assembly-language global variables covered in this volume, with their hexadecimal addresses. *Warning:* The addresses given may be subject to change in future versions of the Toolbox; always refer to these variables by name rather than using the addresses directly.

Variable name	Offset in bytes	Handbook section	Meaning
ApFontID	**$984**	[8.2.1]	True font number of current application font
AppParmHandle	**$AEC**	[7.3.4]	Handle to Finder startup information
CurApName	**$910**	[7.3.4]	Name of current application (maximum 31 characters)
CurApRefNum	**$900**	[7.3.4]	Reference number of application resource file
CurMap	**$A5A**	[6.2.2]	Reference number of current resource file
CurPageOption	**$936**	[7.1.1]	Integer specifying screen and sound buffers
DeskPattern	**$A3C**	[5.1.2]	Screen background pattern
FinderName	**$2E0**	[7.1.3]	Name of program to exit to (maximum 15 characters)
FScaleDisable	**$A63**	[8.3.1]	Disable font scaling if nonzero
Key1Trans	**$29E**	[8.4.4]	Pointer to keyboard configuration routine
Key2Trans	**$2A2**	[8.4.4]	Pointer to keypad configuration routine

Variable name	Offset in bytes	Handbook section	Meaning
MemTop	$108	[3.3.1]	Pointer to end of physical memory
ResErr	$A60	[6.6.1]	Result code from last resource-related call
ResLoad	$A5E	[6.3.4]	Load resources automatically?
ROMFont0	$980	[8.2.1]	Handle to system font
ScrapCount	$968	[7.4.2]	Current scrap count
ScrapHandle	$964	[7.4.2]	Handle to contents of desk scrap
ScrapName	$96C	[7.4.2]	Pointer to scrap file name
ScrapSize	$960	[7.4.2]	Current size of desk scrap
ScrapState	$96A	[7.4.2]	Current state of desk scrap
SPFont	$204	[8.2.1]	True font number of default application font
SysMap	$A58	[6.2.2]	True reference number (not 0) of system resource file
SysMapHndl	$A54	[6.2.2]	Handle to resource map of system resource file
SysResName	$AD8	[6.2.2]	Name of system resource file (string, maximum 19 characters)
Time	$20C	[2.4.1]	Current date and time in "raw" seconds
TopMapHndl	$A50	[6.2.2]	Handle to resource map of most recently opened (not necessarily current) resource file

QuickDraw Globals

The QuickDraw global variables listed below are located at the given offsets relative to the QuickDraw globals pointer, which in turn is pointed to by address register **A5.**

Variable name	Offset in bytes	Handbook section	Meaning
ThePort	0	[4.3.3]	Current graphics port
White	−8	[5.1.2]	Standard white pattern
Black	−16	[5.1.2]	Standard black pattern
Gray	−24	[5.1.2]	Standard gray pattern
LtGray	−32	[5.1.2]	Standard light gray pattern
DkGray	−40	[5.1.2]	Standard dark gray pattern
Arrow	−108	[II:2.5.2]	Standard arrow cursor
ScreenBits	−122	[4.2.1]	Screen bit map
RandSeed	−126	[2.3.5]	"Seed" for random number generation

Glossary

Note: Terms within a definition shown in *italic* are defined elsewhere in this glossary. Simple page numbers in square brackets, such as [278], refer to the Programmer's Guidebook; two- or three-part section numbers, such as [2.1] or [2.2.2], refer to the Reference Handbook. Numbers in angle brackets following a section number, such as [2.1.1<1>], refer to specific notes within that Handbook section. References to Volume Two are preceded by a roman numeral II and a colon: for example, [II:278, II:2.1.1<1>]. Because some terms are found repeatedly in the text and a comprehensive listing would be tedious to the reader, we have, in some cases, given you a sampling of where they are. Each of these listings will be preceded by the word "Sampling:". For those entries with fewer references, the listings will be complete as is.

A5 *world:* Another name for a program's *application global space,* located through a *base address* kept in processor register **A5.**

"*above* A5" *size:* The number of bytes needed between the *base address* in register **A5** and the end of the *application global space,* to hold a program's *application parameters* and *jump table* [303, 7.5.1<4>].

allocate: To set aside a *block* of memory from the *heap* for a particular use [60, 3.2.1].

and: A bit-level operation in which each bit of the result is a **1** if both operands have **1**s at the corresponding bit position, or **0** if either or both have **0**s [24, 2.2.2].

apple mark: A special *control character* (*character code* **$14**) that appears on the Macintosh screen as a small Apple symbol; used for the menu title of *desk accessories* [350, 8.1.1<4>].

application file: A *file* containing the executable code of an application program, with a *file type* of '**APPL**' and the program's own signature as its *creator signature* [310, 312, 313, 7.3.1<5>].

application font: The standard *typeface* used by an application program; normally **Geneva**, but can be changed to some other typeface if desired [354, 8.2.1<7–9>].

application global space: The area of memory containing a program's *application globals*, *application parameters*, and *jump table*, normally situated just before the *screen buffer* in memory and located through a *base address* kept in processor register **A5** [51, 52–54, 302–304, 7.1.1<3>, 7.5.1<5>].

application globals: Global variables belonging to the running application program, which reside in the *application global space* and are located at negative offsets from the *base address* in register **A5** [51, 52, 302–304, 7.1.1<3>, 7.5.1<4>].

application heap: The portion of the *heap* available for use by the running application program [56–57].

application heap limit: The memory address marking the farthest point to which the *heap* can expand, to prevent it from colliding with the *stack* [74, 3.3.4].

application parameters: Descriptive information about the running program, located in the *application global space* at positive offsets from the *base address* in register **A5**. The application parameters are a vestige of the Lisa software environment, and most are unused on the Macintosh; the only ones still used are the *QuickDraw globals pointer* and the *startup handle* [52–54, 97, 303–304].

application resource file: The *resource fork* of a program's *application file*, containing *resources* belonging to the program itself [262, 6.2.1<7>].

arc: A part of an *oval*, defined by a given *starting angle* and *arc angle* [201, 5.3.5].

arc angle: The angle defining the extent of an *arc* or *wedge* [201, 5.3.5<3–7>].

ascent: (1) For a text character, the height of the character above the *baseline*, in pixels [352]. (2) For a *font*, the maximum ascent of any character in the font [356–357, 8.2.2<9>].

ascent line: The line marking a font's maximum *ascent* above the *baseline* [356–357].

ASCII: American Standard Code for Information Interchange, the industry-standard 7-bit character set on which the Macintosh's 8-bit *character codes* are based [349, 8.1.1].

@ operator: An operator provided by Apple's Pascal compiler, which accepts a variable or routine name as an operand and produces a *blind pointer* to that variable or routine in memory [20].

attribute byte: The byte in a *resource map* entry that holds the *resource attributes* [271].

autograph: A *Finder resource* whose *resource type* is the same as a program's *signature* and which serves as the program's representative in the *desktop file;* also called a *version data* resource [312–313, 7.5.4<6–7>].

background pattern: The *pattern* used for *erasing* shapes in a given *graphics port* [181, 185, 4.2.2<9>, 5.1.1<4–6>, 5.1.5<3>].

base address: In general, any memory address used as a reference point from which to locate desired data in memory. Specifically, (1) the address of the *bit image* belonging to a given *bit map* [118, 4.2.1<1>]; (2) the address of a program's *application parameters,* kept in processor register **A5** and used to locate the contents of the program's *application global space* [52, 54, 303–304, 7.1.1<3>, 7.5.1<4>].

baseline: The reference line used for defining the *character images* in a *font,* and along which the *graphics pen* travels as text is drawn [352].

base of stack: The end of the *stack* that remains fixed in memory and is unaffected when items are added and removed; compare *top of stack* [13].

base type: In Pascal, the data type to which a given pointer type is declared to point: for example, the pointer type ^**INTEGER** has the base type **INTEGER**.

"below A5" size: The number of bytes needed between the beginning of the *application global space* and the *base address* in register **A5**, to hold a program's *application globals* [304, 7.5.1<4>].

binary point: The binary equivalent of a decimal point, separating the integer and fractional parts of a *fixed-point number.*

Binary/Decimal Conversion Package: A standard *package,* provided in the *system resource file,* that converts numbers between their internal binary format and their external representation as strings of decimal digits [308, 2.3.4, 7.2.1<10>].

bit image: An array of bits in memory representing the *pixels* of a graphical image [100–101].

bit map: The combination of a *bit image* with a *boundary rectangle.* The bit image provides the bit map's content; the boundary rectangle defines its extent and gives it a system of coordinates [115–120, 121, 4.2.1, 4.2.2<3–5>, 4.3.4<1–3, 8>, 5.1.4, 5.1.5].

bit-mapped display: A video display screen on which each *pixel* can be individually controlled.

blind pointer: A Pascal pointer whose *base type* is unspecified, and which can consequently be assigned to a variable of any pointer type. The standard Pascal constant **NIL** is a blind pointer; two nonstandard features of Apple's Pascal compiler, the **POINTER** function and the **@** *operator,* also produce blind pointers as their results [19–20].

block: An area of contiguous memory within the *heap*, either allocated or free [57].

bottleneck procedure: A specialized procedure for performing a low-level drawing operation in a given *graphics port*, used for *customizing* QuickDraw operations [125, 4.2.2<15>].

boundary rectangle: (1) For a *bit map*, the *rectangle* that defines the bit map's extent and determines its system of coordinates. (2) For a *graphics port*, the boundary rectangle of the port's bit map [103, 115, 173, 185, 191, 4.2.1<4–7>, 4.2.2<4>, 5.1.4<7>, 5.1.5<2>, 5.2.4<6>, 5.3.1<11>].

bounding box: The smallest *rectangle* enclosing a *polygon* or *region* on the coordinate grid [112, 4.1.3<6>, 4.1.5<5>].

bundle: A *Finder resource* that identifies all of a program's other Finder resources, so that they can be installed in the *desktop file* when the program is copied to a new disk [313, 315–316, 7.3.2<4>, 7.5.4].

bundle bit: A flag that tells whether a program has any *Finder resources* that must accompany it when it is copied to a new disk [315, 7.3.2<4>, 7.5.4<5>].

byte: An independently addressable group of 8 bits in memory [7].

Caps Lock key: A *modifier key* on the Macintosh keyboard, used to convert lowercase letters to uppercase while leaving all nonalphabetic keys unaffected.

chain: To start up a new program after reinitializing the *stack* and *application global space*, but not the *application heap*; compare *launch* [320, 7.1.1].

character code: An 8-bit integer representing a text character; compare *key code* [349–350, 8.1.1, Appendix D].

character height: The overall height of a font's *font rectangle*, from *ascent line* to *descent line* [357, 8.2.2<9>].

character image: A *bit image* that defines the graphical representation of a text character in a given *typeface* and *type size* [352–353].

character key: A key on the keyboard or keypad that produces a character when pressed; compare *modifier key* [351, 8.1.3, 8.1.4].

character offset: The horizontal distance, in pixels, from the left edge of the *font rectangle* to that of the *character image* for a given character; equal to the difference between the character's leftward *kern* and the maximum leftward kern in the font [359, 8.2.3<12>].

character origin: The location within a *character image* marking the position of the *graphics pen* when the character is drawn [352].

character style: See *type style*.

character width: The distance in pixels by which the *graphics pen* advances after drawing a character; compare *image width* [352–353, 358, 8.2.3<11>].

check mark: A special *control character* (*character code* **$12**) that appears on the Macintosh screen as a small check symbol; used for marking items on a menu [350, 8.1.1<4>].

clip: To confine a drawing operation within a specified boundary, suppressing any drawing that falls outside the boundary [123, 173, 185, 191, 5.1.4<1, 7–8>, 5.1.5<2>, 5.2.4<6>, 5.3.1<11>].

clipping boundaries: The boundaries to which all drawing in a given *graphics port* is confined, consisting of the port's *boundary rectangle*, *port rectangle*, *clipping region*, and *visible region* [123–124, 173, 185, 191, 4.2.2<4–8>, 5.1.4<7>, 5.1.5<2>, 5.2.4<6>, 5.3.1<11>].

clipping region: A general-purpose *clipping boundary* associated with a *graphics port*, provided for the application program's use [124, 173, 185, 191, 213, 4.2.2<7>, 4.3.6, 5.1.4<7>, 5.1.5<2>, 5.2.4<6>, 5.3.1<11>].

clock chip: A component of the Macintosh, powered independently by a battery, that keeps track of the current date and time even when the machine's main power is turned off [26, 2.4].

code segment: A *resource* containing all or part of a program's executable machine code [301–308, 7.1.2].

Command key: A *modifier key* on the Macintosh keyboard, used in combination with *character keys* to type keyboard equivalents to menu commands.

command mark: A special *control character* (*character code* **$11**) that appears on the Macintosh screen as a "cloverleaf" symbol; used for displaying *Command-key* equivalents of items on a menu [350, 8.1.1<4>].

compaction: The process of moving together all of the *relocatable blocks* in the *heap*, in order to coalesce the available free space [57, 3.3.2].

complement: A bit-level operation that reverses the bits of a given operand, changing each **0** to a **1** and vice versa [2.2.2<12>].

control: An object on the Macintosh screen that the user can manipulate with the mouse to operate on the contents of a window or control the way they're presented.

control character: An ASCII text character with a character code from **$00** to **$1F** (as well as the character **$7F**). Most control characters have no special meaning and no visual representation on the Macintosh, but a few are defined as special-purpose symbols for use on the screen: see *apple mark, check mark, command mark,* and *diamond mark* [349–350, 8.1.1<3–6>].

creator signature: A four-character string identifying the application program a given *file* belongs to, and which should be started up when the user opens the file in the *Finder* [309–310, 7.3.1, 7.3.2<2>].

current port: The *graphics port* in use at any given time, to which most *QuickDraw* operations implicitly apply [Sampling: 178, 191, 359, 361, 4.2.3<1–2>, 4.3.3, 5.1.4<7>, 5.2.1<10>, 5.3.1<3>, 8.2.6<2>].

current resource file: The *resource file* that will be searched first when looking for a requested resource, and to which certain *resource*-related operations implicitly apply [263, 270, 273, 6.2.1<4>, 6.2.2, 6.3.1<3>, 6.3.3<4>, 6.5.3<1>].

cursor: A small (16-by-16-bit) *bit image* whose movements can be controlled with the *mouse* to designate positions on the Macintosh screen.

customize: To redefine an aspect of the Toolbox's operation to meet the specialized needs of a particular program.

dangling pointer: An invalid pointer to an object that no longer exists at the designated address [57].

data fork: The *fork* of a *file* that contains the file's data, such as the text of a document; compare *resource fork* [262, 6.5.1<3>].

date and time record: A data structure representing a calendar date and clock time, with fields for the year, month, day of the month, day of the week, hour, minute, and second; used for reading or setting the Macintosh's built-in *clock chip* [26–27, 2.4.2].

dead character: (1) A text character with a zero *character width*, which doesn't advance the *graphics pen* when drawn [353]. (2) A character (such as a foreign-language accent) that combines with the character following it to produce a single result character (such as an accented letter) [366–367, 8.1.1<8>].

definition file: An assembly-language file containing definitions of Toolbox constants and global variables, to be incorporated into an assembly-language program with an **.INCLUDE** directive [17].

dereference: (1) In general, to convert any pointer to the value it points to. (2) Specifically, to convert a *handle* to the corresponding *master pointer* [85, 361].

descent: (1) For a text character, the distance the character extends below the *baseline*, in pixels [352]. (2) For a *font*, the maximum descent of any character in the font [356–357, 8.2.2<9>].

descent line: The line marking a font's maximum *descent* below *baseline* [357].

desk accessory: A type of *device driver* that operates as a "mini-application" that can coexist on the screen with any other program [260, 262, 316–317, 319, 350, 367, 2.4.1<2>, 2.4.2<2>, 7.4.2<4>, 7.4.3<9>, 7.5.5].

desk scrap: The vehicle by which information is cut and pasted from one application program or *desk accessory* to another [317–319, 320, 7.4].

desktop: (1) The gray background area of the Macintosh screen, outside any window. (2) The arrangement of windows, icons, and other objects on the screen, particularly in the *Finder*.

desktop file: A file containing *Finder*-related information about the files on a disk, including their *file types*, *creator signatures*, and locations on the Finder *desktop* [309, 312, 7.3.2<4>, 7.5.4<5>].

detach: To decouple a *resource* from its *resource file*, so that the resource will remain in memory when the file is closed [266, 6.3.2<2–4>].

device code: An integer identifying the output device a *graphics port* draws on, used in selecting the appropriate *fonts* for drawing text [361, 4.2.2<12>, 8.3.1<11–13>, 8.3.2].

device driver: The low-level software through which the Toolbox communicates with an input/output device; an important special category of device drivers are *desk accessories* [316–317, 7.5.5].

diamond mark: A special *control character* (*character code* **$11**) that appears on the Macintosh screen as a small diamond symbol. This symbol is a vestige of earlier versions of the Macintosh user interface and no longer has any specific use [8.1.1<4>].

disk driver: The *device driver* built into ROM for communicating with the Macintosh's built-in Sony disk drive [316, 7.5.5].

Disk Initialization Package: A standard *package*, provided in the *system resource file*, that takes corrective action when an unreadable disk is inserted into the disk drive, usually by initializing the disk [307, 7.2.1<5>, II:8.4].

dispatch table: A table in memory, used by the *Trap Dispatcher* to locate the various Toolbox routines in ROM [13, 50].

document: A coherent unit or collection of information to be operated on by a particular application program [309, 310].

document file: A *file* containing a *document* [309, 310].

driver reference number: An integer between -1 and -32, used to refer to a particular *device driver*; derived from the driver's *unit number* by the formula **refNum** $= -($**unitNum** $+ 1$) [316, 7.5.5].

empty handle: A *handle* that points to a **NIL** *master pointer*, indicating that the underlying *block* has been *purged* from the heap [74, 265, 275, 276, 3.1.2<5>, 3.3.3<2>, 6.3.1<7>, 6.3.4<2, 7–9>].

empty rectangle: A *rectangle* that encloses no pixels on the coordinate grid [107, 4.1.2<3>, 4.4.4<9>].

empty region: A *region* that encloses no pixels on the coordinate grid [4.1.7<1–2>, 4.4.7<7>].

emulator trap: A form of *trap* that occurs when the *MC68000* processor attempts to execute an *unimplemented instruction;* used to "emulate" the effects of such an instruction with software instead of hardware [12].

enclosing rectangle: The *rectangle* within which an *oval* is inscribed [198, 5.3.4].

erase: To fill a *shape* with the *background pattern* of the *current port* [191, 197, 5.3.1<8>].

error code: A nonzero *result code,* reporting an error of some kind detected by an *Operating System* routine [64, 70, 275, 3.1.2, 6.6.1, Appendix E].

event: An occurrence reported by the Toolbox for a program to respond to, such as the user's pressing the mouse button or typing on the keyboard.

exception: See *trap.*

exclusive or: A bit-level operation in which each bit of the result is a **1** if the corresponding bits of the two operands are different, or **0** if they're the same [2.2.2].

external reference: A reference from one *code segment* to a routine contained in another segment [306].

Fat Mac: A model of *Macintosh* with a memory capacity of 512 kilobytes.

file: A collection of information stored as a named unit on a disk [261–264, 309–316, 319, II:Chapter 8, 6.2, 6.5.1, 6.5.4, 6.6.2, 7.3, 7.4.4, 7.5.3].

file icon: The *icon* used by the *Finder* to represent a *file* on the screen [312–316, 7.5.3].

file reference: A *Finder resource* that establishes the connection between a *file type* and its *file icon* [313, 315, 7.5.3, 7.5.4<4>].

file reference number: An integer used to designate a particular *file,* assigned by the Toolbox when the file is opened and used thereafter to refer to the file [262, 6.2.1<2, 10>, 6.2.2, 6.4.3<4–5>, 6.5.1<2>, 6.5.4<5>, II:Chapter 8].

file type: A four-character string that characterizes the kind of information a *file* contains, assigned by the program that created the file [309–310, 7.3.1, 7.3.2<2>].

fill: To color a *shape* with a specified *pattern* [191, 194, 5.3.1<7>].

fill pattern: A *pattern* associated with a *graphics port,* used privately by *QuickDraw* for *filling* shapes [181, 4.2.2<9>, 5.1.1<4–5,8>].

Finder: The Macintosh program that allows the user to manipulate files and start up applications; normally the first program to be run when the Macintosh is turned on [309–316, 7.3, 7.5.3, 7.5.4].

Finder information record: A data structure summarizing the *Finder*-related properties of a *file,* including its *file type, creator signature,* and location on the Finder *desktop* [309, 7.3.2, 7.3.3].

Finder resources: The *resources* associated with a program that tell the *Finder* how to represent the program's *files* on the screen and which files to transfer when moving the program to another disk. Finder resources include *autographs, icon lists, file references,* and *bundles* [312–316, 5.5.4<3>, 7.3.2<4>, 7.5.3, 7.5.4].

Finder startup handle: See *startup handle.*

Finder startup information: See *startup information.*

fixed-point number: A binary number with a fixed number of bits before and after the *binary point;* specifically, a value of the Toolbox data type **Fixed**, consisting of a 16-bit integer part and a 16-bit fraction [25, 360, 2.3.1, 8.3.1<10>, 8.3.2<4–5>].

floating-point number: A binary number in which the *binary point* can "float" to any required position within the number; the number's internal representation includes a binary exponent, or order of magnitude, that determines the position of the binary point.

Floating-Point Arithmetic Package: A standard *package,* provided in the *system resource file,* that performs arithmetic on *floating-point numbers* in accordance with the *IEEE standard,* using the Standard Apple Numerical Environment *(SANE)* [307, 7.2.1<7>].

folder: An object in a disk's *desktop file,* represented by an icon or a window on the screen, that can contain files or other folders; used for organizing the files on the disk [7.3.2<7>].

folder number: The integer used by the *Finder* to identify a particular *folder* [7.3.2<7>].

font: (1) A *resource* containing all the *character images* and other information needed to draw text characters in a given *typeface* and *type size* [353–359, 8.2.2, 8.2.3, 8.4.5]. (2) Sometimes used loosely (and incorrectly) as a synonym for *typeface,* as in the terms *font number* and *text font.*

font image: A *bit image* consisting of all the individual *character images* in a given *font,* arranged consecutively in a single horizontal row; also called a *strike* of the font [357, 359, 8.2.3].

font number: An integer denoting a particular *typeface* [354, 8.2.1, 8.2.5].

font record: A data structure containing all the information associated with a given *font* [355–359, 8.2.2, 8.2.3].

font rectangle: The smallest rectangle, relative to the *baseline* and *character origin,* that would enclose all the *character images* in a *font* if they were superimposed with their origins coinciding [356, 8.2.2<7–11>].

font-width table: A *resource* containing all the information on the *character widths* in a given *font,* but without the *character images* themselves; used for measuring the width of text without actually drawing it [366, 8.3.4, 8.4.6].

fork: One of the two parts of which every *file* is composed: the *data fork* or the *resource fork* [262, 6.5.1<3-5>].

frame: To draw the outline of a *shape*, using the *pen size, pen pattern,* and *pen mode* of the *current port* [191, 192, 208, 4.1.5<2>, 4.1.6<2-3, 8>, 5.3.1<4>].

free block: A contiguous *block* of space available for allocation within the *heap* [57, 3.1.2<6>, 3.3.1, 3.3.2, 3.3.3<10-11>].

global coordinate system: The coordinate system associated with a given *bit image,* in which the top-left corner of the image has coordinates (**0, 0**); the global coordinate system is independent of the *boundary rectangle* of any *bit map* or *graphics port* based on the image [128, 4.4.2].

glue routine: See *interface routine.*

graphics pen: The imaginary drawing tool used for drawing lines in a *graphics port* [Sampling: 172-183, 192, 204, 352-353, 358, 4.1.4<3-4, 8>, 5.1.5<7>, 5.2, 5.4.2<4, 7>, 8.2.3<12>].

graphics port: A complete drawing environment containing all the information needed for *QuickDraw* drawing operations [Sampling: 120-125, 359-366, 4.2.2, 4.3, 5.1.1<4>, 5.1.3<10>, 5.2.1<1-2>, 5.2.2<3>, 5.2.4<2>, 8.3.1, 8.3.2].

handle: A pointer to a *master pointer,* used to refer to a *relocatable block* [Sampling: 17, 58-63, 70-73, 264-266, 271, 276, 3.1.1<2>, 3.3.3, 6.3.1<1, 4-7>, 6.3.4<2, 7-9>].

heap: The area of memory in which space is allocated and deallocated at the explicit request of a running program; compare *stack* [56-57].

heap zone: An independently maintained area of the *heap,* such as the *application heap* or the *system heap* [58].

icon: A *bit image* of a standard size (32 pixels by 32), used on the Macintosh screen to represent an object such as a disk or file [189, 312-316, 5.4.4, 5.5.3, 5.5.4, 7.5.3<1-3>].

icon list: A *resource* containing any number of *icons;* commonly used to hold a *file icon* and its mask for use by the Finder [313-316, 5.5.4, 7.5.3<2-3>].

identifying information: The properties of a *resource* that uniquely identify it: its *resource type, resource ID,* and (optional) *resource name* [259-260, 271, 6.4.1].

IEEE standard: A set of standards and conventions for *floating-point* arithmetic, published by the Institute of Electrical and Electronic Engineers [307, 7.2.1<7>].

image width: The horizontal extent of a *character image;* the width in pixels of a character's graphical representation. Compare *character width* [352-353, 8.2.3<8>].

Inside Macintosh: The comprehensive manual on the Macintosh *Toolbox,* to be published by Apple Computer, Inc.

interface: A set of rules and conventions by which one part of an organized system communicates with another.

interface file: A text file that contains the declarations belonging to an *interface unit* in source-language form, to be incorporated into a Pascal program with a **uses** *declaration* [15].

interface routine: A routine, part of an *interface unit,* that mediates between the *stack-based* parameter-passing conventions of a Pascal calling program and those of a *register-based* Toolbox routine; also called a "glue routine" [16].

interface unit: A precompiled *unit* containing declarations for Toolbox routines and data structures, making them available for use in Pascal programs [14–15].

International Utilities Package: A standard *package,* provided in the *system resource file,* that helps programs conform to the prevailing conventions of different countries in such matters as formatting of numbers, dates, times, and currency; use of metric units; and alphabetization of foreign-language accents, diacriticals, and ligatures [23, 308, 2.1.2<4>, 2.4.4, 7.2.1<9>].

invert: (1) Generally, to reverse the colors of *pixels* in a graphical image, changing white to black and vice versa. (2) Specifically, to reverse the colors of all pixels inside the boundary of a given *shape* [191, 194, 5.3.1<9>].

invisible bit: A flag that marks a file as invisible, so that the *Finder* will not display it on the screen [7.3.2<5>].

jump table: A table used to direct *external references* from one *code segment* to another to the proper addresses in memory; located in the *application global space,* at positive offsets from the *base address* kept in register **A5** [302–307, 7.1.1<3>, 7.1.2, 7.5.1].

K: See *kilobyte.*

kern: The amount by which a *character image* extends leftward beyond the *character origin* or rightward beyond the *character width* [352, 359, 8.2.3<12>].

key code: An 8-bit integer representing a key on the Macintosh keyboard or keypad; compare *character code* [351, 8.1.3, Appendix D].

key map: An array of bits in memory representing the state of the keys on the keyboard and keypad [8.4.4<5>, II:2.6.1].

keyboard configuration: The correspondence between keys on the Macintosh keyboard or keypad and the characters they produce when pressed [351, 367, 8.1.4, 8.4.4].

kilobyte: A unit of memory capacity equal to 2^{10} (1,024) bytes.

launch: To start up a new program after reinitializing the *stack, application global space,* and *application heap;* compare *chain* [320, 7.1.1].

leading: The amount of extra vertical space between lines of text, measured in pixels from the *descent line* of one to the *ascent line* of the next. Although every *font* specifies a recommended leading value, the recommendation need not be followed when drawing text in a *graphics port* [357, 8.2.2<12–13>].

length byte: The first byte of a *Pascal-format string,* which gives the number of characters in the string, from **0** to **255** [21–22, 2.1.1<1–3>].

LIFO: Last in, first out; the order in which items are added to and removed from the *stack* [13].

ligature: A text character that combines two or more separate characters into a single symbol, such as **æ**.

limit pointer: A pointer that marks the end of an area of memory by pointing to the address following the last byte.

line drawing: Drawing in a *graphics port* by moving the *graphics pen,* using the QuickDraw routines **Move**, **MoveTo**, **Line**, and **LineTo** [172–183, 204, 208, 4.1.3<2>, 4.1.4<2–3, 8>, 4.1.5<2>, 4.1.6<2–3, 8>, 5.2, 5.3.6<2>].

Lisa: A personal computer manufactured and marketed by Apple Computer, Inc.; the first reasonably priced personal computer to feature a high-resolution *bit-mapped display* and a hand-held *mouse* pointing device. Now called *Macintosh XL.*

load: To read an object, such as a *resource* or the *desk scrap,* into memory from a disk file.

local coordinate system: The coordinate system associated with a given *graphics port,* determined by the *boundary rectangle* of the port's *bit map* [125, 4.4.2].

local ID: The identifying number by which a *Finder resource* is referred to by other resources in the same *bundle;* not necessarily the same as its true *resource ID* [313, 315–316, 7.5.3<3>, 7.5.4<3>].

localize: To tailor a program's behavior for use in a particular country [*2/25*, 23, 257, 2.1.2<3–4, 7>, 7.2.1<9>].

location table: A table giving the horizontal position of each *character image* in a *font,* measured in pixels from the beginning of the *font image* [358, 359, 8.2.3<7–9>].

lock: To temporarily prevent a *relocatable block* from being *purged* or moved within the heap during *compaction* [65–69, 265, 272, 361, 3.1.2<7>, 3.2.1<7>, 3.2.4, 3.3.3<3>, 3.3.3<8>, 6.4.2<4>, 8.2.7].

logical shift: A bit-level operation that shifts the bits of a given operand left or right by a specified number of positions, with bits shifted out at one end being lost and **0**s shifted in at the other end [24, 2.2.2<4–7>].

long integer: A data type provided by Apple's Pascal compiler, consisting of double-length integers: 32 bits including sign, covering the range ±2147483647 [18–19].

long word: A group of 32 bits (2 *words*, or 4 *bytes*) beginning at a *word boundary* in memory [7].

Macintosh: A personal computer manufactured and marketed by Apple Computer, Inc., featuring a high-resolution *bit-mapped display* and a hand-held *mouse* pointing device.

Macintosh Operating System: The body of machine code built into the Macintosh *ROM* to handle such low-level tasks as memory management, disk input/output, and serial communications.

Macintosh Software Supplement: A set of software tools for developing Macintosh software on a *Lisa* computer [10].

Macintosh XL: The largest model of the *Macintosh,* with a memory capacity of 512 kilobytes or 1 megabyte and a larger display screen than the standard Macintosh; formerly called the *Lisa.*

MacWorks: The software "emulator" program that enables a *Lisa* to run Macintosh software without modification [10].

main entry point: The point in a program's code where execution begins when the program is first started up [305].

main segment: The *code segment* containing a program's *main entry point* [305].

master pointer: A pointer to a *relocatable block,* kept at a known, fixed location in the *heap* and updated automatically by the Toolbox whenever the underlying block is moved during *compaction.* A pointer to the master pointer is called a *handle* to the block [58, 65, 72, 74, 3.1.1<2>, 3.1.2<5>, 3.2.1<10>, 3.3.3<2>, 3.2.5<5>, 3.3.3<2, 5>].

MC68000: The 32-bit microprocessor used in the Macintosh, manufactured by Motorola, Inc; usually called "68000" for short.

megabyte: A unit of memory capacity equal to 2^{20} (1,048,576) bytes.

menu: A list of choices or options from which the user can choose, by using the mouse.

MiniEdit: The extensive example program developed in Volume Two of this book.

MiniFinder: See *Standard File Package.*

missing character: A character for which no *character image* is defined in a given *font;* represented graphically by the font's *missing symbol* [357, 8.2.3<5–6, 8, 13>].

missing symbol: The graphical representation used for drawing *missing characters* in a given *font* [357, 8.2.3<4, 9, 14>].

modifier key: A key on the Macintosh keyboard that doesn't generate a character of its own, but may affect the meaning of any *character key* pressed at the same time; see *Shift key, Caps Lock key, Option key,* and *Command key* [351, 8.1.3<2>, 8.1.4].

mouse: A hand-held pointing device for controlling the movements of the *cursor* to designate positions on the Macintosh screen.

nonrelocatable block: A *block* that can't be moved within the heap during *compaction,* referred to by single indirection with a simple pointer; compare *relocatable block* [60].

object module: The file containing the compiled code of a Pascal *unit,* to be linked with that of an application program after compilation [15].

offset/width table: A table giving the *character offset* and *character width* for each character in a given *font* [358–359, 8.2.3<10–14>].

Operating System: See *Macintosh Operating System.*

Option key: A *modifier key* on the Macintosh keyboard, used to type special characters such as foreign letters and accents.

or: A bit-level operation in which each bit of the result is a **1** if either or both operands have **1**s at the corresponding bit position, or **0** if both have **0**s [24, 2.2.2].

ORD: A standard Pascal function for converting any scalar value to a corresponding integer (for instance, a character to its equivalent integer character code); on the Macintosh, **ORD** will also accept a pointer and return the equivalent long-integer address [19].

origin: (1) The top-left corner of a *rectangle.* (2) For a *bit map* or *graphics port,* the top-left corner of the *boundary rectangle,* whose coordinates determine the *local coordinate system* [103, 125].

oval: A graphical figure, circular or elliptical in shape; defined by an *enclosing rectangle* [200, 5.3.4].

package: A *resource,* usually residing in the *system resource file,* containing a collection of general-purpose routines that can be loaded into memory when needed; used to supplement the Toolbox with additional facilities that either require too much code or are not used frequently enough to justify taking up space in *ROM* [15, 16, 307–308, 7.2, 7.5.2].

package number: The *resource ID* of a *package;* must be between **0** and **7** [307, 7.2.1<2, 4>, 7.5.2<3>].

package trap: One of the eight Toolbox *traps,* named **_Pack0** to **_Pack7,** used at the machine-language level to call a routine belong to a *package* [308, 2.3.4<7>, 2.4.4<8>, 7.2.1<11>].

paint: To fill a *shape* with the *pen pattern* of the *current port* [191, 194, 5.3.1<6>].

Pascal-format string: A sequence of text characters represented in the internal format used by Apple's Pascal compiler, consisting of a *length byte* followed by from 0 to 255 bytes of *character codes* [21–22, 2.1.1<1–3>, 350, 8.1.2, 8.4.2].

pattern: A small *bit image* (8 pixels by 8) that can be repeated indefinitely to fill an area, like identical floor tiles laid end to end [179–181, 5.1.1, 5.1.2].

pattern list: A *resource* consisting of any number of *patterns* [5.1.2 <4>, 5.5.2].

pattern transfer modes: A set of *transfer modes* used for drawing lines or shapes or filling areas with a *pattern* [180–183, 5.1.3, 5.2.1<5>, 5.2.2<5>].

pen: See *graphics pen.*

pen level: An integer associated with a *graphics port* that determines the visibility of the port's *graphics pen.* The pen is visible if the pen level is zero or positive, hidden if it's negative [178, 191, 4.2.2<11>, 5.2.1<7>, 5.2.3].

pen location: The coordinates of the *graphics pen* in a given *graphics port* [Sampling: 172–174, 191, 352, 358, 361, 4.2.2<10>, 5.1.5<7>, 5.2.1<3>, 8.2.3<12>, 8.3.3<2, 6>].

pen mode: The *transfer mode* with which a *graphics port* draws lines and frames or paints shapes; should be one of the *pattern transfer modes* [181–183, 192, 194, 4.2.2<10>, 5.1.3<10–12>, 5.2.1<5>, 5.2.2, 5.2.4<5>, 5.3.1<4, 6>].

pen pattern: The *pattern* in which a *graphics port* draws lines and frames or paints shapes [179, 191, 192, 194, 4.2.2<10>, 5.1.1<4–5, 7>, 5.2.1<6>, 5.2.2, 5.2,4<5>, 5.3.1<4, 6>].

pen size: The width and height of the *graphics pen* belonging to a *graphics port* [177, 192, 204, 4.2.2<10>, 5.2.1<4>, 5.2.2, 5.2.4<5>, 5.3.1<4>].

pen state: The characteristics of the *graphics pen* belonging to a *graphics port,* including its *pen location, pen size, pen mode,* and *pen pattern* [183, 5.2.1<9–12>].

picture: A recorded sequence of *QuickDraw* operations that can be repeated on demand to reproduce a graphical image [213–214, *7/27*, 5.4.1, 5.4.2, 5.4.3, 5.5.5, 7.4.1<4>].

picture frame: The reference *rectangle* within which a *picture* is defined, and which can be mapped to coincide with any other specified rectangle when the picture is drawn [213, 5.4.1<4>, 5.4.2<2>, 5.4.3<2>].

pixel: A single dot forming part of a graphical image; short for "picture element: [99, 4.2.3].

point: (1) A position on the *QuickDraw* coordinate grid, specified by a pair of horizontal and vertical coordinates [104–105, 4.1.1]. (2) A unit used by printers to measure type sizes, equal to approximately 1/72 of an inch [352].

point size: See *type size*.

POINTER: A function provided by Apple's Pascal compiler, which accepts a *long integer* representing a memory address and returns a *blind pointer* to that address [19].

polygon: A graphical figure defined by any closed series of connected straight lines [111–112, 204–208, 4.1.3, 4.1.4, 4.4.6, 4.4.9<5–6>, 5.3.6].

pop: To remove a data item from the top of a *stack*.

port: (1) A connector on the back of the Macintosh used for serial communication with a peripheral device, such as a printer or modem. (2) Short for *graphics port*.

port rectangle: The rectangle that defines the portion of a *bit map* that a *graphics port* can draw into [122, 173, 185, 191, 4.2.2<5>, 4.3.5, 5.1.4<7>, 5.1.5<2>, 5.2.4<6>, 5.3.1<11>].

printer driver: The *device driver* that communicates with a printer through one of the Macintosh's built-in serial ports [316, 7.5.5].

pseudo-random numbers: Numbers that seem to be random but can be reproduced in the same sequence if desired [26].

purge: To remove a *relocatable block* from the heap to make room for other blocks. The purged block's *master pointer* remains allocated, but is set to **NIL** to show that the block no longer exists in the heap; all existing *handles* to the block become *empty handles* [Sampling: 74, 265, 274, 3.1.2<7>, 3.2.1<4–5>, 3.2.4, 3.2.6<4>, 3.3.1<3–4>, 6.3.4<8–9>, 6.4.2<4>, 6.5.4<10>].

purgeable block: A *relocatable block* that can be *purged* from the heap to make room for other blocks [74, 265, 272, 274, 3.2.4, 3.3.3<3, 9>, 6.3.4<9>, 6.4.2<4>].

push: To add a data item to the top of a *stack*.

pushdown stack: See *stack*.

QuickDraw: The extensive collection of graphics routines built into the Macintosh *ROM* [97–214, 4.1.1–4.4.9, 5.1.1–5.5.5].

QuickDraw globals pointer: A pointer to the global variables used by *QuickDraw*, kept at address **0(A5)** in the *application global space* and initialized with the **InitGraf** routine [54, 97, 4.3.1].

RAM: See *random-access memory*.

random-access memory: A common but misleading term for *read/write memory*.

read-only memory: Memory that can be read but not written; usually called *ROM*. The Macintosh has 64K of ROM containing the built-in machine code of the *Macintosh Operating System*, *QuickDraw*, and the *User Interface Toolbox*.

read/write memory: Memory that can be both read and written; commonly known by the misleading term *random-access memory,* or *RAM.* The standard Macintosh has 128K of read/write memory, the *Fat Mac* has 512K, and the *Macintosh XL* has 512K or 1 megabyte.

reallocate: To allocate fresh space for a *relocatable block* that has been *purged,* thus updating the block's *master pointer* to point to its new location. Only the space is reallocated; the block's former contents are not restored [74, 3.3.3<4–8>].

rectangle: A four-sided graphical figure defined by two *points* specifying its top-left and bottom-right corners, or by four integers specifying its top, left, bottom, and right edges [105, 4.1.2, 4.4.3, 4.4.4, 4.4.5, 4.4.9<5–6>, 5.3.2].

region: A graphical figure that can be of any arbitrary shape. It can have curved as well as straight edges, and can even have holes in it or consist of two or more separate pieces [111–114, 208, 4.1.5, 4.1.6, 4.1.7, 4.4.3<1–3>, 4.4.7, 4.4.8, 4.4.9<5–6>, 5.3.7].

register-based: Describes a Toolbox routine that accepts its parameters and returns its results directly in the processor's registers; compare *stack-based* [15–16, 18].

release: To deallocate a *block* of memory that's no longer needed, allowing the space to be reused for another purpose [57, 60, 266, 3.2.2, 6.3.2].

relocatable block: A *block* that can be moved within the heap during *compaction,* referred to by double indirection with a *handle;* compare *nonrelocatable block* [59–60].

resource: A unit or collection of information kept in a *resource file* on a disk and *loaded* into memory when needed [Sampling: 257–277, 301, 316, 350, 2.3.4<6>, 5.1.1<9–15>, 7.1.1<2–3>, 8.1.2<3–4>, 8.4, Appendix B].

resource attributes: A set of flags describing various properties of a *resource,* kept in the *attribute byte* of its *resource map* entry [271–273, 6.4.2].

resource compiler: A utility program that constructs *resources* according to a coded definition read from a text file [259].

resource data: The information a *resource* contains [260].

resource editor: A utility program with which *resources* can be defined or modified directly on the Macintosh screen with the mouse and keyboard [259].

resource file: A collection of *resources* stored together as a unit on a disk; technically not a *file* as such, but merely the *resource fork* of a particular file.

resource file attributes: A set of flags describing various properties of a *resource file* [273, 276–277, 6.6.2].

resource fork: The *fork* of a *file* that contains the file's *resources;* usually called a *resource file.* Compare *data fork* [262, 6.5.1<3–5>].

resource ID: An integer that uniquely identifies a particular *resource* within its *resource type* [259–260, 6.4.1].

resource map: The table that summarizes the contents of a *resource file,* stored as part of the file itself and read into memory when the file is opened [Sampling: 261, 263, 264, 266, 270–271, 273–274, 275–276, 6.2.1<3, 8>, 6.3.1<4, 7>, 6.6.2<5>].

resource name: An optional string of text characters that uniquely identifies a particular *resource* within its *resource type,* and by which the resource can be listed on a *menu* [261, 6.4.1].

resource specification: The combination of a *resource type* and *resource ID,* or a *resource type* and *resource name,* which uniquely identifies a particular resource [259].

resource type: A four-character string that identifies the kind of information a *resource* contains [259–260, 6.1.1, 6.4.1].

result code: An integer code returned by an *Operating System* routine to signal successful completion or report an error [63–64, 70, 275, 3.1.2, 6.6.1, Appendix E].

return link: The address of the instruction following a routine call, to which control is to return on completion of the routine [14].

ROM: See *read-only memory.*

rounded rectangle: A graphical figure consisting of a *rectangle* with rounded corners; defined by the rectangle itself and the dimensions of the *ovals* forming the corners [201, 5.3.3].

routine selector: An integer used to identify a particular routine within a *package* [308, 2.3.4<7>, 2.4.4<8>, 7.2.1<11>].

row width: The number of bytes in each row of a *bit image* [101, 118, 4.2.1<2–3>].

SANE: The Standard Apple Numeric Environment, a set of routines for performing arithmetic on *floating-point numbers* in accordance with the *IEEE standard;* available on the Macintosh through the *Floating-Point Arithmetic Package* [307, 7.2.1<7>].

scrap count: An integer maintained by the Toolbox that tells when the contents of the *desk scrap* have been changed by a *desk accessory* [319, 7.4.2<4>, 7.4.3<9>].

scrap handle: A *handle* to the contents of the *desk scrap,* kept by the Toolbox in a *system global* [318, 320, 7.1.1<5>, 7.1.3<3>, 7.4.2<3>].

scrap information record: A data structure summarizing the contents and status of the *desk scrap* [318, 7.4.2].

screen buffer: The area of memory reserved to hold the *screen image* [51, 101].

screen image: The *bit image* that defines what is displayed on the Macintosh screen [101].

screen map: The *bit map* representing the Macintosh screen, kept in the QuickDraw global variable *ScreenBits*. Its *bit image* is the *screen image;* its *boundary rectangle* has the same dimensions as the screen, with the *origin* at coordinates (**0, 0**) [120, 4.2.1<8–10>].

scroll: To move the contents of a *window*, changing the portion of a document or other information that is visible within the window [186, 188–189, 5.1.5].

scroll bar: A *control* associated with a *window* that allows the user to *scroll* the window's contents.

seed: The starting value used in generating a sequence of *pseudo-random numbers* [26, 2.3.5].

segment header: Information at the beginning of a *code segment* identifying which entries in the program's *jump table* belong to this segment [306, 7.5.1<3–4>].

segment number: The *resource ID* of a *code segment* [302, 7.1.2<3, 7>, 7.5.1<2>].

segment 0: A special *code segment* containing the information needed to initialize a program's *application global space* [303–304, 7.1.1<3>, 7.5.1<5>].

serial driver: The *device driver* built into ROM for communicating with peripheral devices through the Macintosh's built-in serial ports [316, 7.5.5].

shape: Any of the figures that can be drawn with QuickDraw *shape-drawing* operations, including *rectangles, rounded rectangles, ovals, arcs* and *wedges, polygons,* and *regions* [189–213, 5.3].

shape drawing: Drawing *shapes* in a *graphics port*, using the operations *frame, paint, fill, erase,* and *invert* [189–213, 4.1.5<2>, 4.1.6<2–3, 8>, 5.3].

Shift key: A *modifier key* on the Macintosh keyboard, used to convert lowercase letters to uppercase or to produce the upper character on a nonalphabetic key.

68000: See *MC68000*.

signature: A four-character string that identifies a particular application program, used as a *creator signature* on files belonging to the program and as the *resource type* of the program's *autograph* resource [309–310, 312, 7.3.1, 7.3.2<2>, 7.5.4<6>].

SIZEOF: A function provided by Apple's Pascal compiler, which accepts a variable or type name as a parameter and returns the number of bytes of memory occupied by that variable or by values of that type [21].

sound buffer: The area of memory whose contents determine the sounds to be emitted by the Macintosh speaker [51, 7.5.5].

sound driver: The *device driver* built into ROM for controlling the sounds emitted by the Macintosh speaker [316, 7.5.5].

source transfer modes: A set of *transfer modes* used for transferring pixels from one *bit map* to another or for drawing text characters into a bit map [183–184, 5.1.3, 5.1.4<3>, 8.3.1<8>].

stack: (1) Generally, a data structure in which items can be added (*pushed*) and removed (*popped*) in *LIFO* order: the last item added is always the first to be removed. (2) Specifically, the area of Macintosh *RAM* that holds parameters, local variables, return addresses, and other temporary storage associated with a program's procedures and functions; compare *heap*. One end of the stack (the *base*) remains fixed in memory, while items are added or removed at the other end (the *top*); the *stack pointer* always points to the current top of the stack [13–14, 54, 56].

stack-based: Describes a Toolbox routine that accepts its parameters and returns its results on the *stack*, according to Pascal conventions; compare *register-based* [15, 17].

stack pointer: The address of the current top of the *stack*, kept in process register **A7** [13].

Standard File Package: A standard *package*, provided in the *system resource file*, that provides a convenient, standard way for the user to supply file names for input/output operations; also called the *MiniFinder* [307, 7.2.1<6>, II:8.3].

standard fill tones: A set of five *patterns* representing a range of homogeneous tones from solid white to solid black, provided as global variables by the *QuickDraw* graphics routines [181, 4.3.1, 5.1.2].

standard patterns: The 38 *patterns* included on the standard MacPaint pattern palette, available as a *pattern list* resource in the *system resource file* [181, 5.1.2].

starting angle: The angle defining the beginning of an *arc* or *wedge* [201, 5.3.5<3-7>].

startup handle: A *handle* to a program's *startup information*, passed to the program by the *Finder* as an *application parameter* [54, 311, 7.3.4].

startup information: A list of files selected by the user to be opened on starting up an application program [310–312, 7.3.4].

strike: See *font image*.

string list: A *resource* consisting of any number of *Pascal-format strings* [8.4.3].

system font: The *typeface* (**Chicago**) used by the Toolbox for displaying its own text on the screen, such as window titles and menu items [354, 8.2.1<4-6>].

system globals: Fixed memory locations reserved for use by the Toolbox [50].

system heap: The portion of the *heap* reserved for the private use of the Macintosh Operating System and Toolbox [56].

system resource file: The *resource fork* of the file **System**, containing shared resources that are available to all programs [Sampling: 181, 262, 264, 307–308, 367, 2.3.4<6>, 5.1.1<15>, 6.2.1<7, 10–12>, 6.4.3<5>, 7.2.1<3>, 7.5.2<4>].

text characteristics: The properties of a *graphics port* that determine the way it draws text characters, including its *text face*, *text size*, *text style*, and *text mode* [359–361, 8.3.1, 8.3.2].

text face: The *typeface* in which a *graphics port* draws text characters [125, 360, 4.2.2<12>, 8.3.1<2>, 8.3.2].

text file: A file of file type '**TEXT**', containing pure text characters with no additional formatting or other information [310, 7.3.1<6>].

text font: Term sometimes used loosely (and incorrectly) as a synonym for *text face.*

text mode: The *transfer mode* with which a *graphics port* draws text characters [125, 360, 4.2.2<12>, 8.3.1<8>, 8.3.2].

text size: The *type size* in which a *graphics port* draws text characters [125, 360, 4.2.2<12>, 8.3.1<3>, 8.3.2].

text style: The *type style* in which a *graphics port* draws text characters [125, 360, 4.2.2<12>, 8.3.1<6–7>, 8.3.2].

Toolbox: (1) The *User Interface Toolbox*. (2) Loosely, the entire contents of the Macintosh *ROM*, including the *Macintosh Operating System* and *QuickDraw* in addition to the *User Interface Toolbox* proper.

top of stack: The end of the *stack* at which items are added and removed; compare *base of stack* [13].

Transcendental Functions Package: A standard *package*, provided in the *system resource file*, that calculates various transcendental functions on *floating-point numbers*, such as logarithms, exponentials, trigonometric functions, compound interest, and discounted value [307, 7.2.1<8>].

transfer mode: A method of combining *pixels* being transferred to a *bit map* with those already there [182, 360, 5.1.3, 8.3.1<8>, 8.3.2].

translate: To move a *point* or a graphical figure a given distance horizontally and vertically [125].

trap: An error or abnormal condition that causes the *MC68000* processor to suspend normal program execution temporarily and execute a *trap handler* routine to respond to the problem; also called an *exception* [11–13, 16, 64, 306, 308, 7.2.1<11>].

Trap Dispatcher: The *trap handler* routine for responding to the *emulator trap*, which examines the contents of the *trap word* and jumps to the corresponding Toolbox routine in ROM [12–13].

trap handler: The routine executed by the *MC68000* processor to respond to a particular type of *trap* [11].

trap macro: A macroinstruction used to call a Toolbox routine from an assembly-language program; when assembled, it produces the appropriate *trap word* for the desired routine. Trap macros are defined in the assembly-language interface to the Toolbox and always begin with an underscore character (_) [16–17, Appendix F].

trap number: The last 8 or 9 bits of a *trap word*, which identify the particular Toolbox routine to be executed; used as an index into the *dispatch table* to find the address of the routine in ROM [12].

trap vector: The address of the *trap handler* routine for a particular type of *trap*, kept in the *vector table* in memory [*2/5*, 11, 50].

trap word: An *unimplemented instruction* used to stand for a particular Toolbox operation in a machine-language program. The trap work includes a *trap number* identifying the Toolbox operation to be performed; when executed, it causes an *emulator trap* that will execute the corresponding Toolbox routine in ROM [12, 15, 16, 2.1.2<10>, 2.3.4<7>, Appendix F].

type size: The size in which text characters are drawn, measured in printer's *points* and sometimes referred to as a "point size" [352].

type style: Variations on the basic form in which text characters are drawn, such as bold, italic, underline, outline, or shadow [352].

typecasting: A feature of Apple's Pascal compiler that allows data items to be converted from one data type to another with the same underlying representation (for example, from one pointer type to another) [20, 67, 4.4.3<6>].

typeface: The overall form or design in which text characters are drawn, independent of size or style. Macintosh typefaces are conventionally named after world cities, such as **New York**, **Geneva**, or **Athens** [352, 8.2.1].

unimplemented instruction: A machine-language instruction whose effects are not defined by the *MC68000* processor. Attempting to execute such an instruction causes an *emulator trap* to occur, allowing the effects of the instruction to be "emulated" with software instead of hardware [12].

unit: A collection of precompiled declarations that can be incorporated wholesale into any Pascal program [14].

unit number: The *resource ID* of a *device driver;* an integer between **0** and **31**, related to the *driver reference number* by the formula **refNum** = −(**unitNum** + 1) [316, 7.5.5].

unload: To remove an object, such as a *code segment* or the *desk scrap,* from memory, often (though not necessarily) by writing it out to a disk file.

unlock: To undo the effects of *locking* a *relocatable block,* again allowing it to be moved within the heap during *compaction* [65, 361, 3.2.4].

unpurgeable block: A *relocatable block* that can't be *purged* from the heap to make room for other blocks [74, 3.2.4].

update: (1) To write a new version of a *resource file* to the disk, incorporating all changes made in the file's resources in memory [123–124, 6.5.4]. (2) To redraw all or part of a *window* that has been exposed to view on the screen as a result of the user's manipulations with the mouse [189, 5.1.5<8>, II:3.4].

update region: The *region* defining the portion of a *window* that must be redrawn when *updating* the window [189, 5.1.5<8>, II:3.4.1, II:3.4.2].

user: The human operator of a computer.

user interface: The set of rules and conventions by which a human *user* communicates with a computer system or program.

User Interface Toolbox: The body of machine code built into the Macintosh *ROM* to implement the features of the standard *user interface.*

uses *declaration:* A declaration that incorporates the code of a pre-compiled *unit* into a Pascal program [15].

vector table: A table of *trap vectors* kept in the first kilobyte of RAM, used by the *MC68000* processor to locate the *trap handler* routine to execute when a *trap* occurs [11].

version data: Another name for a program's *autograph* resource, so called because its *resource data* typically holds a string identifying a program's version and date.

visible region: A *clipping boundary* that defines, for a *graphics port* associated with a *window,* the portion of the *port rectangle* that's exposed to view on the screen. The visible region is maintained entirely by the Toolbox, and should never be manipulated by a running program [123, 173, 185, 191, 4.2.2<6>, 4.2.3<4>, 5.1.4<7>, 5.1.5<2>, 5.2.4<6>, 5.3.1<11>].

wedge: A graphical figure bounded by a given *arc* and the lines joining its end points to the center of its *oval* [202, 5.3.5].

wide-open region: A rectangular *region* extending from coordinates (**−32768**, **−32768**) to (**32767**, **32767**), encompassing the entire QuickDraw coordinate plane [123, 4.3.6<7>].

window: An area of the Macintosh screen in which information is displayed, and which can overlap and hide or be hidden by other windows.

word: A group of 16 bits (2 *bytes*) beginning at a *word boundary* in memory [7].

word boundary: Any even-numbered memory address. Every *word* or *long word* in memory must begin at a word boundary.

Index

513

DATE DUE

FEB 28 1990			
4/28/91			
DEC 06 1998			
GAYLORD			PRINTED IN U.S.A